WebWork in Action

WebWork in Action

PATRICK LIGHTBODY
JASON CARREIRA

MANNING
Greenwich
(74° w. long.)

For online information and ordering of this and other Manning books, please visit
www.manning.com. The publisher offers discounts on this book when ordered in
quantity. For more information, please contact:

Special Sales Department
Manning Publications Co.
209 Bruce Park Avenue   Fax: (203) 661-9018
Greenwich, CT 06830   email: manning@manning.com

Manning Publications Co.   Copyeditor: Tiffany Taylor
209 Bruce Park Avenue   Typesetter: Gordan Salinovic
Greenwich, CT 06830   Cover designer: Leslie Haimes

ISBN 1-932394-53-2

Printed in the United States of America
1 2 3 4 5 6 7 8 9 10 – VHG – 10 09 08 07 06 05

brief contents

contents

PART 2 CORE CONCEPTS 75

foreword

Building a framework is difficult. On the one hand, the framework needs to be flexible enough to cater to a wide variety of needs; on the other hand, it needs to be solid enough that it doesn't fall prey to the beast of complexity—the urge to make it the solution to conquer all other solutions. In today's development environment, a multitude of frameworks is available to help you deal with various aspects of creating complex and useful enterprise software. Each framework provides something unique that makes it cover its particular field of application in a (more or less) human-friendly manner; in addition, each framework must work within its boundaries, relating to other frameworks in a software ecology that is constantly changing as needs and requirements change.

In order to accomplish this seemingly impossible task, it is necessary to acknowledge and study past efforts that a framework is supposed to replace and/or extend. In the case of WebWork, there were, and still are, a number of different approaches and frameworks that I looked at before I set to work. The idea was to create a new framework that allowed developers to get their job done with as little work as possible and perform each task efficiently without needing an unnecessarily complex framework to work against. Simple things should be simple to do while allowing complex things to be possible.

Another important aspect of WebWork is that it should allow developers as much freedom as possible to use other technologies—for example, to render output. A number of rendering alternatives are available, and it's impossible—and futile—to determine which one is best in all situations; such an alternative simply doesn't, and can't, exist. Being open minded in this regard is crucial, and it has paid off: WebWork has now been successfully integrated with a wide variety of rendering technologies, including some that don't target HTML or the Web. It has grown beyond its initial purpose, which is always gratifying for a parent.

WebWork started as an itch that I needed to personally scratch. However, with its second generation it has expanded into a fully grown community project, where developers add and improve WebWork by leveraging the structure provided by the framework. No framework of this kind, in today's competitive environment, can be successful without the input and ideas of a multitude of developers, because it's important that it be able to handle the real issues that people face in their daily work. As a result, WebWork now has a life of its own and is growing steadily as a community effort.

A book covering such a framework needs to be able to deal with all the intricacies of framework construction and convey the reasoning behind why it works the way it does; it must also demonstrate in action how all the theoretical stuff works in practice. Theory has no point if it ain't practically applicable. This book explains in reasonable detail the rationale for how WebWork is constructed, but it's mainly focused on showing you in practical terms how to use WebWork, from the simple to the complex. Time is always of the essence, and this book is a great investment if you're interested in learning about web framework construction, or if you want to make a killer web app that blows everyone's mind. Anything is possible!

RICKARD ÖBERG

preface

It's been almost 10 years since I developed my first web-based application. The program was a simple online shopping cart written in Perl. I still have the code lying around, and I look at it occasionally—I do this to remind myself of where I was and to keep myself focused on where I want to go. The application was horrible. It consisted of one extremely large Perl file (over 10,000 lines!), and it printed out HTML using lots of `print` statements. Looking at it today, it's impossible for me to understand.

And yet, 10 years ago, I managed to put together something that not only was functional but also made sense to me. This growth is typical of what most professional developers go through, Jason and me included. The "hacks" I wrote made sense at the time, but as the months and years went on, the code became a rat's nest and maintenance was a nightmare. This problem is bad enough when you're developing non-GUI programs, but it's worse when bad code that handles business logic is mixed with bad code that handles the GUI. And it's even worse when your GUI is written in HTML, and you're relying on linearly spitting out HTML tags instead of using object orientation or componentization.

Why is this important? Because, like all other developers, Jason and I have grown from novice programmers hacking in Perl and PHP (and not really knowing what we were doing) to experienced developers with a deep understanding of what it takes to build a maintainable web-based application.

Jason and I didn't create WebWork. It was developed by Rickard Öberg, one of the original authors of JBoss, after he decided there had to be a better way to develop web applications. What came from Rickard was a framework built around the philosophy that the correct way to do something should also be the easiest option, that the path of least resistance is a good thing, and that there is a fine balance between too much flexibility and too little.

Jason and I found WebWork through different means, but the end result was the same: We were captivated by its functionality and grace. Over time, we evolved from users to contributors to developers, and now to published authors. In the process, we've learned better ways to do things. And similarly, WebWork has also evolved. Jason and I spent endless nights creating version 2.0, which has become a major upgrade and has set the groundwork for doing much more with the Web-Work platform.

Today, WebWork is much more than it was in the past. And tomorrow, it will be even better. In this book, you'll learn the techniques, best practices, and concepts that go with the WebWork framework. You'll see why we spent so much energy on type conversion and how it relates to HTTP. You'll learn about how common challenges in the world of HTML (such as the double-submit problem) were solved using interceptors—a feature unique to WebWork. You'll understand why building reusable templates that generate HTML is the best way to quickly create maintainable web applications.

Mostly, though, you'll learn a better way to build web applications. Whether you're already a WebWork user, or you use an alternative Java framework, or you don't use Java at all, this book provides the concepts and techniques that are the foundation of WebWork. We hope this book serves as a WebWork reference and also as a great tool for sharpening your development skills.

PATRICK LIGHTBODY

acknowledgments

This book wouldn't have been possible if it weren't for the tremendous community at OpenSymphony and all the software developers who continue to push for innovation in the Java web space. To everyone who uses WebWork or other OpenSymphony projects: Thank you for the appreciation and support through the years; with this book we'll continue to drive innovation even further.

Of course, this book also couldn't have been possible without a publisher. To everyone at Manning, thank you for believing in us and in WebWork. This experience has been the most fulfilling project we've ever completed. We'd like to recognize the tireless efforts of our editor, Jackie Carter. As we closed in on the final weeks and months, we couldn't have pulled it off without the amazing proofreading, editing, marketing, and coordination provided by Liz Welch, Tiffany Taylor, Karen Tegtmeyer, and Mary Piergies. And finally, thank you to Marjan Bace for having the faith that, even through delays and setbacks, Manning could offer a book that would benefit so many software developers.

We also want to make a special mention of Carlos Whitt, who, with little notice, was kind enough to step in and take on the role of technical editor at the last minute. Thanks to Carlos's diving catch, we received valuable feedback and insightful comments. Carlos, your input was more valuable than we can possibly describe. Thank you. In addition to Carlos's heroic effort, we want to thank each and every reviewer who provided feedback during the entire process: Jack Herrington, Drew McAuliffe, Bill Lynch, Dick Zetterberg, Steve Poll, Ryan Daigle,

Peter White, Luigi Viggiano, Matthew Payne, Joseph B. Ottinger, Hani Suilman, Mark Woon, Berndt Hamboeck, Andrew Oswald, and Dag Liodden. Your feedback led to some major changes in how this book was structured, and we're forever in your debt for your wisdom. Finally, special thanks and words of appreciation to Rickard Öberg for agreeing to write the foreword to our book.

Patrick would also like to thank all his coworkers at Cisco Systems, Spoke Software, and Jive Software. Without their support, both verbal and technical, he could never have invested the time and energy in a project like WebWork and would certainly have never written a book on the subject. He also thanks his friends and family, who, no matter how much of a hermit he became, stood by his side through the entire process. And finally, many thanks to his girlfriend and best friend, Megan. Without her honesty, encouragement, and love, this book would never have been realized.

Jason would first and foremost like to thank his wife, Cyndy, without whose love, support, and nagging, his work on WebWork and this book would not have been possible. He would also like to thank his children, who had to spend too much time watching their dad work on his laptop instead of playing with them. He'd like to thank his former coworkers at Notiva and current coworkers at ePlus, whose wise decision to use WebWork allowed him to put theory to practice in creating great web applications. Finally, he'd like to thank Patrick for picking up his slack at the end when the real world intruded too heavily.

about this book

This book is very much what the title says: a book about *working* on *web-based* applications, using real-world examples along the way. That's what WebWork emphasizes: *working* on your project, not *wrestling* with your framework. Although it isn't the most-used web framework in the Java world, WebWork is widely known as the most refined, and it's gaining momentum every day. We'll show you how you can stop wrestling and get your framework to begin working for you.

In this book, we'll walk you through the basics of writing web applications, starting with simple forms and form processing. However, we know you've probably done that stuff a million times, and you're looking to sink your teeth into meatier problems. As such, we quicken the pace and look at advanced features such as validation, data-type conversion, resource dependencies, loose coupling of web application components, and a treasure chest of ways to deal with common challenges unique to the Web.

This book stays focused on a single application: CaveatEmptor. This is a modified version of the same application used in *Hibernate in Action* (Christian Bauer and Gavin King, Manning, 2004). By focusing on a tangible, growing application that you can download and modify, you get the benefit of taking part of an evolutionary process that goes beyond the pages of this book. You can expect that for the years following the publication of this book, the CaveatEmptor application will continue to lead the way for showcasing best practices for common web- and persistence-related problems.

Roadmap

Chapter 1 provides a basic overview required to help you get started with Web-Work. In addition to answering the hows, whys, and whats, we compare WebWork to other frameworks and outline the philosophy set by Rickard Öberg when he first created WebWork.

In chapter 2, we run through several iterations of a basic "Hello, World" application, starting from an extremely simple read-only example and going all the way to a more advanced input workflow complete with data validation and error reporting.

In chapter 3, we begin to look at the configuration options WebWork provides. This chapter covers how to configure individual actions, interceptors, and results, as well as general framework-related options such as what URL pattern to bind to.

Chapter 4 improves on the configuration lessons and hands-on experience from the previous two chapters and provides concrete examples of how to create your own WebWork actions. In this chapter we dive deeper into the basic form validation, error handling, and localization provided by the ActionSupport base class. We also look at handling alternative data elements in your actions, such as file uploads.

By this point, you'll be comfortable writing applications in WebWork. In the remaining chapters, our goal is to help you use the advanced WebWork features that were created to address everyday problems. In chapter 5, we explore interceptors and how they can add behavior to your actions without your needing to change the action classes or subclass.

Chapter 6 explores the Inversion of Control (IoC) pattern and how WebWork provides native support for it while also integrating into other popular IoC frameworks, such as Spring.

At this point, we shift gears and begin to focus on issues relating to user interfaces. We begin by looking at the concept of *results* in chapter 7. Results include common technologies like JSP but also uncommon ones: template languages such as Velocity and FreeMarker, and reporting engines such as JasperReports.

Displaying results isn't very useful if you can't include your data. In chapter 8, we take an in-depth look at Object Graph Navigation Language (OGNL): Web-Work's de facto expression language (EL). We also look at how EL shortcuts can save you a ton of time when you're rendering web-based forms.

Chapter 9 covers all the utility JSP tags that come with WebWork, from the familiar (if/elseif/else) to the unfamiliar (push, pop, action, and set). Even if you choose to develop in a template language such as FreeMarker rather than in

JSP, this chapter is still important, because similar concepts exist in those other technologies.

Now we'll be almost ready to look at the other half of the JSP tags: the UI tags. However, because they're implemented in Velocity, we spend chapter 10 presenting the basics so that you're well prepared. Chapter 10 is also a good way for you to get up to speed on JSP alternatives.

In chapter 11, we look at one of the most important features in WebWork: the UI tags. These tags let you componentize your HTML elements in to easy-to-reuse pieces. Building maintainable and scalable web applications hinges on use of these tags.

Chapter 12 examines common issues of type conversion—a challenge all web developers face, regardless of what programming language you're using. That's because HTTP is untyped, meaning all inputs are effectively Strings.

Chapter 13 looks at advanced validation techniques, focusing on ways to get data *validation* logic away from your code data *manipulation* logic.

Chapter 14 discusses techniques and features related to internationalization (i18), also known as *localization*.

Finally, in chapter 15, we pull it all together and look at common problems in the web environment and how everything you've learned can solve them. We take on the double-submit problem many web developers have faced. We also look at innovative ways to handle long-running processes rather than just asking the user to please wait. In addition to these common problems, we explore testing and debugging techniques that are useful when you're building WebWork-powered applications.

Who should read this book?

This book is for anyone who's fed up with web development, or at least wondering if there's a better way. Specifically, we expect that readers have a basic understanding of Java and the commonly used Java APIs, such as the Java Collections API. Because WebWork is all about the Web, a minimum level of understanding of HTML, JavaScript, and CSS is required.

Those who don't work on the web portion of their applications but have coworkers who do are also encouraged to read this book. With advanced features like type conversion, WebWork shows that you may not have to compromise on the design of your application's API just to appease the framework the web developers use.

Our hope is that both novice and experienced software developers—even those who aren't from a primarily Java-based background—can pick up this book and be productive right away.

Code conventions and downloads

This book provides many examples in various formats found in web applications powered by WebWork: Java code, HTML, XML snippets, JSPs, and template files written in Velocity. All source code in listings or in text is in a fixed-width font like this to separate it from ordinary text. Additionally, Java method names, JavaBean properties, XML elements, and attributes in text are presented using this same font.

Java, HTML, and XML can be verbose. In many cases, the original source code (available online) has been reformatted; we've added line breaks and reworked indentation to accommodate the available page space in the book. In rare cases even this was not enough, and listings include line-continuation markers. Additionally, many comments and JavaBean setters and getters have been removed from the listings.

Code annotations accompany some of the source code listings, highlighting important concepts. In a few cases, numbered bullets link to explanations that follow the listing.

WebWork is an open source project released under the very liberal OpenSymphony License. Directions for downloading WebWork, in source or binary form, are available from the WebWork web site: http://www.opensymphony.com/webwork.

The source code for all the CaveatEmptor examples in this book is available from http://www.manning.com/lightbody. The CaveatEmptor example application is a derivative of the one used in *Hibernate in Action*, found at http://caveatemptor.hibernate.org. You can find many versions of CaveatEmptor, using various deployment techniques (EJB, non-EJB), but the one found at the Manning web site should be the one you use as the companion to this book. Once you're finished reading the book, we highly recommend taking a peak at other versions of CaveatEmptor if you're at all curious about Hibernate or future versions of WebWork.

Author Online

Purchase of *WebWork in Action* includes free access to a private web forum run by Manning Publications where you can make comments about the book, ask technical questions, and receive help from the author and from other users. To access the forum and subscribe to it, point your web browser to http://www.manning.com/lightbody. This page provides information on how to get on the forum once you are registered, what kind of help is available, and the rules of conduct on the forum.

Manning's commitment to our readers is to provide a venue where a meaningful dialog between individual readers and between readers and the authors can take place. It is not a commitment to any specific amount of participation on the part of the authors, whose contribution to the AO remains voluntary (and unpaid). We suggest you try asking the authors some challenging questions lest their interest stray!

The Author Online forum and the archives of previous discussions will be accessible from the publisher's web site as long as the book is in print.

About the authors

PATRICK LIGHTBODY   Heading up Jive Software's Professional Services organization, Patrick has worked for various technology companies, ranging from well-established giants such as Cisco Systems to tiny Silicon Valley startups. He is the author of Java Open Source Programming and spends his spare time contributing to various OpenSymphony projects, including WebWork and OSWorkflow. While he grew up in the heart of the Silicon Valley, Patrick now resides in Portland, Oregon.

JASON CARREIRA   Jason has been developing and architecting J2EE applications for six years. For the last five, he's been designing and building enterprise financial software products from the ground up. He recently joined ePlus where he is working on the next generation of eProcurement solutions. In his spare time, Jason is a core developer of the XWork command pattern framework and Web-Work MVC web framework at OpenSymphony. He lives in Rochester, New York, with his wife Cyndy and three children.

a look at the future

In the open source world, innovation never stops. Although this can be a great thing, it can make it terribly difficult for people to keep up—even more so in the printed media. When we began working on this book over a year ago, WebWork 2.1 was just coming out and had huge momentum behind it. Today, WebWork 2.2 is just around the corner, and many new things are coming with it.

With that in mind, we specifically focused this book on things we knew would be important no matter what version of WebWork you're using—or even if you aren't using WebWork at all. The concepts and techniques introduced here—such as decoupled validation and type conversion—are important in any web environment.

This book is based on WebWork 2.1.7, but we took several steps to prepare you for the upgrade to 2.2. Most important, we use the optional altSyntax feature in WebWork 2.1.7 that will become standard in 2.2 and beyond. This feature simplifies how the tag libraries work. Because this feature was optional in 2.1, it's extremely important that you enable it before attempting to use any of the examples in this book. In chapter 3, "Setting up WebWork," we show you how to enable this feature.

Another step we took to make sure concepts learned here can be taken beyond the pages of this book is to use derivative of the sample application used in *Hibernate in Action*. Both the Hibernate and WebWork teams have committed to improving and evolving CaveatEmptor; so, after you're finished reading this book, you can look at new versions of CaveatEmptor to see how the same application was built using WebWork 2.2 features.

about the title

By combining introductions, overviews, and how-to examples, the *In Action* books are designed to help learning and remembering. According to research in cognitive science, the things people remember are things they discover during self-motivated exploration.

Although no one at Manning is a cognitive scientist, we are convinced that for learning to become permanent it must pass through stages of exploration, play, and, interestingly, retelling of what is being learned. People understand and remember new things, which is to say they master them, only after actively exploring them. Humans learn in action. An essential part of an *In Action* guide is that it is example-driven. It encourages the reader to try things out, to play with new code, and explore new ideas.

There is another, more mundane, reason for the title of this book: our readers are busy. They use books to do a job or to solve a problem. They need books that allow them to jump in and jump out easily and learn just what they want just when they want it. They need books that aid them *in action*. The books in this series are designed for such readers.

about the cover illustration

The figure on the cover of *WebWork in Action* is a "Dancer from Constantinople." The illustration is taken from a collection of costumes of the Ottoman Empire published on January 1, 1802, by William Miller of Old Bond Street, London. The title page is missing from the collection and we have been unable to track it down to date. The book's table of contents identifies the figures in both English and French, and each illustration bears the names of two artists who worked on it, both of whom would no doubt be surprised to find their art gracing the front cover of a computer programming book...two hundred years later.

The collection was purchased by a Manning editor at an antiquarian flea market in the "Garage" on West 26th Street in Manhattan. The seller was an American based in Ankara, Turkey, and the transaction took place just as he was packing up his stand for the day. The Manning editor did not have on his person the substantial amount of cash that was required for the purchase and a credit card and check were both politely turned down.

With the seller flying back to Ankara that evening the situation was getting hopeless. What was the solution? It turned out to be nothing more than an old-fashioned verbal agreement sealed with a handshake. The seller simply proposed that the money be transferred to him by wire and the editor walked out with the bank information on a piece of paper and the portfolio of images under his arm. Needless to say, we transferred the funds the next day, and we remain grateful and impressed by this unknown person's trust in one of us. It recalls something that might have happened a long time ago.

The pictures from the Ottoman collection, like the other illustrations that appear on our covers, bring to life the richness and variety of dress customs of two centuries ago. They recall the sense of isolation and distance of that period‹and of every other historic period except our own hyperkinetic present.

Dress codes have changed since then and the diversity by region, so rich at the time, has faded away. It is now often hard to tell the inhabitant of one continent from another. Perhaps, trying to view it optimistically, we have traded a cultural and visual diversity for a more varied personal life. Or a more varied and interesting intellectual and technical life.

We at Manning celebrate the inventiveness, the initiative, and, yes, the fun of the computer business with book covers based on the rich diversity of regional life of two centuries ago, brought back to life by the pictures from this collection.

Part 1

Introduction to WebWork

This part of the book eases you into the basics of WebWork and the problems it tries to solve. Chapter 1 looks at the high-level architecture of WebWork and why the Model-View Controller design pattern helps when you're building web applications. In chapter 2, we apply these concepts in a concrete manner and walk you through the creation of a simple read-only WebWork example. We then modify that example and add data input and validation and the corresponding page workflow. Once you're comfortable building basic web apps, we examine the various forms of configuration you can use to build your own applications.

An overview of WebWork

Imagine you just built an entire web application and shipped version 1.0. Your biggest customer is now demanding that in version 1.1, the user interface must change dramatically to fit with their corporate usability standards—everything from the number of fields in data-entry forms to button and image locations to the number of steps in various wizards. And the customer wants the changes made by next week.

Depending on how your web application was built, you might not even break a sweat. Or, you might be beefing up your resume. In the early days of building web applications, developers often used scripting languages like Perl and printed out content they wanted to display directly within their scripts—the same place where critical business logic was located. It soon became clear that this technique too tightly coupled the core business code with the presentation.

These days, libraries exist for Perl, PHP, JSP, ASP, and every other web-enabled programming language, to try to solve the problem of separating business code from presentation code. Depending on the library you use and how well you've taken advantage of it, fulfilling your customer's demands might be a walk in the park.

In this book, you'll learn how to use one of Java's most popular web frameworks: WebWork. WebWork is an advanced framework based on the philosophy that common tasks should be easy to do and advanced designs should be possible to build. More than anything, the developers of WebWork wanted to provide a framework that works *for* you, not *against* you.

To help you learn WebWork, we'll show you how we utilized its basic and advanced features to build a second-generation version of the sample application used in the book *Hibernate in Action* (Manning Publications, 2004, www.manning.com/bauer). Hibernate is an Object-Relational Mapping (ORM) framework that provides easy database access. The authors, Christian Bauer and Gavin King, demonstrated the features of Hibernate using an online auction application named CaveatEmptor. Although CaveatEmptor is a complete application, it lacks any sort of web-based interface.

In this book, we'll demonstrate how we used the features of WebWork to add a web front end on top of the original CaveatEmptor code. We chose to introduce WebWork and its features this way for several reasons. First, many WebWork users also use Hibernate, so expanding on CaveatEmptor allows the community to see optimal ways to integrate the two. In addition, the original CaveatEmptor application contains no web user interface, and many readers of *Hibernate in Action* might want to learn how to add one. Those who know how to write back-end code quite well but aren't experts with the front end can consult this book to see how it's done.

However, before we can explore WebWork's features and CaveatEmptor, we'll first examine the general ideas behind web application frameworks. In chapter 2, "HelloWorld, the WebWork way," we'll walk through the familiar "Hello, World" tutorial to show you the basics of using WebWork. For the remainder of the book, we'll focus entirely on WebWork's features and how we used them in the CaveatEmptor application.

But before we can do that, you need to understand what WebWork is and what it's trying to accomplish. At the core, WebWork solves the problem of separating presentation logic from domain logic. But what does that mean? Why is it important? Where did this concept come from? More to the point, what is MVC, the pattern on which WebWork is based?

1.1 Why MVC is important

The issue of separating the domain model from presentation isn't unique to web applications. The *Model-View-Controller* (MVC) pattern was originally developed by the SmallTalk community to solve this problem for desktop GUI applications. MVC seeks to break an application into three parts and define the interactions between these components, thereby limiting the coupling between them and allowing each one to focus on its specific responsibilities without worrying about the others.

Although the original MVC pattern worked well for desktop GUI applications, it failed to map directly to the World Wide Web. As developers continued to refine their web development techniques, MVC variations evolved to address the behaviors specific to the request/response model that makes up the HyperText Transport Protocol (HTTP). The core concerns of MVC haven't changed as these evolutions have taken place, and WebWork continues to champion the same motivations that SmallTalk developers faced decades ago.

MVC tries to keep the more generally reusable domain model code and the view-specific code from being too aware of each other. It does this by introducing a controller to sit between the view and the model. The controller handles events from the view, such as button clicks, and maps them to model changes. The controller also registers the view to receive notifications of changes to the domain model, so that the view can refresh. This allows, for instance, a different view to be applied without changing the underlying model or controller layers.

MVC frameworks have become the dominant architecture for web application development. WebWork is an MVC framework. Other popular Java-based MVC web application frameworks include Struts (no longer in active development), Tapestry, RIFE, and JavaServer Faces (JSF). Before we look at web-based MVC designs, let's briefly examine the original MVC design that was used for desktop GUI applications. Knowing the flow of the original MVC will help you understand the importance of the changes and updates MVC has faced as it has been applied to WebWork—and, specifically, as it's implemented in WebWork.

1.1.1 *Classic MVC becomes outdated*

Figure 1.1 shows the event flow in classic MVC. The user interacts with the view, filling in data and clicking buttons. The controller receives events from the view and performs actions on the model, updating it with the data the user has provided. The view is notified of model-change events so that it can refresh from the model, showing the result of their work back to the user. Multiple views and controllers may be configured to use the same shared model by registering more event listeners. This pattern works well for applications where the entire application runs on the user's machine and everything runs and is refreshed in real time. The classic MVC pattern breaks down, however, in the Web world, where the view is rendered in a browser on the client side while the controller and model are on the server. Figure 1.1 shows a very clean design approach. Unfortunately, it doesn't work in the world of HTTP and HTML. Instead, web applications, using an HTTP request/response model, require a very different dwesign that borrows its name and some aspects from classic MVC.

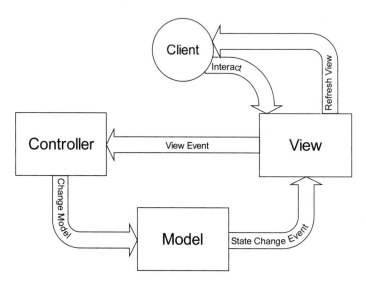

Figure 1.1   Event flow for the classic MVC pattern

1.1.2 Classic MVC gets an update: the Front Controller

In the web version of MVC, views can't make direct calls to controllers, as shown in figure 1.1, but are mapped based on web requests to URLs. The view isn't an object to be updated, but a web page that is redrawn only when the client makes a new request. The model also can't notify the view about changes, because it's rendered in the user's browser on a different machine; so, the view is forced to re-render every time for all the latest data.

Figure 1.2 shows the event flow in MVC as it's applied to web application frameworks. The classic application of MVC to the Web world is implemented using the *Front Controller* pattern. This involves a dispatcher (implemented as a servlet in Java web MVC implementations) that maps

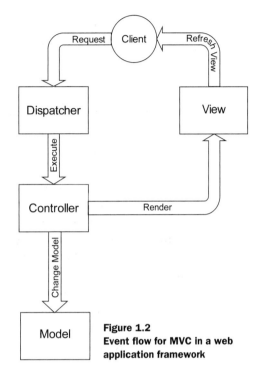

**Figure 1.2
Event flow for MVC in a web application framework**

request URLs to command instances to be executed. The command instances, which are actions in WebWork or Struts, interact with backend services of the system, which can be generally grouped together as the model. The command instance returns a return code after doing its processing, which is mapped to a view (usually a web page template such as a JSP). The view is provided with the controller and model to render for the user and often uses custom tag libraries to easily access these values.

1.1.3 MVC evolves: the Page Controller

A somewhat different implementation of MVC has been popularized by frameworks like Microsoft's ASP.NET[1]. Rather than have requests go through a dispatcher

---

[1] Microsoft has an interesting discussion of presentation tier design patterns at http://msdn.microsoft.com/practices/type/Patterns/Enterprise/EspWebPresentationPatterns/. They include both the Page Controller and Front Controller patterns; but the Page Controller is built into their framework, whereas a Front Controller implementation must be built from scratch.

to look up a controller to execute, the view is hit directly and calls its controller before continuing to render. Although this pattern gives up some of the decoupled nature of a more classic MVC implementation, it should gain in productivity and tool support (especially in Microsoft Visual Studio). This type of development can also be supported by WebWork by using the `<webwork:action>` custom tag (see chapter 9, "Tag libraries," for a discussion of the WebWork tag library).

Front Controller versus Page Controller

Figures 1.3 and 1.4 show how a dashboard might be implemented differently using the Front Controller or Page Controller design. The Page Controller may look more modular due to the split of the X, Y, and Z responsibilities, but good use of object-oriented design could allow for a modular Front Controller design as well. If you're familiar with Struts, the Front Controller pattern will look very familiar. Even if you aren't familiar with other web frameworks, this technique should seem to be the most linear way to gather data and present it. However, some frameworks are embracing the Page Controller, shown in figure 1.4, because of the way it encourages encapsulation. Fortunately, WebWork supports both implementations, giving you the best of both worlds.

In our experience, frameworks can greatly increase your productivity. In order to meet your customers' requirements and be ready for all the challenges an ever-changing business world throws at you, we recommend that you take advantage

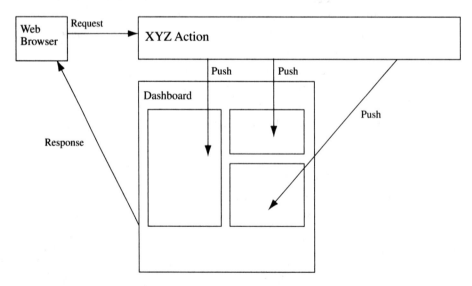

Figure 1.3 A dashboard implemented using the Front Controller MVC design

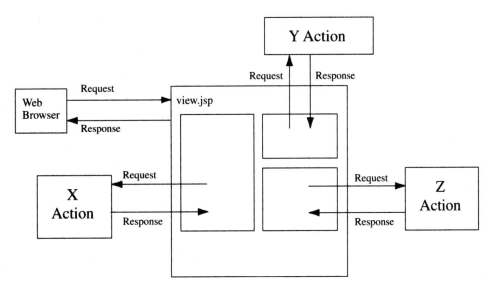

Figure 1.4   A dashboard implemented using the Page Controller MVC design

of the MVC design pattern when building web applications. Rather than build an MVC framework from scratch, most developers choose to leverage an existing one, such as WebWork.

1.2   Understanding frameworks and containers

WebWork is, at its very heart, an MVC *framework*. But it's also a lightweight *container*. To help you better understand the difference between a framework and a container, we're going to look at the functionality each one provides as well as several alternative or related technologies for both categories.

1.2.1   What is a framework?

When he was building the original version of WebWork, Rickard Öberg (the creator of WebWork and co-founder of JBoss) said, "A framework's power comes not from what it allows, but from what it does not allow." What Rickard meant explains what a framework is: Frameworks are meant to bring structure to what would otherwise be chaos. In the case of web application frameworks, the goal is to encourage developers to use a supplied set of base classes and tag libraries, thereby avoiding a potential mess of tangled JSPs.

In the framework of a house, too many wooden beams will leave you with no options when expanding your home with new rooms, adding new windows and doorways, or accessorizing your living room with a fireplace. Too few beams and too little structure will leave you with many options, but you probably won't feel safe keeping your family under that roof during the middle of a storm or an earthquake. Frameworks are a delicate balance between structure and creativity.

As a framework mandates more structure, your creativity wiggle room begins to shrink. One extreme is the absence of a framework: chaos. The other extreme is a framework that restricts you to so few choices that you can't finish your application. Clearly, a middle ground exists somewhere between these two extremes, and that is what WebWork and all other MVC frameworks are trying to find.

WebWork encourages creativity

Struts, a popular Java web framework, shares many similarities with WebWork. However, it doesn't offer the amount of wiggle room that is often needed when you're building large-scale web applications. For example, consider the case of comparing the tags that both frameworks use to print out an internationalized message. In both frameworks, internationalized text can be parameterized with dynamic values such as a price, number, and date.

Suppose we wish to display an airplane ticket confirmation in the following form:

```
Your {0} ticket(s) for flight {1} have been booked.
The total cost is {2}. Your confirmation number is {3}.
Your flight leaves at {4} and arrives at {5}
```

In Struts, <bean:message> is the tag used to do this. Unfortunately, Struts only allows messages to be parameterized with five values, meaning our message must be split into two parts:

```
<bean:message key="confirmation.msg1"
            arg0="count" arg1="flightNumber" arg2="cost"/>
<bean:message key="confirmation.msg2"
            arg0="confirmation" arg1="departure" arg2="arrival"/>
```

In WebWork, we use the <ww:text> tag. However, rather than limit messages to a fixed number of parameters, WebWork allows unlimited parameters:

```
<ww:text name="confirmation.msg">
    <ww:param value="count"/>
    <ww:param value="flightNumber"/>
    <ww:param value="cost"/>
    <ww:param value="confirmation"/>
    <ww:param value="departure"/>
```

```
        <ww:param value="arrival"/>
    </ww:text>
```

This may seem like an extremely trivial difference—and it is. But it helps show how a framework can provide more options without falling closer to the chaos that no framework leaves us with. A good framework provides certain features that restrict what the developer can do but is also careful to give as many *good* options as possible. As any veteran developer can attest, some tremendous software development achievements can be accomplished by making a lot of minor but intelligent decisions. Frameworks can assist by making many of these decisions for you.

WebWork strikes a balance

Through years of experience in building web applications, the authors of this book have found that WebWork provided the best compromise, but some other frameworks are worth looking at—if not to be used, at least to be learned from.

> **NOTE** We recommend that if you wish to explore other frameworks, the most interesting are JSF and Tapestry. You can learn more about Tapestry from *Tapestry in Action* by Howard Lewis-Ship (Manning Publications, 2004, www.manning.com/catalog/view.php?book=lewisship).

1.2.2 What a container can do

Frameworks are often defined by what they can't do. *Containers*, on the other hand, are most often defined by what they *can* do. Let's look at the container most web application developers are familiar with: the servlet container. Many different servlet containers have been built: Tomcat, Orion, Resin, WebLogic, WebSphere … the list goes on. They differ in many ways: cost, performance, support, and so forth. But beyond economics, each container provides its own unique value-added features. Some do clustering better than others. Some provide better support for developers. Some support the 2.3 specification, whereas others support the newer 2.4 spec.

The point is that a container is designed to contain some of your code and provide unique features to that code. The more useful features, the better the container. What does it mean when we say that WebWork is both a framework and a container?

WebWork's lightweight container

Servlet containers provide features that the specification requires or that the developers of the container provided. The same goes for other J2EE containers, such as the EJB container. A *lightweight container* is different—it gives you the ability to add features to a generic container, thereby making a unique container that fits the needs of your application.

Let's consider a more concrete example. Suppose you aren't using EJB but you still want to provide simple transactional support to developers who are working on your project. You could build into a lightweight container transactional support for any object that is contained. Now you have a unique container that provides some of the benefits of EJB. It gets much more interesting when you start providing features unique to your application that EJB or other specifications would never have dreamed of.

In addition to being an MVC framework, WebWork comes with a small, light-weight container designed to let you build these kinds of features. It's designed to make life simple for other developers, allowing them to easily take advantage of your unique container. In chapter 6, "Inversion of Control," we'll show you how to use WebWork's container to provide highly custom solutions to your development team.

Competing containers

WebWork isn't the only lightweight container on the block. Others include Jakarta HiveMind (and before that, Jakarta Avalon), PicoContainer, and Spring. Although each container is unique, they all try to provide the same thing: a simple, customizable environment in which your objects can exist and be managed independently and passively. Lightweight containers are only recently being recognized as something exciting.

NOTE   For more on the excellent Spring container, we recommend *Spring in Action* by Craig Walls (Manning Publications, 2005, www.manning.com/walls2).

Jumping back to the framework discussion for a minute, remember that there is a delicate balance between providing too many features and too few. Although WebWork comes with its own lightweight container, it also allows for alternative containers to be plugged in. That means you can use WebWork's framework and PicoContainer together without any problems.

In a purely technical sense, WebWork's container isn't a core part of WebWork and is considered optional. Replacing it and integrating it with an alternative container is fairly simple. Many of these types of integrations are done through Web-Work's support for interceptors. In chapter 5, "Adding functionality with interceptors," you'll learn about interceptors and discover the huge amount of power and flexibility they offer while still maintaining a rigid framework on which your applications can be built.

You can better understand the difference between WebWork's container and framework aspects if you know how WebWork evolved. Let's take a moment to examine the history of WebWork and the community revolving around WebWork; in doing so, you'll learn the core parts of WebWork, where XWork came from, and when and why the Inversion of Control container was added.

1.3 WebWork: past, present, and future

To better understand the direction and philosophy that WebWork follows, let's look at the roots of WebWork, how it evolved, and where it's going. In doing so, we'll identify an underlying component, XWork, which provides the foundation on which WebWork is built. Although it's fundamentally important to WebWork, we'll only examine XWork at a high level in this chapter. Finally, we'll explore some ideas and concepts being discussed today, to give you a better idea of what WebWork might look like in the future.

1.3.1 The history of WebWork

Even though WebWork 2.0 was released in February 2004, WebWork was first created a long time ago (long being a relative term when applied to Java open-source technologies). WebWork was first publicly available in the fall of 2000 as version 0.92. It was originally created by Rickard Öberg after he faced many frustrations with other Java web frameworks.

As more developers began to use WebWork, it joined the OpenSymphony group and continued releasing new versions until 1.3. At that point, it was widely recognized that one of WebWork's main benefits was the fact that it wasn't truly tied to the web, despite its name. In the winter of 2003, in an effort to separate the web and nonweb portions, a roadmap for WebWork 2.0 was created. Version 2.0 was designed to continue to use all the principles of the 1.x version but to be built on a non-web-based component called XWork.

> **NOTE** Between the release of 1.3 and 2.0, the WebWork 1.x branch continued to be supported and used by many users. Version 1.4 has since been released, and the 1.x branch will continue to be maintained. However, all new major enhancements and features have been planned for the 2.x branch, and as such this book is purely about WebWork 2.0 and beyond.

1.3.2 Understanding the XWork core

Although XWork is an important and critical part of WebWork, we won't be explicitly discussing XWork in this book. (We want to avoid confusion around the

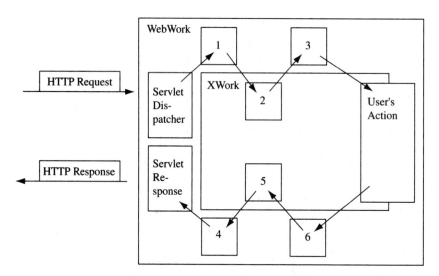

Figure 1.5 A high-level demonstration of the interactions between XWork and WebWork, including how XWork and WebWork interceptors work together as the action invocation is processed

terms *XWork* and *WebWork*, given that unless you plan to dig deep into the core implementation of both projects, you probably won't need to know the difference.) To give you an idea of how WebWork and XWork relate, figure 1.5 shows a high-level representation of the interactions between them.

An HTTP request goes to WebWork's servlet dispatcher. The request is converted to an action command, which is then routed through a series of WebWork and XWork *interceptors* (1–3). The command is finally executed in the form of user code that sits on top of both XWork and WebWork. After the action executes, the response is routed through another series of interceptors (4–6) and finally converted to a web-aware response (such as a JSP) via WebWork's servlet response.

As you can see, the interaction between XWork and WebWork can be complex. Rather than ask you to continue to context-switch between XWork and WebWork, we'll merely refer to everything as *WebWork*, because it's the higher-level component of the two.

If you're interested in learning more about XWork, plenty of good online documents and resources can help you get started. XWork is far from a WebWork-only component. In fact, it's supported in another web framework called JPublish and OpenSymphony's workflow engine (OSWorkflow), and it's even being used as the basis for a Swing GUI framework (being developed at the time of this writing) called Pendulum.

1.3.3 *Future directions*

A Swing framework built on top of WebWork was one of the many grand visions conceived from the very start of WebWork. Some people have already done this in limited ways. It's expected that in the future, the number of such developers will increase around XWork and WebWork, providing even more user interface options for your UI-agnostic action classes.

Other future work on WebWork includes more integrated support for Java-Script on the client browser, tool integration to enable rapid application development, and better support for third-party libraries and containers. Other future features might include support for alternative web-enabled view technologies, such as Macromedia Flash. In general, the driving force will always be to allow you to fulfill your customers' changing needs quickly and safely, while giving you as much freedom as possible without breaking down into chaos.

Having glanced at the future, let's take a moment to look at the primary basis for all the example code in this book. By knowing what the application does, what domain models are used, and how the application is packaged, you'll have a much easier time following along with the examples in the rest of the book.

1.4 *The CaveatEmptor application*

As we mentioned at the start of this chapter, this book bases many of its examples on a web-enabled version of the CaveatEmptor application that was the foundation of the book *Hibernate in Action*. CaveatEmptor is a fictitious online auction application. It contains domain models like `Item`, `Bid`, and `User`, which we'll focus on in this book.

The original CaveatEmptor application detailed in *Hibernate in Action* didn't have a web interface. For the purpose of this book, we implemented parts of the web interface to demonstrate many WebWork features. You don't need to be familiar with Hibernate to understand the examples in this book, because all the Hibernate-specific code is cleanly abstracted away in a `PersistenceManager` component (detailed in chapter 6). Similarly, you won't need the original CaveatEmptor source code; you don't even need to be familiar with it. However, if you do find yourself with a copy of both books, you'll find some continuity in the examples and domain objects.

Speaking of domain objects, of all the objects found in CaveatEmptor, we'll spend the most time (by far) discussing the `User` domain object and the various actions and web user interfaces that interact with it. The `User` object isn't special by any means: It's a simple JavaBean with properties like `firstName`, `lastName`, email, age, birthDate, and so on. These properties, however, represent the most common domain properties around which you'll often write web applications.

We'll look at use cases such as updating a user's profile, registering for an account, logging in and out, and creating multiple users at a time (batch processing). We'll also examine a few non-user-specific use cases, such as pagination, displaying wait pages while background searches take place, and gracefully handling double-click form submissions. All the actions and the view files (JSPs, in this case) are found in the CaveatEmptor download available from this book's web site. Let's look at how the download is organized so you can quickly get up to speed on the examples in this book.

1.4.1 How CaveatEmptor is organized

Because this book focuses so much on this application, let's go over what you'll find once you download the application. The download is in the form of a .zip file. You'll need to extract it using a standard tool like WinZip, Windows XP's zip tool, Java's jar tool, or StuffIt Expander for the Mac OS. Once you extract the contents, you'll find this directory structure:

```
CaveatEmptor
 - lib
    - core
    - resin*
 - src
    - java
       - org
          - hibernate
             - auction
                - ...
    - webapp
       - WEB-INF
       - ...
 - build.xml
```

All the source code we present in this book is found in the src directory. If the example is a Java file, it's in src/java and probably somewhere in the org.hibernate.auction.web package. JSPs and Velocity templates, as well as any other web-specific files, are found in src/webapp. Configuration files, such as xwork.xml and webwork.properties, are located in src/java; they're packaged into a single JAR file, which is included in WEB-INF/lib when the entire WAR is packaged.

Every JAR required for the application is found in lib/core. In addition to these JARs, we also provide instructions in the form of a README.TXT file in lib/resin. These instructions show you how to quickly launch the application *without* running Ant or packaging the application as a WAR. The instructions also explain how to download additional Resin JAR files needed to launch the application quickly. This will let you open up the examples and modify them as you read the book, playing with different options on the fly. When you do want to package the application as a WAR, you can use the supplied build.xml file in the root of the download; invoking `ant war` from the command line will do the trick.

> **NOTE** We'll continue to update CaveatEmptor after this book has been published. You can always download the latest version at Manning's web site.

1.5 *Summary*

Building reusable frameworks is a tough job—they can't be custom tailored, they can't be too rigid, and they can't be too flexible. The framework that can best allow your development team to meet your customer's requirements is the one you should use. In this book, we'll show you many WebWork features, tips, and techniques, demonstrating that you that if you build your applications using WebWork, meeting that next week's deadline might not be nearly as difficult as it sounds.

You've now seen the history of MVC, how it evolved, and why, when applied to the Web, it enforces important design decisions that make building your next web application much easier. Because WebWork provides both Front Controller and Page Controller support, you should be able to use WebWork exactly as you want to and not be limited by the framework.

In addition to the framework that WebWork provides, we also explored the concept of passive management of resources in containers. Because WebWork is both a framework and a container, it can both address the need to narrow the scope of certain functionality (such as a WebWork action) and broaden the scope of other functionality (such as a passively managed persistence layer).

Differentiating the need to sometimes be restricted and other times be totally free is an important characteristic of WebWork. WebWork has evolved and will continue to evolve, but this key characteristic continues to be the driving motivation for WebWork and all pragmatic programmers.

We also explained our motivation for using a new version of the CaveatEmptor application to demonstrate WebWork. This book focuses on the `User` domain model for most examples, but a few examples aren't user related. It's important to remember that although the examples in this book may be narrowed in scope to just users, the concepts can be applied to any domain object.

Before we can dig in to CaveatEmptor, let's take some smaller steps. In chapter 2, you'll build a simple "Hello, World" web application using WebWork. After getting your feet wet, we'll then explore some of WebWork's architecture so you can make more informed decisions when building WebWork-enabled applications. Then we'll dive headfirst into the features WebWork offers, all of which are designed to make your job easier. Our aim is to show how you can build web applications faster and smarter and be better prepared for change.

HelloWorld,
the WebWork way

This chapter covers
- How to set up a WebWork project
- How to create your first WebWork action
- Input and output of data from your action
- An introduction to the WebWork JSP tag library

In this chapter, we'll walk through a brief example that demonstrates the basics of WebWork. By the end of this chapter, you should have enough understanding of WebWork to build simple web-based applications. Later in the book, you'll expand on what you learned here to do more advanced configurations and take advantage of advanced features including validation, internationalization, scripting, type conversion, and support for display formats other than HTML, such as PDF.

2.1 Downloading WebWork

Before you begin, you must download WebWork. You can find the latest version (2.1.7 at the time of this writing) at http://webwork.dev.java.net/servlets/Project-DocumentList. Once you've downloaded the distribution binary, such as web-work-2.1.7.zip, you need to unzip it. Inside, you'll find sample applications, documentation, and the source code of the framework so you can see how it works. You'll also find all the JAR files required to get WebWork running.

We highly recommend that you examine all the documentation and sample code, but for now we're only concerned with the required libraries and the Web-Work JAR. Let's begin by preparing the basic web application file structure so that you can start building applications.

2.2 Preparing the skeleton

The basic web application file structure, also known as the *skeleton*, is the bare minimum required to begin building the sample applications you'll explore in this chapter. You need the files listed in table 2.1, which are found in the downloadable WebWork distribution.

Table 2.1   **Files required to set up a WebWork web application**

Filename	Description
xwork.jar	XWork library on which WebWork is built
commons-logging.jar	Commons logging, which WebWork uses to support transparently logging to either Log4J or JDK 1.4+
oscore.jar	OSCore, a general-utility library from OpenSymphony
velocity-dep.jar	Velocity library with dependencies
ognl.jar	Object Graph Navigation Language (OGNL), the expression language used throughout WebWork

Table 2.1   Files required to set up a WebWork web application *(continued)*

Filename	Description
xwork.xml	WebWork configuration file that defines the actions, results, and interceptors for your application
web.xml	J2EE web application configuration file that defines the servlets, JSP tag libraries, and so on for your web application

Some files, especially configuration files, aren't included in the distribution; you'll create them in a moment. Also note that the version numbers of the dependent JAR files (such as oscore.jar and ognl.jar) can be found in the distribution in the file versions.txt, located in the lib directory.

As usual for J2EE web applications, JARs go in the WEB-INF/lib directory and web.xml goes in the WEB-INF directory. As is most often the case, configuration elements such as xwork.xml go in the WEB-INF/classes directory. Having done that, your directory layout should appear as follows:

```
/ (Root)
|---WEB-INF
    |---web.xml
    |---classes
    |    |---xwork.xml
    |---lib
    |    |---webwork-2.1.7.jar, xwork.jar, oscore.jar, ognl.jar, ...
```

NOTE   Now that the directory structure is set, you must configure your web application server (such as Resin, Orion, or Apache Tomcat) to deploy the web app starting from the location marked Root. How you deploy it depends on the server you're using and whether you zip the directory layout as a WAR beforehand. Consult your server's documentation for detailed instructions on deploying web apps such as this one. We also suggest that you consult your IDE's documentation to be able to deploy your web application directly from the IDE, either by using a plug-in or by starting the container's main class as an executable.

2.2.1 *Creating the web.xml deployment file*

In order for WebWork to work properly, it needs to be deployed in such a way that certain URL patterns, such as `*.action`, map to a WebWork servlet that is responsible for handling all WebWork requests. A URL *pattern* is a pattern that is matched against all incoming HTTP requests (such as from web browsers). If the location, also known as a *resource*, matches the pattern, the associated servlet is invoked. Without this servlet, WebWork wouldn't function.

You must first add the following entry to web.xml:

```
<servlet>
    <servlet-name>webwork</servlet-name>
    <servlet-class>
        com.opensymphony.webwork.dispatcher.ServletDispatcher
    </servlet-class>
</servlet>
```

The next step is to map the servlet to a URL pattern. The pattern you choose can be anything you want, but the most typical pattern is `*.action`. You can configure the pattern the servlet will match by adding the following to web.xml:

```
<servlet-mapping>
    <servlet-name>webwork</servlet-name>
    <url-pattern>*.action</url-pattern>
</servlet-mapping>
```

Finally, in order to use WebWork's tag library, you must add an entry to web.xml indicating where the tag library definition can be found:[1]

```
<taglib>
    <taglib-uri>webwork</taglib-uri>
    <taglib-location>/WEB-INF/lib/webwork-2.1.7.jar
    </taglib-location>
</taglib>
```

You can add many other optional configuration items to web.xml, such as support for JasperReports, Velocity, FreeMarker, and other view technologies. Because you're building a skeleton application with no other files or configuration elements, the final web.xml file should look like the following:

```
<?xml version="1.0" encoding="ISO-8859-1"?>
 <!DOCTYPE web-app PUBLIC
    "-//Sun Microsystems, Inc.//DTD Web Application 2.3//EN"
    "http://java.sun.com/dtd/web-app_2_3.dtd">
 <web-app>
    <servlet>
        <servlet-name>webwork</servlet-name>
        <servlet-class>
            com.opensymphony.webwork.dispatcher.ServletDispatcher
        </servlet-class>
    </servlet>
    <servlet-mapping>
        <servlet-name>webwork</servlet-name>
        <url-pattern>*.action</url-pattern>
```

---

[1] In newer servlet containers that fully support the JSP 1.2 specification, the taglib should be automatically picked up without any configuration.

```
        </servlet-mapping>
        <taglib>
            <taglib-uri>webwork</taglib-uri>
            <taglib-location>/WEB-INF/lib/webwork-2.1.7.jar
            </taglib-location>
        </taglib>
    </web-app>
```

This is the most basic web.xml file you can use for a WebWork application. Most likely, your web.xml will quickly grow to include additional servlets, tag libraries, event listeners, and so on.

2.2.2 Creating the xwork.xml configuration file

Now that you've configured web.xml correctly, you need to set up a skeleton configuration for WebWork itself. Because WebWork is based on a subproject, XWork, the configuration file is named xwork.xml and is located in WEB-INF/classes, as previously shown. We'll discuss configuration in more detail in chapter 3, "Setting up WebWork," so don't worry too much about the contents of this file. For now, the skeleton setup requires just the following in xwork.xml:

```
<!DOCTYPE xwork PUBLIC "-//OpenSymphony Group//XWork 1.0//EN"
"http://www.opensymphony.com/xwork/xwork-1.0.dtd">
<xwork>
    <include file="webwork-default.xml"/>

    <package name="default" extends="webwork-default">
        <default-interceptor-ref name="completeStack"/>
    </package>
</xwork>
```

The key thing to note here is that a file, webwork-default.xml, is included. Doing this ensures that all the WebWork additions built on top of XWork are available to you. This file contains the standard configuration for WebWork, so it's very important that it be included. Without this file, WebWork wouldn't function as you'd expect, because it wouldn't be correctly configured. Note that you don't need to have a file named webwork-default.xml—it's already included in the WebWork JAR file.

2.2.3 Creating the webwork.properties configuration file

Just as you placed xwork.xml in WEB-INF/classes, you also need to add a file called webwork.properties to that directory. Like other aspects of WebWork configuration, the contents of this file are discussed in chapter 3. For now, add the following line to webwork.properties:

```
webwork.tag.altSyntax = true
```

This line is required because every example in this chapter (and the rest of the book) is given with the assumption that webwork.tag.altSyntax is set to true. We did this to let you have the most up-to-date information about a framework that is always evolving. At the time of this writing, WebWork 2.1.7 is the latest released version. However, we already know that as of WebWork 2.2, altSyntax will become standard; so, we felt it would be best to cover this syntax now rather than teach something that is on the verge of changing.

2.2.4 *Tips for developing WebWork apps*

You're now ready to begin building your first example application. In order to do so, you must compile Java sources and copy the resulting .class files to WEB-INF/ classes. There are several ways to do this, including executing javac by hand, using an Ant build script, or using an IDE such as Eclipse or JetBrains IntelliJ IDEA (formerly IntelliJ IDEA). You should choose whatever method you're most comfortable with. In the CaveatEmpt●r example used in the rest of the book, you'll find project files for IDEA as well as an Ant build script to help you get started. Feel free to use and modify the supplied build scripts and project files for your own projects.

Using an IDE may be a better approach because you can launch the application server, debug, and edit all within the same environment. Without these features, you have to manually stop and start your application server from the command line whenever you make changes to the code in your applications. If you haven't tried using a full-featured IDE with J2EE application server support, we highly recommend doing so.

2.3 *Your first action*

Let's start by creating a simple WebWork action. An *action* is a piece of code that is executed when a particular URL is requested. After actions are executed, a *result* visually displays the outcome of whatever code was executed in the action. A result is generally an HTML page, but it can also be a PDF file, an Excel spreadsheet, or even a Java applet window. In this book, we'll primarily focus on HTML results, because those are most specific to the Web. As Newton's Third Law states, every action must have a reaction.[2] Although not "equal and opposite," a result is always the reaction to an action being executed in WebWork.

Suppose you want to create a simple "Hello, World" example in which a message is displayed whenever a user goes to a URL such as http://localhost/

---

[2] An action doesn't technically have to have a result, but it generally does.

helloWorld.action. Because you've mapped WebWork's servlet to `*.action`, you need an action named `helloWorld`. To create the "Hello, World" example, you need to do three things:

1 Create an action class: `HelloWorld`.

2 Create a result: hello.jsp.

3 Configure the action and result.

Let's begin by writing the code that creates the welcome message.

2.3.1 *Saying hello, the WebWork way*

Start by creating the action class, HelloWorld.java, as shown in listing 2.1.

Listing 2.1 HelloWorld.java

```
package ch2.example1;

import com.opensymphony.xwork.Action;

public class HelloWorld implements Action {
    private String message;

    public String execute() {
        message = "Hello, World!\n";
        message += "The time is:\n";
        message += System.currentTimeMillis();
        return SUCCESS;
    }

    public String getMessage() {
        return message;
    }
}
```

The first and most important thing to note is that the `HelloWorld` class implements the `Action` interface. All WebWork actions must implement the `Action` interface, which provides the `execute()` method that WebWork calls when executing the action.

Inside the `execute()` method, you construct a "Hello, World" message along with the current time. You expose the message field via a `getMessage()` JavaBean-style getter. This allows the message to be retrieved and displayed to the user by the JSP tags.

Finally, the `execute()` method returns `SUCCESS` (a constant for the `String` "success"), indicating that the action successfully completed. This constant and others, such as `INPUT` and `ERROR`, are defined in the `Action` interface. All WebWork actions must return a *result code*—a `String` indicating the outcome of the action execution. Note that the result *code* doesn't necessarily mean a result will be executed, although generally one is. You'll soon see how these result codes are used to map to results to be displayed to the user. Now that the action is created, the next logical step is to create an HTML display for this message.

2.3.2 *Displaying output to the web browser*

WebWork allows many different ways of displaying the output of an action to the user, but the simplest and most common approach is to show HTML to a web browser. Other techniques include displaying a PDF report or a comma-separated value (CSV) table. You can easily create a JSP page that generates the HTML view:

```
<%@ taglib prefix="ww" uri="webwork" %>
<html>
    <head>
        <title>Hello Page</title>
    </head>
    <body>
    The message generated by my first action is:
    <ww:property value="message"/>
    </body>
</html>
```

The taglib definition in the first line maps the prefix *ww* to the URI *webwork*. (Note that the URI is the same as that in the web.xml file.) A prefix of *ww* indicates that all the WebWork tags will start with `ww:`.

As you can see, this is a simple JSP page that uses one custom WebWork tag: `property`. The `property` tag takes a `value` attribute and attempts to extract the content of that expression from the action. Because you created a `getMessage()` method in the action, a `property` value of `message` results in the return value of a `getMessage()` method call. Save this file in the root of your web application, and call it hello.jsp.

Again, this example is extremely basic. In later chapters, we'll go over many other WebWork tags that can help you create dynamic web sites without using any Java code in your JSPs, using a simple expression language called the Object Graph Navigation Language (OGNL).

2.3.3 *Configuring your new action*

Now that you've created both the action class and the view, the final step is to tie the two together. You do so by *configuring* the action to a particular URL and mapping the SUCCESS result to the JSP you just created. Recall that when you created the skeleton layout, you generated a nearly empty xwork.xml file. You'll now add some meaningful values to this file and see the final WebWork action work.

When you're configuring a WebWork action, you must know three things:

- The full action class name, including the complete package
- The URL where you expect the action to exist on the Web
- All the possible result codes the action may return

As you know from the previous Java code, the action class name is ch2.example1.HelloWorld. The URL can be anything you like; in this case, we choose /helloWorld.action. You also know that the only possible result code for this action is SUCCESS.

Armed with this information, let's modify xwork.xml to define the action:

```
<!DOCTYPE xwork PUBLIC "-//OpenSymphony Group//XWork 1.0//EN"
 "http://www.opensymphony.com/xwork/xwork-1.0.dtd">
 <xwork>
     <include file="webwork-default.xml"/>

     <package name="default" extends="webwork-default">
         <default-interceptor-ref name="completeStack"/>

         <action name="helloWorld"
                 class="ch2.example1.HelloWorld">
             <result name="success">hello.jsp</result>
         </action>
     </package>
 </xwork>
```

In this file, you've now made a direct correlation between an action name (helloWorld) and the class you wish to be executed. So, any HTTP request to /helloWorld.action will invoke your new action class. You also made a direct correlation between the result code SUCCESS (a String constant for "success") and the JSP that you just created to display the message.

With xwork.xml saved, the action class compiled and copied to WEB-INF/classes, and hello.jsp added to the root of the web application, you're ready to fire up the application server and try this new action. Consult your application server's documentation for detailed instructions on how to start, stop, and deploy web applications like this one.

Figure 2.1
The first "Hello World" action

And that's it! You can now point your web browser to the action URL, such as http://localhost/helloWorld.action,[3] to see the final product shown in figure 2.1.

> **NOTE** The message returned by this action isn't very friendly to the eye: The time (displayed as 1073357910) is pretty hard to read. Don't despair—in chapter 14, "Internationalization," we'll show you how easy it is to display locale-specific dates to the user.

As you can see, this isn't the most exciting web page, so let's spice it up. You'll make the greeting generated by this action customizable by letting users enter their name and be personally greeted. Up to this point, you've seen an action that is read-only; now you'll learn how to handle inputs and read-write actions.

2.4 Dealing with inputs

Now that you know how to build a simple action, let's take it up one notch and add the ability to personalize the message. You'll build on the existing code. First, create another HTML page that asks for the user's name. Create the following file, name.jsp, in the same directory as hello.jsp:

---

[3] Depending on the servlet container and the configuration, this URL could include a port number like 8080.

```
<html>
    <head>
        <title>Enter your name</title>
    </head>
    <body>
        Please enter your name:
        <form action="helloWorld.action">
            <input type="textfield"
                    name="name"/>
            <input type="submit"/>
        </form>
    </body>
</html>
```

Note that the form is being submitted to helloWorld.action—the same location you used to display the previous example. Since you're expanding on the previous example, you'll continue to use this location. Another important point is that the textfield input is named name. Just as message was the property you used to display (get) the message, name is the property you use to write (set) the user's name.

Next, you need to tweak the HelloWorld action to construct the personalized message. The new action code looks like this:

```
package ch2.example1;

import com.opensymphony.xwork.Action;

public class HelloWorld implements Action {
    private String message;
    private String name;

    public String execute() {
        message = "Hello, " + name + "!\n";
        message += "The time is:\n";
        message += System.currentTimeMillis();
        return SUCCESS;
    }

    public String getMessage() {
        return message;
    }

    public void setName(String name) {
        this.name = name;
    }
    public String getName(){
        return this.name;
    }
}
```

This code adds two things to the previous example. The first new item is a field and corresponding JavaBean-style set method named `name`. This must match exactly the name of the textfield you used in name.jsp. You also personalize the message that is constructed by including the name in the message during the `execute()` method. In WebWork, values are always set (via the `setXxx()` methods such as `setName()`) before the `execute()` method is called. That means you can use the variables in the `execute()` method while assuming they have already been populated with the correct value.

That's it! Recompile the action class, and start your application server. Now point your web browser to http://localhost/name.jsp, enter a name, and see that the message (shown in figure 2.2) is now personalized.

As easy as that was, a few problems can result. For instance, what if the user doesn't enter any data? The greeting will end up saying "Hello, !" Rather than show an ugly message, it might be better to send the user back to the original page and ask them to enter a real name. Let's add some advanced control flow to this action.

Figure 2.2
The new greeting is personalized. In this case, we used the name Patrick as the input.

2.5 *Advanced control flow*

Because you want the action to show either the message result (hello.jsp) or the original input form (name.jsp), you have to define another result in xwork.xml. You do this by changing the action entry to the following:

```
<action name="helloWorld"
        class="ch2.example1.HelloWorld">
    <result name="success">hello.jsp</result>
    <result name="input">name.jsp</result>
</action>
```

Now, if the execute() method in the HelloWorld action returns the String "input" (also defined as a constant, INPUT, in the method), the result of the action will be name.jsp rather than hello.jsp. In order to spice up this example a little more, let's also not allow the String "World" to be entered as a name. Editing the action to support these checks results in the following execute() method:

```
public String execute() {
    if (name == null || "".equals(name)
        || "World".equals(name)) {
        return INPUT;
    }

    message = "Hello," + name + "!\n";
    message += "The time is:\n";
    message += System.currentTimeMillis();
}
```

If the name doesn't pass your validation rules, you return a result code of INPUT and don't prepare the message. With just a couple lines of code, the control flow of this action has doubled the number of possible results the action can display. However, this still isn't as interesting as it could be, for two reasons:

- When you return to the INPUT, users can't see why they're back on this page. Essentially, there is no error message.

- Users can't tell what they originally entered as the name value. It might be nothing, or it might be *World*. It would be better if the input box displayed what the user original entered.

In order to address both concerns, let's modify the input result to display an error message. You can reuse the message property from the success result. Then, add logic to display an error message as well as make the textfield input display the previous name in the event of an error. With the modifications in place, name.jsp now looks like this:

```
<%@ taglib prefix="ww" uri="webwork" %>
<html>
    <head>
        <title>Enter your name</title>
    </head>
    <body>
        <ww:if test="message != null">
            <font color="red">
                <ww:property value="message"/>
            </font>
        </ww:if>
        Please enter your name:
        <form action="/helloWorld.action">
            <input type="textfield"
                    name="name"
                    value="<ww:property value="name"/>"/>
            <input type="submit"/>
        </form>
    </body>
</html>
```

This code adds two significant things to the JSP. First, if an error message exists, it's printed in a red font. You use the `ww:if` tag to see whether the `message` property exists; if it does, you print it. If a user goes to this page directly, the test fails, and no error message is reported—exactly the behavior you're striving for.

Second, you add a `value` attribute to the input HTML element. This attribute defines the default value to be displayed when the page is first loaded. Because the `ww:property` tag returns an empty `String` if a property isn't found, it also results in the desired behavior. After the action has been submitted once, the property exists. As such, if the INPUT result occurs, the value previously entered is displayed.

Finally, let's modify the action's `execute()` method one more time. This time, you'll make sure an error message is set in the `message` property just before the action returns with the INPUT code. The new method looks like this:

```
public String execute() {
    if (name == null || "".equals(name)
        || "World".equals(name)) {
        message = "Blank names or names of 'World' are not allowed!";
        return INPUT;
    }

    message = "Hello," + name + "!\n";
    message += "The time is:\n";
    message += System.currentTimeMillis();
    return SUCCESS;
}
```

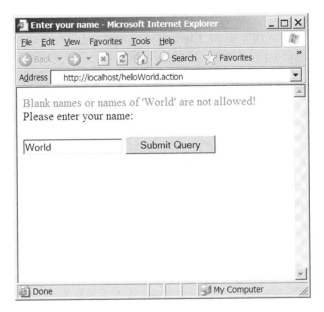

Figure 2.3
The "Hello World" example when an invalid name is entered

The most important thing to note here is that the execute() method is prevented from finishing and returns with INPUT if the name fails the validation check.

With these small changes, you're ready to try the new behaviors. Start your application server, and point your browser to http://localhost/name.jsp. Enter in the value World for the name textfield and submit the form, and you should see the screen shown in figure 2.3.

This type of control flow, validation, and error reporting is often required for forms in web applications. Rather than leave the developer to handle these tasks, WebWork provides help that does almost all the work for you. In the next section, we'll explore how you can convert this example to use the reusable components that WebWork provides.

2.6 *Letting WebWork do the work*

One of the most common tasks developers want to perform when building web applications is to build input widgets, such as drop-down selection boxes or textfields, that all have a standard behavior. This includes displaying error messages about data as well as ensuring the original value is displayed in the case of an error. In addition, developers almost always want the widgets to have a common look and feel.

Because this is such a common need, WebWork provides support for it. Rather than code all the if-else error message logic in your JSPs and actions, you can take advantage of WebWork's helper classes and JSP tags to do the work for you. You'll now convert the previous example to use these classes and tags so you can see the most common way WebWork applications are built.

2.6.1 *Taking advantage of ActionSupport*

You'll start by converting the `HelloWorld` action to take advantage of a helper class called `ActionSupport`. Rather than implement the `com.opensymphony.xwork.Action` interface, you'll modify your class to extend `com.opensymphony.xwork.ActionSupport`. `ActionSupport` provides a method called `addFieldError()` that you can use to report error messages. Listing 2.2 shows the modified class.

Listing 2.2   HelloWorld.java, modified to extend `ActionSupport`

```java
package ch2.example1;

import com.opensymphony.xwork.ActionSupport;

public class HelloWorld extends ActionSupport {
    private String message;
    private String name;

    public String execute() {
        if (name == null || "".equals(name)
            || "World".equals(name)) {
            addFieldError("name",
                "Blank names or names of 'World' are not allowed!");
            return INPUT;
        }

        message = "Hello," + name + "!\n";
        message += "The time is:\n";
        message += System.currentTimeMillis();
        return SUCCESS;
    }

    public String getMessage() {
        return message;
    }

    public void setName(String name) {
        this.name = name;
    }
}
```

As you can see, little has changed. In fact, only two lines have been modified: The action now extends `ActionSupport`, and you no longer set the error message to the `message` property but rather call `addFieldError()`, which is provided by `ActionSupport`. This new method takes two arguments:

- `name`—The property to which this error message relates
- `message`—The error message itself

Because the error message is about the `name` property, you pass the `String` "name" as the first argument. The second argument is the same error message you previously assigned to the `message` property. Although there isn't a significant difference between the old action code and the new code, keep in mind that you're only reporting an error on a single property. Imagine that you have 10 or 15 properties—do you really want to maintain 10 or 15 error message properties as well?

2.6.2 *Intermediate modifications to the JSP*

The next step is to modify the JSP to take advantage of the new `ActionSupport` class structure. Because `ActionSupport` provides a method, `getFieldErrors()`, that returns a `java.util.Map` of error messages, the new JSP looks like this:

```
<%@ taglib prefix="ww" uri="webwork" %>
<html>
    <head>
        <title>Enter your name</title>
    </head>
    <body>
        <ww:if test="fieldErrors['name'] != null">
            <font color="red">
                <ww:property value="fieldErrors['name']"/>
            </font>
        </ww:if>
        Please enter your name:
        <form action="/helloWorld.action">
            <input type="textfield"
                    name="name"
                    value="<ww:property value="name"/>"/>
            <input type="submit"/>
        </form>
    </body>
</html>
```

The code includes only one change: In the area where the error message is printed, the `value` attribute has changed from `message` to `fieldErrors['name']`. Right about now, you may be asking yourself, "Didn't they say this was supposed to be *better*?" You're right that this code looks more confusing. Fortunately, you're not finished changing the JSP. Don't worry; it gets easier—a lot easier.

We're showing you this JSP so you can begin to understand what's going on in the background. Because `ActionSupport` has a field called `fieldErrors` that is a `Map`, you can reference values in that `Map` by using the notation `map[key]`. Because the key is always the first argument of the `addFieldError()` method call, you pass in a `String` "name". Now that you have a basic understanding of what's going on, let's create the final version of the JSP.

2.6.3 *Exploring the UI tag library*

At this point, the change you made to the JSP has added more complexity rather than made it easier to work with. But you're not finished with it. WebWork comes with a complete UI tag library that helps you quickly write web applications with a standard look and feel. Let's add a UI tag to take care of the textfield input as well as display the error message:

```
<%@ taglib prefix="ww" uri="webwork" %>
<html>
    <head>
        <title>Enter your name</title>
    </head>
    <body>
        <ww:form action="helloWorld">
            <ww:textfield label="Please enter your name:"
                            name="name"/>
            <input type="submit"/>
        </ww:form>
    </body>
</html>
```

You may be looking at the previous JSP and wondering, "Where did everything go?" Without getting into too much detail (you'll learn all about UI tags in chapter 11), we'll explain what the new `ww:textfield` tag does.

The WebWork UI tag library contains a tag for every HTML form element (select, textfield, checkbox, and so on), and you can even write custom components easily. Each tag provides a standard label, error reporting, font coloring, and more. In this case, you've replaced the hand-coded HTML for error reporting, labeling, and font coloring with a single call to a UI tag that does all this for you.

These tags assume that the action extends `ActionSupport` (or at least provides a `getFieldErrors()` method) to show error messages for that field. This is the primary reason that 99 percent of all WebWork actions extend `ActionSupport` rather than implement the `Action` interface. Using the UI tag library and `ActionSupport`, you can create large, complex forms in almost no time.

2.7 Summary

In this chapter, we showed you how to build a simple web application and then expand on it to introduce more complex flow control and validation rules. By doing this, you discovered what a typical WebWork application looks like—one that takes advantage of `ActionSupport` and the UI tag library. Whereas the first two examples were simple in nature, the third example provided more functionality and a better look and feel, all while containing less code. The idea that less is more and that simplicity can be achieved through component reuse is a theme in WebWork that will reoccur throughout this book.

Setting up WebWork

This chapter covers

- Configuring actions, results, and interceptors
- Describing required and optional libraries
- Creating reusable WebWork modules
- Configuring WebWork behaviors and features
- Using the default configuration that comes with WebWork

In chapter 2, "HelloWorld, the WebWork way," you built a simple WebWork application. In addition to creating the necessary Java and JSP code, you also configured web.xml and xwork.xml. In this chapter, we'll dive deeper into WebWork's configuration and setup. This includes the basic concepts of actions, results, and interceptors—all of which are configured in xwork.xml. We'll also look at how you can split large applications into smaller modules through the use of packages, namespaces, and includes.

In addition to xwork.xml, we'll discuss the other two configuration files necessary to use WebWork: web.xml and webwork.properties. As you saw in chapter 2, web.xml must be configured to instruct the servlet container that you wish to use WebWork. In addition, you use webwork.properties to configure specific features for WebWork, such as how certain tags render and how file uploads happen.

Finally, we'll explain how to package a WebWork-powered web application, including which JAR files are required and which are optional. By the end of this chapter, you should have a good grasp of the core concepts of WebWork. In addition, you'll know how to create a new project that uses WebWork.

3.1 Configuring actions, results, and interceptors

Recall that when you built the simple "Hello World" application, you created both an action and a result: the action in Java and the result in JSP. You tied them together in the xwork.xml file. In addition to results and actions, WebWork includes a third important type of object: interceptors. In this section, we'll discuss what these objects do and how you can configure them to work together.

3.1.1 Overview of terminology

At the core of WebWork are *actions*. Actions are responsible for implementing the logic for your web-based application. They're implemented in Java and almost always extend the class `com.opensymphony.xwork.ActionSupport`. Actions are invoked whenever an HTTP request is made to WebWork's `ServletDispatcher`. In the "Hello World" example, requests to `/hello.action` invoked `HelloWorld`'s `execute()` method.

Once an action has finished executing, it returns a result code, such as SUCCESS, INPUT, or error. These result codes tell WebWork what to do next, as defined in xwork.xml. This next step is called a *result*. WebWork supports many different *result types*, which allow you to use your choice of template technologies, such as JSP, Velocity, or FreeMarker. In the "Hello World" example, you implemented your results in JSP and as such used the servlet dispatcher result type, which is used to dispatch to a JSP or another servlet.

Surrounding the execution of an action and its result is an *interceptor*. An interceptor is invoked before (and possibly after) the action is executed and can control how or whether the action is executed. Interceptors provide loose coupling of logic such as security, logging, and validation. They can also do work after the action and result have finished—allowing for them to provide functionality such as database transactions.

WebWork allows for multiple interceptors to be grouped together in the form of an *interceptor stack*. These stacks can be reused with many different actions, letting you provide sweeping behavior modifications across many different actions. We'll discuss interceptors, including the default ones bundled with WebWork, in chapter 5 ("Adding functionality with interceptors"). For now, you'll learn how to configure these three critical parts of WebWork.

3.1.2   *Actions*

At the most basic level, configuring an action requires only two pieces of information: the action name and the action class. When these two items are added to xwork.xml, an action mapping is created. Listing 3.1 contains the most basic xwork.xml file possible; the name `login` is mapped to the `Login` class.

> **Listing 3.1   Action mapping at the most basic level**

```
<!DOCTYPE xwork PUBLIC "-//OpenSymphony Group//XWork 1.0//EN"
  "http://www.opensymphony.com/xwork/xwork-1.0.dtd">
<xwork>
  <package name="default">
    <action name="login"
            class="org.hibernate.auction.web.actions.users.Login"/>
  </package>
</xwork>
```

Except in a few rare cases when you're using the `<ww:action/>` tag (discussed in chapter 9, "Tag libraries"), an action without results isn't very useful. An action-result mapping must be provided before your action can display anything to a user. Although WebWork lets you create your own result types (as you'll see in section 3.1.3), it also comes with a common set of result types that's typically all you'll need. Listing 3.2 shows the `login` action again, but this time with the result mappings for the SUCCESS and INPUT result codes.

Listing 3.2 Login action with two result mappings

```
<!DOCTYPE xwork PUBLIC "-//OpenSymphony Group//XWork 1.0//EN"
 "http://www.opensymphony.com/xwork/xwork-1.0.dtd">
<xwork>
  <include name="webwork-default.xml"/>
  <package name="default" extends="webwork-default">
    <default-interceptor-ref name="defaultStack"/>
    <action name="login"
            class="org.hibernate.auction.web.actions.users.Login">
      <result name="input">login.jsp</result>
      <result name="success"
              type="redirect">/secure/dashboard.action</result>
    </action>
  </package>
</xwork>
```

This example includes two important changes: the inclusion of webwork-default.xml and the addition of two `result` elements. Let's set aside discussing webwork-default.xml and packages for the moment and focus on the new `result` elements. Nested in the action mapping, you've added two result mappings. Each result mapping has a required name, an optional type, and a value. When a result type isn't specified, the default result type (as defined in the package or superpackage) is used. In this case, the default result type is `dispatcher`, as dictated by webwork-default.xml.

Here, if the named result returned by the `Login`'s `execute()` method is SUC-CESS, then the user will be redirected to a `dashboard` action (not yet defined). If the return result is INPUT, the browser will display the login.jsp page again to prompt the user to fix any invalid data, such as a bad username or password. Note that the INPUT result maps to a relative path, whereas the SUCCESS result maps to an absolute path. Your result mappings can be absolute or relative; this will become more important when we begin to discuss the notion of namespaces later in this chapter.

> **NOTE** From this point on, our examples of xwork.xml won't include the Document Type Definition (DTD) DOCTYPE at the start of the file. We recommend that you always specify the DTD so you get the added benefit of XML validation; but for the sake of brevity, we won't reprint it every time. We may also exclude irrelevant parts of xwork.xml, such as packages and other actions, in certain examples.

Aliasing actions

Remember that each `action` element in xwork.xml is an action mapping. Nothing stops you from mapping multiple names to the same action class. This is often a great way to reuse the same action logic but provide different results or interceptor logic, a technique called *action aliasing*. Even more powerful than providing two action aliases for the same action's `execute()` method, WebWork also lets you provide alternative methods in your action classes to which you can alias.

Recall that WebWork is an implementation of a generic command pattern framework (see the appendix, "WebWork architecture," for detailed information on this topic). Each WebWork action encapsulates a single instruction, or command. Although this is typically enough, sometimes you may have many actions that perform similar tasks. You can end up with many classes that have a similar form, especially if they all deal with the same inputs and outputs. This situation is most common when you're writing actions to deal with Create, Read, Update, and Delete (CRUD) data operations.

By default, WebWork invokes the `execute()` method of your action classes. However, WebWork lets you pass in an optional `method` attribute in your action mappings that indicates which method WebWork should invoke. The method specified must adhere to the same format that the `execute()` method does: return a `String` result code, and optionally throw any type of `Exception` (uncaught exceptions are handled by WebWork). Listing 3.3 shows two aliases of the `Search` action class.

> **Listing 3.3   Search action class aliased twice with different configurations**

```
<action name="search" class="org.hibernate.auction.web.actions.Search">
  <interceptor-ref name="default"/>
  <interceptor-ref name="execAndWait"/>
  <result name="wait">search-wait.jsp</result>
  <result name="success" type="redirect">moreResults.action</result>
</action>

<action name="moreResults"
        class="org.hibernate.auction.web.actions.Search"
        method="moreResults">
  <result name="success">search.jsp</result>
</action>
```

Using aliases, you implement these two search functions using one class rather than two separate classes. Disregard the search action's interceptor configuration for now; we'll go over interceptors in a moment. Listing 3.4 shows the `Search` class (some helper methods are omitted).

Listing 3.4   Search action with two methods mapped to different action aliases

```
public class Search extends ActionSupport
                    implements ItemDAOAware, SessionAware {
    public static final String RESULTS = "__search_results";

    List items;
    String query;
    int page = 1;
    int pages;

    ItemDAO itemDAO;
    Map session;

    public String execute() throws Exception {
        List results = itemDAO.search(query);
        session.put(RESULTS, results);
        cutPage(results);

        return SUCCESS;
    }

    public String moreResults() throws Exception {
        List results = (List) session.get(RESULTS);
        cutPage(results);

        return SUCCESS;
    }

    // helper methods omitted
}
```

Here you see the two methods used in the two action mappings: `execute()` and `moreResults()`, both of which adhere to the requirement that they return a `String` result code.

NOTE   WebWork maps methods in xwork.xml two ways: by looking for any method with the name provided in the `method` attribute and also for any method of the format `doMethod()`. In listing 3.4, WebWork looks for the method `moreResults()` first; if it isn't found, it then looks for a method named `do-MoreResults()`. This is partly because of legacy behavior from older versions of WebWork but also because some commonly desired method aliases, such as `default`, can't be used due to the Java language syntax.

Because WebWork uses reflection to execute any method other than `execute()`, you should take care when refactoring actions that contain aliases. Although IDEs such as IDEA and Eclipse contain powerful tools for refactoring, they typically have no way of updating the action mapping with the new method name. Consequently, when you're creating a method intended to be used as an alias, the name of the method should describe what action it performs and the method should be clearly marked as a method intended for use as an alias.

Aliasing without configuration

It's common to want to use a method alias for an action without wishing to create a new action mapping in xwork.xml. WebWork makes this easy by providing a special syntax for requesting actions from a web browser. Typically, actions are requested in the form of `name.action`, where `name` is the name of the action mapping. WebWork also supports the form `name!method.action`.

When a request is made in this form, such as to `search!moreResults.action`, the `search` action mapping is used. Everything about the action execution is the same as a request to `search.action` would be, except for the fact that `moreResults()` is invoked instead of `executed()`.

This feature is commonly used when you wish to use the same action mapping without the actual action execution to show the initial, or default, view of a form. For example, a user may be sent to the URL `login!default.action` when initially logging in. The method `doDefault()` in the action then returns INPUT, which directs the user to login.jsp. Then, in login.jsp, the form submits to `login.action`, which invokes the `execute()` method this time around. If the data is invalid or missing, the method returns INPUT, causing the page flow to repeat. Otherwise, SUCCESS is returned, and the flow completes.

> **NOTE** Because any method can be executed from the URL, a malicious user can easily invoke a method you may not intend to be invoked. Always assume that action methods are completely open for users to call, and never expose a way for an attacker to gain access to critical data. Always protect your data and business logic with a solid security layer, especially when building public-facing web applications.

Customizing actions with parameters

Actions can be customized, or *parameterized*, by using the `<param>` element. Parameterized actions are especially useful if you have many actions that perform similar tasks. Rather than having to write multiple actions, you can write a single action that varies its behavior based on parameters provided.

For example, suppose you've written an action to handle Web Service (SOAP) requests. You may want to bind different instances of this action to different URLs. You may also want a separate timeout value for each action. Using the <param> tag, you can use the same WebServiceAction. Listing 3.5 shows a parameterized action configuration.

Listing 3.5   Parameterizing an action with the param element

```
<action name="service" class="com.example.WebServiceAction">
  <result name="success">/success.jsp</result>
  <param name="url">http://somesite.com/service.wsdl</param>
  <param name="timeout">30</param>
</action>
```

In this example, you created two parameters: url and timeout. In order for these parameters to be set on the action, you must provide JavaBean-style setters, as shown in listing 3.6.

Listing 3.6   Setters for the parameters shown in listing 3.5

```
public class WebServiceAction {
  private String url;
  private long timeout;

  public void setUrl(String url) {
    this.url = url;
  }

  public void setTimeout(long timeout) {
    this.timeout = timeout;
  }

  public String execute() {
    // perform task here
  }
}
```

When the action executes, WebWork automatically calls these setters with the value specified in the action mapping. Remember that the values in the action mapping are in the form of a string and therefore contain no data-typing information. For example, the timeout parameter is the string "30". But WebWork does its best to convert this value to the type represented in the action—in this case, long. This is called automatic *type conversion* and it's a useful WebWork feature. Consult chapter 12, "Type conversion," for more information on advanced type conversion.

> **NOTE** All the examples thus far assume that the complete xwork.xml file represented in listing 3.2 is still being used, with the inclusion of webwork-default.xml, the default-interceptor-ref, and the extension of the web-work-default package. This is the case because webwork-default.xml, which is covered later in this chapter, provides a set of default result types and interceptors that are commonly used.

Now that you see how action mappings are configured, let's examine result mappings and result types.

3.1.3 Results

Consider listing 3.2, reprinted here:

```
<xwork>
  <include name="webwork-default.xml"/>
  <package name="default" extends="webwork-default">
    <default-interceptor-ref name="defaultStack"/>
    <action name="login"
            class="org.hibernate.auction.web.actions.users.Login">
      <result name="input">login.jsp</result>
      <result name="success"
              type="redirect">/secure/dashboard.action</result>
    </action>
  </package>
</xwork>
```

In this example, you see two results: One doesn't specify a type, and the other is type redirect. It's important to remember that result configuration is made up of two parts: *result mappings*, which you've already seen associated with an action mapping; and *result types*. We'll now look at how result types are configured. Results and result configuration are explained in much more detail in chapter 7, "Using results."

Configuring result types

Every package in WebWork can be associated with one or more result types. Using listing 3.2 as a starting point, listing 3.7 shows how a new result type might be configured.

> **Listing 3.7 With two result types configured**

```
<xwork>
  <include name="webwork-default.xml"/>
  <package name="default" extends="webwork-default">
```

```
<result-types>
  <result-type name="dispatcher" class="..." default="true"/>
  <result-type name="redirect" class="..."/>
</result-types>

<default-interceptor-ref name="defaultStack"/>

<action name="login"
        class="org.hibernate.auction.web.actions.users.Login">
  <result name="input">login.jsp</result>
  <result name="success"
          type="redirect">/secure/dashboard.action</result>
</action>
  </package>
</xwork>
```

In this example, two result types are configured for the package default. We've left out the values for the class attribute for the sake of brevity—you'll see the real values in a moment when we discuss webwork-default.xml.[1] The first result type, dispatcher, is declared as the default result. That means whenever a result mapping in this package doesn't specify a result type, the dispatcher result type is used. The second result type, redirect, is also declared.

Looking at the login action in listing 3.7, you can see how both result types are being used. The INPUT mapping uses the dispatcher result type implicitly, whereas the SUCCESS mapping uses the redirect result type explicitly. Both forms are acceptable, but using the implicit default result helps reduce the amount of configuration required.

Reducing configuration duplication with global result mappings

Another way to reduce the amount of configuration in xwork.xml is through the use of global result mappings. Web applications often have a common set of results that are used across many actions. Common results include redirects to login actions and permission-denied pages. Rather than define each of these results in every action mapping, WebWork lets you centralize the definitions for the common pages, as shown in listing 3.8.

---

[1] This is just an example of defining result types. In a real application, you don't have to repeat the definition of these result types, which are already defined in webwork-default.xml.

Listing 3.8 Global result mappings for `login` and `unauthorized` result codes

```
<package name="default" extends="webwork-default">
  <global-results>
    <result name="login"
            type="redirect">/login!default.action</result>
    <result name="unauthorized">/unauthorized.jsp</result>
  </global-results>
  <!-- other package declarations -->
</package>
```

You can define any number of global result mappings for each package. Because global results are searched after local results, you can override any global result mapping by creating a local result mapping for a specific action. Recall that results can point to locations using relative or absolute paths. Because you may not know the context in which they're being invoked, it's best to use absolute paths for global results, as in listing 3.8.

Let's look next at interceptors, a concept we haven't spent much time on until now.

3.1.4 Interceptors

Recall that interceptors wrap around the execution of an action *and* a result. As with results, interceptors are important for customizing and using WebWork, but you typically don't need to use them when you're doing day-to-day development of new actions. Typically, you'll create a group, or *stack*, of interceptors that you'll then apply globally to all your actions. Before we can discuss stacks and default interceptors, let's look at how an interceptor is defined. For a more in-depth discussion of interceptors, see chapter 5.

Defining interceptors

As with results, each package may contain a set of interceptors. To define an interceptor, you need to first create an `<interceptors>` element within your package that contains your interceptors. Once you've done that, you can create your interceptors by using the `<interceptor>` element and specifying a reference name along with the implementation class.

Listing 3.9 provides the sample configuration for defining two interceptors for the `default` package: `timer` and `logger`.

Listing 3.9   Two sample interceptors defined for the `default` package

```
<package name="default" extends="webwork-default">
  <interceptors>
    <interceptor name="timer" class=".."/>
    <interceptor name="logger" class=".."/>
  </interceptors>

  <!-- result-types, global-results, and action mappings -->
</package>
```

Class names have been left out for the moment. Once you've defined the interceptor names, you can configure action mappings in the package to use the interceptors, as shown in listing 3.10.

Listing 3.10   The `login` action, configured to use two interceptors

```
<package name="default" extends="webwork-default">
  <interceptors>
    <interceptor name="timer" class=".."/>
    <interceptor name="logger" class=".."/>
  </interceptors>

  <action name="login"
        class="org.hibernate.auction.web.actions.users.Login">
    <interceptor-ref name="timer"/>
    <interceptor-ref name="logger"/>
    <result name="input">login.jsp</result>
    <result name="success"
          type="redirect">/secure/dashboard.action</result>
  </action>
</package>
```

When the `login` action is invoked, the `timer` and `logger` interceptors are invoked as well.

Naming individual interceptors can become tedious, especially considering that WebWork provides more than 10 commonly used prebuilt interceptors. Fortunately, you can group interceptors together.

Grouping interceptors as stacks

With most web applications, you'll find yourself wanting to apply the same interceptors over and over. Rather than declare numerous `interceptor-refs` for each action, you can bundle these interceptors together using an interceptor stack. An interceptor stack consists of a set of interceptors that are executed in the same order they're defined in the stack. In listing 3.11, the `timer` and `logger` interceptors are grouped into a stack called `myStack`.

Listing 3.11　Grouping the `timer` and `logger` interceptors

```
<interceptors>
  <interceptor name="timer" class=".."/>
  <interceptor name="logger" class=".."/>
  <interceptor-stack name="myStack">
    <interceptor-ref name="timer"/>
    <interceptor-ref name="logger"/>
  </interceptor-stack>
</interceptors>
```

Consider listing 3.10 again, as shown in listing 3.12, this time using the stack instead of the individual interceptors.

Listing 3.12　The `login` action, configured to use the `myStack` interceptor stack

```
<package name="default" extends="webwork-default">
  <interceptors>
    <interceptor name="timer" class=".."/>
    <interceptor name="logger" class=".."/>
    <interceptor-stack name="myStack">
      <interceptor-ref name="timer"/>
      <interceptor-ref name="logger"/>
    </interceptor-stack>
  </interceptors>

  <action name="login"
          class="org.hibernate.auction.web.actions.users.Login">
    <interceptor-ref name="myStack"/>
    <result name="input">login.jsp</result>
    <result name="success"
            type="redirect">/secure/dashboard.action</result>
  </action>
</package>
```

Note that when you compare listings 3.10 and 3.12, individual interceptors and interceptor stacks are both referenced as `interceptor-refs`. This is the case because WebWork doesn't distinguish between the two when referencing interceptors, making it easy to define one stack by including another stack and adding to it.

Reducing configuration duplication with default interceptor-refs

As with global results, interceptors also have a way to declare a default interceptor stack, allowing you to avoid repeating the same information for every action mapping. For every package, you can establish a default `interceptor-ref`, as shown in listing 3.13.

Listing 3.13 Defining the default interceptor stack as myStack

```
<package name="default" extends="webwork-default">
  <interceptors>
    <interceptor name="timer" class=".."/>
    <interceptor name="logger" class=".."/>
    <interceptor-stack name="myStack">
      <interceptor-ref name="timer"/>
      <interceptor-ref name="logger"/>
    </interceptor-stack>
  </interceptors>

  <default-interceptor-ref name="myStack"/>

  <action name="login"
          class="org.hibernate.auction.web.actions.users.Login">
    <result name="input">login.jsp</result>
    <result name="success"
            type="redirect">/secure/dashboard.action</result>
  </action>
</package>
```

Now, each action in this package no longer needs to define any interceptors. However, it's extremely important to note that if even one interceptor is defined, the default interceptor reference won't be used. This is a common mistake that many new WebWork users commit: They think they can *add* interceptor-refs in an action mapping, which will be invoked in addition to the default `interceptor-ref`. This is incorrect: The new `interceptor-refs` *replace* the default reference, and only those will be invoked. Listing 3.14 shows how to properly add a single interceptor for an individual action mapping.

Listing 3.14 The proper way to add an interceptor for an individual action mapping

```
<package name="default" extends="webwork-default">
  <interceptors>
    <interceptor name="timer" class=".."/>
    <interceptor name="logger" class=".."/>
    <interceptor name="foo" class=".."/>
    <interceptor-stack name="myStack">
```

```
            <interceptor-ref name="timer"/>
            <interceptor-ref name="logger"/>
        </interceptor-stack>
    </interceptors>

    <default-interceptor-ref name="myStack"/>

    <action name="login"
            class="org.hibernate.auction.web.actions.users.Login">
        <interceptor-ref name="foo"/>
        <interceptor-ref name="myStack"/>
        <result name="input">login.jsp</result>
        <result name="success"
                type="redirect">/secure/dashboard.action</result>
    </action>
</package>
```

In this example, the `login` action is configured to work with both the `foo` interceptor and the entire `myStack` interceptor. If no interceptors were defined, then only the `myStack` interceptor reference would be used. If only the `foo` interceptor were defined for the `login` action, then only the `foo` interceptor would be used.

More complete information on interceptors, interceptor stacks, and configuration is provided in chapter 5. We've completed the tour of configuring the three core objects of WebWork: actions, results, and interceptors. It's time to look at more advanced configuration, including the concept of packages and namespaces.

3.2 Advanced configuration

You've seen the basic configuration that WebWork provides; thus far, everything is focused around individual action mappings. Once an action is defined in xwork.xml, you can apply result mappings and interceptor references to it. However, WebWork goes beyond focusing on individual action mappings and provides ways to group actions together into packages and namespaces, which can then in turn be stored in separate files to promote modular design. In this section, we'll discuss the advanced configuration WebWork provides and explain why these advanced features are useful when you're building large applications.

3.2.1 The xwork.xml DTD

Before we get started with advanced configuration topics, let's examine the WebWork DTD file. A Document Type Definition (DTD) file defines the structure of an XML document type. The contents of the DTD, currently version 1.0, are located

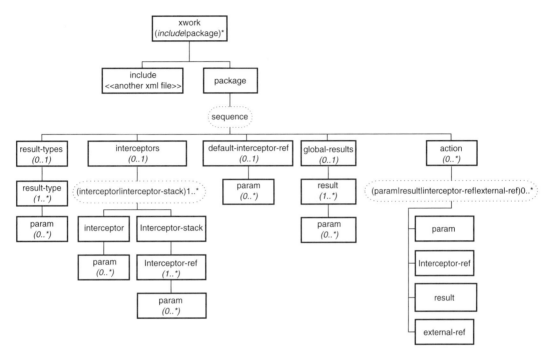

Figure 3.1   A visual representation of the WebWork configuration DTD

at www.opensymphony.com/xwork/xwork-1.0.dtd. Feel free to look at the DTD and get a feel for how WebWork groups actions, results, and interceptors together in packages. We've also provided a visual representation of the DTD in figure 3.1.

As you can see in figure 3.1, and as you saw throughout section 3.1, actions, results, and interceptors are bound by package declarations. It's time to understand what packages are used for.

3.2.2   Namespaces and packages

WebWork packages are similar to Java packages in many ways. They typically represent a cohesive set of functionality. They let you simplify maintenance and promote reusability by providing a means to organize a multitude of actions into a single module. Within xwork.xml, all configurations are organized in packages. Each package contains definitions for all the actions, results, and interceptors that it will use.

In the CaveatEmptor example WebWork application, three major packages are defined: `default`, `public`, and `secure`. The `default` package doesn't have any action mappings but instead provides the basis from which the `public` and secure packages can extend. The `public` package contains actions that are available without logging in, whereas the `secure` package contains protected actions. Listing 3.15 provides parts of the package definitions.

Listing 3.15   CaveatEmptor's three main packages: `default`, `public`, and `secure`

```
<xwork>
  <include file="webwork-default.xml"/>
  <include file="config-browser.xml"/>

  <package name="default" extends="webwork-default">
    <interceptors>
      <interceptor name="auth"
                   class="org.hibernate.auction.web.interceptors.
              ➥AuthenticationInterceptor"/>
    </interceptors>

    <global-results>
      <result name="login"
              type="redirect">/login!default.action</result>
    </global-results>
  </package>

  <package name="public" extends="default">
    <default-interceptor-ref name="completeStack"/>

    <!-- public facing actions -->
  </package>

  <package name="secure" extends="default" namespace="/secure">
    <interceptor-stack name="default">
      <interceptor-ref name="auth"/>
      <interceptor-ref name="completeStack"/>
    </interceptor-stack>

    <default-interceptor-ref name="default"/>

    <!-- protected actions -->
  </package>
</xwork>
```

Using this example, we'll discuss the purpose of packages and namespaces. Let's talk about how the public package in listing 3.15 extends the default package and what that means.

TIP   Package names must be unique. You can't have two packages with the same name in a single xwork.xml file.

Extending packages

Unlike a Java package, a WebWork package can extend other packages. A Web-Work package may specify a comma-separated list of packages to extend in the `extends` attribute. When a WebWork package extends another package, it copies all the definitions—including all interceptor, interceptor-stack, result, and action configurations—from the package being included and adds them to the definitions it already has. This enables you to centralize the configuration of common elements and improves the readability of derived packages by reducing the contents of the package to just those items that define the package.

> **NOTE** WebWork packages are evaluated sequentially down the document, so parent packages must be defined before their child package.

When WebWork looks for specific identifiers within a package, it first looks in the package declaration and then at the packages that are extended in the order they're extended. The first matching identifier is used. This enables derived packages to override the behavior of a parent package in much the same way that a derived class can override methods from the parent class.

To make packages more self-describing, you can mark them as abstract by setting the `boolean` attribute abstract to true. An abstract package behaves like a non-abstract package in every way except that WebWork doesn't map actions in abstract packages. This makes them useful for setting up default values without making the actions available from that package.

For a concrete example of this behavior, see listing 3.15. In this example, the default package defines a custom interceptor, `auth`, and also a global result mapping for the `login` result code. Then the `public` and `secure` packages extend the default package and inherit those configuration elements. Let's look at that `namespace` attribute that the secure package defines but the public package doesn't.

Mapping namespaces

To put it simply, WebWork uses namespaces to map URLs to actions. WebWork identifies actions by the name of the action and the namespace it belongs to. If no `namespace` attribute has been defined by the package, then the default namespace, `""`, is assigned. When WebWork receives an incoming request, it divides the requested URL into a namespace and an action name. WebWork then attempts to find an action associated with this namespace/action name pair. If no action exists for the namespace/action name pair, WebWork searches for the action name in the default namespace.

For example, let's say you've deployed the CaveatEmptor example application to the /caveat context path. If your URL looks like this

```
http://www.somesite.com/caveat/public/categoryPicker.action
```

then the namespace is /public and the name of the action is categoryPicker. To find the action, WebWork first searches for an action named categoryPicker in the namespace /public. Finding none, it then searches for and finds the category-Picker action in the default namespace. This means the following URL also maps to the same categoryPicker action:

```
http://www.somesite.com/caveat/some/path/categoryPicker.action
```

Since no action named categoryPicker has been mapped to the namespace /some/path, WebWork falls back and searches for categoryPicker in the default namespace (note that WebWork doesn't then search for the /some namespace—it searches in only two places). In smaller applications, this isn't a problem. In larger applications, you should minimize the number of actions defined in the default namespace. The most useful actions in the default namespace are those that aren't context sensitive, such as logging in/out or having a password reminder sent.

Unlike package names, which must be unique, more than one package can map to the same namespace. If the namespace attribute isn't used to specify which namespace a package belongs to, WebWork places the package in the default namespace. Having namespaces declared separately from package names means that changing a namespace doesn't break any references used by derived packages. This is important when you're trying to provide a flexible approach for managing your web application's URL resource space.

For a concrete example of why namespaces are useful, let's again look at listing 3.15. Recall that the secure package has the namespace /secure. This means only HTTP requests in the pattern /secure/xxx.action will invoke any actions in this package. The CaveatEmptor application takes advantage of this behavior and provides a servlet filter in web.xml that maps to /secure/* and that prevents unauthenticated users from logging in. In addition to the servlet filter, the secure package has a second line of defense in the form of the auth interceptor.

Now that you know what packages and namespaces are all about, it's time to come clean: Listing 3.15 isn't *exactly* what the real xwork.xml file looks like in CaveatEmptor. It's close, but with one major difference: The real version componentizes the public and secure packages using includes. Let's talk about how you can break your application into modules using this technique.

3.2.3 *Componentization using the include tag*

As a web application gets larger, so to does the task of managing the project. To simplify this task, web applications are frequently subdivided into smaller modules. Often these modules are organized on logical boundaries, such as member versus administrative functionality. However, the specifics vary depending on a number of factors including the size and complexity of your application.

To support breaking applications into more manageable modules, WebWork provides an include facility to enable you to separate the xwork.xml file into multiple files. Each of these subfiles can then be associated with a module. You can include the subfiles into the xwork.xml configuration file using the `<include>` tag by specifying the file that contains the subfile. WebWork looks for the specified file in the application's classpath. Listing 3.16 shows the complete CaveatEmptor xwork.xml file.

Listing 3.16   CaveatEmptor's complete xwork.xml file

```xml
<?xml version="1.0" encoding="ISO-8859-1"?>
<!DOCTYPE xwork PUBLIC "-//OpenSymphony Group//XWork 1.0//EN"
 "http://www.opensymphony.com/xwork/xwork-1.0.dtd">
<xwork>                                                webwork-default.xml
  <include file="webwork-default.xml"/>    ←――――――――| include
  <include file="config-browser.xml"/>     ←――――――――― config-browser.xml
                                                       | include
  <package name="default" extends="webwork-default">
    <interceptors>
      <interceptor name="auth"
                 class="org.hibernate.auction.web.interceptors.
              ⇒AuthenticationInterceptor"/>
    </interceptors>

    <global-results>
      <result name="login"
              type="redirect">/login!default.action</result>
      <result name="invalid.token">/invalidToken.jsp</result>
    </global-results>
  </package>

  <include file="xwork-public.xml"/>    ←――――――――― xwork-public.xml include

  <include file="xwork-secure.xml"/>    ←――――――――― xwork-secure.xml include
</xwork>
```

This example uses four include declarations. The first is one you've already seen: webwork-default.xml. We'll discuss this include in more detail in a moment. The next include, config-browser.xml, is a helpful utility that comes with WebWork and is also discussed in a moment.

The last two includes, xwork-public.xml and xwork-secure.xml, are a repackaging of the packages from listing 3.15 into their own standalone XML files. Listing 3.17 contains part of the contents of xwork-secure.xml.

Listing 3.17 Partial contents of CaveatEmptor's xwork-secure.xml file

```
<!DOCTYPE xwork PUBLIC "-//OpenSymphony Group//XWork 1.0//EN"
 "http://www.opensymphony.com/xwork/xwork-1.0.dtd">
<xwork>
  <package name="secure" extends="default" namespace="/secure">
    <interceptor-stack name="default">
      <interceptor-ref name="auth"/>
      <interceptor-ref name="completeStack"/>
    </interceptor-stack>

    <default-interceptor-ref name="default"/>

    <!-- protected actions -->
  </package>
</xwork>
```

In this example, note that xwork-secure.xml is a complete and valid XML document that validates against the DTD. This shows that the `<include>` declaration doesn't simply copy the contents of the file over but merges two well-formed Web-Work configuration files. Thus two modules can be independently developed and then packaged together at a later date.

Because WebWork looks for includes in your application's classpath, you can place included XML files in the JARs located in your application's WEB-INF/lib directory. Using includes, you can take large, monolithic applications and divide them into smaller modules in the form of individual JAR files. Each module can contain its package and action configuration, the action class files, and possibly even result files if the views are written in a template language like Velocity or FreeMarker.

If you decide to take this modular approach to building your web application, it's important to note that you can't name the configuration files for each module xwork.xml. Rather, you must give them each a unique name and then provide a single xwork.xml file that includes all the modules. For example, suppose you have a project with three modules: Foo, Bar, and Baz. Their Java packages are `com.acme.foo`, `com.acme.bar`, and `com.acme.baz`, respectively. You can place xwork-foo.xml in com/acme/foo, xwork-bar.xml in com/acme/bar, and xwork-baz.xml in com/acme/baz.

In your web application project, you can place foo.jar, bar.jar, and baz.jar in the WEB-INF/lib directory. Finally, an xwork.xml file in WEB-INF/classes can then include all three modules, as shown in listing 3.18.

Listing 3.18   An xwork.xml file that includes three hypothetical modules

```
<!DOCTYPE xwork PUBLIC "-//OpenSymphony Group//XWork 1.0//EN"
 "http://www.opensymphony.com/xwork/xwork-1.0.dtd">
<xwork>
  <include name="webwork-default.xml"/>
  <include name="com/acme/foo/xwork-foo.xml"/>
  <include name="com/acme/bar/xwork-bar.xml"/>
  <include name="com/acme/baz/xwork-baz.xml"/>
</xwork>
```

Let's now look at the most common WebWork include file: webwork-default.xml.

WebWork's default configuration

As you've already seen in many examples in this chapter and in chapter 2, including webwork-default.xml in your xwork.xml is a common thing to do. This section explains what's in this file and why it's so commonly used. Listing 3.19 contains the entire contents of webwork-default.xml, which specifies result types, interceptors, and interceptor stacks.

Listing 3.19   The entire contents of webwork-default.xml

```
<!DOCTYPE xwork PUBLIC "-//OpenSymphony Group//XWork 1.0//EN"
 "http://www.opensymphony.com/xwork/xwork-1.0.dtd">

<xwork>
  <package name="webwork-default">
    <result-types>
      <result-type name="dispatcher"
                class="com.opensymphony.webwork.dispatcher.
              ➥ServletDispatcherResult" default="true"/>
      <result-type name="redirect"
                class="com.opensymphony.webwork.dispatcher.
              ➥ServletRedirectResult"/>
      <result-type name="velocity"
                class="com.opensymphony.webwork.dispatcher.
              ➥VelocityResult"/>
      <result-type name="chain"
                class="com.opensymphony.xwork.
              ➥ActionChainResult"/>
      <result-type name="xslt"
                class="com.opensymphony.webwork.views.xslt.
```

```
                                ➥XSLTResult"/>
        <result-type name="jasper"
                    class="com.opensymphony.webwork.views.
                ➥jasperreports.JasperReportsResult"/>
        <result-type name="freemarker"
                    class="com.opensymphony.webwork.views.freemarker.
                ➥FreemarkerResult"/>
        <result-type name="httpheader"
                    class="com.opensymphony.webwork.dispatcher.
                ➥HttpHeaderResult"/>
        <result-type name="stream"
                    class="com.opensymphony.webwork.dispatcher.
                ➥StreamResult"/>
    </result-types>

    <interceptors>
      <interceptor name="timer"
                    class="com.opensymphony.xwork.interceptor.
                ➥TimerInterceptor"/>
      <interceptor name="logger"
                    class="com.opensymphony.xwork.interceptor.
                ➥LoggingInterceptor"/>
      <interceptor name="chain"
                    class="com.opensymphony.xwork.interceptor.
                ➥ChainingInterceptor"/>
      <interceptor name="static-params"
                    class="com.opensymphony.xwork.interceptor.
                ➥StaticParametersInterceptor"/>
      <interceptor name="params"
                    class="com.opensymphony.xwork.interceptor.
                ➥ParametersInterceptor"/>
      <interceptor name="model-driven"
                    class="com.opensymphony.xwork.interceptor.
                ➥ModelDrivenInterceptor"/>
      <interceptor name="component"
                    class="com.opensymphony.xwork.interceptor.
                ➥component.ComponentInterceptor"/>
      <interceptor name="token"
                    class="com.opensymphony.webwork.
                ➥interceptor.TokenInterceptor"/>
      <interceptor name="token-session"
                    class="com.opensymphony.webwork.interceptor.
                ➥TokenSessionStoreInterceptor"/>
      <interceptor name="validation"
                    class="com.opensymphony.xwork.validator.
                ➥ValidationInterceptor"/>
      <interceptor name="workflow"
                    class="com.opensymphony.xwork.interceptor.
                ➥DefaultWorkflowInterceptor"/>
      <interceptor name="servlet-config"
                    class="com.opensymphony.webwork.interceptor.
```

```xml
                  ServletConfigInterceptor"/>
<interceptor name="prepare"
             class="com.opensymphony.xwork.interceptor.
             PrepareInterceptor"/>
<interceptor name="conversionError"
             class="com.opensymphony.webwork.interceptor.
             WebWorkConversionErrorInterceptor"/>
<interceptor name="fileUpload"
             class="com.opensymphony.webwork.interceptor.
             FileUploadInterceptor"/>
<interceptor name="execAndWait"
             class="com.opensymphony.webwork.interceptor.
             ExecuteAndWaitInterceptor"/>

<!-- Basic stack -->
<interceptor-stack name="defaultStack">
  <interceptor-ref name="servlet-config"/>
  <interceptor-ref name="prepare"/>
  <interceptor-ref name="static-params"/>
  <interceptor-ref name="params"/>
  <interceptor-ref name="conversionError"/>
</interceptor-stack>

<!-- Sample validation and workflow stack -->
<interceptor-stack name="validationWorkflowStack">
  <interceptor-ref name="defaultStack"/>
  <interceptor-ref name="validation"/>
  <interceptor-ref name="workflow"/>
</interceptor-stack>

<!-- Sample file upload stack -->
<interceptor-stack name="fileUploadStack">
  <interceptor-ref name="fileUpload"/>
  <interceptor-ref name="defaultStack"/>
</interceptor-stack>

<!-- Sample Inversion of Control stack -->
<interceptor-stack name="componentStack">
  <interceptor-ref name="component"/>
  <interceptor-ref name="defaultStack"/>
</interceptor-stack>

<!-- Sample model-driven stack  -->
<interceptor-stack name="modelDrivenStack">
  <interceptor-ref name="model-driven"/>
  <interceptor-ref name="defaultStack"/>
</interceptor-stack>

<!-- Sample action chaining stack -->
<interceptor-stack name="chainStack">
  <interceptor-ref name="chain"/>
```

```
            <interceptor-ref name="defaultStack"/>
          </interceptor-stack>

          <!--
          Sample execute and wait stack.
          Note: execAndWait should always be the *last* interceptor.
          -->
          <interceptor-stack name="executeAndWaitStack">
            <interceptor-ref name="defaultStack"/>
            <interceptor-ref name="execAndWait"/>
          </interceptor-stack>

          <!--
          A complete stack with all the common interceptors in place.
          Generally, this stack should be the one you use, though it
          may process additional stuff you don't need, which could
          lead to some performance problems. Also, the ordering can be
          switched around (ex: if you wish to have your components
          before prepare() is called, you'd need to move the component
          interceptor after up
          -->
          <interceptor-stack name="completeStack">
            <interceptor-ref name="prepare"/>
            <interceptor-ref name="servlet-config"/>
            <interceptor-ref name="chain"/>
            <interceptor-ref name="model-driven"/>
            <interceptor-ref name="component"/>
            <interceptor-ref name="fileUpload"/>
            <interceptor-ref name="static-params"/>
            <interceptor-ref name="params"/>
            <interceptor-ref name="conversionError"/>
            <interceptor-ref name="validation"/>
            <interceptor-ref name="workflow"/>
          </interceptor-stack>
        </interceptors>
      </package>
    </xwork>
```

The result types defined in this file are described briefly in table 3.1. Consult chapter 7 for more detailed descriptions of results, including the common results that make up part of webwork-default.xml.

In addition to result types, WebWork provides a selection of default interceptors that you can take advantage of if you include webwork-default.xml in your

Table 3.1 Default result types included with WebWork

Name	Description
chain	Chains to another WebWork action
dispatcher (default)	Standard ServletDispatcher include
freemarker	Renders a FreeMarker template
httpheader	Sends back HTTP header commands
jasper	Renders a JasperReports report
redirect	Sends HTTP redirects
velocity	Renders a Velocity template
xslt	Processes XML through XSL translations

configuration *and* extend the webwork-default package. Those interceptors are described in table 3.2.

Table 3.2 Default interceptors included with WebWork

Name	Description
chain	Copies parameters from one action to another
component	Applies IoC logic to the action
conversionError	Adds field errors if any type-conversion errors occurred
execAndWait	Spawns a separate thread to execute the action
fileUpload	Sets uploaded files as action files (`File` objects)
logger	Logs the start and finish of an action's execution
model-driven	Pushes the action model onto the stack
params	Applies HTTP parameters to action instances
prepare	Calls the action's `prepare()` method
servlet-config	Provides access to common HTTP objects (request, response, and so on)
static-params	Applies action-mapping parameters to action instances
timer	Times action execution
token	Basic form-duplication prevention
token-session	Advanced form duplication prevention

Table 3.2   **Default interceptors included with WebWork** *(continued)*

Name	Description
validation	Validates fields in the action
workflow	Automatically returns to the INPUT view if there are errors

Building on these interceptors, WebWork provides eight example interceptor stacks that you can use to get started. Table 3.3 describes all eight stacks; `completeStack` is the best candidate to start with.

Table 3.3   **Default interceptor stacks included with WebWork**

Name	Description
defaultStack	Basic interceptor stack.
validationWorkflowStack	Example using the validation and workflow interceptors.
fileUploadStack	Example using the `fileUpload` interceptor.
componentStack	Example using the `component (IoC)` interceptor.
modelDrivenStack	Example using the `model-driven` interceptor.
chainStack	Example using the `chain` interceptor.
execAndWaitStack	Example using the `execAndWait` interceptor.
completeStack	Complete interceptor stack using `chain`, `model-driven`, `IoC`, `fileUpload`, `validation`, and `workflow`. This can almost always be your stack of choice.

As you can see, including webwork-default.xml provides you with easy access to all the major features included with WebWork. It's highly recommended that when you start any WebWork project, you begin by including this file.

Example: configuration browser

The config-browser.xml file can also be useful when you're getting started with WebWork. Let's look at what it does and how WebWork's configuration browser is a simple example of how to package together web application modules. This module lets you visually browse your xwork.xml settings.

    To add this functionality to your web application, drop webwork-config-browser.jar into your WEB-INF/lib directory, and add the following your xwork.xml:

```
<include file="config-browser.xml"/>
```

In your velocity.properties[2] file, add an entry to your `velocimacro.library` property for `tigris-macros.vm`:

```
velocimacro.library = webwork.vm, tigris-macros.vm
```

Now, launch your web application and point your browser to http://localhost/config-browser/actionNames.action. You'll be greeted by something like the window shown in Figure 3.2.

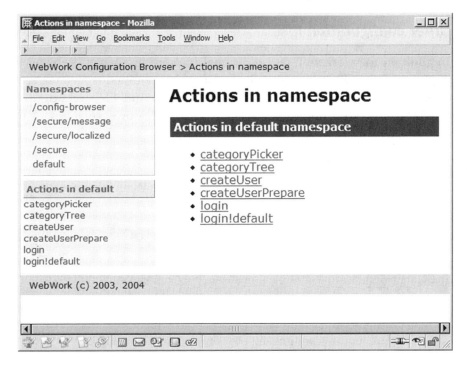

Figure 3.2   The configuration browser shows the action mappings for your application.

That's it—you've added a module to your application. We'll look more at the configuration browser in chapter 15, "Best practices."

NOTE   The edit to velocity.properties is required due to the way the configuration browser was created. It's possible to build modules that only require editing xwork.xml.

---

[2] See chapter 12 for details about configuring Velocity.

Because the results for this module were written in Velocity, they were included in the JAR file. This makes packaging modules easy. If you're thinking about breaking your application into modules using WebWork includes, we recommend that you think about using a template language like Velocity or FreeMarker.

We've completed the tour of xwork.xml, looking at everything from basic action mappings to complex modular packaging. Let's move on to the rest of the configuration files that are important when you're setting up a WebWork project.

3.3 *Other configuration files*

In addition to xwork.xml, two additional files are important: web.xml and webwork.properties. The first file, web.xml, must be modified before the servlet container can be made aware of WebWork. The second file, webwork.properties, provides access to configure many of WebWork's features, such as its UI tags and file upload support.

3.3.1 *Web-app configuration: web.xml*

In chapter 2, you saw how to configure web.xml. We summarize those changes here, in listing 3.20.

> **Listing 3.20 Required changes to web.xml**

```xml
<?xml version="1.0" encoding="ISO-8859-1"?>
<!DOCTYPE web-app PUBLIC
  "-//Sun Microsystems, Inc.//DTD Web Application 2.3//EN"
  "http://java.sun.com/dtd/web-app_2_3.dtd">
<web-app>
    <servlet>
        <servlet-name>webwork</servlet-name>
        <servlet-class>com.opensymphony.webwork.dispatcher.
    ➥ServletDispatcher</servlet-class>
    </servlet>
    <servlet-mapping>
        <servlet-name>webwork</servlet-name>
        <url-pattern>*.action</url-pattern>
    </servlet-mapping>
    <taglib>
        <taglib-uri>webwork</taglib-uri>
        <taglib-location>
            /WEB-INF/lib/webwork-2.1.7.jar
        </taglib-location>
    </taglib>
</web-app>
```

Only two things are happening in listing 3.20: the servlet mapping to *.action and the declaration of the WebWork JSP tag library. If you wish to map the `webwork` servlet to another servlet mapping, such as *.jspa, which is a popular alternative, keep in mind that you must also indicate this nonstandard mapping in webwork.properties.

Using WebWork's JSP taglib

If you wish to use the WebWork JSP tag library (see chapters 9 and 11 for a complete description of the tags provided by WebWork), you need to put a taglib declaration in web.xml. The recommended way is to use the taglib file included in the WebWork JAR file. The taglib is included in the JAR at META-INF/taglib.tld and is automatically found, as per the JSP specification.

Depending on your IDE and/or how you structure your web application during development, it may be beneficial to refer directly to the WebWork Tag Library Definition (TLD) rather than the JAR file containing it. You can do so by extracting the TLD from META-INF/taglib.tld and copying it to WEB-INF/webwork.tld in your web application. The taglib declaration in web.xml now looks like this:

```
<taglib>
    <taglib-uri>webwork</taglib-uri>
    <taglib-location>/WEB-INF/webwork.tld</taglib-location>
</taglib>
```

Both approaches are valid; however, if you refer to the TLD directly, remember to upgrade the TLD file after each upgrade of the WebWork JAR file.

3.3.2 Feature configuration: webwork.properties

Remember: xwork.xml defines the configuration for your action mappings and applies interceptors and results to them. On the other hand, webwork.properties is used to define application-wide settings and to configure parameters that change the behavior of the framework. (Note that webwork.properties isn't required and is only necessary if you wish to configure any of the options outlined here.)

WebWork first loads the contents of com/opensymphony/webwork/default.properties, which is found in the WebWork JAR file. It then loads webwork.properties and overrides any configuration settings defined in that file. Listing 3.21 contains the complete contents of default.properties and will give you a good understanding of which settings can be changed.

> **Listing 3.21   The complete contents of WebWork's default configuration file**

```
###
### Webwork default properties
```

```
### (can be overridden by a webwork.properties
###  file in the root of the classpath)
###

### This can be used to set your default locale and encoding scheme
#webwork.locale=en_US
webwork.i18n.encoding=ISO-8859-1

### Parser to handle HTTP POST requests,
### encoded using the MIME-type multipart/form-data
#webwork.multipart.parser=cos
#webwork.multipart.parser=jakarta
webwork.multipart.parser=pell
# uses javax.servlet.context.tempdir by default
webwork.multipart.saveDir=
webwork.multipart.maxSize=2097152

### Load custom property files
### (does not override webwork.properties!)
#webwork.custom.properties=application,com/webwork/extension/custom

# extension for actions
webwork.action.extension=action

# use beta alternative syntax that requires %{} in most places
# to evaluate expressions for String attributes for tags
webwork.tag.altSyntax=false

### Standard UI theme
# Change this to reflect which path should be
# used for JSP control tag templates by default
webwork.ui.theme=xhtml
webwork.ui.templateDir=template
#sets the default template type. Either vm or jsp
webwork.ui.templateSuffix=vm

### Configuration reloading
# This will cause the configuration to
# reload xwork.xml when it is changed
webwork.configuration.xml.reload=false

### Location of velocity.properties file.
### Defaults to velocity.properties
#webwork.velocity.configfile = velocity.properties

### Comma separated list of VelocityContext
### classnames to chain to the WebWorkVelocityContext
#webwork.velocity.contexts =

# used to build URLs, such as the UrlTag
webwork.url.http.port = 80
```

```
webwork.url.https.port = 443

### Load custom default resource bundles
#webwork.custom.i18n.resources=testmessages,testmessages2
```

The default configuration file is mostly self-describing, but we outline the important configuration options in table 3.4. Some of these configuration options are discussed in greater detail in future chapters.

Table 3.4   Common WebWork configuration options

Property	Default Value	Description
webwork.locale	none	Default locale to use for i18n. (See chapter 14.)
webwork.i18n.encoding	ISO-8859-1	WebWork's character encoding set.
webwork.multipart.parser	pell	Used for file upload support. Possible values are pell, cos, and jakarta. Although not yet the default, jakarta is highly recommended. (See chapter 4.)
webwork.multipart.saveDir	none	Directory in which temporary uploaded files are stored. By default, this value is the temp directory associated with your web application by the servlet container.
webwork.multipart.maxSize	2097152	Maximum size of allowed uploaded files (in bytes).
webwork.custom.properties	none	Other properties files to load in addition to webwork.properties. Useful if you're making packaged applications that are designed to be customized.
webwork.action.extension	action	Mapping extension used in web.xml.
webwork.tag.altSyntax	false	When set to true, WebWork's JSP tags use the new alternative syntax that is set to become standard in WebWork 2.2. *In this book,* altSyntax *is assumed to be set to true.*
webwork.ui.theme	xhtml	Default UI tag theme to use. (See chapter 11.)
webwork.ui.templateDir	template	Directory and/or classpath location to search for UI tag themes.
webwork.ui.templateSuffix	vm	Suffix in which the UI templates are implemented.
webwork.configuration.xml.reload	false	When set to true, WebWork checks configuration files to see if they need to be reloaded. This setting is helpful for development and debugging.
webwork.velocity.configfile	velocity.properties	Where to look for Velocity-related configuration.

Table 3.4 Common WebWork configuration options *(continued)*

Property	Default Value	Description
webwork.velocity.contexts	none	Additional VelocityContexts to chain together (see chapter 10).
webwork.url.http.port	80	HTTP port for the URLTag. (See chapter 9.)
webwork.url.https.port	443	HTTPS port for the URLTag. (See chapter 9.)
webwork.custom.i18n.resources	none	Additional i18n resource bundles to search for if no resource is found elsewhere. (See chapter 14.)

The most important thing to note is that throughout this book, every example is given with the assumption that webwork.tag.altSyntax is set to true. We did this to allow you to have the most up-to-date information on a framework that is always evolving. At the time of this writing, WebWork 2.1.7 was the latest released version. However, we know that as of WebWork 2.2, altSyntax will become standard; so, we felt it would be best to cover this syntax now rather than teach something that is on the verge of changing.

We've now explored every configuration option that WebWork offers. The last thing to do when setting up WebWork is to place these configuration files and the WebWork library files in the correct places.

3.4 Setting up your web app

We're finally going to look at how you set up your web application in order to start using WebWork. Specifically, we'll explain where the various configuration files—including xwork.xml, webwork.properties, and web.xml—must be placed. In addition, we'll outline which JAR files are required and which are optional. For the optional libraries, we'll also discuss which features require them so you can choose only the libraries you need.

3.4.1 General layout

A J2EE web application has the following basic structure:

- WEB-INF/*lib*—JAR files
- WEB-INF/*classes*—Classes and configuration files
- WEB-INF—web.xml and configuration files
- *Everything else*—JSPs, images, HTML, and so on

In sections 3.4.2 and 3.4.3, we discuss which files must be placed into WEB-INF/lib. All files that aren't configuration files or JAR files can be placed wherever you'd like. As with all web applications, you must place web.xml in WEB-INF.

Configuration files

The two configuration files discussed in this chapter (xwork.xml and web-work.properties) must be placed in your application's classpath. This typically is WEB-INF/classes, but some people like to package these files into a JAR file and then place the JAR file in WEB-INF/lib. Both methods work, because both have the same result: the configuration files are accessible via the classpath. Unless you have a specific need, we recommend placing the files in WEB-INF/classes.

Next, let's look at the required libraries that must be added to WEB-INF/lib.

3.4.2 Required libraries

Table 3.5 lists all the required libraries needed to run WebWork 2.1.7. You may try newer versions of the dependant libraries, but only the specific version outlined here is guaranteed to work. Most minor revisions tend to be backward compatible and work quite well with WebWork.

Table 3.5 Required JAR files for WebWork 2.1.7

Name	Version	Description
commons-logging.jar	1.0.4	Apache Jakarta Commons-Logging; can be used to plug into any other logging system
ognl.jar	2.6.7	OGNL Expression Language (see chapter 8)
oscore.jar	2.2.4	OSCore, a utility library used by many of the OpenSymphony projects
webwork-2.1.7.jar	2.1.7	WebWork JAR
xwork.jar	1.0.5	XWork project, which WebWork is built on

Because WebWork requires OSCore, it might be a good idea to familiarize yourself with that project. It must be included anyway, so it can't hurt to look at what the package has to offer and use some of the utilities that come with it. Some particularly useful classes are GUID, TextUtils, and Yarrow (used for strong random number generation). You can learn more about OSCore at www.opensymphony.com/oscore.

3.4.3 *Optional libraries*

Table 3.6 lists the optional libraries that WebWork 2.1.7 supports. Just as with the required libraries, you are free to try to use newer versions of these libraries, but you do so at your own risk.

Table 3.6   Optional JAR files for WebWork 2.1.7

Name	Version	Description
velocity-dep.jar	1.3.1	Required if you wish to use the Velocity result type or Web-Work's UI tags. See chapters 7, 10, and 11.
cos-multipart.jar	N/A	Three multipart libraries to choose from for multipart file-upload support (see webwork.properties configuration). You only need to include the JAR that matches the implementation you choose.
pell-multipart.jar	N/A	
commons-fileupload.jar	1.0	
bsh.jar	1.2 b6	Libraries needed by the JasperReports result (see chapter 7).
commons-beanutils.jar	1.5	
commons-collections.jar	2.1	
commons-digester.jar	1.3	
jakarta-poi.jar	2.0	
jasperreports.jar	0.6.3	
itext.jar	1.0.1	
freemarker.jar	2.3.2	Required for the FreeMarker result (see chapter 7).

Refer back to this table as we cover the optional features of WebWork and you begin experimenting with them.

3.5 *Summary*

In this chapter, we discussed how to configure WebWork actions, results, and interceptors. You saw strategies for simplifying WebWork configuration using global results, interceptor stacks, and default interceptors. We looked at modularizing WebWork configuration using packages and breaking up the xwork.xml file using includes. Finally, we discussed setting up a WebWork web application, including the application file structure and the required and optional libraries.

By now, you should have a good idea of the core WebWork concepts and how to set up and configure a new WebWork project. Although we've explored WebWork concepts including actions, interceptors, and results, we have yet to touch on their full features and capabilities; we'll do this in chapters 4, 5, and 7, respectively.

We hope that the practice of building modular web application modules is now something that you understand and can begin to attempt. At this point, we recommend that you take a break from the book and try to build a few simple actions based on the information you've seen in this chapter and in chapter 2; then come back and get ready to dig into the fun and interesting features Web-Work provides.

Part 2

Core concepts

This part of the book digs into the core concepts of WebWork. We don't spend much time on the user interface or displaying data; instead, we focus on how that data is processed. Chapter 4 looks at how to create actions, including concepts such as how action fields are mapped to forms and how you can handle file uploads. Chapter 5 discusses how you can add functionality in a loosely coupled manner using interceptors. Extending the theme of loose coupling, chapter 6 examines the Inversion of Control pattern and why it's important for dependency management.

Implementing
WebWork actions

WebWork actions are the central unit of programming in WebWork. They represent what you want your web application to do. Actions are responsible for both holding data/state (in the form of getters and setters) and executing logic.

In this chapter, we'll look at how actions are implemented and how they provide the common functionality required in web applications. In addition to the Action interface, WebWork actions may also choose to implement optional interfaces that let WebWork provide functionality like internationalization, validation, complex workflow, and error-message handling. We'll examine the ActionSupport base class, which implements the Action interface and provides default implementations of many of these optional interfaces. We'll also look at how actions are designed to provide input and output using JavaBean properties and how you can handle file uploads.

4.1   *The Action interface*

The only requirement for WebWork actions is to implement the com.opensymphony.xwork.Action interface. The Action interface defines one method:

```
public String execute() throws Exception
```

This single method defines the contract for executing actions in WebWork. Actions for which a method other than execute() is configured to be called must also implement the Action interface, and those methods must have the same signature and contract as the execute() method.

NOTE   In future versions of WebWork, the Action interface may no longer be a requirement. The interface dates back to earlier versions of WebWork, but it's no longer needed now that WebWork, which acts as a command pattern implementation (see the appendix), can execute any method name.

4.1.1   *Result codes*

The execute() method must return a String return code, which can be any value. This result code is then used to map to a result based on the action mapping specified in xwork.xml. Let's look at the EditCategory action from the CaveatEmptor example application. Listing 4.1 shows the saveCategory() method.

Listing 4.1   The EditCategory action's saveCategory() method returns one of two result codes.

```
public String saveCategory() {
    if (category == null) {
        return INPUT;
```

```
        }
        categoryDAO.makePersistent(category);
        return SUCCESS;
    }
```

You see two return statements here, one returning INPUT and the other returning SUCCESS. These are static final Strings defined in the Action interface that can be used as predefined default result codes. Listing 4.2 shows the action mapping defined in xwork.xml; here, these return codes are mapped to different results.

Listing 4.2 Action mapping for the EditCategory example

```
<action name="saveCategory"
        class=
          "org.hibernate.auction.web.actions.categories.EditCategory"
        method="saveCategory">
  <interceptor-ref name="crudStack"/>
  <result name="input">createCategory.jsp</result>
  <result name="success" type="redirect">dashboard.action</result>
</action>
```

Note that if the action returns input, the createCategory.jsp page is rendered; if success is returned, the user is redirected back to the dashboard action. This works because the INPUT and SUCCESS values are input and success, respectively.

4.1.2 *Handling exceptions*

The execute() method of the Action interface declares that it throws java.lang.Exception. This allows your action subclasses to throw any application-specific exception without having to catch and rethrow a WebWork-specific exception type. Action subclasses can also choose to not declare any Exception types or any specific Exception subclasses to be thrown. Because of the laws of Java inheritance, implementing classes can only declare that they throw fewer than or the same exceptions as the interface or parent class, not more. Therefore, if the Action interface didn't declare throws Exception, your action subclasses would be required to catch any exceptions and wouldn't be able to indicate that a system error occurred.

4.2 *Using the ActionSupport base class*

`ActionSupport` serves as a quick-start base class for your action classes. It includes default implementations of many of the optional services an action can provide; this makes it easier to start developing your own actions, because you don't have to provide implementations. You can override the implementations of any of these optional interface methods while keeping the default implementations of the others. Actions are *not* required to extend `ActionSupport`, nor are they required to implement any of the extra interfaces (besides `com.opensymphony.xwork.Action`) that `ActionSupport` implements. Due to the prebuilt functionality that comes out of the box with `ActionSupport`, our example actions all extend `ActionSupport` (or some subclass of `ActionSupport`), as do 99% of WebWork users' actions. `ActionSupport` implements the following optional interfaces:

- `com.opensymphony.xwork.Validateable`—Provides a `validate()` method to allow your action to be validated

- `com.opensymphony.xwork.ValidationAware`—Provides methods for saving and retrieving action- and field-level error messages

- `com.opensymphony.xwork.TextProvider`—Provides methods for getting localized message texts

- `com.opensymphony.xwork.LocaleProvider`—Provides a `getLocale()` method to provide the locale to use for getting localized messages

We'll present examples as we discuss these interfaces and the implementation provided by `ActionSupport`.

4.3 *Understanding basic validation*

One of the basic requirements of a web application framework is validating user input and informing the user of any invalid values. In chapter 13, "Validating form data," we'll discuss validation in depth, including the metadata-driven XWork Validation Framework; but here, we'll look at basic action validation. This involves two steps:

1 Automatically validate your action.

2 Collect and report any errors to the user.

Let's examine these steps.

4.3.1 *Validating an action: Validateable*

It's often necessary to validate the data provided by the user before executing business logic. This validation can be anything from a simple `field x is required` to `The document creation date must be before the document due date and after the parent document creation date`. To perform this validation automatically, WebWork provides a mechanism to call a method on your action before the `execute()` method (or whatever method you've told WebWork to call) is called. This mechanism is provided by the `com.opensymphony.xwork.Validateable` interface, which includes one method:

```
public void validate()
```

The `Validateable` interface marks the action to be automatically validated using that method. Let's look at the `CreateUser` action from CaveatEmptor to see how you can use this `validate()` method. The original `execute()` method of the `CreateUser` action is shown in listing 4.3.

Listing 4.3   The `CreateUser` action's `execute()` method

```
public String execute() throws Exception {                  Validation
    // see if the name already exists          ◁──────┐     logic
    User existing = userDAO.findByUsername(this.user.getUsername());
    if (existing != null) {
        addFieldError("user.username", "The user already exists");
        return INPUT;
    }

    userDAO.makePersistent(user);
    return SUCCESS;
}
```

The part of the code identified in listing 4.3 isn't performing the function of the action—it's validating the user input. Therefore, you should separate this code out from the `execute()` method. Listing 4.4 shows the refactored code.

Listing 4.4   The `CreateUser` action, refactored to use the `validate()` method

```
public void validate() {
    // see if the name already exists
    User existing = userDAO.findByUsername(this.user.getUsername());
    if (existing != null) {
        addFieldError("user.username", "The user already exists");
    }
}
```

```
public String execute() throws Exception {
    userDAO.makePersistent(user);
    return SUCCESS;
}
```

The validation code has been moved out into a validate() method. Because this action extends ActionSupport, this implementation of validate() overrides the default implementation in ActionSupport, which is empty. Notice that there is no call to the validate() method and that the

```
return INPUT;
```

line is missing from this code. This is the case because calling this method and shortcutting the rest of the action processing are handled by interceptors, assuming the proper interceptors are in place. This shows a common pattern in Web-Work: an optional interface, and an interceptor that can be applied to use that interface. We'll look more at interceptors in chapter 5, "Adding functionality with interceptors"; for now, it's important to know that if DefaultWorkFlowInterceptor is applied to your action, it will do the following:

1   Call the validate() method on the action if the action implements Validateable.

2   If the action has errors, return INPUT; otherwise, execute the action.

The validate() method is called before your action is executed, and the action is executed only if no error messages are added to it. You'll see in the next section on ValidationAware how error messages are added to and retrieved from the action. These methods are also used to determine whether any problem occurred in validating the action; so, if you want your action validation to work with the DefaultWorkflow interceptor, you should use the methods described next to add error messages and let the framework know about any problems. Now, let's look at the methods used to add error messages and check for their existence.

4.3.2 *Displaying error messages: ValidationAware*

One of the major features provided by ActionSupport is collecting error messages for display to the user. Error messages can be collected at both the class (action) level and the field level. The validate() method you just refactored checks the value of the username property; if the value is invalid, validate() calls addFieldError(). This method is implemented by `ActionSupport` and is defined in the `com.opensym-phony.xwork.ValidationAware` interface, shown in listing 4.5.

Listing 4.5   The com.opensymphony.xwork.ValidationAware interface

```
/**
 * ValidationAware classes can accept Action (class level) or field
 * level error messages. Action level messages are kept in a
 * Collection. Field level error messages are kept in a Map from
 * String field name to a List of field error msgs.
 *
 * @author $Author: mbogaert $
 * @version $Revision: 1.11 $
 */
public interface ValidationAware {
    //~ Methods //////////////////////////////////////////////////////////////

     /**
      * Set the Collection of Action-level String error messages.
      *
      * @param errorMessages
      */
     void setActionErrors(Collection errorMessages);

     /**
      * Get the Collection of Action-level error messages for this
      * action. Error messages should not be added directly here, as
      * implementations are free to return a new Collection or an
      * Unmodifiable Collection.
      *
      * @return Collection of String error messages
      */
     Collection getActionErrors();

     /**
      * Set the Collection of Action-level String messages (not
      * errors).
      */
     void setActionMessages(Collection messages);

     /**
      * Get the Collection of Action-level messages for this action.
      * Messages should not be added directly here, as
      * implementations are free to return a new Collection or an
      * Unmodifiable Collection.
      *
      * @return Collection of String messages
      */
     Collection getActionMessages();
```

```
/**
 * Set the field error map of fieldname (String) to Collection
 * of String error messages.
 *
 * @param errorMap
 */
void setFieldErrors(Map errorMap);

/**
 * Get the field specific errors associated with this action.
 * Error messages should not be added directly here, as
 * implementations are free to return a new Collection or an
 * Unmodifiable Collection.
 *
 * @return Map with errors mapped from fieldname (String) to
 * Collection of String error messages
 */
Map getFieldErrors();

/**
 * Add an Action-level error message to this Action.
 *
 * @param anErrorMessage
 */
void addActionError(String anErrorMessage);

/**
 * Add an Action-level message to this Action.
 */
void addActionMessage(String aMessage);

/**
 * Add an error message for a given field.
 *
 * @param fieldName    name of field
 * @param errorMessage the error message
 */
void addFieldError(String fieldName, String errorMessage);

/**
 * Check whether there are any Action-level error messages.
 *
 * @return true if any Action-level error messages have been
 * registered
 */
boolean hasActionErrors();

/**
 * Checks whether there are any Action-level messages.
 *
```

```
     * @return true if any Action-level messages have been
     * registered
     */
    boolean hasActionMessages();

    /**
     * Note that this does not have the same meaning as in WW 1.x.
     *
     * @return (hasActionErrors() || hasFieldErrors())
     */
    boolean hasErrors();

    /**
     * Check whether there are any field errors associated with
     * this action.
     *
     * @return whether there are any field errors
     */
    boolean hasFieldErrors();
}
```

Actions should implement this interface to signal parts of the framework (such as the Validation Framework [discussed in chapter 13] and parts of the type-conversion support [discussed in chapter 12, "Type conversion"]) to add error messages.

As you can see from the JavaDoc comments in listing 4.5, the `ValidationAware` interface requires an implementation to maintain two collections of error messages. The `actionErrors` property is a `java.util.Collection` of `String` error messages that apply to the entire action instance. The `fieldErrors` property is a `java.util.Map` mapping `String` field names to `java.util.List`'s of `String` error messages for each field. In addition to methods to get and set the collections and to add error messages, `boolean` methods check whether the action has action errors and/or field errors. The `hasErrors()` method (which checks for either action-level or field-level error messages) is used by the `DefaultWorkFlowInterceptor` to determine whether the action should be executed. `ValidationAware` actions also provide for action-level messages that can be displayed to the user but that aren't errors.

`ActionSupport` provides a simple default implementation of this interface that collects error messages for action-level and field-level error messages. If you choose not to extend `ActionSupport`, but you want a quick way to implement `Validation-Aware`, your code can do the same as `ActionSupport` and delegate all the methods in this interface to an instance of `com.opensymphony.xwork.ValidationAwareSupport`, which collects error messages for you. This class is a base implementation of

ValidationAware that maintains the lists of action-level error messages and non-error messages and the Map of field-level error messages. This implementation has been separated from ActionSupport to make it easy for action classes that don't extend ActionSupport to easily implement the ValidationAware interface.

4.4 Using localized message texts

This chapter's example has been using messages that are coded directly into your actions. What if you want to use the same application to support users in different countries, who speak different languages? It would be inefficient to create a different version of the application for each language and location; instead, you want to make the texts external to the code and enable the code to determine at runtime which text to return to the user based on their language and location.

4.4.1 Retrieving the user's locale: LocaleProvider

The first hurdle is to determine what language and location the user expects. In Java, this information is encapsulated in the java.util.Locale class. The com.opensymphony.xwork.LocaleProvider interface allows an action to determine which locale to use for getting message texts with its one method:

```
public Locale getLocale()
```

The default implementation of this method, in ActionSupport, uses the ActionContext to get this value by calling ActionContext.getContext().getLocale(). (You'll learn more about what ActionContext does in section 4.7.) The locale is associated with the WebWork action call by consulting the HttpServletRequest and calling its getLocale() method.

This is a good default, in most cases, because it's based on the locales the user's browser has indicated it can support in the HTTP request headers. Your action classes can choose, instead, to override this method to provide a different implementation, perhaps one that pulls a user's Locale information from a user profile stored in a database.

4.4.2 Displaying the localized text: TextProvider

Now you know the user's locale, but how do you get the text of your message for that locale? The standard Java technique for getting localized text messages is to use java.util.ResourceBundle. The most commonly used implementation of the ResourceBundle interface is java.util.PropertyResourceBundle, which reads message texts from a set of like-named .properties files.

The com.opensymphony.xwork.TextProvider interface (see listing 4.6) provides methods for getting localized text messages.

```
public interface TextProvider {

    /**
     * Gets a message based on a message key, or null if no message
     * is found.
     *
     * @param key the resource bundle key that is to be searched
     * for
     * @return the message as found in the resource bundle, or null
     * if none is found.
     */
    String getText(String key);

    /**
     * Gets a message based on a key, or, if the message is not
     * found, a supplied
     * default value is returned.
     *
     * @param key the resource bundle key that is to be searched for
     * @param defaultValue the default value which will be returned
     * if no message is found
     * @return the message as found in the resource bundle, or
     * defaultValue if none is found
     */
    String getText(String key, String defaultValue);

    /**
     * Gets a message based on a key using the supplied args, as
     * defined in {@link java.text.MessageFormat}, or null if no
     * message is found.
     *
     * @param key the resource bundle key that is to be searched
     * for
     * @param args a list of args to be used in a
     * {@link java.text.MessageFormat} message
     * @return the message as found in the resource bundle, or null
     * if none is found.
     */
    String getText(String key, List args);

    /**
     * Gets a message based on a key using the supplied args, as
     * defined in {@link java.text.MessageFormat}, or, if the
     * message is not found, a supplied default value is returned.
     *
```

```
      * @param key the resource bundle key that is to be searched
      * for
      * @param defaultValue the default value which will be returned
      * if no message is found
      * @param args a list of args to be used in a
      * {@link java.text.MessageFormat} message
      * @return the message as found in the resource bundle, or
      * defaultValue if none is found
      */
     String getText(String key, String defaultValue, List args);

     /**
      * Gets a message based on a key using the supplied args, as
      * defined in {@link java.text.MessageFormat}, or, if the
      * message is not found, a supplied default value is returned.
      * Instead of using the value stack in the ActionContext this
      * version of the getText() method uses the provided value
      * stack.
      *
      * @param key the resource bundle key that is to be searched for
      * @param defaultValue the default value which will be returned
      * if no message is found
      * @param args a list of args to be used in a
      * {@link java.text.MessageFormat} message
      * @param stack the value stack to use for finding the text
      * @return the message as found in the resource bundle, or
      * defaultValue if none is found
      */
     String getText(String key, String defaultValue,
                 List args, OgnlValueStack stack);

    /**
     * Get the named bundle, such as "com/acme/Foo".
     *
     * @param bundleName the name of the resource bundle, such as
     * "com/acme/Foo"
     */
    ResourceBundle getTexts(String bundleName);

    /**
     * Get the resource bundle associated with the implementing
     * class (usually an action).
     */
    ResourceBundle getTexts();
}
```

As you can see in listing 4.6, the TextProvider interface consists mostly of different sets of method arguments to getText() methods, which can be used to look up a localized message text. The default implementation of `TextProvider`, `com.opensymphony.xwork.TextProviderSupport`, uses the `PropertyResourceBundle` implementation of `ResourceBundle` by using property files named based on the action class.

Let's look at an example by pulling the text messages out of the `CreateUser` example and putting them into property files. First let's examine the .properties file that will hold the default message texts. Property files for action message texts are in the same package as the class with the same name, so the `org.hibernate.auction.web.actions.users.CreateUser` class has a CreateUser.properties file in the org/hibernate/auction/web/actions/users directory, right next to the CreateUser.java file:

```
user.exists=The user already exists
```

This properties file contains one message. To see how this message is used, let's look at the refactored `CreateUser`'s `validate()` method (see listing 4.7).

Listing 4.7 A refactored `CreateUser` action that uses `getText()` to get a localized message text

```
public void validate() {
        // see if the name already exists
        String username = this.user.getUsername();
        User existing = userDAO.findByUsername(username);
        if (existing != null) {
            addFieldError("user.username", getText("user.exists"));
        }
    }
```

The hard-coded text has been replaced by a call to `getText()`, which loads the message from the CreateUser.properties file. The message is looked up in the `validate()` method if a user already exists with the given username and added to the field error map for the user.username field.

4.4.3 *Providing messages for other languages*

You've pulled your messages out of your action class, but you still don't have support for any other languages. Let's look at what you have to do to add another translation. Later, in chapter 14 ("Internationalization"), we'll present a more complete internationalization example using French, Spanish, and German; here, let's examine a German translation. The translated texts will go in a file named

CreateUser_de.properties in the same directory with your original CreateUser.properties file and the CreateUser.java source code. Here's an example:

```
user.exists=Der benutzer besteht bereits
```

The earlier message has been translated and put into another .properties file with a similar name, except that the _*de* part tells `PropertyResourceBundle` that this is the German language translation (those of you who can speak or read German can blame Google's translate tool). This .properties file contains the same message key, `user.exists`, but a different message body. These message bodies will be retrieved when a user attempts to use your application and is using a German language browser. Similarly, you can translate into other languages and create more .properties files—there are many more options than the simple one-`Resource-Bundle`-per-action strategy. We'll go into more depth about the details of building a localized web application in chapter 14.

4.5 Advanced inputs

Applications often use JavaBeans to provide representations of objects within a domain. Examples of these types of classes include `Address`, `Bid`, and `BankAccount`. These application-specific classes, or domain objects, form the building blocks of most applications. Much of what a web application does involves getting information into and out of these domain objects. This process is also known as *data binding*.

With web applications, the two common approaches to data binding are to use intermediary objects or to access the domain objects directly.

4.5.1 Intermediary objects

Intermediary objects provide a bridge between user input and the domain objects. In most cases, the fields within the intermediary object are either `String`s or `Booleans`. This simplifies prepopulation of HTML forms. As temporary containers for user input, intermediary objects are often called upon to perform a number of different roles such as data validation, type transformation, and firewalling (allowing only certain properties to be changed by the user).

Using intermediary objects isn't without drawbacks, however. The largest disadvantage is the proliferation of small intermediary classes that usually mirror the domain objects. Your `Address`, `Bid`, and `BankAccount` domain objects would need corresponding `AddressForm`, `BidForm`, and `BankAccountForm` objects.

4.5.2 *Using domain objects directly*

The alternative approach is to use the domain objects directly. Doing so pushes many of the responsibilities of the intermediary objects (such as data validation and type transformation) to the application container—in our case, WebWork. Although this technique makes the container more complicated, it has the advantage of significantly reducing the development time for applications. WebWork supports both intermediary objects and using domain objects directly, but the authors of this book believe the best practice is to use domain objects. However, both security concerns and design decisions come into play when you do this. We'll discuss these issues further throughout this book.

Suppose you're attempting to collect some information about a user. You already have a domain object, User, which you'd like to take advantage of. Listing 4.8 shows how you might create a form (using localized texts, as discussed earlier).

Listing 4.8 WebWork tags let you directly access the properties of your domain objects.

```
<ww:form action="createUser">
 <ww:textfield label="%{getText('username')}" name="user.username"/>
 <ww:password label="%{getText('password')}" name="user.password"/>
 <ww:textfield label="%{getText('firstname')}"
               name="user.firstname"/>
 <ww:textfield label="%{getText('lastname')}" name="user.lastname"/>
 <ww:textfield label="%{getText('email')}" name="user.email"/>
 <ww:submit value="Submit"/>
</ww:form>
```

Listing 4.9 shows the CreateUser action, which exposes the User object via a Java-Bean getter and setter.

Listing 4.9 The CreateUser action exposes the User object via the getUser() and setUser() JavaBean property accessors.

```
public class CreateUser extends ActionSupport
                        implements UserDAOAware {
    User user;

    ...

    public String execute() throws Exception {
        userDAO.makePersistent(user);
        return SUCCESS;
    }
```

```
        public User getUser() {
            return user;
        }

        public void setUser(User user) {
            this.user = user;
        }
    }
```

With WebWork's data binding, passing a request parameter of

```
user.username
```

is equivalent to calling:

```
action.getUser().setUsername(...);
```

Note, however, that you never created an instance of a User object, so you should have received the dreaded NullPointerException. Fortunately, as WebWork traverses the request parameter, it automatically instantiates any object along the way that it needs to populate data. For example, events happen in this order when WebWork tries to set the user's username property:

```
action.getUser();
action.setUser(newUser());
action.getUser().setUsername(...);
```

WebWork first attempts to get a reference to the User. Noting that User is null, it creates a User using the zero-argument constructor. WebWork can now populate the username field.

You can see that by being able to use your domain objects directly, you can reduce the amount of work required to implement this functionality. The object instantiation feature that you saw for Users works to any depth and could be used to automatically create instances to any level. For example, an expression of user.address.street would call

```
getUser().getAddress().setStreet(...)
```

It would create the User object, as you saw earlier, but it would also create the Address object so the street property could be set on it. Although this is a simplified example, you can see how using this technique will significantly improve code readability.

Advantages of using domain objects

WebWork allows you to use your actions to directly edit domain objects, rather than having an intermediate layer of value objects or FormBeans as is often required in web applications built on frameworks such as Struts. These value objects or FormBeans are used for carrying data between the core business logic and the presentation layer, and they offer little real value; avoiding them saves the overhead of maintaining them without losing anything. This can save time not only in the value object classes you don't have to create but also in the layer of mapping code you would need to create to build domain objects from the value objects. You can also take advantage of common code, such as domain model validators, rather than have to duplicate this code for your value objects.

The power of using domain objects is enabled by the powerful type conversion and dynamic expression evaluation provided by the WebWork framework. Many web frameworks use `String`-based FormBeans or other value objects because their type conversion support isn't sufficient to support true domain objects. True domain objects often have complex property types and may require different type conversion rules on a property-by-property basis, even if the different properties are of the same type. WebWork's type conversion, as described in full in chapter 12, provides this flexible support and allows you to use complex object types to back your actions and web pages.

Along with supporting complex types when converting type values from web requests, WebWork's support for Object Graph Navigation Language (OGNL), as described more fully in chapter 8, allows your web pages to navigate complex object models, getting and setting subproperties easily. This allows you to use complex types as easily as a flat FormBean with only `String` properties. Thus your model objects can be your rich domain objects and automatically set the properties and subproperties.

Considerations when using domain objects

Along with the convenience of using domain objects directly in your web tier come some issues that you must consider. These considerations are applicable not only to domain objects, as you've seen previously, but also to `ModelDriven` actions, as you'll see in the next section.

One of the major issues when using domain objects is the order of interceptors and what you're trying to get them to do. Let's think about the ideal order of operations when you're editing a domain object:

1   Get the object's identifier from the user input.

2   Load the object from the database with the supplied identifier.

3   Update the properties of the object from the user input submitted from the form.

The problem is that you're looking at the parameters twice: once to get the object ID and again to set the object's properties. You'll see a concrete example when we discuss implementing a Create, Read, Update, and Delete (CRUD) action in chapter 15; but in general, one pattern that supports this order of operations is to use the parameter interceptor twice in one interceptor stack:

1   The `parameter` interceptor sets the object ID on the action. The other properties can't be set because the domain object is currently null.

2   The `prepare` interceptor calls `prepare()` on the action so the action can load the object from the database. The domain object is no longer null.

3   The `parameter` interceptor sets the other properties on the domain object. Because the domain object is no longer null, the additional properties can now be set.

As you can see, many different problems can be overcome by a creative usage of interceptors.

Another issue to consider when directly using domain objects in your web tier is security. When you're taking the user's request parameters and setting them on a domain object before saving it back to the database, you have to be careful not to let the user modify properties they shouldn't. For instance, what if the user put in `saveUser.action?userId=100&user.id=1`? The `userId` parameter might be used to load the `User` object, but then the `user.id` parameter might overwrite the `id` of the `User` object. Similarly, there are other properties you may not wish the user to set.

Currently, no single right answer exists for this problem. One option is to have no getter for the domain object; instead, you put the getters and setters for the properties you want the user to be able to set on the action and have them delegate to the domain object properties, like this:

```
public String getUsername() {
    return user.getUsername();
}

public void setUsername(String username) {
    user.setUsername(username);
}
```

Although this approach effectively protects the properties you don't want modified, you've lost a lot of advantages of using the domain object, because you need to duplicate the getters and setters for the properties on your action.

Another option that is being worked on is using dynamic proxies to expose only the methods on interfaces implemented by the domain object. Using Aspect-Oriented Programming (AOP), these proxies can be built automatically without your having to do it manually in your code. If you have an interface named `User` with getters and setters for the properties `username`, `firstname`, `lastname`, and `email`, and a class named `UserImpl` that implements the `User` interface but adds properties with getters and setters for `id`, `version`, `lastUpdate`, and `createDate`, then the proxy implementing `User` will block access to these `UserImpl`-specific properties. Because the proxy only implements the `User` interface, only the getters and setters for `username`, `firstname`, `lastname`, and `email` will be accessible. Again, this is a work in progress; for the current status of this functionality, your best source is the WebWork forums at http://forums.opensymphony.com.

4.6 *Working with ModelDriven actions*

One of WebWork's key features is that it doesn't require you to use special classes to back your form fields on your web pages. The properties can instead be on your action and can include complex objects with subproperties of their own. This can be valuable because you don't have to write FormBean classes, which are just more boilerplate code to be maintained. Actions (which handle the form data) and FormBeans (which hold the form data) are so tightly bound anyway, it makes sense to combine them.

Another option exists, however. If you want to have an object backing your form, your action can implement `com.opensymphony.xwork.ModelDriven`. This backing object doesn't have to be a weak, all-string-property pseudo-object; it can be a domain model object or other rich object. `ModelDriven` is an optional interface that `ActionSupport` doesn't implement, but subclasses of `ActionSupport` can choose to implement it. `ModelDriven` lets you work directly with your application's domain objects, allowing you to use the same objects in your web tier and your core business logic. Rather than having to map back and forth to another layer of FormBean objects, your web application can directly view and edit your domain objects.

4.6.1 *Implementing ModelDriven actions*

The `ModelDriven` interface has one method:

```
public Object getModel()
```

You can use this method to return the model that will back your web page. The properties of this model object are directly available by name for getting and setting from the web page; you don't have to make them (the model's properties) available from the action. This is another example of an optional interface that an action can choose to implement along with a corresponding interceptor. In this case, the interceptor is `com.opensymphony.xwork.interceptor.ModelDrivenInterceptor`, and its job is to put the model onto the value stack. We haven't looked fully at interceptors (see chapter 5), but the code in listing 4.10 (from the `ModelDrivenInterceptor`) should be straightforward.

> **Listing 4.10 The `before()` method of the `ModelDrivenInterceptor` is called before the action and result are executed.**

```
protected void before(ActionInvocation invocation)
    throws Exception {
    Action action = invocation.getProxy().getAction();

    if (action instanceof ModelDriven) {
        ModelDriven modelDriven = (ModelDriven) action;
        OgnlValueStack stack = invocation.getStack();
        stack.push(modelDriven.getModel());
    }
}
```

As you can see, the `ModelDrivenInterceptor` only does its work if the action implements `ModelDriven`. If it does, the model object is retrieved and pushed onto the value stack.

In addition to the properties of your action being visible directly to the JSP tags, your model object as returned from `getModel()` will also be available. As you can see in figure 4.1, the model object is on the top of the value stack, with the action instance just below, so the model properties are seen first by expressions that access property values.

Let's look at an example of a `ModelDriven` action. Listing 4.11 shows the `UpdateUser` action before it's refactored to implement `ModelDriven`.

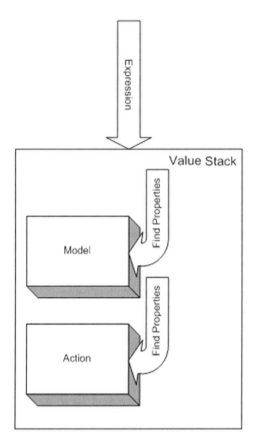

Figure 4.1
A representation of the value stack with the model object on top and the action below it. Queries for property values look first on the model and then on the action.

Listing 4.11 The `UpdateUser` action before it's refactored to implement `ModelDriven`

```
public class UpdateUser extends ActionSupport
                    implements UserDAOAware, Preparable,
                                   SessionAware {
    UserDAO userDAO;
    Map session;

    User user;

    public void setSession(Map session) {
        this.session = session;
    }

    public void setUserDAO(UserDAO userDAO) {
```

```
        this.userDAO = userDAO;
    }

    public void prepare() throws Exception {
        Long id = ((User)
session.get(AuthenticationInterceptor.USER)).getId();
        user = userDAO.getUserById(id, false);
    }

    public String execute() throws Exception {
        userDAO.makePersistent(user);
        return SUCCESS;
    }

    public String doDefault() throws Exception {
        return INPUT;
    }

    public User getUser() {
        return user;
    }
}
```

Listing 4.12 shows the `UpdateUser` action after it has been refactored to implement `ModelDriven`.

Listing 4.12   The `UpdateUser` action after it's been refactored to implement `ModelDriven`

```
public class UpdateUser extends ActionSupport
                        implements UserDAOAware, Preparable,
                                   SessionAware, ModelDriven {
    UserDAO userDAO;
    Map session;

    User user;

    public void setSession(Map session) {
        this.session = session;
    }

    public void setUserDAO(UserDAO userDAO) {
        this.userDAO = userDAO;
    }

    public void prepare() throws Exception {
        Long id = ((User)
session.get(AuthenticationInterceptor.USER)).getId();
```

```
        user = userDAO.getUserById(id, false);
    }

    public String execute() throws Exception {
        userDAO.makePersistent(user);
        return SUCCESS;
    }

    public String doDefault() throws Exception {
        return INPUT;
    }

    public Object getModel() {        ◁──────┐   Change to getModel()
        return user;                         │   to return User object
    }
}
```

In listing 4.12, the only changes needed make the action implement `ModelDriven` and change the `getUser()` method to `getModel()`. Now let's look at the changes in the JSP. Listing 4.13 shows updateProfile.jsp before it's refactored to support the `ModelDriven` version of the `UpdateUser` action.

Listing 4.13 updateProfile.jsp before it's refactored to support the `ModelDriven` version of the `UpdateUser` action

```
<ww:form action="updateProfile" method="post">
<ww:textfield label="%{getText('firstname')}"
            name="user.firstname"/>
<ww:textfield label="%{getText('lastname')}" name="user.lastname"/>
<ww:textfield label="%{getText('email')}" name="user.email"/>
<ww:radio label="%{getText('gender')}" name="user.gender"
        list="#{0 : getText('gender.male'),
                1 : getText('gender.female')}"/>
<ww:textfield label="%{getText('address.street')}"
            name="user.address.street"/>
<ww:textfield label="%{getText('address.zipcode')}"
            name="user.address.zipcode"/>
<ww:textfield label="%{getText('address.city')}"
            name="user.address.city"/>
<ww:select label="%{getText('address.state')}"
        name="user.address.state"
        list="{'Californa', 'Oregon'}"/>
<ww:select label="%{getText('address.country')}"
        name="user.address.country"
        list="{'USA', 'Canada', 'Mexico', 'Other'}"/>
<ww:checkbox label="%{getText('address.poBox')}"
            name="user.address.poBox"
            fieldValue="true"/>
```

```
<ww:submit value="%{getText('updateProfile')}"/>
</ww:form>
```

Each of the form fields is mapped to one of the properties of the User object using the user.* notation. To support the new ModelDriven action, all you need to do is to remove these user. prefixes from the property names. Listing 4.14 shows the refactored updateProfile.jsp.

Listing 4.14 The refactored updateProfile.jsp directly accesses the properties of the User object.

```
<ww:form action="updateProfile" method="post">
<ww:textfield label="%{getText('firstname')}"
              name="firstname"/>
<ww:textfield label="%{getText('lastname')}" name="lastname"/>
<ww:textfield label="%{getText('email')}" name="email"/>
<ww:radio label="%{getText('gender')}" name="gender"
          list="#{0 : getText('gender.male'),
                  1 : getText('gender.female')}"/>
<ww:textfield label="%{getText('address.street')}"
              name="address.street"/>
<ww:textfield label="%{getText('address.zipcode')}"
              name="address.zipcode"/>
<ww:textfield label="%{getText('address.city')}"
              name="address.city"/>
<ww:select label="%{getText('address.state')}"
           name="address.state"
           list="{'Californa', 'Oregon'}"/>
<ww:select label="%{getText('address.country')}"
           name="address.country"
           list="{'USA', 'Canada', 'Mexico', 'Other'}"/>
<ww:checkbox label="%{getText('address.poBox')}"
             name="address.poBox"
             fieldValue="true"/>
<ww:submit value="%{getText('updateProfile')}"/>
</ww:form>
```

The JSP form is essentially the same, but you can now directly access the properties of the User object, so you don't need the user.* prefix.

4.6.2 Considerations when using ModelDriven

This isn't to say that ModelDriven should be used in all circumstances. You may find scenarios where there are no existing business objects and it isn't worthwhile to create any. The search action is a common example. Most search actions take a

query and build a list of found items. You could create an object to hold these values, but usually it's easier to directly use the properties, as in listing 4.15.

Listing 4.15   A search action doesn't need a domain model object to back it.

```
public class Search extends ActionSupport
                    implements ItemDAOAware, SessionAware {
    List items;
    String query;

    public String execute() throws Exception {
        List results = itemDAO.search(query);

        return SUCCESS;
    }



    public List getItems() {
        return items;
    }

    public void setQuery(String query) {
        this.query = query;
    }
}
```

Another consideration when using `ModelDriven` concerns how the model is handled. For consistency, the value returned by `getModel()` shouldn't change over the
course of a request. Because `execute()` is called after a reference to the model is
returned, the `execute()` method may not replace the model. Consider the example in listing 4.16.

**Listing 4.16   The value returned from `getModel()` shouldn't change over the lifetime
             of the action.**

```
//Example 1: This is wrong:
public class ViewHeadlineAction implements Action, ModelDriven {
    Headline headline = new Headline();

    public Object getModel() {
        return this.headline ;
    }

    // ...

    public String execute() {
```

```
        headline = headlineFactory.findLatest();
        return SUCCESS;
    }
}


//Example 2: This is correct:
public class ViewHeadlineAction implements Action, ModelDriven {
    Headline headline = new Headline();

    public Object getModel() {
        return this.headline ;
    }

    // ...

    public String execute() {
        headlineFactory.updateToLatest(headline);
        return SUCCESS;
    }
}
```

Example 1 attempts to change the instance that getModel() returns. However, because getModel() is called before execute() and before the object is pushed onto the value stack, the reference that WebWork uses is the original instance, created by new Headline(), not the instance loaded from the HeadlineFactory. The second example resolves this issue by updating the existing instance rather than having headline point to a new instance.

4.7 Accessing data through the ActionContext

Until now, we've shown how information can be retrieved and set via the fields in your action and/or model. Although 90% of the time this is all the data you'll need access to, in some cases additional data access is required (for example, to the data stored in an HttpSession). In this section, we'll cover the basics of accessing this type of information. The key is in the ActionContext class.

> **NOTE**   For more information about how ActionContext works, including how it guarantees data consistency, consult appendix, "WebWork architecture."

4.7.1 CaveatEmptor: accessing the session

Let's look at the Login action in CaveatEmptor. This action uses WebWork's Inversion of Control container to delegate to the username/password verification. (For now, ignore the UserDAO, but know that it's one of many components built for

CaveatEmptor. In chapter 6, we discuss Inversion of Control and a couple of the components that are part of CaveatEmptor.) In listing 4.17, the important thing is the call to `ActionContext`.

Listing 4.17 Login action using `ActionContext`

```
public class Login extends ActionSupport
    implements UserDAOAware {

    User user;
    UserDAO userDAO;

    public String execute() throws Exception {
        user = userDAO.findByCredentials(user.getUsername(),
                                          user.getPassword());
        if (user ==  null) {
            return INPUT;
        } else {
            Map session = ActionContext.getContext().getSession();
            session.put("user", user);
            return SUCCESS;
        }
    }

    public String doDefault() throws Exception {
        return INPUT;
    }

    public User getUser() {
        return user;
    }

    public void setUserDAO(UserDAO dao) {
        this.userDAO = dao;
    }
}
```

As you can see, `ActionContext` provides a static method `getContext()`, which returns an instance of `ActionContext`. Once you have a handle on this object, you can call several of its methods, which provide access to data associated with the action invocation. One of those methods, `getSession()`, provides access to session-scoped data. You use the session `Map` to then store the `User` object and indicate that the user has been authenticated.

Although `ActionContext` can be handy, it's sometimes cumbersome to use. It has two big problems: It's hard to test, and it can lead to bad designs. Specifically, because `ActionContext` is statically accessed and is implemented as a `ThreadLocal`, automated unit tests for your actions require more work to set up.

Also, because you can technically access the `ActionContext` at any point in the thread call stack, as you can with any `ThreadLocal`, if you rely on it too much you may find yourself calling out to it deep in code that has nothing to do with your WebWork actions. This is a bad design, but it's easy to get caught up. Trust us— we've been caught by it many times.

But don't despair! WebWork provides simple alternatives to getting access to the values stored in the `ActionContext`. Listing 4.18 shows the use of the `Session-Aware` interface, which uses Inversion of Control to give the action a handle to the session `Map`. In chapter 5, we'll explain which interceptor provides this functionality; for now, know that using the `completeStack` outlined in chapter 3 is sufficient.

Listing 4.18 Login action using `SessionAware`

```
public class Login extends ActionSupport
    implements com.opensymphony.webwork.interceptor.SessionAware,
        UserDAOAware {

    Map session;
    User user;
    UserDAO userDAO;

    public void setSession(Map session) {
        this.session = session;
    }

    public String execute() throws Exception {
        user = userDAO.findByCredentials(user.getUsername(),
                                         user.getPassword());
        if (user ==  null) {
            return INPUT;
        } else {
            session.put("user", user);
            return SUCCESS;
        }
    }

    public String doDefault() throws Exception {
        return INPUT;
    }

    public User getUser() {
        return user;
    }
```

```
        public void setUserDAO(UserDAO dao) {
            this.userDAO = dao;
        }
    }
```

The major change is that you no longer access `ActionContext`. Instead, the action now implements `SessionAware`, which tells WebWork that the action needs the session `Map` to be set on the action *before* it's executed. This makes unit testing much easier because you can pass in a `HashMap` and verify the contents after `execute()` has completed. For more information about testing practices with WebWork, consult chapter 15.

You've now seen two ways to access the session in your action, but using `SessionAware` is the recommended approach. Note that the session is represented as `Map` rather than the servlet-specific `HttpSession`, although the `Map` merely wraps the `HttpSession`. Let's see what needs to happen to get access to objects that are specific to servlet environments.

4.7.2 *Example: accessing the request and response*

Let's continue with the Login example, but this time access the `HttpSession` directly rather than use the wrapper `Map` provided by WebWork. Start again by using `ActionContext`:

```
public String execute() throws Exception {
    user = userDAO.findByCredentials(user.getUsername(),
                                     user.getPassword());
    if (user ==  null) {
        return INPUT;
    } else {
        ActionContext ctx = ActionContext.getContext();
        HttpServletRequest req =
            ctx.get(ServletActionContext.HTTP_REQUEST);
        HttpSession session = req.getSession();
        session.setAttribute("user", user);
        return SUCCESS;
    }
}
```

In order to get the servlet-specific session object, you first need access to the `HttpServletRequest` that is associated with this request. You can do so by asking the `ActionContext` for the object associated with the `ServletActionContext.HTTP_REQUEST` key, which is a string. Once you get the object, the standard servlet APIs are used to set the user in the session.

NOTE The complete class name for ActionContext is com.opensympho-
ny.xwork.ActionContext. Similarly, the complete class name for Servlet-
ActionContext is com.opensymphony.webwork.ServletActionContext.
However, we recommend that you avoid using both of these classes unless
absolutely necessary.

The ServletActionContext class contains a bunch of keys, such as HTTP_REQUEST,
as well as helper methods, which work in tandem with the ActionContext to provide servlet-specific objects such as the request and response. It even provides a
helper method that simplifies the previous example down to the following:

```
public String execute() throws Exception {
    user = userDAO.findByCredentials(user.getUsername(),
                                     user.getPassword());
    if (user ==  null) {
        return INPUT;
    } else {
        HttpServletRequest req = ServletActionContext.getRequest();
        HttpSession session = req.getSession();
        session.setAttribute("user", user);
        return SUCCESS;
    }
}
```

ServletActionContext.getRequest() returns the request associated with the current thread's ActionContext. You can simplify this example one more time by
employing the same Inversion of Control pattern, shown in listing 4.19.

Listing 4.19 Login action using ServletRequestAware

```
import com.opensymphony.webwork.interceptor.ServletRequestAware;

public class Login extends ActionSupport
                implements ServletRequestAware, UserDAOAware {

    HttpServletRequest req;
    User user;
    UserDAO userDAO;

    public void setServletRequest(HttpServletRequest req) {
        this.req = req;
    }

    public String execute() throws Exception {
        user = userDAO.findByCredentials(user.getUsername(),
                                         user.getPassword());
        if (user ==  null) {
            return INPUT;
```

```
        } else {
            HttpSession session = req.getSession();
            session.setAttribute("user", user);
            return SUCCESS;
        }
    }

    public String doDefault() throws Exception {
        return INPUT;
    }

    public User getUser() {
        return user;
    }

    public void setUserDAO(UserDAO dao) {
        this.userDAO = dao;
    }
}
```

This listing uses the same pattern of implementing an `Aware` interface to get access to the request object without accessing any static methods. Just like when you access the session `Map`, we recommend using the `Aware` interface approach to get access to this data rather than using `ServletActionContext`. In addition to getting access to the request, you can implement `ServletResponseAware` to get access to the `HttpServletResponse` object. Access to these servlet-specific objects is sometimes important, especially when you're dealing with file uploads. Let's now look at how WebWork handles that process.

4.8 Handling file uploads

You've just seen how WebWork can allow simple access to the servlet request object. This is important when you're dealing with *multipart requests*—better known as *file uploads*. Just as with the `ActionContext` examples in section 4.7, there are two ways to get access to uploaded files. We'll start with the more straightforward approach, and then we'll show you the recommended approach by taking advantage of WebWork's interceptors.

4.8.1 Accessing uploaded files through the request wrapper

Before a file can be uploaded, it's important to remember that your HTML form *must* submit the request in the proper form. Marking your HTML form with the encoding type of `multipart/form-data` does this:

```
<form action="upload.action"
    enctype="multipart/form-data"
    method="post">
    <input type="file" name="doc"/>
    ...
</form>
```

This tells the web browser to send the HTTP request encoded in such a manner that uploaded files can be processed. WebWork automatically recognizes these types of requests and wraps the HttpServletRequest object with a special MultiPartRequestWrapper (in the package com.opensymphony.webwork.dispatcher.multipart). This object properly parses out the files from the rest of the request, allowing you to get a handle on the uploaded temporary java.io.File object as well as the file's content-type and original filename. An example of an action that does this is shown here:

```
public class DocUpload extends ActionSupport
    implements ServletRequestAware {

    HttpServletRequest req;

    public void setServletRequest(HttpServletRequest req) {
        this.req = req;
    }

    public String execute() throws Exception {
        MultiPartRequestWrapper wrapper =
            (MultiPartRequestWrapper) req;
        File doc = null;
        try {
            doc = wrapper.getFiles("doc")[0];
            String contentType = wrapper.getContentTypes("doc")[0];
            String filename = wrapper.getFilesystemNames("doc")[0];

            // do something with the file, content-type, and filename
        } finally {
            doc.delete();
        }

        return SUCCESS;
    }
}
```

In this example, the first thing to notice is that the request object is cast to MultiPartRequestWrapper. This is necessary to get access to the file, content-type, and filename. Note that the wrapper's method calls are all in the plural form, such as getFiles() and getContentTypes(). This is because a form could potentially upload several files using the same parameter name (doc in this case). Because you know your form is sending only one file for that parameter, you can safely use the array index 0 to get a handle on the data.

Once you have access to the File object, the action needs to do something with it, such as copy the contents to a permanent location (a database, for example). The File object that is handed off with the request will *not* be deleted (unless you're using the FileUploadInterceptor, which we'll discuss in the next section). The try/finally block ensures that the temporary file is removed once it has been processed.

This approach works, but it obviously isn't graceful to have to clean up uploaded files every time. WebWork has features that can make file uploads easier to handle, as we'll now discuss.

4.8.2 *Automating file uploads*

WebWork provides an interceptor, FileUploadInterceptor, which automates the retrieval and cleanup of uploaded files. Using this interceptor, your action no longer needs to worry about request objects, request wrappers, or even cleaning up the File objects. We discuss interceptors more in chapter 5; but the fileUpload interceptor is automatically configured in webwork-default.xml and is part of the completeStack outlined in chapter 3. Provided you configure your actions to use the completeStack or some other stack that includes the fileUpload interceptor, the following modifications to the previous example are valid:

```
public class DocUpload extends ActionSupport {
    File doc;
    String docContentType;
    String docFileName;

    public String execute() throws Exception {
        // do something with the file, content-type, and filename

        return SUCCESS;
    }

    public void setDoc(File doc) {
        this.doc = doc;
    }

    public void setDocContentType(String docContentType) {
        this.docContentType = docContentType;
    }

    public void setDocFileName(String docFileName) {
```

```
        this.docFileName = docFileName;
    }
}
```

This example is much simpler. Using the interceptor, you can treat uploaded files (and their associated metadata: content-type and filename) like normal form parameters. Also, the action is no longer required to delete the uploaded files— the `fileUpload` interceptor automatically handles that.

The field names in the action must follow a specific pattern. In this example, the `form` element is named `doc`, so the `File` field must also be named `doc`. Similarly, the content-type and filename must be in the form `[element]ContentType` and `[element]FileName`, respectively. If you don't need the content-type or original filename, you can omit the fields and setters in your actions.

Uploading multiple files with the same parameter names is also supported. All you have to do is change your action fields to arrays: that is, `File` becomes `File[]`, and the two strings become string arrays. The three arrays are always the same length, and their order is the same, meaning that index 0 for all three arrays represents the same file and file metadata.

4.8.3 *Configuration settings*

Although WebWork supports file uploading without any modifications, three configuration options are available to tune how WebWork handles files. We discussed these items in chapter 3, but we'll go over them here in more detail now that you've seen a real file-upload example. These three properties are defined in webwork.properties:

- `webwork.multipart.parser`—Configures the underlying multipart request parser. Possible values are `pell`, `cos`, and `jakarta`.

- `webwork.multipart.saveDir`—The directory to which WebWork saves temporary uploaded files. If this isn't specified, WebWork saves files to the directory specified by the `javax.servlet.context.tempdir` system property.

- `webwork.multipart.maxSize`—The maximum size of the uploaded files, measured in bytes. Defaults to 2097152, or roughly 2MB.

The most important configuration for file uploads is the parser you choose. Although `pell` is the default for WebWork 2.1.7 and below, as of WebWork 2.2 `jakarta` will be the default choice. This is the case because that implementation is the only one that supports multiple files with the same parameter name. We recommend that you configure your WebWork application to also use the `jakarta` parser in preparation for the upgrade to WebWork 2.2 when it's released and also because it's the best implementation of the three.

NOTE In order to use the file-upload feature, you must include the correct JAR file for the multipart parser you've chosen. For `jakarta`, that file is included with WebWork as commons-fileupload.jar.

4.9 Summary

Actions are the core unit of functionality in WebWork. At their heart, actions are nothing more than classes with an `execute()` method, but your action classes can choose to implement a number of optional interfaces to take advantage of other services provided by the framework. Several of these optional interfaces follow a common pattern in WebWork: an optional interface paired with an interceptor that applies to actions implementing this interface. This is a powerful pattern to remember for your code as you pull common code out into interceptors. Although you can implement these optional interfaces, the overriding message we hope to convey is that WebWork should provide 99% of your desired functionality in the form of the `ActionSupport` base class.

We also looked at another way of building your web applications using `Model-Driven` actions. The model-driven approach will start to introduce you to the robust parameter mapping and type conversion that WebWork offers. This allows you to directly use your domain objects in your web applications, gaining the advantage of code reuse and reducing code duplication. WebWork's powerful type conversion and dynamic expression evaluation make this a valuable alternative to putting your form properties on actions as fields.

You now know that the `ActionContext` contains additional information that your action doesn't necessarily have access to. Although it's possible to access it directly, it's recommended that you use the `Aware` interfaces that WebWork provides. These interfaces are described in more detail in chapter 5.

Finally, using the `fileUpload` interceptor rather than directly talking to WebWork's `MultiPartRequestWrapper` is the simplest way to support uploaded files in your web applications. The `pell` parser is the default choice at this moment, but we highly recommend that you use the `jakarta` parser: it's more feature-rich, has fewer bugs, and will be the default in future versions of WebWork.

Adding functionality with interceptors

5

This chapter covers

- How interceptors are called
- Using the prepackaged interceptors
- Using the prepackaged interceptor stacks
- Customizing interceptor stacks for specific needs
- Building your own interceptors

Interceptors are one of WebWork's most powerful features—one that sets it apart from other frameworks. Interceptors allow you to do some processing before and/or after the action and result are executed, and they also let you modularize common code out into reusable classes. Many of the core features of WebWork are implemented as interceptors, including setting parameters and chaining action properties. Interceptors, including your own custom interceptor classes, may be applied in any order to provide the exact functionality required for each action.

As you'll see in this chapter, WebWork comes with many interceptors to provide both the common functionality of a web application framework and several advanced features. We'll also look at an example that shows how you can build a custom interceptor and how interceptors can be used to integrate other libraries and frameworks with WebWork.

5.1 *How interceptors are called*

When we're discussing interceptors throughout the rest of this chapter, it's important to understand the lifecycle of an action's execution and when interceptors are called in that execution. When a request comes into the WebWork `Servlet-Dispatcher`, WebWork looks up the configuration for that action and builds a list of the interceptors applied for that action configuration. Figure 5.1 shows that WebWork starts the call to the list of interceptors, which calls each of the interceptors in order.[1]

Because interceptors wrap around the execution of the action and the result, when the action and result are finished, each interceptor regains control in reverse order until the interceptor that was first on the way in is the last on the way out. If you're familiar with servlet filters, interceptors are similar in that each interceptor has the option to continue the execution of the rest of the interceptors or to short-circuit the execution of the rest of the interceptors and the action/result by just returning. By returning, an interceptor can prevent the rest of the interceptors and the action from executing. The return value from either the action or a short-circuiting interceptor is used to look up the result configured in xwork.xml for that return code.

---

[1] Note that this is a highly simplified view of how interceptors and the action and result are called. For a more detailed look at the architecture of WebWork, see the appendix ("WebWork architecture").

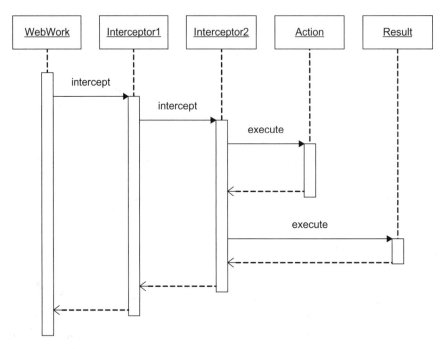

Figure 5.1   Each interceptor wraps the execution of the remainder of the interceptors and the action and result.

5.2 *Using the prepackaged interceptors*

WebWork comes packaged with a number of interceptors that provide much of the core functionality as well as optional advanced features. As you saw in chapter 3, "Setting up WebWork," these interceptors are defined in the webwork-default.xml file. Some default interceptor stacks, or named groups of interceptors, are also defined; you can use them to provide a set of functionality or extend them for your own custom interceptor stacks. Remember, interceptor stacks are just ordered lists of interceptors mapped to a name; they can be referenced by name anywhere where an interceptor can be referenced. The prepackaged interceptors are shown in table 5.1.

Table 5.1 Prepackaged interceptors, grouped by functionality

	Interceptor alias	Description
Utility interceptors	`timer`	Times the execution of the rest of the `ActionInvocation` and logs the time.
	`logger`	Logs a message before and after the rest of the `ActionInvocation` for trace logging.
Property setting interceptors	`params`	Sets the properties of the action using the request parameters. Request parameters are mapped to the same named properties of the action, if they exist, and the values are converted to the proper type.
	`static-params`	Sets any parameters defined in the xwork.xml action configuration onto the action instance
	`component`	Calls the Inversion of Control (IoC) container to have all the action's dependencies set with component instances managed by the container. Chapter 6 discusses the IoC container built into WebWork.
	`chain`	Copies all the properties from previous actions to the current action. This interceptor is usually applied to an action that is chained to using a chain result to automatically copy the property values from the previous action to the new action.
	`conversionError`	Adds a field error message to the action for every type conversion error.
	`servlet-config`	Sets the `HttpServletRequest`, `HttpServletResponse`, parameter map, session map, and application map on the action if it implements `ServletRequestAware`, `ServletResponseAware`, `ParameterAware`, `SessionAware`, and `ApplicationAware`, respectively. An action may choose to implement some or all of these to get the ones it needs.
	`fileUpload`	Handles multipart file uploads, allowing your action to use the uploaded file without needing to parse the multipart request.

Table 5.1 **Prepackaged interceptors, grouped by functionality** *(continued)*

	Interceptor alias	Description
Workflow interceptors	workflow	Defines a default workflow for actions. If the action implements the Validateable interface, the interceptor calls validate() on the action. If the action implements ValidationAware, the interceptor checks to see whether the action has any error messages using the hasErrors() method. If the action does have any errors, the interceptor returns input without letting the action execute.
	validation	Invokes the validation framework to read the *-validation.xml files and apply the validations declared in them.
	prepare	Calls prepare() on your action if the action implements Preparable. This is useful for setting up resources before other interceptors (such as params) are called and before the action is executed. As an example, you could create a model object in prepare() into which the params interceptor sets parameters.
	model	Calls getModel() on your action if it implements the ModelDriven interface, and pushes the model object onto the value stack. This allows your form fields to directly access the model's properties without your having to precede the property names with model.*.
	token	Checks for a valid form token in the request parameters. This form token is generated using the <ww:token> JSP tag; it sets an expected value in the session and creates a hidden input field in the form. The token interceptor verifies that the form token is in the request parameters and that it hasn't been used before. If the token isn't valid, the token interceptor returns invalid.token without executing the action. This is useful for preventing duplicate form submissions.
	token-session	Extends the token interceptor. When there is a valid token, it saves the ActionInvocation in the session; then, if a duplicate form submission comes in, it re-renders the same page as the first time without executing the action.
	execAndWait	Spawns a new thread to execute the action, and returns wait as the result code. The wait result can be mapped to a page that has a meta refresh, telling the browser to try again every few seconds. When the Thread executing the action finishes, the next request from the browser returns the result of the original action invocation.

5.2.1 *Utility interceptors*

The utility interceptors listed in table 5.1 are the simplest interceptor classes; so, as we begin to look at how interceptors are built and used, they make a good starting point. Using these interceptors is as easy as applying them in your xwork.xml action configurations, as you saw in chapter 3.

Timing your actions

One of the simplest and most frequently used interceptors is also one of the classic usage examples for the interceptor pattern: execution timing. The `timer` interceptor is the most basic direct implementation of the `Interceptor` interface. Here's its `intercept()` method, which logs the time it takes to execute the action and result:[2]

```
public String intercept(ActionInvocation invocation)
            throws Exception {
    long startTime = System.currentTimeMillis();
    String result = invocation.invoke();
    long executionTime = System.currentTimeMillis() - startTime;
    ... log the time ...
}
```

As you can see, it's basically very simple. The `intercept()` method calls `System.currentTimeMillis()` before executing the rest of the `ActionInvocation` (including the rest of the interceptors applied to this action) by calling `invocation.invoke()`. After the action and result have executed and returned, the `timer` interceptor gets the time it took by subtracting the start time from the current time and building a message to log the execution time.

The AroundInterceptor

Rather than directly implement the `Interceptor` interface, like the `TimerInterceptor` does, most of the prebuilt interceptors extend `com.opensymphony.xwork.interceptor.AroundInterceptor`. We'll look at when to extend `AroundInterceptor` and when to directly implement the interceptor interface later in this chapter. For now, let's take a quick look at what it does, to better understand the other interceptors that come bundled with WebWork (see listing 5.1).

---

[2] This code sample is simplified to show only the pertinent parts.

Listing 5.1   `AroundInterceptor`: a useful base class for interceptors

```
public abstract class AroundInterceptor implements Interceptor {
    public String intercept(ActionInvocation invocation)
            throws Exception {
        String result = null;

        before(invocation);
        result = invocation.invoke();
        after(invocation, result);

        return result;
    }

    /**
     * Called after the invocation has been executed.
     *
     * @param result the result value returned by the invocation
     */
    protected abstract void after(
            ActionInvocation dispatcher,
            String result)
            throws Exception;

    /**
     * Called before the invocation has been executed.
     */
    protected abstract void before(ActionInvocation invocation)
            throws Exception;
}
```

As you can see in listing 5.1, the `AroundInterceptor` defines two callback methods, `before()` and `after()`. The `before()` method is called, surprisingly, before the rest of the invocation is called, and the `after()` method is called afterward. This allows for subclasses to implement these two abstract methods to put the code they want to execute before and after the action in the correct spots. As you look at the prebuilt interceptors that follow, you'll see examples of this, along with several interceptors that need only `before()` or `after()`.

Logging action executions

In addition to execution timing, the other classic example for the interceptor pattern is logging. The `com.opensymphony.xwork.interceptor.LoggingInterceptor` implements logging a message before and after the action is executed by extending the `AroundInterceptor` and implementing the `before()` and `after()` methods, as shown here:

```
protected void after(ActionInvocation invocation, String result)
    throws Exception {
    logMessage(invocation, FINISH_MESSAGE);
}

protected void before(ActionInvocation invocation) throws Exception {
    logMessage(invocation, START_MESSAGE);
}
```

5.2.2 Setting parameters

As we said earlier, interceptors handle even core features such as setting properties on your action instance so that their order can be customized via configuration in xwork.xml. Several interceptors set properties on your action, depending on the source of the values to be set—the configuration, the request, or the container.

Setting properties from the request parameters

The com.opensymphony.xwork.interceptor.ParametersInterceptor, which is mapped as params in webwork-defaults.xml, is responsible for setting properties on your action from the request parameters. Suppose you have a text field named foo defined like this:

```
<ww:textfield label="Foo" name="foo"/>
```

When that form is submitted to an action with the parameter interceptor applied, it will try to call a setFoo() method on your action with the value from the form field.

Listing 5.2 shows the heart of the ParametersInterceptor, which takes the request parameters and iterates through them, setting the value for each name using the value stack. As explained in more detail in the appendix, the value stack uses the name of the property passed in as an Object Graph Navigation Language (OGNL) expression and traverses object relationships using getters to find the final property to be set.

Listing 5.2 ParametersInterceptor sets the properties of the action from the request parameters.

```
if (parameters != null) {
    final OgnlValueStack stack =
        ActionContext.getContext().getValueStack();

    for (Iterator iterator = parameters.entrySet().iterator();
            iterator.hasNext();) {
        Map.Entry entry = (Map.Entry) iterator.next();
```

```
            stack.setValue(entry.getKey().toString(), entry.getValue());
        }
    }
```

This parameter interceptor is responsible for turning the name-value pair `user.name->John` that comes in the HTTP request into a call of `getUser().set-Name("John")`.

Setting properties from the configuration

A similar interceptor is the `com.opensymphony.xwork.interceptor.StaticParame-tersInterceptor`, which is mapped with the name `static-params` in webwork-default.xml. This interceptor does the same thing as `ParametersInterceptor`; but instead of using the request parameters, it uses the parameters from the action configuration in xwork.xml. For example, suppose you have an action defined like this in xwork.xml:

```
<action name="exampleAction" class="example.ExampleAction">
    <param name="firstName">John</param>
    <param name="lastName">Doe</param>
</action>
```

The `static-params` interceptor is called with these two name-value pairs. If the action has properties named `firstName` and `lastName` with setters, then they will be set with the supplied values.

Setting components into your action from the IoC container

The `com.opensymphony.xwork.interceptor.component.ComponentInterceptor` also sets properties on your action, but in this case they are instances of component classes that are managed by an IoC container. Chapter 6 discusses Inversion of Control and the IoC container that comes with WebWork.

Setting properties on your action from a chained action

Another interceptor that sets property values on actions is `com.opensym-phony.xwork.interceptor.ChainingInterceptor`. The `ChainingInterceptor` can be used as part of chaining from one action to another if you want to copy the property values of the executed action along to the new action. This process is discussed in detail in chapter 7, "Using results"; but the general idea of this interceptor is to use reflection to find all the properties of the first action and try to set them into properties with the same name on the next action.

Getting at the HTTP-specific objects when you need them

The `ServletConfigInterceptor` works with actions that implement any or all of five interfaces:

1 `com.opensymphony.webwork.interceptor.ServletRequestAware`

2 `com.opensymphony.webwork.interceptor.ServletResponseAware`

3 `com.opensymphony.webwork.interceptor.ParameterAware`

4 `com.opensymphony.webwork.interceptor.SessionAware`

5 `com.opensymphony.webwork.interceptor.ApplicationAware`

Each of these interfaces contains one method—a setter—for (respectively) the `HttpServletRequest`, the `HttpServletResponse`, a map of the request parameters, a map wrapping the `HttpSession`, and a map wrapping the `ServletContext`'s attributes. If your action needs to directly access any or all of these, you can pick and choose which of these interfaces to implement and apply the `servlet-config` interceptor to put them into your action. Listing 5.3 shows an action that implements `ServletRequestAware`. The `servlet-config` interceptor puts the `HttpServletRequest` into this action before it's executed, so it can just use the request.

Listing 5.3   An action that implements `ServletRequestAware`

```
public class ServletConfigAction extends ActionSupport
            implements ServletRequestAware {
    private HttpServletRequest request;
    private String contextPath;

    public void setServletRequest(HttpServletRequest request) {
        this.request = request;
    }

    public String getContextPath() {
        return contextPath;
    }

    public String execute() throws Exception {
        contextPath = request.getContextPath();
        return SUCCESS;
    }
}
```

Listing 5.4 shows the `ServletConfigInterceptor` checking for each of these interfaces and calling the appropriate method if it's found.

Listing 5.4 `ServletConfigInterceptor` sets servlet-specific parameters onto an action.

```
protected void before(ActionInvocation invocation)
throws Exception {
        Action action = invocation.getAction();
        ActionContext context = ActionContext.getContext();

        if (action instanceof ServletRequestAware) {
            HttpServletRequest request =
              (HttpServletRequest) context.get(HTTP_REQUEST);
            ((ServletRequestAware) action)
                .setServletRequest(request);
        }

        if (action instanceof ServletResponseAware) {
            HttpServletResponse response =
                (HttpServletResponse)
                   ➥context.get(HTTP_RESPONSE);
            ((ServletResponseAware) action)
                ➥.setServletResponse(response);
        }

        if (action instanceof ParameterAware) {
            ((ParameterAware) action)
                ➥.setParameters(context.getParameters());
        }

        if (action instanceof SessionAware) {
            ((SessionAware) action)
                ➥.setSession(context.getSession());
        }

        if (action instanceof ApplicationAware) {
            ((ApplicationAware) action)
                ➥.setApplication(context.getApplication());
        }
    }
```

The `ServletConfigInterceptor` is the best method when you need to get direct access to the HTTP-specific classes. If at all possible, you should avoid tying your actions to the Web like this, because it makes testing more difficult and ties you to a servlet container for deployment. At times, however, this approach may be necessary to get below the abstractions provided by the framework—for instance, to set custom HTTP headers on the response.

Handling file uploads

As you saw in chapter 3, the `fileUpload` interceptor automates the handling of multipart file uploads. It parses the file(s) from the request and sets them, along with the filenames and content types, into your action. Refer to chapter 3 for more information about how to use the `fileUpload` interceptor.

5.2.3 Defining workflow

Several interceptors change the workflow of an action's execution. By *workflow*, here we mean the method calls that your action receives—both which ones are called and the order in which they are called. Some add more workflow steps, such as calling optional methods on actions that implement certain interfaces, whereas the `DefaultWorkflowInterceptor` can prevent the action from executing altogether.

Using the default workflow

Here's the `intercept()` method of the `com.opensymphony.xwork.interceptor.DefaultWorkflowInterceptor`, which validates an action and checks for any error messages:

```
public String intercept(ActionInvocation invocation)
        throws Exception {
    Action action = invocation.getAction();

    if (action instanceof Validateable) {
        Validateable validateable = (Validateable) action;
        validateable.validate();
    }

    if (action instanceof ValidationAware) {
        ValidationAware validationAwareAction =
            (ValidationAware) action;

        if (validationAwareAction.hasErrors()) {
            return Action.INPUT;
        }
    }

    return invocation.invoke();
}
```

The `DefaultWorkflowInterceptor` implements a common best practice in Web-Work actions and also maintains backward compatibility with the 1.x WebWork development line. In WebWork 1.x, `ActionSupport` encapsulated much of the functionality pulled into interceptors in WebWork 2.0 and later. Included in the functionality in `ActionSupport` was some workflow that called a `validate()`

method on the action and then checked for any action-level or field-level error messages in the action. If the action contained any errors, `ActionSupport` automatically returned `Action.INPUT`.

The `validate()` method has been pulled into the `com.opensymphony.xwork.Validateable` interface, which `ActionSupport` in WebWork 2.x implements. If an action implements this interface, the `DefaultWorkflowInterceptor` calls `validate()` on the action before it's executed. If the action implements `com.opensymphony.xwork.ValidationAware`, which is the interface that defines methods for managing action- and field-level error messages, then the `Default-WorkflowInterceptor` calls `hasErrors()` to check for any error messages and returns `Action.INPUT` without executing the action if any error messages exist.

Validating your action using the validation framework

The `DefaultWorkflowInterceptor` with the `Validateable` interface is one method of validating user input before executing your action. Another way of doing validation is to use the `com.opensymphony.xwork.validator.ValidationInterceptor`. This interceptor calls into the XWork Validation Framework, which lets you define your validations in external XML files, keeping your validation separate from your code. The details of the validation framework are discussed in chapter 13, "Validating form data," along with the pros and cons of each approach and when the two approaches can be used together.

Preparing your actions

The `PrepareInterceptor`, like the `ServletConfigInterceptor`, calls an optional method on your action if the action implements the correct interface. The `Prepare-Interceptor` acts on actions that implement `com.opensymphony.xwork.Preparable`. The `Preparable` interface implements only one method:

```
void prepare() throws Exception
```

As you can see, the `PrepareInterceptor` looks for classes implementing this interface and calls `prepare()` on them:

```
protected void before(ActionInvocation invocation)
    throws Exception {
    Action action = invocation.getAction();

    if (action instanceof Preparable) {
        ((Preparable) action).prepare();
    }
}
```

The `Preparable` interface can be helpful for setting up resources or values before your action is executed. For instance, if you have a drop-down list of available values that you look up in the database, you may want to do this in the `prepare()` method so that the values will be populated for rendering to the page even if the action isn't executed because the `DefaultWorkflowInterceptor` found error messages.

Making your actions ModelDriven

The final interceptor that calls methods on your action to set up state before executing the action is `com.opensymphony.xwork.interceptor.ModelDrivenInterceptor`. We looked at the `ModelDrivenInterceptor` in chapter 4, "Implementing WebWork actions," when we discussed `ModelDriven` actions. As we showed then, the `ModelDrivenInterceptor` looks for actions that implement `com.opensymphony.xwork.ModelDriven`; it calls `getModel()` from that interface to get an object that's pushed onto the value stack to allow its properties to be directly accessed via OGNL expressions. (See section 4.6 in chapter 4 for the details.)

Preventing duplicate form posting using form tokens

The `token` and `token-session` interceptors can be used as part of a system to prevent duplicate form submissions. Duplicate form posts can occur when users click the Back button to go back to a previously submitted form and then click the button again, or when they click the button more than once while waiting for a response. The `token` interceptors look for valid tokens submitted with your form and allow them to be used only once. On subsequent form posts, the `token` interceptors identify the invalid requests and give you two options for handling them: You can either show an error page or save the original result to be re-rendered for the user. We look in detail at the `token` JSP tag and the `token` interceptors in chapter 15, section 15.6.

Executing long-running actions without making the user wait

The `token` and `token-session` interceptors can help prevent duplicates posts from being submitted and processed, but there is another common problem with web applications and users who click too frequently: Long-running pages are often resubmitted multiple times. As you'll see in chapter 15, the `token-session` interceptor can transparently address this issue; but sometimes, having a simple *Please wait* page while the action executes gives the user more confidence about your application. The `execAndWait` interceptor does exactly that. This interceptor is an advanced feature of WebWork and is explained in detail in chapter 15, section 15.7.

5.3 *Using prepackaged interceptor stacks*

In addition to the prepackaged interceptors, webwork-default.xml includes prepackaged combinations of these interceptors in named interceptor stacks. Table 5.2 lists the prepackaged interceptor stacks defined in webwork-default.xml.

Table 5.2 **The prepackaged interceptor stacks define starter recipes for interceptor stacks.**

Interceptor alias	Description

`defaultStack`
 	
```<interceptor-stack name="defaultStack">   <interceptor-ref name="servlet-config"/>   <interceptor-ref name="prepare"/>   <interceptor-ref name="static-params"/>   <interceptor-ref name="params"/>   <interceptor-ref name="conversionError"/></interceptor-stack>```
	Defines the basic interceptor stack. It gives the action any servlet-specific dependencies it has, calls `prepare()` on it if it implements `Preparable`, sets configuration and request parameters on the action, and finds any type conversion errors.

`validationWorkflowStack`
 	
```<interceptor-stack name="validationWorkflowStack">   <interceptor-ref name="defaultStack"/>   <interceptor-ref name="validation"/>   <interceptor-ref name="workflow"/></interceptor-stack>```
	Builds on the `defaultStack` and adds `validation` and `workflow` interceptors. The interceptor-ref to `defaultStack` includes all of the interceptors from that stack. The `validation` interceptor calls the XWork validation framework, and the `workflow` interceptor adds the validation and error-checking workflow we looked at earlier.

`fileUploadStack`
 	
```<interceptor-stack name="fileUploadStack">   <interceptor-ref name="fileUpload"/>   <interceptor-ref name="defaultStack"/></interceptor-stack>```
	Prepends the `fileUpload` interceptor to the default stack to handle a multipart file upload. See chapter 4 for details of handling file uploads.

`componentStack`
 	
```<interceptor-stack name="componentStack">   <interceptor-ref name="component"/>   <interceptor-ref name="defaultStack"/></interceptor-stack>```
	Adds the `component` interceptor, which invokes the Inversion of Control container to provide the dependencies for the action.

Table 5.2   The prepackaged interceptor stacks define starter recipes for interceptor stacks. *(continued)*

Interceptor alias	Description

`modelDrivenStack`
 	
```<interceptor-stack name="modelDrivenStack">   <interceptor-ref name="model-driven"/>   <interceptor-ref name="defaultStack"/> </interceptor-stack>```
	Prepends the `model-driven` interceptor to the default stack to get the model object and put it onto the value stack, as you saw in chapter 4.

`chainStack`
 	
```<interceptor-stack name="chainStack">   <interceptor-ref name="chain"/>   <interceptor-ref name="defaultStack"/> </interceptor-stack>```
	Adds the `chain` interceptor to copy the properties from a previous action or actions to the current action when chaining actions.

`executeAndWaitStack`
 	
```<interceptor-stack name="executeAndWaitStack">   <interceptor-ref name="defaultStack"/>   <interceptor-ref name="execAndWait"/> </interceptor-stack>```
	Adds the `execAndWait` interceptor to run the rest of the action in a separate thread. It's very important that the `execAndWait` interceptor be the last interceptor in the stack, because no further interceptors will be executed after it.

`completeStack`
 	
```<interceptor-stack name="completeStack">   <interceptor-ref name="prepare"/>   <interceptor-ref name="servlet-config"/>   <interceptor-ref name="chain"/>   <interceptor-ref name="model-driven"/>   <interceptor-ref name="component"/>   <interceptor-ref name="fileUpload"/>   <interceptor-ref name="static-params"/>   <interceptor-ref name="params"/>   <interceptor-ref name="conversionError"/>   <interceptor-ref name="validation"/>   <interceptor-ref name="workflow"/> </interceptor-stack>```
	Defines an all-purpose stack of interceptors. The interceptor order has been designed to be good for general-purpose use.

These interceptor stacks aren't meant to be the only ones you use. You may not use any of them as is, but they provide a starting point for understanding interceptor ordering and interceptor stack design. By understanding what each of the interceptors does as described here, you'll learn about the interactions between the interceptors and how interceptor stacks are put together to create a certain order of events that produce the required outcome. Chapter 15 has some examples of advanced usages of interceptors and interceptor stacks.

5.4 *Building your own interceptors*

One of WebWork's most powerful features is the ability to create your own interceptor classes and apply them to the execution of your actions. This allows you to modularize repeated code without having to build up brittle class hierarchies of abstract parent actions, delegating part of the processing to the subclass after surrounding it with some pre- and post-processing. The class hierarchy approach works fine for small applications; but as the size and complexity of your web application grows, it becomes difficult to pull together the right class hierarchy to provide two or more optional services for your action class. With interceptors, these optional services can be pulled out into interceptor classes and applied wherever, and in whatever combination and order, they are required.

For example, just to provide all combinations of security checking and Hibernate Session setup, you would need four base classes (one with neither, one with security but no Hibernate Session, one with the Hibernate Session but no security, and one with both). Adding another optional service brings this number to eight, and so on.

As we continue with this section, keep in mind the most important rule of building interceptors: *Interceptors must be stateless and not use anything outside of the* ActionInvocation *provided in the API.*

Remember that, and interceptors will be simple to understand and build. Forget this rule, and you'll be seeing (and trying to debug) strange results. As an example, suppose you have a timer interceptor that does this:

```
public class BadTimingInterceptor extends AroundInterceptor {
    private long startTime;
    protected void after(
            ActionInvocation dispatcher,
            String result)
            throws Exception {
        long totalTime = System.currentTimeMillis() - startTime;
        LOG.debug("Processed Action in " +
            (totalTime / 1000) + " seconds.")
    }

    protected void before(ActionInvocation invocation)
            throws Exception {
```

```
        startTime = System.currentTimeMillis();
    }
}
```

The problem is that because more than one invocation can be running through the interceptor at a time, you may get incorrect times when another `Thread` comes in and sets the `startTime`. Compare this to the real `TimerInterceptor`:

```
public String intercept(ActionInvocation invocation)
        throws Exception {
    long startTime = System.currentTimeMillis();
    String result = invocation.invoke();
    long executionTime = System.currentTimeMillis() - startTime;
    ... log the time ...
}
```

The real `TimerInterceptor` avoids this problem by keeping the scope of the `startTime` variable inside the single method, so it's not shared between calls to the interceptor.

5.4.1 *Using the AroundInterceptor as a base*

As you saw in section 5.1, many of the prebuilt interceptor classes extend `com.opensymphony.xwork.interceptor.AroundInterceptor`. This class provides what most interceptor implementations really want: callbacks for `before()` and `after()` the action is executed. To refresh your memory, listing 5.5 shows the `intercept()` method from the `AroundInterceptor` again.

Listing 5.5 AroundInterceptor: a useful base class for interceptors

```
public String intercept(ActionInvocation invocation)
        throws Exception {
    String result = null;

    before(invocation);
    result = invocation.invoke();
    after(invocation, result);

    return result;
}

/**
 * Called after the invocation has been executed.
 *
 * @param result the result value returned by the invocation
 */
protected abstract void after(
        ActionInvocation dispatcher,
```

```
            String result)
        throws Exception;

/**
 * Called before the invocation has been executed.
 */
protected abstract void before(ActionInvocation invocation)
        throws Exception;
```

This method calls the `before()` method and then lets the rest of the `ActionInvocation` continue by calling `invocation.invoke()`. It saves the result code, and then calls `after()`, passing in the `ActionInvocation` and the result code.

This is fine for most interceptors. Many don't even need both `before()` and `after()` and only do real work in one of these methods. However, sometimes your interceptor needs to remember something across both the before and after code—for example, the `TimerInterceptor` needs to know the start time in order to calculate the total time in the code after the action has executed. Keep in mind the first rule for building interceptors: Interceptors *must* be stateless and not use anything outside of the `ActionInvocation`.

These interceptors can't extend the `AroundInterceptor` because there is no clean way to save state between these two method calls.[3] In this case, as well as in the `DefaultWorkflowInterceptor` shown earlier, it makes more sense to directly implement the interceptor interface. It's important to remember these examples as well as the simpler examples of interceptors when building your own interceptors.

5.4.2 *Looking at an example custom interceptor*

We've discussed how the bundled interceptors are implemented and talked about some considerations for implementing custom interceptors, but where would you need a custom interceptor, and what might it look like? One use for implementing a custom interceptor might be integrating another library with WebWork. Whether it's for resource management, setting up data for the action to use, or, as in the example we'll look at, security, an interceptor allows you to set up or control access to resources.

Most web applications share a need to control who uses them. The process of checking a username and some credential, such as a password or certificate, is called *authentication*. Authentication is the first step to controlling access to your

---

[3] Yes, yes, it *could* save it in the `ActionContext` `ThreadLocal` or in the `ActionInvocation`, but that's hardly "clean."

application, because it's impossible to say what the user can or can't do if you don't know who they are. The AuthenticationInterceptor used in the CaveatEmptor example application is relatively simple, as authentication goes. Listing 5.6 shows the AuthenticationInterceptor, which checks that the user has been logged on and returns a special result without executing the action otherwise.

Listing 5.6 AuthenticationInterceptor: checks the user logon

```java
public class AuthenticationInterceptor implements Interceptor {
    public static final String USER = "user";

    public void destroy() {
    }

    public void init() {
    }

    public String intercept(ActionInvocation actionInvocation)
            throws Exception {
        Map session = actionInvocation.getInvocationContext()
            .getSession();
        User user = (User) session.get(USER);
        if (user == null) {
            return Action.LOGIN;
        } else {
            Action action = actionInvocation.getAction();
            if (action instanceof UserAware) {
                ((UserAware)action).setUser(user);
            }
            return actionInvocation.invoke();
        }
    }
}
```

As you can see, the AuthenticationInterceptor doesn't actually *do* the authentication. It's responsible for checking whether the user has already been logged in, and, if not, returning the built-in default LOGIN result code. In the xwork.xml file for CaveatEmptor, the login result is mapped as a global-result and is available for all actions, as shown here:

```xml
<global-results>
    <result name="login" type=
        "redirect">/login!default.action</result>
    <result name="invalid.token">/invalidToken.jsp</result>
</global-results>
```

The AuthenticationInterceptor works together with the Login action to handle the whole authentication process. Listing 5.7 shows the Login action, which takes a username and password that are set onto an empty User object and verifies that there's a user in the database with those values.

Listing 5.7 Login action: checks whether the user exists in the database

```
public class Login extends ActionSupport
        implements SessionAware, UserDAOAware {
    Map session;
    User user;
    private UserDAO userDAO;

    public void setSession(Map session) {
        this.session = session;
    }

    public String execute() throws Exception {
        user = userDAO.findByCredentials(
            user.getUsername(),
            user.getPassword());
        if (user ==  null) {
            return INPUT;
        } else {
            session.put(AuthenticationInterceptor.USER, user);
            return SUCCESS;
        }
    }

    public String doDefault() throws Exception {
        return INPUT;
    }

    public User getUser() {
        return user;
    }

    public void setUser(User user) {
        this.user = user;
    }

    public void setUserDAO(UserDAO dao) {
        this.userDAO = dao;
    }
}
```

The other responsibility of the `AuthenticationInterceptor` is to check whether the action implements `UserAware` and, if so, to give the action the `User` object using the `setUser()` method. This is an important difference between an interceptor and a servlet filter, because the interceptor has easy access to the action instance and can provide it with needed dependencies.

5.4.3 Getting callbacks before the result is executed with the PreResultListener

When you're implementing interceptors, sometimes it's important to know when the action has finished executing but the result hasn't executed yet. For example, this is important in exception handling. During the execution of the action, exceptions are probably system exceptions due to back-end processing. During the execution of the result, exceptions are generated due to rendering the view to the user, rather than due to system problems.[4]

Listing 5.8 shows an `ExceptionInterceptor` that deals with exceptions differently before and after the result begins. Before the result starts, you can change the return code used to look up a result from the action configuration; so, you want to catch the exception and return `Action.ERROR`, because it's the common practice in WebWork apps to use `Action.ERROR` as a mapping for a page describing an error to the user. After the result has started, the return code from the interceptor isn't particularly important, but you capture the result code passed back to you from the `beforeResult()` call and return that. One thing to note in this example is that because the interceptor must be stateless, it creates a new `ExceptionHandler` object for each `ActionInvocation` to hold state specific to that `ActionInvocation`.

Listing 5.8 `ExceptionInterceptor`: handles exceptions differently before and after the result is called

```
public class ExceptionInterceptor implements Interceptor {
    public String intercept(ActionInvocation invocation)
        throws Exception {
        ExceptionHandler handler = new ExceptionHandler(invocation);
        return handler.invoke();
    }

    private class ExceptionHandler implements PreResultListener {
```

---

[4] Note that the Open Session in View pattern (where the database connection is available while rendering the page to load lazy-initialized relationships) can make this distinction blurry, because you can get exceptions due to mappings or database problems while rendering the view. Every pattern has its drawbacks.

```
private ActionInvocation invocation;
private boolean beforeResult = true;
private String result = Action.ERROR;

public ExceptionHandler(ActionInvocation invocation) {
    this.invocation = invocation;
    invocation.addPreResultListener(this);
}

String invoke() {
    try {
        result = invocation.invoke();
    } catch (Exception e) {
        if (beforeResult) {
            LOG.warn(
                "There was an error executing the Action");
            return Action.ERROR;
        } else {
            LOG.error(
              "There was an error executing the result.");
            // it doesn't really matter what we return,
            // since the result has already been mapped
            return result;
        }
    }
    return result;
}

public void beforeResult(
    ActionInvocation invocation,
    String resultCode) {
    beforeResult = false;
    result = resultCode;
}

}
}
```

5.4.4 Looking out for interceptor interactions

With interceptors, it's important to understand what each interceptor is doing, because the order *definitely* matters. We provide some prebuilt interceptor stacks that are set up with the correct order to provide certain services to your actions; but as you begin to add your own interceptors and build up custom interceptor stacks, it's vital to understand the interactions between interceptors' side effects.

The ModelDrivenInterceptor is one whose interactions give people the most trouble. For instance, you don't want to put the parameter interceptor before the `model` interceptor, because the model properties won't be available to be directly set on the value stack yet. But what if you want the parameters to influence which model type you return from `getModel()`? One way to do this is to use the parameter interceptor twice:

1. ParameterInterceptor
2. ModelDrivenInterceptor
3. ParameterInterceptor
4. …

Another way to do this is to make your action implement `Preparable` and apply the `prepare` interceptor. In your `prepare()` method, your action can look in the parameter map from the `ActionContext` (that is, `ActionContext.getContext().getParameters()`) and use this to determine what type of model to return. You can also combine these two, as you'll see in chapter 15, section 15.8, when we look at implementing data admin operations.

Another interceptor that needs special attention is the `DefaultWorkflowInterceptor`. It's important to remember that if there are any error messages, none of the rest of the interceptors or the action will be executed. Also remember that any validations that should affect whether the action should execute should happen before this interceptor is executed, so that it can check for error messages.

Overall, it's important to understand what the interceptors you are applying are going to do. Interceptor stacks should be carefully designed to provide specific sets of functionality and reused throughout your application to reduce the number of unexpected interactions.

5.5 *Interceptors vs. servlet filters*

We often hear the question, "How are interceptors different from servlet filters?" One of the key differences is that interceptors aren't tied to a servlet container. This may seem like a small thing when you're building a web application, but when you're *unit testing* your web application, it makes things much easier. One of the key tenets of WebWork is to make things simple and loosely coupled. Having interceptors outside the servlet container makes integration testing much simpler. You can test the combination of your action, configuration, and interceptors by directly calling the framework from your unit test.

Another advantage is that your interceptor has access to your `ActionContext`, your action, the value stack, and so on. When we looked at the `Authentication-Interceptor`, you saw how this can be useful for giving the action some context—

in this case, the identity of the user who made this web request. Your interceptors can access your business objects and set up resources for your actions in a way that would be much more difficult with servlet filters. When you're managing resources with a servlet filter, you would have to set up the resources in the servlet request, and your action would need to retrieve them from there, requiring lookup code in your action. Interceptors are also aligned with the lifecycle of your action, whereas filters are aligned with the lifecycle of the servlet request. For example, the servlet filter won't be called again between actions in an action chain, whereas the interceptors for the second action will be.

You don't have to make a choice between interceptors and filters, though. Sometimes filters are a better alternative, and nothing in WebWork stops you from using them. Using a GZIP filter to compress the output of your web pages can reduce the amount of bandwidth your servers use. SiteMesh, which is a servlet filter–based page-decoration framework from OpenSymphony, lets you give a common look to all the pages in your site and easily change it in just one place. For each requirement, you should weigh the pros and cons of using an interceptor versus a servlet filter.

5.6 *Summary*

Interceptors let you encapsulate common functionality in classes and reuse that functionality by applying the interceptors to your actions in the xwork.xml configuration. Interceptors are called as part of the execution of the action and are nested wrappers around the execution of your action and its result. Many of the core features of WebWork are implemented as interceptors, including setting parameters on the action and applying workflow before and after the action. You can specify which interceptors are applied and in what order on a per-action level in the xwork.xml file; or, you can save and reuse these lists of interceptors across many actions. In addition to the prebuilt interceptors that come with WebWork, you can build custom interceptors and apply them to your actions. These custom interceptors can provide any needed functionality and are often useful for integrating other libraries with WebWork. It's important to understand what interceptors are available and what they do. Designing interceptor stacks to be reused throughout your application is as important as designing the classes in your application.

Inversion of Control

In chapter 5, "Adding functionality with interceptors," you learned that interceptors are very useful when you wish to separate cross-cutting logic from your actions. Typically, things like logging, security, and transactions consist of code segments interspersed in your other code. With interceptors, you can separate those concerns from your core action logic. Once you've begun to use interceptors, a common pattern that begins to take place is a crude form of Inversion of Control (IoC). In fact, you've probably seen forms of IoC if you've ever written EJB code. We also explored a little of IoC when we demonstrated the `ServletConfigInterceptor`.

In this chapter, we'll take a closer look at the pattern that evolved in the `ServletConfigInterceptor`. Then, we'll demonstrate how this pattern can be applied a general terms rather than as an interceptor for specific needs (such as supplying HTTP-related objects to the action).

6.1 *Examining the pattern*

In order to help you understand the IoC pattern, we must first look at how alternative resource management patterns work and what IoC brings to the table. IoC doesn't solve every resource management problem; so even if you choose to build your applications using IoC, like any other technology decision, knowing the alternatives is important.

Finally, we'll explore one of the biggest reasons why IoC is ideal: testing. WebWork was designed from the ground up to make testing your code as simple as possible. This can be seen in design decisions such as keeping your actions separated from the servlet APIs. IoC is also an effective way to make unit-testing your code accessible.

6.1.1 *Common patterns for active resource management*

Before we explore IoC in detail, let's look at the evolution of various resource management patterns. The most primitive form of managing resources is not managing them at all! Imagine that you want to write a class called `BalanceChecker`, which needs to provide a method that determines whether enough money is in a bank account. The class might look like the following:

```
public class BalanceChecker {
    private BankAccountManager mgr;

    public BalanceChecker() {
        mgr = new BankAccountManager();
    }
```

```
    public boolean hasEnoughMoney(int bankAccountId, double money) {
        BankAccount account = mgr.getBankAccount(bankAccountId);

        return account.getBalance() >= money);
    }
}
```

The method takes two arguments, bankAccountId and money. It uses bankAccountId to ask a BankAccountManager for a BankAccount object so it can then compare the balance of the account to the money parameter. Although this approach is hypothetically correct, there is something interesting to note: Each new BalanceChecker creates a new BankAccountManager.

Many projects include classes that don't need to be created all the time—they provide stateful logic and can be reused by multiple objects and threads, occasionally at the same time. This might sound an awful lot like a static method, and in fact you could have changed the hasEnoughMoney() method to just call a hypothetical static method, instead:

```
public boolean hasEnoughMoney(int bankAccountId, double money) {
    BankAccount account = BankAccountManager.getBankAccount(bankAccountId);

    return account.getBalance() >= money;
}
```

However, static methods often aren't friendly to work with in terms of both testability and providing options to the programmer. For example, if you choose to use static methods, you can no longer pass around a BankAccountManager object to other objects, thereby forcing those other objects to be *tightly coupled* to BankAccountManager. For some systems, this might be acceptable—but for most applications, tight coupling is something to be avoided.

Singleton pattern

The *Singleton pattern* is used to find a balance between the desire to have only a single instance of an object (conceptually, a collection of static methods and fields) and being able to use that code as a regular object. The Singleton pattern allows only one instance of an object to exist through the use of a private constructor and a single static method used to retrieve the single instance of the class. The follow Widget class is a Singleton:

```
public class Widget {
    private static Widget instance = new Widget();

    public static Widget getInstance() {
        return instance;
```

```
        }

        private Widget() {
        }

        public int doSomething(int x, int y) {
            return x + y;
        }
    }
```

Widget's constructor is private, meaning only the static method getInstance() can create a Widget object. Because the instance field is static, there can by definition be only one instance. The first call to getInstance() creates a new Widget, and all subsequent calls return that instance.

Rewriting the previous BalanceChecker example to use a Singleton pattern produces the following:

```
public class BalanceChecker {
    private BankAccountManager mgr;

    public BalanceChecker() {
        mgr = BankAccountManager.getInstance();
    }

    public boolean hasEnoughMoney(int bankAccountId, double money) {
        BankAccount account = mgr.getBankAccount(bankAccountId);

        return account.getBalance() >= money);
    }
}
```

By using a Singleton, you've eliminated unnecessary object creation. However, this pattern still ties you to using the BankAccountManager implementation, leaving you still tightly coupled. It's common to need to be able to easily swap out different types of BankAccountManagers without having to rewrite much code. The most frequent need for this type of behavior is when writing tests for your code.

Because BankAccountManager might connect to a database, it might be much easier to replace the normal manager class with a much simpler *mock* manager. However, the current state of BalanceChecker would require that its code be changed to replace BankAccountManager with, say, BankAccountManagerMock.

NOTE   *Mocking* a class is the technique of replacing a complex class with a simple one that is designed to assist with writing test code. Often, mocks are used to allow a tester to easily introduce otherwise hard-to-reproduce situations. They're also commonly used because they make running tests much faster: Heavy resources (such as a database) are no longer necessary; the behavior they provide can be mocked.

In order to *decouple* BalanceChecker from BankAccountManager, we need to look to another pattern that is designed to provide various configurations of similar resources.

Factory pattern

Because the Singleton pattern doesn't assist with decoupling your code, you need to provide code that is designed to do this. You want a class that can be *configured* to produce either a BankAccountManager or BankAccountManagerMock for when you're writing tests. The *Factory pattern* is exactly this.

Suppose that BankAccountManager is now an interface, and the two implementing classes are BankAccountManagerImpl and BankAccountManageMock. Also assume that there is a factory called BankAccountManagerFactory. The code might now look like this:

```
public class BalanceChecker {
    private BankAccountManager mgr;

    public BalanceChecker() {
        mgr = BankAccountManagerFactory.getManager();
    }

    public boolean hasEnoughMoney(int bankAccountId, double money) {
        BankAccount account = mgr.getBankAccount(bankAccountId);

        return account.getBalance() >= money);
    }
}
```

As you can see, you utilize a static method getManager() to return an implementation of BankAccountManager. This code isn't aware of whether this is a concrete implementation or just a simple mock. You've successfully decoupled BalanceChecker from BankAccountManagerImpl. You can now add more methods to BankAccountManagerFactory to let you configure the type of object to be returned when getManager() is called:

```
BankAccountManagerFactory.setMock(true);
```

Doing this might tell the factory that instead of producing normal objects, it should produce mock objects. Making a call to this method just before running a test would give you much more control over the test.

Factories aren't just useful for tests, though. Suppose you have two kinds of banks in your application: international and domestic banks. It might be desirable to tell the factory which type of account manager you want to be produced.

Registry pattern and WebWork's ActionContext

Factories are nice for decoupling code, but once you have many factories, it becomes unwieldy to handle all the various classes. Rather than try to understand all the options for assorted factories, you can create a single class called a *registry* to act as a central repository for all the components you wish to choose from.

In its simplest form, a registry is nothing more than a mapping of keys to objects. Once a registry is set up, rather than passing around resources through method calls or depending on classes to understand all the factory semantics, you can pass a single object—the registry—that provides access to every resource through a simple method like get(String key).

A registry is also good for abstracting how code accesses a resource, thereby allowing all the logic of *how* a resource is obtained to be placed in a single place to better modularize your code. WebWork's ActionContext is a perfect example of the Registry pattern. Rather than passing the ServletRequest, HttpSession, or parameters map all the way through the interceptors, action class, and result, it's better to dump everything in the ActionContext so that there is only one object to worry about.

In the next section, you'll see how ActionContext (and its wrapper, Servlet-ActionContext) can be replaced by inverting the logic for resource management.

6.1.2 Inverting resource management

Now that we've discussed the patterns that exist to help you manage resources, let's look at how you can get a handle to an HttpServletRequest object in your Web-Work action. You can do this two ways in WebWork: *actively* and *passively*. We'll look at both techniques to demonstrate the concept of inversion that is central to IoC.

Actively requesting ActionContext

To actively request the HttpServletRequest object, all you need to do is look in the ActionContext. For every WebWork action, the ActionContext is given a bunch of information pertinent to the current request, including the request object itself. This means the following code, when executed inside the scope of an action, is correct:

```
public class SomeAction implements Action {
    public String execute() throws Exception {
        HttpServletRequest request =
            ServletActionContext.getHttpServletRequest();
        request.setAttribute("foo", "bar");
        return SUCCESS;
    }
}
```

Note that you use the `ServletActionContext` instead of `ActionContext` because it provides a simple wrapper that retrieves the request object from the `ActionContext` using the correct key. `HttpServletRequest` is an interface, so you can mock the request object by setting the request with a different instance:

```
ServletActionContext.setHttpServletRequest(
    ➥new HttpServletRequestMock());
```

Through these examples, you can see that the `ActionContext` provides many of the same benefits that the factory and registry patterns do. Now let's look at the passive technique for gathering this information.

Passively telling WebWork

Rather than write code that says, "I am going to get object X," an alternative is to write code that says, "Hey, give me X when I need it." The difference between active and passive is that one gets the object itself, whereas the other states that something should *inject* the resource when the time comes.

> **NOTE**   Martin Fowler recently wrote an article indicating that the term *Inversion of Control* might be overloaded and that *Dependency Injection pattern* would be a better-suited name (see http://www.martinfowler.com/articles/injection.html). We use IoC in this book because the alternative name hasn't yet caught on. However, the concept of *injecting* objects is important and must be recognized regardless of which name you choose.

Let's look at the previous action rewritten in the form of IoC. No longer will the code actively retrieve the request object from the `ActionContext`; rather, it will state that it *needs* the request object. It's up to a process external to this action class to make sure the needs of all action classes are handled:

```
public class SomeAction implements Action, ServletRequestAware {
    private ServletRequest request;

    public void setServletRequest(ServletRequest request) {
```

```
        this.request = request;
    }

    public String execute() throws Exception {
        request.setAttribute("foo", "bar");
        return SUCCESS;
    }
}
```

By implementing the interface `ServletRequestAware` and providing the `setServletRequest()` method, you indicate to WebWork that this action should be given a `ServletRequest` object before `execute()` is called.

Inversion in J2EE APIs

It turns out that this concept is seen in various J2EE APIs you may already be familiar with. In fact, WebWork's IoC implementation (as well as alternatives) is often called a *container*, just like J2EE servers are called servlet and/or EJB containers. But rather than being specifically about servlets or EJBs, these containers are designed to let the developer shape and mold what services they provide.

In the EJB world, the container is required to call a method such as `setEntityContext(EntityContext ec)` or `setSessionContext(SessionContext sc)` on your entity or session beans. EJB containers also make method calls to `ejbActivate()`, `ejbPassivate()`, `ejbLoad()`, and `ejbStore()`. As you'll learn in a moment, one of the major features that a container must provide is *lifecycle*—when to start and stop code. In EJB, these methods are used to provide code that responds to certain lifecycle events.

In the servlet world, there are many interfaces you can implement when building a listener, such as `ServletContextListener`, `HttpSessionListener`, and `HttpSessionAttributeListener`. These interfaces are used as flags to tell the servlet container what information your class requires. It's up to the container to then find that data and call the methods the interface defines. Examples of such methods are `contextInitialized(ServletContext sc)`, `contextDestroyed(ServletContext sc)`, and `sessionCreated(HttpSessionEvent e)`.

Other J2EE specifications, such as JMS, also provide similar techniques in their API. The point isn't that J2EE is using a unique and special concept, but rather to show that this style of depending on external container management is common and should not be foreign to you. Next we'll look at how IoC, especially generalized IoC like that found in WebWork, can assist with testing.

6.1.3 *How IoC helps with testing*

When we introduced the Factory pattern, we showed how you can configure the factory to produce mock instances of whatever resource it was responsible for. We also hinted at how testing might be done when we actively grabbed the request object from the `ActionContext`. Let's look at how you can test the previous action in both forms.

Testing without inversion

Regardless of whether you use IoC, testing a WebWork action was designed to be easy. Because actions are simple objects with an `execute()` method and JavaBean-style getters and setters, testing is as straightforward as instantiating a new object, setting any data via the setters, and then calling `execute()`.

   In the following example, a mock object is created and then inserted into the `ActionContext`. When `execute()` is called, you know that the request object returned by `ActionContext` will be the mock object you just set up. This is the most typical way to test a WebWork action that isn't using IoC:

```
SomeAction action = new SomeAction();
ServletRequestMock mockReq = new ServletRequestMock();
ServletActionContext.setServletRequest(mockReq);
action.execute();
String foo = mockReq.getAttribute("foo");
if ("bar".equals(foo)) {
    // test passed
} else {
    // test failed
}
```

Testing with inversion

Testing with inversion is almost exactly the same; but rather than indirectly hand the resource to the action via the `ActionContext`, you can directly set the resource on the action object itself. This subtle yet powerful difference makes up the foundation of IoC:

```
SomeAction action = new SomeAction();
ServletRequestMock mockReq = new ServletRequestMock();
Action.setServletRequest(mockReq);
action.execute();
String fooattrValue = mockReq.getAttribute("foo");
if ("bar".equals(foo)) {
    // test passed
} else {
    // test failed
}
```

It's important to note that even though we're demonstrating the difference that inversion brings to the table through the use of tests, IoC's usefulness isn't limited to people who write a lot of unit tests (although writing tests is almost never a bad thing). Rather, you use tests to show the fundamental difference in how the resources are *wired* to the object. The difference in wiring (how the resource finally reaches its destination) is the most obvious visual difference between IoC and non-IoC code.

6.2 IoC essentials

Although not an entirely new pattern, Inversion of Control didn't become an officially recognized pattern under that name or under the name *Dependency Injection* until recently. However, the problems it addresses are common, and you should have no trouble relating to them. Before we dive into the two main parts of IoC—*dependencies* and *scope and lifecycle*—let's briefly explore the history that led to a marriage between WebWork and IoC.

6.2.1 WebWork's IoC history

Before the 2.0 branch of WebWork (this book is based on the current version, 2.1.7), the WebWork 1.x line existed and didn't have any support for interceptors or IoC. However, it did support something similar to interceptors, which was the basis for the interceptor support in WebWork today.

The sample PetStore application in the book *Java Open Source Programming* (Walnes, Cannon-Brookes, Abrahamian, Lightbody; Wiley, 2003) was built on WebWork 1.3. Because the book is primarily about Test-Driven Development (also known as Test-First Development), the code evolved over time. Eventually, a plug-in for WebWork 1.3 evolved that did a simple job of identifying whether an action needed a particular class and, if so, supplied it via a setter.

Hard-coded resources

The initial version of this plug-in was trivially simple—the resources it supported were hard-coded. After spending a bit of time generalizing the concept and borrowing many ideas from the Apache Avalon framework, an IoC implementation similar to WebWork's was born. We're telling you this history so you can better understand the thought process behind building an IoC framework and thus better grasp IoC as well.

The important thing to note is that IoC can be achieved without using an IoC framework (including WebWork's) in WebWork by creating an interceptor that decides when to apply resources to the action. This is what the early versions of the IoC support were doing when bundled with the PetStore application. Today, you could write an interceptor that manages their specific resources Foo, Bar, and Baz, as follows:

```
public FooBarBazInterceptor extends AroundInterceptor {
    public void before(Action action) {
        if (action instanceof FooAware) {
            ((FooAware) action).setFoo(new Foo());
        }

        if (action instanceof BarAware) {
            ((BarAware) action).setBar(new Bar());
        }

        if (action instanceof BazAware) {
            ((BazAware) action).setBaz(new Baz());
        }
    }
}
```

From this point on, any action that implemented one of those three `*Aware` interfaces automatically had a resource applied to it. This approach works well; but eventually it becomes tedious because for every new resource, more code must be written. The first stab at WebWork's IoC implementation did nothing more than generalize this behavior.

Aware interfaces

Even before IoC was a twinkle in WebWork's eye, the idea of interfaces that declare what the action needs was well accepted. For compatibility as well as ease, WebWork still has all the interfaces that it supported long before IoC. These interfaces are called *aware interfaces* because the interface names always end with *Aware* and the interfaces require that a single setter method be implemented so the resource may be applied.

Common aware interfaces that WebWork supports are as follows:

- `ParametersAware`—Indicates that the action requires the HTTP request parameter `Map`

- `ServletRequestAware`—Indicates that the action requires the `ServletRequest` object, as previously seen

- `SessionAware`—Indicates that the action requires the `HttpSession` object

- `ApplicationAware`—Indicates that the action requires the `ServletContext` object

Following in the pattern of aware interfaces, WebWork's IoC support requires an aware interface to be implemented, as you'll see in a moment. But before we examine WebWork's specific implementation (many other implementations are available to use), let's look at the concept of dependencies.

6.2.2 *Dependencies*

Let's tweak the previous example to give more concrete names to each resource. Foo will become PersistenceManager, Bar will be TransactionManager, and Baz will be AuthenticationManager. With names like these, it isn't hard to imagine that TransactionManager and AuthenticationManager require PersistenceManager in order to work properly. However, looking at the simple FooBarBazInterceptor, neither would be given a handle to the PersistenceManager you just created.

Rewriting the interceptor to support this more complex dependency results in a much more complicated piece of code, as shown in listing 6.1.

Listing 6.1   Complex dependency example

```
public void before(Action action) {
    PersistenceManager pm = null;
    if (action instanceof PersistenceManagerAware) {
        pm = new PersistenceManager();
        ((PersistenceManagerAware) action)
            .setPersistenceManager(pm);
    }

    if (action instanceof TransactionManagerAware) {
        TransactionManager tm = new TransactionManager();
        if (pm == null) {
            pm = new PersistenceManager();
        }
        tm.setPersistenceManager(pm);
        ((TransactionManagerAware) action)
            .setTransactionManager(tm);
    }

    if (action instanceof AuthenticationManagerAware) {
        AuthenticationManager am = new AuthenticationManager();
        if (pm == null) {
            pm = new PersistenceManager();
        }
        am.setPersistenceManager(pm);
        ((AuthenticationManagerAware) action)
            .setAuthenticationManager(am);
    }
}
```

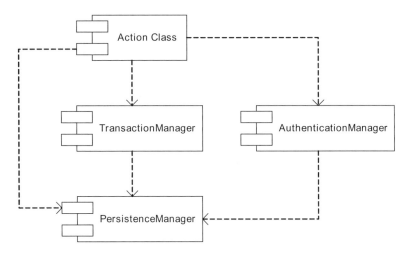

Figure 6.1 A simple dependency graph between resources and an action class

Whoa! Often, you write code that depends on other classes without fully realizing the dependencies that you're introducing. Sometimes, if the dependencies get too complicated, you end up with the scientifically named *spaghetti code*. A visual representation of these dependencies, shown in figure 6.1, helps explain.

When looking at this dependency graph, you can see that `PersistenceManager` must be created before anything else. Another way to say it is that the *life* of the `PersistenceManager` must start *before* the life of the other resources. This means the *lifecycle* of an object is intimately tied in to its dependencies As such, we can't talk about dependencies without also talking about lifecycle.

6.2.3 Scope and lifecycle

As you just learned, lifecycle is tied closely to the dependencies between objects. It turns out that not only is lifecycle important, but *scope* also affects when that lifecycle goes through its various stages. Let's first look at what lifecycle is; then we'll examine how scope affects lifecycle.

Lifecycle

In life, all things go through many stages, but at least two events are guaranteed: birth and death. As such, when we talk about lifecycle, we're talking about a minimum of these two states. Objects don't exactly give birth (or die, although sometimes we all wish we could kill our code—or someone else's!), so let's call these states *initializing* and *disposing*.

There are many other lifecycle states that you might be interested in; a few that come to mind are *reset, pause, stop,* and *start.* Every time one of these events takes place, you'd like to notify the object so that it might do the appropriate work needed. This can be done with methods such as init() and dispose(), which all objects that wish to participate in lifecycle must provide.

Scope

Often you want to exert some level of control over when these lifecycle events (especially initialize and dispose) take place. The initialize and dispose lifecycle events control the entire span of the object's life. This span is often called the object's *scope.* Just like in programming languages, where variables can have scopes such as global, object, method, or just a code block, resources can also have varying scopes.

The scope of a resource depends on what the resource has to do. If the resource is a cache, it would be sensible for the cache to have a global scope, meaning that it will live the entire lifetime of the application. If the resource is a transaction, it makes more sense for the scope to be much more constrained, because having a transaction open for an extended period is costly and often not the desired behavior.

Figure 6.2 shows a timeline for two different users accessing a web application. On the first request, 1A, the session and application scopes are started and

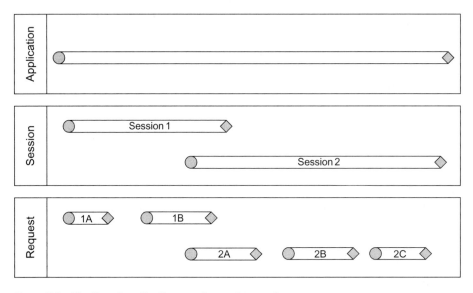

Figure 6.2 Timeline of application, session, and request scopes

initialized. On the second request, 2A, a new session is created. Note that no new application scope is started because application scope is global, meaning there is only one instance.

On the third request, 1B, the user logs out, and the associated session is destroyed (disposed). The fourth request, 2B, does nothing in the session or application scope. The fifth request, 2C, logs out the second user, causing the associated session to end as well. Finally, the application is shut down, and the application scope is disposed.

6.3 *Using WebWork's IoC framework*

Now that we've introduced the general concepts common in all IoC frameworks, let's look at the WebWork IoC implementation. Because WebWork's IoC framework is optional, it isn't ready to be used initially. We'll first discuss the configuration changes you need to make in order to use WebWork's IoC. We'll then examine the step-by-step instructions for creating a new component that can be plugged into the IoC container. Finally, we'll look at advanced topics such as complex dependencies and using WebWork's IoC on objects other than actions.

6.3.1 *Configuration*

Before you can begin to use WebWork's IoC, it must be properly configured. Two major parts are equally important when you're configuring this optional Web-Work feature: configuring the servlet container through web.xml, and configuring WebWork through xwork.xml. We'll first look at the web.xml changes and explain why they're necessary.

Modifying web.xml

WebWork's IoC container understands three scopes: *request, session,* and *application.* Their hierarchy is as follows: All requests have one session, and all sessions have one application. The opposite isn't true. In order for WebWork to be aware of these three scopes, you must configure the servlet container to notify WebWork when they operate.

You'll start with application scope. Adding the following entry to web.xml lets objects get application-scoped resources:

```
<listener>
    <listener-class>
        com.opensymphony.webwork.lifecycle.
        ➥ApplicationLifecycleListener
```

```
    </listener-class>
</listener>
```

Listeners are part of the servlet specification and allow custom code to act on various servlet-related events, such as the application starting or stopping. In this case, the ApplicationLifecycleListener is configured to respond to application-scope-related events.

NOTE Be sure you place this XML snippet in the correct location to ensure that web.xml is well formed and validates against the Servlet 2.3 specification DTD. Listeners are defined to be *after* <filter-mapping> elements and *before* <servlet> elements.

Next, you configure the session scope. Like application scope, this is done with a listener:

```
<listener>
    <listener-class>
        com.opensymphony.webwork.lifecycle.
        ➥SessionLifecycleListener
    </listener-class>
</listener>
```

This listener, appropriately named SessionLifecycleListener, is configured to respond to events related to session scope, such as a new session starting or a session ending (for example, a user logging out of your application).

Last is request scope. Rather than provide another listener, you can best monitor for the start and end of a request by using a filter. You first define the filter with the following addition to web.xml:

```
<filter>
    <filter-name>container</filter-name>
    <filter-class>
        com.opensymphony.webwork.lifecycle.RequestLifecycleFilter
    </filter-class>
</filter>
```

After the filter is defined, you need to map it to a URL pattern. To ensure that WebWork's IoC container is accessible under all circumstances, you should choose a mapping to allow all requests access. In this example, you'll choose /*, although you're free to limit your mapping to a more narrow URL pattern if you have a specific need to do so:

```
<filter-mapping>
    <filter-name>container</filter-name>
    <url-pattern>/*</url-pattern>
</filter-mapping>
```

Now that web.xml is configured, WebWork's IoC container is officially ready to begin to work. However, in order for your actions to get access to the container, you must modify the interceptor stack so that an interceptor can apply resources according to the `Aware` interfaces that your actions implement.

ComponentManager

Before we show you how the WebWork IoC container uses the items you configured in web.xml, let's first take a quick look at the main interface to WebWork's IoC: the `ComponentManager`. This interface—and the associated implementation, `Default-ComponentManager`—is responsible for deciding whether an object needs a resource handed to it, as well as managing all resource lifecycles and dependencies.

In WebWork, each scope (request, session, or application) gets a `Component-Manager` (CM) associated with it. Each CM has a parent CM that it consults when making decisions about how to manage and apply resources. The request-scoped CM has a session-scoped CM, which in turn has an application-scoped CM.

This means that applying an object to the request-scoped CM makes sure that it also gets resources that are session- or application-scoped. Each scope has the CM saved in the *attribute map*, which is accessible via `setAttribute()` and `get-Attribute()` methods on the `ServletRequest` object, the `HttpSession` object, or the `ServletContext` object.

Modifying xwork.xml

In addition to being placed in `ServletRequest`'s attribute map, the request-scoped CM is also placed in the `ActionContext`, which is a `ThreadLocal` that only exists for the lifetime of a request. As such, an interceptor that applies an action to the request-scoped CM is shown in the following code:

```
ComponentManager container =
    (ComponentManager) ActionContext.getContext()
        .get(ComponentManager.KEY);

if (container != null) {
    container.initializeObject(dispatcher.getAction());
}
```

In fact, this interceptor is included with WebWork. All you need to do to start using IoC-aware actions is to configure xwork.xml to include this interceptor in your interceptor stack. The interceptor is already configured in webwork-default.xml with the name `component`. If you plan to use IoC for all your applications, add the following to your base package:

```
<interceptors>
    <interceptor-stack name="defaultComponentStack">
        <interceptor-ref name="component"/>
        <interceptor-ref name="defaultStack"/>
    </interceptor-stack>
</interceptors>

<default-interceptor-ref name="defaultComponentStack"/>
```

If you don't intend to use IoC for all actions, you can just as easily apply the component interceptor as you see fit. Now that everything is configured, it's time to see how to create a new component.

> **PITFALL**   A *very* common mistake when using WebWork's IoC container is to not include the component interceptor in your action's interceptor stack. If, while debugging a program, you encounter a NullPointerException when a method call is made on a dependent resource, it's almost guaranteed to be because the interceptor didn't run.

6.3.2 *Creating a new component*

Creating a new component involves four steps: creating the component, creating the component interface, creating the *enabler interface* (also known as the aware interface), and telling WebWork about these new classes by editing components.xml.

Imagine that you need to create a miniature online banking system. In order to do so, you require a single Bank resource and a BankManager that is used to make transactions with the bank. Because there is only a single Bank, application scope is the best choice for the Bank instance. The BankManager, on the other hand, is transactional, and therefore should be request-scoped so that each request can do a unique transaction (and potentially roll back the transaction). Let's start by creating the component classes as well as their interfaces.

Creating the component and component interface

For each component (Bank and BankManager), you'll create a concrete class as well as an interface that the class will implement. You're using interfaces for these components purely to promote testability of your objects. You don't have to separate the interface from your component, but doing so makes your code many times more testable and loosens the coupling of your objects.

Let's start with the Bank interface. In this example, Banks are trivially simple: They only contain whole dollars, and you may only get the balance in an account, add money to an account, or subtract money from an account:

```
public interface Bank {
    int balance(String account);

    void add(String account, int dollars);

    void subtract(String account, int dollars);
}
```

The next step is to write an implementation for this interface. A real implementation would, of course, store to a database and offer much better security; but for the sake of a simple example, you'll allow the bank to store all its account balances in memory:

```
public class BankImpl implements Bank {
    HashMap balances = new HashMap();

    int balance(String account) {
        Integer b = (Integer) balances.get(account);
        return (b == null) ? 0 : b.intValue();
    }

    void add(String account, int dollars) {
        Integer b = (Integer) balances.get(account);
        if (b == null) {
            balances.put(account, new Integer(dollars));
        } else {
            balances.put(account,
                new Integer(b.intValue() + dollars));
        }
    }

    void subtract(String account, dollars) {
        add(account, -dollars);
    }
}
```

Because the Bank resource is application-scoped, as long as the application is running, the account balances are shared across all classes that use the Bank resource. Let's now create the BankManager interface and class implementation. You'll support two operations in the BankManager: transferring money and rolling back transactions:

```
public interface BankManager {
    void transfer(String account1, String account2, int dollars);

    void rollback();
}
```

When writing the implementation, let's assume that any operation on a BankManager is committed at the end of its lifecycle unless the rollback() method has been called. Because you want to do an operation at the end of this resource's life, you can take advantage of the lifecycle support that WebWork offers:

```
public class BankManagerImpl implements BankManager, Disposable {
    ArrayList transfers = new ArrayList();
    Bank bank;
    boolean rolledBack = false;

    public void transfer(String account1,
                         String account2,
                         int dollars) {
        Transfer t = new Transfer();
        t.account1 = account1;
        t.account2 = account2;
        t.dollars = dollars;
        transfers.add(t);
    }

    public void rollback() {
        rolledBack = true;
    }

    public void dispose() {
        if (!rolledBack) {
            for (Iterator it = transfers.iterator();
                 it.hasNext;()) {
                Transfer t = (Transfer) it.next();
                bank.add(t.account1, t.dollars);
                bank.subtract(t.account2, t.dollars);
            }
        }
    }
}

class Transfer {
    String account1;
    String account2;
    int dollars;
}
}
```

Although not exactly up to snuff for the needs of a real bank, the example provides a good demonstration of how a resource might depend on another resource as well as how tying in to lifecycle events can be very important to the object's behavior. The only thing missing from BankManager is the fact that it has no way to get Bank objects. For that to happen, you need to create enabler interfaces that let the BankManager advertise to WebWork that it requires a Bank object in order to successfully complete.

Creating the enabler interface and tying the resources together

To give `BankManager` access to the `Bank`, you'll create an enabler interface called `BankAware`. Likewise, you'll also create an enabler interface called `BankManager-Aware` so that WebWork actions can get a handle to the `BankManager` associated with the current request. The `BankAware` interface is a single setter method:

```
public interface BankAware {
    void setBank(Bank bank);
}
```

The `BankManagerAware` interface is also a single setter method:

```
public interface BankManagerAware {
    void setBankManager(BankManager mgr);
}
```

With these two enabler interfaces, you can modify `BankManagerImpl` to implement `BankAware`, so the container can identify that `BankManagerImpl` requires `Bank` in order to work properly. The code now looks like this:

```
public class BankManagerImpl implements BankManager,
                                        Disposable,
                                        BankAware {
    ArrayList transfers = new ArrayList();
    Bank bank;
    boolean rolledBack = false;

    void setBank(Bank bank) {
        this.bank = bank;
    }

    ...
}
```

The enabler interface not only lets WebWork know that `BankManager` has a dependency on `Bank`, but it also provides a method to allow WebWork to wire the dependent resource correctly. Note that enablers should always have exactly one method that is in the form of `setXxx()`, where the one and only parameter is either the resource itself (`BankImpl`, in this case) or something equivalent, such as an interface for the resource (`Bank`).

Editing components.xml

The next step is to tell WebWork about all these new classes by modifying (creating, in this case) the components.xml file. The three things WebWork needs to know about are the scope, the enabler interface, and the resource class. Because

these are the first components you created, you need to create a new compo-
nents.xml file. The file should read as follows:

```
<components>
    <component>
        <scope>application</scope>
        <class>ch6.example1.BankImpl</class>
        <enabler>ch6.example1.BankAware</enabler>
    </component>
    <component>
        <scope>request</scope>
        <class>ch6.example1.BankManagerImpl</class>
        <enabler>ch6.example1.BankManagerAware</enabler>
    </component>
</components>
```

Notice that you never refer to any of the interfaces that your resources implement
(`Bank` and `BankManager`). Again, that's because although it's nice to separate interface from implementation, it isn't necessary and isn't specific to the configuration. The last step is to save this file in the same location where xwork.xml is
located, WEB-INF/classes.

   With components.xml created, all configuration is completed. At this point,
you're free to implement the enablers in your actions; WebWork will automatically take care of all the lifecycle, dependency, and scope complexities for you. As
you've already seen, WebWork will also handle the resource dependency requirements of other resources, just like the `BankManager` depends on the `Bank`. In fact,
WebWork's IoC container isn't just for actions and resources, but can be used on
any object.

6.3.3 *Using IoC on any object*

Although out-of-the-box WebWork only supports applying resources to actions
and resources themselves, you can use the `ComponentManager` to apply resources to
any object you need. Recall the implementation of the component interceptor
from the previous section. All that is needed is to look up the CM from the
`ActionContext` and then pass the object you wish to be managed by the container
through to the CM's `initializeObject()` method.

   The key required to pass `ActionContext`'s `get()` method is in the `ComponentMan-`
ager interface. However, sometimes using `ActionContext` isn't ideal. For example,
you may want to get a handle to the CM, but the request isn't going through an
action. That means an `ActionContext` doesn't exist, and therefore you can't get the
CM the way you've previously seen. However, the request-scoped CM is applied to the
`ServletRequest` object for all requests you've mapped the filter to (in the case of this

chapter, you mapped it to all requests). Getting the CM from the `ServletRequest` is as simple as calling `getAttribute()` with the same key, `ComponentManager.KEY`.

Because WebWork's IoC implementation can be used anywhere, even outside of WebWork, it offers a great deal of power. Next, we'll look at how it handles complex dependencies and what it can and can't do.

6.3.4 *Dealing with complex dependencies*

Odds are, if you use IoC even moderately, you'll begin building up a lot of components. Many of those components will probably depend on each other in various ways. Eventually, you'll find yourself with a pretty complex and deep dependency graph. Knowing how WebWork handles complex dependencies will help you better design your components to support the capabilities of WebWork.

A complex example

Look at the dependency graph shown in figure 6.3. Suppose a request comes to an action that implements the `FAware` interface. In order to identify how the resources will be initialized on the first request as well as subsequent requests, you must understand a bit about the implementation of the WebWork IoC container. WebWork uses a *depth-first search* (DFS) algorithm when identifying the order in which lifecycles should be managed. WebWork also uses *lazy initialization*, meaning that even if a scope opens, no resources are initialized until they're needed. Once a resource has been initialized, that same object instance is used again and again until it's disposed and its scope is closed.

Knowing that WebWork uses the DFS algorithm to handle dependencies and also uses lazy initialization, let's pretend that the application has just started and

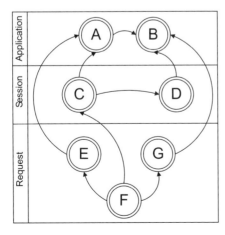

Figure 6.3
A complex dependency graph spanning all three scopes

no requests have been issued yet. A request then comes in that causes WebWork to retrieve the F component. Assuming that ties are broken in alphabetical order, the order of initialization for the first request is as follows: B, A, C, D, E, G, F. If you're having trouble seeing this order, try working your way up from F until you no longer have any outgoing arrows; then cross off each resource as you work your way backward.

It's important to note here that even though the B resource is a dependency for many other resources, it's only initialized once. All other resources, such as C and G, are given the same B resource that A got.

Now, let's assume a second request has come through from the same user (same session). The order of initialization is E, G, F. Far fewer resources are initialized this time because only the request scope is opening; all the other resources that were initialized from the previous request are still open and in their respective scopes. Likewise, a request from a new user (new session) will yield C, D, E, G, F.

Now that you know how WebWork manages dependencies, let's look at some of the dependencies that are problematic and aren't supported.

Circular dependencies

A circular dependency is one that yields a dependency graph in the shape of a circle. Sometimes the circle is *tight*, meaning that it's obvious a circular dependency exists. A tight circle is when X depends on Y and Y depends on X. These are usually easy to find and eliminate, often by introducing a common component Z that both X and Y can depend on.

The harder-to-find and trickier circles are *loose*, meaning that there may be multiple circles that go several levels deep before they loop. Figure 6.4 illustrates an example. Can you see the circle?

Actually, although this graph is complex, it's almost legal. The only link that is invalid is the dependency of G on F. If that link could be broken, WebWork would be able to handle even this complex dependency chart. Finding these kinds of dependency errors requires a careful eye.

Your best bet is to draw out the graph and then, starting at the lowest-level node, begin working your way up the graph. As you pass each node, place a checkmark next to each item. Cross off any node that no longer has any dependencies that haven't been crossed off. As you work your way up the graph, if you come across a node that has a checkmark but hasn't yet been crossed off, you have a circular dependency.

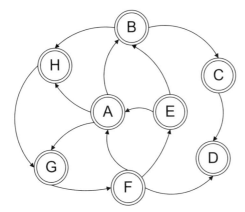

**Figure 6.4
A complex (and invalid) circular
dependency graph**

Scope dependencies

Another kind of dependency isn't allowed by WebWork: *lower-scope* dependencies.
These are usually easier to identify but sometimes harder to solve. As we've discussed previously and also showed in figure 6.3, objects in the request scope may
depend on objects in the session scope, just as session scope may depend on application scope. However, the opposite doesn't hold true. Let's examine why this is
the case and how you can get around it when it crops up.

Sometimes it makes logical sense for a higher-level scope to depend on a scope
below it. For example, a ShoppingCart in session scope might want to depend on a
Transaction in request scope. Individually, it makes sense for each object to be in
its respective scope, session, and request. The problem comes up when you want
ShoppingCart to implement TransactionAware.

At first this might seem like a feasible situation, especially given that during
development, there is almost zero traffic on your site. But what if two requests
come in at almost the same time from the same use? This case can easily happen—a common situation is when the user double-clicks a link or a Submit button. Imagine that a user clicks Submit twice, and the following two requests come
in at almost exactly the same time (see table 6.1).

Table 6.1 A race condition using inverse-scoped dependencies

Time	Request 1	Request 2
T=0	Transaction t1 is initialized	
T=1		Transaction t2 is initialized.
T=2	cart.setTransaction(t1) is called.	

Table 6.1 A race condition using inverse-scoped dependencies *(continued)*

Time	Request 1	Request 2
T=3		`cart.setTransaction(t2)` is called.
T=4	`cart.checkOut()` is called.	
T=5		`cart.checkOut()` is called.

A *race condition* is occurring: There is a chance that Request 1 is getting Request 2's `Transaction` object, which may cause strange behavior. These types of multithreading bugs are very difficult to track down and can result in you and other developers banging your heads on your desks for many days. As such, WebWork doesn't support this type of dependency.

When this situation comes up—and it will—the simplest resolution is to remove the dependency entirely and change the method signatures of the methods that need the resource so that they accept the resource directly. In the case of `ShoppingCart`, rather than having a `checkOut()` method, you change it to have a `checkOut(Transaction t)` method instead. Doing so guarantees that the correct resource is wired correctly and no race conditions can occur.

NOTE   There has been some talk on the WebWork mailing lists about changing WebWork to allow these types of reverse-scope dependencies. Because the nature of the relationship between request, scope, and application is very specific (one-to-many relationship between application-and-session and session-and-request), it's theoretically possible, using complex synchronization logic, to allow these kinds of dependencies. However, we're unsure whether the effort is worth it, because depending on lower-scoped resource is usually a dangerous game, and promoting it could be a slippery slope.

6.4 An example from CaveatEmptor

Let's look at two components in CaveatEmptor that provide that base persistence support using Hibernate. If you're not familiar with Hibernate, don't worry—the ideas presented here could work with any persistence layer.

The first thing to pay special attention to is that Hibernate has a concept of a `Session` and a `SessionFactory`. The `Session` is open only as long as it needs to work with the database. The `SessionFactory`, on the other hand, is created once and then used over and over, providing the backbone for advanced caching and session management.

In CaveatEmptor, we decided to create two IoC components to encapsulate these two objects: the `HibernateSessionFactory` and the `PersistenceManager`. Let's first talk about the `SessionFactory` implementation.

6.4.1 *The HibernateSessionFactory component*

Before you create the classes of any component (or any object, for that matter), it's important to make sure you understand the *role* of the component. That is, you must ask yourself, "What is the purpose of the object?" Considering the introduction to this section, you can assume that this particular component is responsible for managing Hibernate's `SessionFactory` for the CaveatEmptor application.

With that said, you can start to define a simple interface first. Listing 6.2 provides the complete `HibernateSessionFactory` interface.

Listing 6.2   The HibernateSessionFactory interface

```
package org.hibernate.auction.persistence.components;

import net.sf.hibernate.SessionFactory;

public interface HibernateSessionFactory {
    SessionFactory getSessionFactory();
}
```

As you can see, the interface is very simple: All it does is return a `SessionFactory` object. Now that you have defined the interface, let's implement the interface (see listing 6.3). Keep in mind that this component's job is to manage the single `SessionFactory` that should be associated with the entire application.

Listing 6.3   The HibernateSessionFactory implementation

```
package org.hibernate.auction.persistence.components;

import com.opensymphony.xwork.interceptor.component.Initializable;
import com.opensymphony.xwork.interceptor.component.Disposable;
import net.sf.hibernate.cfg.Configuration;
import net.sf.hibernate.SessionFactory;
import net.sf.hibernate.HibernateException;
import org.apache.commons.logging.Log;
import org.apache.commons.logging.LogFactory;

public class HibernateSessionFactoryImpl
    implements HibernateSessionFactory, Initializable, Disposable {
    private static final Log LOG =
        LogFactory.getLog(HibernateSessionFactoryImpl.class);
```

```
SessionFactory sessionFactory;

public void init() {
    try {
        Configuration configuration = new Configuration();
        sessionFactory = configuration.configure()
            .buildSessionFactory();
        // We could also let Hibernate bind it to JNDI:
        // configuration.configure().buildSessionFactory()
    } catch (Throwable e) {
        // We have to catch Throwable, otherwise we'll miss
        // NoClassDefFoundError and other subclasses of Error
        LOG.error("Building SessionFactory failed.", e);
        throw new ExceptionInInitializerError(e);
    }
}

public SessionFactory getSessionFactory() {
    return sessionFactory;
}

public void dispose() {
    try {
        sessionFactory.close();
    } catch (HibernateException e) {
        LOG.error("Closing SessionFactory failed.", e);
    }
}
}
```

Let's break down listing 6.3 so you understand what's going on. First, let's examine the interfaces this class implements. The expected `HibernateSessionFactory` interface is there, but it also includes two new interfaces: `Initializable` and `Disposable`. It turns out that the rest of the implementation of this class is merely satisfying the requirements of these three interfaces: `getSessionFactory()` for your `HibernateSessionFactory`, `init()` for `Initializable`, and `dispose()` for `Disposable`.

WebWork's two lifecycle events: initialize and dispose

WebWork's IoC implementation has two optional lifecycle events: *initialize* and *dispose*. Initialize is called after the component has been created and all its dependencies have been set and also initialized. Dispose is called just before the component lifecycle has ended and the object is about to be no longer accessible by any other objects in the system.

These two lifecycle events are optional; you can hook into them by implementing the `com.opensymphony.xwork.interceptor.component.Initializable` and `com.opensymphony.xwork.interceptor.component.Disposable` interfaces, respectively. These events are very important and allow you to easily implement rules like transactions, as you'll see in a moment.

The HibernateSessionFactory lifecycle

Now that you understand what these events are, let's look at what they're doing. On initialization, the component asks Hibernate to configure itself and create a `SessionFactory` object, which it then stores in a local field. You make this field accessible via the `getSessionFactory()` method required by `HibernateSession-Factory`. Because `init()` is called only once during the entire lifetime of this component, you know that only one `SessionFactory` will be made available.

Hibernate requires that when a `SessionFactory` will no longer be used, it must be closed. This lets Hibernate cleanly disconnect any open connections from the database and flush any outstanding caches. You make sure this contract is honored by calling the `close()` method in the dispose event, as shown in the `dispose()` method.

Combined, the `init()` and `dispose()` methods make sure the `SessionFactory` contract is honored. Let's now look at how you can create a second component that utilizes this `HibernateSessionFactory` component.

6.4.2 The PersistenceManager component

A Hibernate `SessionFactory` does only one thing: It creates Hibernate `Session`s. However, a Hibernate `Session` has a few more responsibilities: It handles transactions, reads data from a database, stores data in the database, and communicates with its `SessionFactory` for caching strategies.

Because you want to encapsulate this behavior, you create an interface like that seen in listing 6.4. Specifically, you provide access to the `Session` but also allow control over transactional behaviors: starting, committing, and rolling back transactions.

Listing 6.4 The PersistenceManager interface

```
package org.hibernate.auction.persistence.components;

import net.sf.hibernate.Session;

public interface PersistenceManager {
    Session getSession();
```

```
void begin();

void commit();

void rollback();

}
```

■

The `PersistenceManager` interface is simple enough. Let's now look at the implementation, provided in listing 6.5. Remember, this implementation is responsible for a few tasks:

- Declaring that it requires a `HibernateSessionFactory` component
- Opening a new `Session` object
- Optionally supporting the transaction features: begin, commit, and rollback
- Closing the `Session` properly

Listing 6.5   The `PersistenceManager` implementation

```
package org.hibernate.auction.persistence.components;

import com.opensymphony.xwork.interceptor.component.Initializable;
import com.opensymphony.xwork.interceptor.component.Disposable;
import net.sf.hibernate.*;
import org.apache.commons.logging.Log;
import org.apache.commons.logging.LogFactory;

public class PersistenceManagerImpl
    implements PersistenceManager, HibernateSessionFactoryAware,
            Initializable, Disposable {
    private static final Log LOG =
        LogFactory.getLog(PersistenceManagerImpl.class);

    SessionFactory sessionFactory;
    Session session;
    Transaction transaction;
    boolean rollback;
    boolean commited;

    public void setSessionFactory(
        HibernateSessionFactory sessionFactory) {
        this.sessionFactory = sessionFactory.getSessionFactory();
    }

    public void init() {
```

```
    try {
        session = sessionFactory.openSession();
        session.setFlushMode(FlushMode.NEVER);
    } catch (HibernateException e) {
        LOG.error("Could not open Hibernate session.", e);
        throw new ExceptionInInitializerError(e);
    }
}

public Session getSession() {
    return session;
}

    public void begin() {
    try {
        transaction = session.beginTransaction();
    } catch (HibernateException e) {
        LOG.error("Could not begin transaction.", e);
        throw new ExceptionInInitializerError(e);
    }
}

public void commit() {
    if (transaction == null) {
        throw new RuntimeException("Transaction must be " +
                                  "started before it can " +
                                  "be committed!");
    }

    if (!commited) {
        try {
            session.flush();
            transaction.commit();
            commited = true;
        } catch (HibernateException e) {
            LOG.error("Could not commit transaction.", e);
        }
    }
}

public void rollback() {
    if (transaction == null) {
        throw new RuntimeException("Transaction must be " +
                                  "started before it can " +
                                  "be rolled back!");
    }

    if (!commited) {
        try {
            transaction.rollback();
            rollback = true;
```

```
            } catch (HibernateException e) {
                LOG.error("Could not roll transaction back.", e);
            }
        }
    }

    public void dispose() {
        try {
            if (transaction != null) {
                commit();
            }

            session.close();
        } catch (HibernateException e) {
            LOG.error("Could not close Hibernate session.");
        }
    }
}
```

Beginning again with the interfaces that the implementation implements again, you see the three familiar interfaces: PersistenceManager, Initializable, and Disposable. However, there is also a fourth interface: HibernateSessionFactoryAware. This is the aware interface, which indicates that this particular class (Persistence-ManagerImpl) requires a HibernateSessionFactory implementation before it can be initialized.

The rest of the implementation is fairly straightforward. The transactional state is kept in the rollback, committed, and transaction fields. All persistence sessions start the same way, as shown in init(), but not all are ended the same way. As you can see in dispose(), if a transaction is still open, it's closed out before the session is closed.

Unlike the previous examples in this chapter, this implementation combines the persistence and transaction duties into a single component. Both approaches are perfectly acceptable. Now that you've seen the two component interfaces and implementations, let's examine how they're configured to work together.

6.4.3 *Configuring the components*

Remember that the SessionFactory is a one-time thing, whereas you need a new Session every time the database is accessed. Armed with this information, it's time to determine the *scope* of these components. You already know how they behave in their lifetime, based on how the init() and dispose() methods were implemented. But you haven't yet declared when and how often those methods are called. Listing 6.6 contains the <component> configurations for both components.

**Listing 6.6   Configuration for the `SessionFactory` and
`PersistenceManager` components**

```
<component>
  <scope>request</scope>
  <class>
    org.hibernate.auction.persistence.components.
    ➥PersistenceManagerImpl
  </class>
  <enabler>
        org.hibernate.auction.persistence.components.
        ➥PersistenceManagerAware
  </enabler>
</component>

<component>
  <scope>application</scope>
  <class>
    org.hibernate.auction.persistence.components.
    ➥HibernateSessionFactoryImpl
  </class>
  <enabler>
    org.hibernate.auction.persistence.components.
    ➥HibernateSessionFactoryAware
  </enabler>
</component>
```

The important thing to note here is the scopes of the two components. The `Session-Factory`, which is implemented only once, has an expected scope of *application*. On the other hand, a new `Session` is created on every request, also as expected.

6.4.4   *Using the new components*

You already saw, in section 6.4.2, how the `PersistenceManagerImpl` declared that it required the `HibernateSessionFactory` by using the aware interface for that component. The way CaveatEmptor was designed, no other components should need to talk to the `HibernateSessionFactory`. However, many components *and* actions need access to the `PersistenceManager` to function properly. You declare this need the same way, by implementing the proper `Aware` interface—in this case, `PersistenceManagerAware`, shown in listing 6.7.

Listing 6.7 The aware interface for the `PersistenceManager` component

```
package org.hibernate.auction.persistence.components;

public interface PersistenceManagerAware {
    void setPersistenceManager(PersistenceManager persistenceManager);
}
```

All other components declared in components.xml can implement this interface to get access to the `PersistenceManager`, provided those components are also in the request scope. If an action needs access to this component, it too must implement the same interface. However, remember to place the component interceptor in the action's stack, or the component won't be wired up.

WebWork's IoC container isn't the only kid on the block. There are others that are more configurable and might be worth looking at if you start to find WebWork's IoC container limiting. In the next section, we outline the types of containers available and the projects that are most closely associated with those types.

6.5 Alternatives

WebWork's IoC container is far from the only way to handle complex object dependency and lifecycle needs. We want to spend a bit of time pointing you to alternatives in the form of both IoC and non-IoC implementations. Inversion of Control and lightweight containers are surrounded by a lot of hype, so be careful that you don't get caught up in the hype as well. For some needs, IoC makes a lot of sense—for others, it doesn't. Look at the alternatives, and decide for yourself what technique will work best for you and your development team.

6.5.1 Alternative IoC containers

Now that you're familiar with the concepts of IoC as well as how to use WebWork's IoC container, let's examine some alternative IoC containers that are available in the Java open source community. Because WebWork's IoC container is optional, you're free to not use it and instead integrate with any other container. It's generally accepted that three types of IoC are available to use. The type of IoC is based on how resources are given to objects:

- *Type 1*—Interfaces
- *Type 2*—Setter methods
- *Type 3*—Constructor

WebWork is considered a Type 1 IoC implementation, although it may be changed in the future to support Type 2 and possibly Type 3 in the future. We'll now look at what each type means by briefly examining open source projects that use them.

Type 1: A look at Avalon

The original IoC framework for Java is Apache Avalon. Like WebWork, Avalon requires that an interface expose a single method, such as `injectWidget(Widget w)`, which will be used by the container. Because this style is just like WebWork's, we won't spend much more time on it here.

The important thing that Avalon brings to the table is a large suite of well-defined lifecycle events. WebWork currently provides only two lifecycle events: initializing and disposing. Avalon goes much further and provides many more lifecycle events, thereby possibly allowing much greater external control over your components.

> **NOTE** You can find Avalon at http://jakarta.apache.org/avalon. However, as of late 2004, the Avalon project has closed down. Look toward Spring and Pico for alternative IoC implementations. In addition, EJB 3.0 is strongly influenced by Spring and can be expected to offer many IoC features in the future.

Type 2: A look at Spring

After Avalon, some people began to wonder why implementing an interface was necessary—and they found that it wasn't. Spring uses setter methods to pass resources to objects and doesn't require that an interface expose a method that provides access. Instead, Spring uses reflection to call the appropriate `setWidget(Widget w)` method if it exists.

Spring also contains its own MVC implementation, although it isn't uncommon for people to use WebWork's MVC and Spring's IoC together. You can find Spring at http://www.springframework.org. You can also learn more about Spring in the book *Spring in Action* (Manning, 2005).

Type 3: A look at Pico

Shortly after the development of WebWork's IoC container, someone asked, why should I do this

```
MyObject o = new MyObject();
o.setWidget(new Widget());
```

when I can do this?

```
MyObject o = new MyObject(new Widget());
```

And thus Type 3 IoC was born. Instead of using methods to pass resources in to an object, Type 3 IoC promotes the notion that if an object such as `MyObject` can't exist without a resource such as `Widget`, that object should be passed in through its constructor and not via a method after the object is already created.

Pico is an IoC implementation that promotes this type of implementation. It's freely available at http://pico.codehaus.org.

6.5.2 *Non-IoC alternatives*

IoC doesn't claim to be anything it isn't. It doesn't do more than a Turing machine can do, it doesn't solve world hunger, and definitely no one is claiming that it *must* be used to develop a clean, modular, decoupled application. So the logical question is, "What is an alternative that offers benefits *similar* to those of IoC?"

At the beginning of this chapter, we discussed several patterns that have influenced and led to the usage of IoC. However, those same influences also led to another pattern that is widely used: the *Service Locator pattern*. This pattern is the dual of Inversion of Control. That is, it offers all the same benefits of IoC, but instead of assuming that a container is passively handing resources to your code, it requires your code to actively get those resources.

Active resource management doesn't make your code more or less coupled together. The only part that is more coupled is the coupling between your code and the service location, but that is so minor that it can be often be dismissed. Before we end this chapter, let's look at what this pattern is, so you at least have a different perspective on the problems IoC is attempting to solve. If you decide that IoC isn't useful for your project, then it might be helpful to look toward this important pattern as an alternative.

Recall the Factory pattern discussed at the start of this chapter. If you need to write a block of code that requires access to a `FooService`, a `BarService`, and a `BazService`, the code might look like the following if you implement it using factories:

```
FooService foo = FooServiceFactory.getFooService();
BarService bar = BarServiceFactory.getBarService();
BazService baz = BazServiceFactory.getBazService();
foo.doSomeThing();
bar.doAnotherThing();
baz.doThisAndThat();
```

This code is decoupled from the service implementations themselves but is now tightly coupled to three factories. Worse, if the factories end up becoming more complicated, such as having more configuration options, managing the factories may become a problem. Using IoC, you would assume that local, private fields in the class already had the services populated, so the code would just be as follows:

```
// 3 setters have already been called
foo.doSomeThing();
bar.doAnotherThing();
baz.doThisAndThat();
```

This is nice because the code is completely decoupled from the implementation of the `foo`, `bar`, and `baz` services and their factories. But there is another way to do this without using IoC: the Service Locator pattern. The idea is to take the logic (complex and simple) of each factory and place it in a single class. The resulting code is

```
FooService foo = ServiceLocator.getFooService();
BarService bar = ServiceLocator.getBarService();
BazService baz = ServiceLocator.getBazService();
foo.doSomeThing();
bar.doAnotherThing();
baz.doThisAndThat();
```

This code isn't tied to the factories or the service implementations, and so it has almost all the same benefits your IoC example does. In fact, this example is nicer for some developers because it's much more straightforward—nothing is going on behind the scenes that is required to make the code work. What you see is what you get.

The only downside to this code is that it's coupled closely to the `ServiceLocator` class. The only downside to the IoC code is that it isn't totally straightforward or obvious. Otherwise, both techniques are conceptually the same. It's up to you to decide where and how you wish to handle resource management (or service management, in this case). Neither approach is right or wrong—they're just two different ways to skin a cat.

6.6 Summary

In this chapter, we looked at the incremental steps that took engineers from crude resource management to advanced techniques such as Inversion of Control. By first examining patterns such as the Singleton and Factory patterns, we were able to explore the relationship between the problems these patterns were trying to solve and those that IoC tries to solve.

You also saw how two important components in CaveatEmptor were created. These components, `PersistenceManager` and `HibernateSessionFactory`, both demonstrate dependencies, scoping, and lifecycles in an easy-to-follow manner.

In addition to showing you how to use WebWork's IoC container, we introduced the general concept of how complex dependencies and lifecycles work in a highly componentized architecture. The fact is that no matter how hard you try to componentize your code, if you don't deal with the basic issues of when the components are created and destroyed, as well as how they depend on each other, your code will inevitably fall back into a state of disarray. We hope that the technique of Inversion of Control has excited you about ways you can cleanly handle resource and component management.

Part 3

Displaying content

This part covers how data is displayed after it has been processed. Chapter 7 looks at the kinds of results WebWork supports, such as JSP, Velocity, and Jasper-Reports. This chapter goes into great detail about the pros and cons of different methods for displaying your content. Chapter 8 explains how WebWork's expression language (EL) can be used in those result pages, regardless of the view technology. The EL provides a very loose coupling between your presentation layer and your data.

Once you've gained a solid grasp of the EL, chapter 9 puts it to good use by showing you the non-UI tags WebWork supplies. Chapter 10 presents a quick overview of Velocity; it's a prerequisite for the next chapter. Chapter 11 discusses UI tags; you'll see how the tags and features covered in chapters 8 and 9 come together to let you create rich, componentized, reusable templates.

Using results

This chapter covers

- The relationship between actions and their results
- How to chain multiple actions together in a single request
- How to redirect to a new page after an action has completed
- Alternatives to JSP, such as Velocity and FreeMarker
- How to render reports in PDF, Excel, XML, and HTML using JasperReports

Newton's third law of thermodynamics states that an action can't happen without a reaction. In the world of WebWork, an action usually shouldn't happen without a *result*. A result is a piece of code that is executed after your action has already completed and returned a value such as success or error. But unlike actions, you won't find yourself writing many results while building your web application. Rather, WebWork comes with most, if not all, of the results you'll need. In this chapter, we'll discuss how results work in general; then we'll examine the common results (such as "servlet dispatcher," used for JSPs, and Velocity) as well as alternative results such as FreeMarker and Jasper Reports (in PDF, XML, and HTML).

7.1 *Life after the action*

Before we discuss complex results, such as those that render a JSP page or produce a PDF chart, you need to understand not only how to configure a result but also how results operate. This will be necessary if you want to write your own result and also if you plan to write any interceptors or other add-ons to WebWork.

7.1.1 *A simple result*

All results must implement a single interface: com.opensymphony.xwork.Result. This interface, like the Action interface, is simple:

```
package com.opensymphony.xwork;

public interface Result {
    public void execute(ActionInvocation invocation)
        throws Exception;
}
```

Just as in the Action interface, there is only a single execute() method. One difference, however, is that the execute() method in Action returns a String, whereas the execute() method here returns void. This is the case because in an action, the return code determines which result to execute. In results, there is no need to determine what to do next, so no return value is necessary.

Let's run through a simple exercise that involves creating a new type of result called debug. By going through this exercise, we'll dive head first into the topic of results. We'll come up for air afterward and then take a detailed look at the topics glossed over in this quick example.

Imagine that you have an action that is behaving erratically, and you need to determine the values of various properties in the action (see listing 7.1). This action returns SUCCESS, INPUT, or ERROR with an equally random chance. It also sets up the properties foo, bar, and baz to have a value that contains that random number.

Listing 7.1   An action that simulates random or erratic behavior

```
package examples.chap07;

import com.opensymphony.xwork.ActionSupport;

import java.util.Random;

public class TestAction extends ActionSupport {
    private String foo;
    private String bar;
    private String baz;

    public String execute() throws Exception {
        int random = new Random().nextInt(100);

        foo = "foo-" + random;
        bar = "bar-" + random;
        baz = "baz-" + random;

        if (random <= 33) {
            return SUCCESS;
        } else if (random <= 66) {
            return ERROR;
        } else {
            return INPUT;
        }
    }

    // getters and setters for all the properties
    ...
}
```

Debugging an action often involves trying to determine the values of various properties after execution. To make your job of debugging easier, let's build a custom result that lets you see the values of a specified property (see listing 7.2).

Listing 7.2   A complete result that prints out the value of a specified property

```
package examples.chap07;

import com.opensymphony.xwork.Result;
import com.opensymphony.xwork.ActionInvocation;
import com.opensymphony.xwork.Action;
```

```
import java.lang.reflect.Method;

public class DebugResult implements Result {
    public static final String DEFAULT_PARAM = "property";

    String property;

    public void execute(ActionInvocation invocation)
        throws Exception {
        String resultCode = invocation.getResultCode();
        System.out.println("Result code: " + resultCode);

        Action action = invocation.getAction();
        String methodName = "get" +
            property.substring(0, 1).toUpperCase() +
            property.substring(1);
        Method method = action.getClass()
            ➥.getMethod(methodName, new Class[0]);
        Object o = method.invoke(action, new Object[0]);
        System.out.println(property + ": " + o);
    }

    public void setProperty(String property) {
        this.property = property;
    }
}
```

NOTE   In listing 7.2, a static string defined as DEFAULT_PARAM exists. Ignore it for now; we'll come back to it in a second when we take a detailed look at configuring results.

Recall that getter methods for properties are in the form of getXxx(). This code converts a property name from the form xxx to a method name of getXxx. It then invokes the corresponding getter to retrieve the property's value. Finally, the property name (in the form of xxx) and the value are printed to standard output. This result is useful if you're trying to debug what the state of your action looks like after it has been executed. Let's now look at how it would be configured in xwork.xml so that you might use it.

7.1.2 *Configuring a result*

Just like actions and interceptors, you configure a result in xwork.xml. Results are specified in packages and are inherited. You can also configure a default result per package, meaning that specifying the `type` attribute for your most common result isn't necessary. Listing 7.3 shows a configuration that uses your newly created result.

Listing 7.3 A configuration that ties your actions in with the result you just created

```
<!DOCTYPE xwork PUBLIC "-//OpenSymphony Group//XWork 1.0//EN"
    "http://www.opensymphony.com/xwork/xwork-1.0.dtd">
<xwork>
    <include file="webwork-default.xml"/>
    <package name="default" extends="webwork-default">
        <result-types>
            <result-type name="debug"
                         class="examples.chap07.DebugResult"
                         default="true"/>
        </result-types>

        <action name="test" class="examples.chap07.TestAction">
            <result name="success" type="debug">
                <param name="property">foo</param>
            </result>
            <result name="error">
                <param name="property">bar</param>
            </result>
            <result name="input">baz</result>
        </action>
    </package>
</xwork>
```

Reading from top to bottom, the first important thing to note is the `<result-types>` section. In it, all results are defined. All the other results you have been using and will use are already defined in webwork-default.xml, which is why you extend that package. In this section, you define the name of the result type as well as the class in listing 7.2. Finally, you decide to make this result the default, meaning that if a result type isn't specified, this one will be assumed.

NOTE In webwork-default.xml, the default result type is `dispatcher` or the servlet dispatch result. We'll discuss this result in a moment, but it's almost always a good idea to leave it as your default result for web applications build using JSPs. We changed the default in this example to showcase the effects of a default result.

The next thing to look at in listing 7.3 is the result for the action. This is where the result code is mapped to an actual result. You've defined three mappings in this case: `success`, `error`, and `input`. In each of these mappings, a value for the `property`

property is specified (foo, bar, baz). This means that when the result is instantiated, it will have setProperty() called with the value specified.

The mapping for success is the most verbose form of defining a result: The type has been specified, and the property parameter has been explicitly called out. The error mapping is a bit less verbose in that the default result type is assumed and therefore not specified. The input mapping is the least verbose because it assumes the default result as well as the default parameter. You'll use this last form most frequently when you're building web applications.

Recall that listing 7.2 defined a DEFAULT_PARAM static string. This string defines the default parameter name for DebugResult. This allows results to be specified in the much more simplified form of the input mapping. All results that are included with WebWork have a DEFAULT_PARAM specified. We'll look at those results, as well as their default parameters, in section 7.2. In chapter 2, you already saw results specified in this form:

```
<result name="success">/hello.jsp</result>
```

That's all there is to configuring and using results. Now let's come up for a breath of fresh air and look at some of the common results you'll most likely be using when building a WebWork-powered application.

7.2 Common results

WebWork comes bundled with most if not all of the result types you'll need when building web applications. Although the DebugResult has some usefulness, you can't build applications without displaying something to the user. The most common way to do this is with a JSP page. The three most common results are as follows:

- Dispatching to a page from within the same HTTP request
- Redirecting the browser to a page
- Directly chaining to another WebWork action

7.2.1 Dispatching to a page

Because the ActionContext and the value stack in particular are ThreadLocal and therefore associated with a single request, any page that needs to display dynamic data prepared by an action must be rendered in the same HTTP request. Displaying a different page (whether a JSP or a servlet or anything else) under the same HTTP request is possible using the Servlet APIs and the RequestDispatcher class.

In webwork-default.xml, the default result type is dispatcher, which does exactly that: It makes a request and renders the output of that request in the same response that the original HTTP request came from. Figure 7.1 illustrates how a RequestDispatcher works when used in the result of an action.

Configuring a dispatch result

As long as you're including webwork-default.xml and your packages inherit (directly or indirectly) from webwork-default, no configuration should be required to use the dispatcher result. This is because webwork-default.xml includes the following entry in the webwork-default package:

```
<result-type name="dispatcher"
            class="com.opensymphony.webwork.dispatcher.
                ⇒ServletDispatcherResult"
            default="true"/>
```

Notice that this result type is configured to be the default result. So, if you don't specify the result type in the results for your actions, it will be assumed to be a dispatcher result. As you saw in chapter 2, a result definition can look like this:

```
<result name="success">/hello.jsp</result>
```

As we noted in section 7.1, most WebWork results have a DEFAULT_PARAM defined, allowing for a much simpler configuration form. In the case of the dispatcher result, the default parameter is location. This means a more formal way to dispatch to hello.jsp would be

```
<result name="success" type="dispatcher">
    <param name="location">/hello.jsp</param>
</result>
```

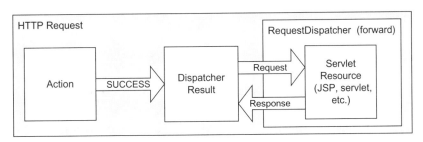

Figure 7.1   A request for an action that invokes a RequestDispatcher

Parsing variables

In addition to the `location` parameter, there is another supported parameter called `parse`. This parameter is a boolean and is true by default. When set to false, the `dispatcher` result won't parse the `location` parameter for variable replacement. *Variable replacement* is the act of changing a string such as `"/view-Cart.jsp?ID=${ID}"` in to `"/viewCart.jsp?ID=54"`. The `dispatcher` result looks in the location string for anything matching the form `${...}` and extracts the Object Graph Navigation Language (OGNL) expression between the curly braces. It then evaluates the expression against the value stack and replaces the entire thing with the result of the evaluation.

> **NOTE** For `dispatcher` results, parsing variables in the location isn't important because the same information can be retrieved in the JSP by using the property tag. However, as you'll see in a moment, it's extremely powerful when redirecting to another page.

This gives you the ability to use dynamic pages and URLs for your results. Setting the `parse` parameter to false tells the result not to do any parsing, leaving the final location that the `RequestDispatcher` attempts to find complete with the `${...}` characters. Unless you have a specific need to turn off parsing, it's recommended you leave it on.

Context matters

Depending on the context in which the `dispatcher` result is called, *how* the dispatch occurs may be slightly different. This is because the Servlet specification has a few restrictions about how the two types of dispatching (includes and forwards) can happen. The `dispatcher` result checks for and acts on three types of contexts:

- JSP context
- Normal context
- Included context

The JSP *context* is automatically discovered with the presence of a `PageContext` object in the `ActionContext`. If a `PageContext` exists, then its `include()` method is called with the location specified in the result. This allows for a JSP to include an action and its corresponding result as a component, as illustrated in figure 7.2 and demonstrated in listing 7.4.

Remember that the `dispatcher` result is responsible for sending arbitrary requests to any servlet resource. Typically you'll dispatch to JSPs, as shown in figure 7.2. However, you could theoretically dispatch to any resource, such as other

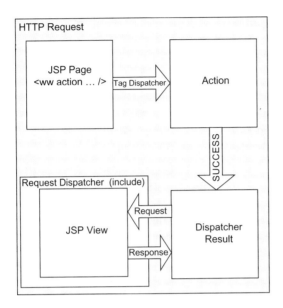

Figure 7.2
**The dispatcher result when under
the JSP context**

servlets, HTML files, Velocity or FreeMarker templates, or even other actions. WebWork provides other results, which we go over later in this chapter, for more specialized uses, such as rendering a template in Velocity or invoking a second action (called *action chaining*).

Listing 7.4   A JSP that invokes an action under a JSP context

```
<%@ taglib uri="webwork" prefix="ww" %>
<html>
    <head>
        <title>JSP Context</title>
    </head>
    <body>
        The following content was included because it is in a JSP
        context:
        <hr/>
            <ww:action name="helloWorld" executeResult="true" />
        </hr>
    </body>
</html>
```

Don't worry about the ww:action tag just yet (it will be covered in chapter 9, "Tag libraries"). Just know that a call to this tag effectively invokes an action and its result, thereby creating the JSP context the dispatcher result needs to be aware of. The outcome is that the output of that action will stream directly into this JSP in the form of a `RequestDispatcher` include.

In the *normal context,* an action executes due to a direct request from a web browser, and the result is a `dispatcher` result. There is no `PageContext` in the `ActionContext`. Under this context, the `RequestDispatcher` is used to forward to another resource. That resource, for example, might be a JSP, which in turn invokes another action, resulting in the JSP context previously described. Such a scenario of an action-JSP-action is presented in figure 7.3.

A third, rarer, context is the *included context.* This occurs whenever the request for an action is due to an include rather than a forward. This context is similar to the JSP context, except that instead of executing the action in the JSP, the action is executed because of a `RequestDispatcher` include. This can happen when a JSP uses `jsp:include` rather than `ww:action` to display a resource for an action. The difference is subtle, but it can create different contexts in which the `dispatcher`

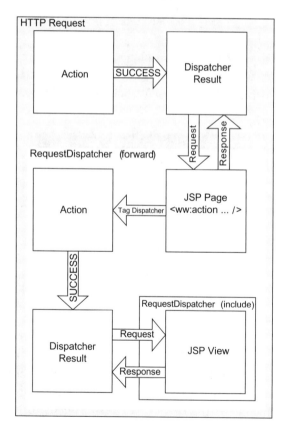

Figure 7.3
The `dispatcher` result under a normal context and a JSP context

result is invoked. To demonstrate the difference, listing 7.5 shows a JSP that causes both a JSP context and an included context.

Listing 7.5   A JSP that invokes an action under the included context

```
<%@ taglib uri="webwork" prefix="ww" %>
<html>
    <head>
        <title>Included Context</title>
    </head>
    <body>
        The following content was included because it is in an
        included context:
        <hr/>
        <jsp:include page="helloWorld.action"/>
    </body>
</html>
```

The key thing to note is that the included context uses the `*.action` extension to identify the action request. This is because an actual `RequestDispatcher` must be used to execute the action *and* its view. In figure 7.2, only one `RequestDispatcher` must be used, thereby making everything simpler and faster. Figure 7.4 demonstrates how the page in listing 7.5 would be executed. As you can see, the JSP and normal context are a bit simpler (and more common) than the included context.

NOTE The differences between a forward and an include can sometimes be difficult to understand. A close read of the Servlet specification as well as the API documentation will clear things up. But if you want to avoid reading that information, the main difference between the two to keep in mind is this: Forwards can happen unlimited times until an include takes place, after which only includes may occur. The `dispatcher` result obeys this rule and never calls for a forward after an include has already taken place.

Error cases

In the case where an error occurs in either finding the resource specified in the dispatcher `location` parameter or when executing the particular page, WebWork will notify you. The `dispatcher` result only knows to return a 404 when it's unable to get a handle to a `RequestDispatcher` object. Depending on the implementation of your servlet container, this may or may not happen when the resource you're dispatching to doesn't exist. If the servlet container tries to serve content that doesn't exist, a 404 won't be returned; rather, a general exception will take place when the result tries to dispatch the request.

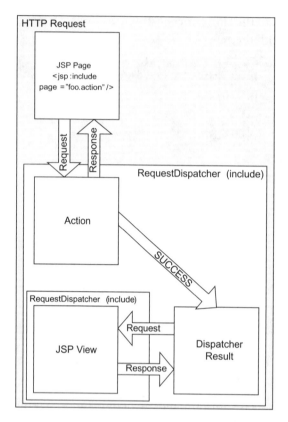

Figure 7.4
The `dispatcher` result under the included context

General exceptions produce a 500 error code. These errors happen whenever WebWork encounters an unknown error of any form. A stack trace is included that will help you track down where the error occurred. In the case of a resource not being found, the servlet container reports that fact in the exception being thrown. In the case where your resource (such as a JSP) is causing an error, the stack trace includes the exception message. If you're working with JSPs, the trace may include the JSP filename and line number, further helping you debug the problem.

7.2.2 *Redirecting to a page*

Although `dispatcher` results are important and even required when you need to display data that was generated or retrieved from an action, many times all you need to do is point the browser to a new location. You can do this by using the `redirect` result that is included with WebWork (see figure 7.5).

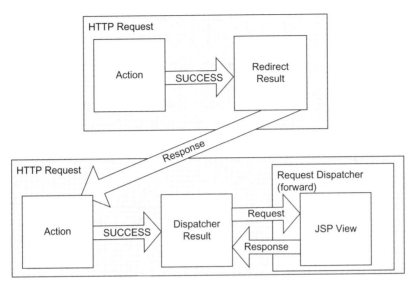

Figure 7.5 A request for an action that calls `HttpServletResponse.sendRedirect()`

NOTE Although figure 7.5 is a diagram of a `redirect` result type sending the browser off to another action, this isn't always the case. You're free to redirect the user to *any* URL, even a URL that isn't part of your web application (such as http://www.google.com).

Configuring a redirect

Just like with the `dispatcher` result, as long as you're including webwork-default.xml and your packages inherit (directly or indirectly) from `webwork-default`, no configuration should be required to use the `dispatcher` result. The entry in webwork-default.xml that is part of the `webwork-default` package is as follows:

```
<result-type name="redirect"
            class="com.opensymphony.webwork.dispatcher.-
ServletRedirectResult"/>
```

Notice that unlike the `dispatcher` result, this result type isn't configured to be the default. Thus in the results for your actions, you must specify the result type as `redirect` in order to use this result. A sample usage looks like this:

```
<result name="success" type="redirect">/hello.jsp</result>
```

As we stated before, all WebWork results have a default parameter specified. For `redirect` results, the default parameter is the same as the `dispatcher` result: `location`. The `redirect` result also takes the other optional parameter that `dispatcher` does: parse. This means the redirect result is also capable of generating requests dynamically by evaluating expressions that use data from the value stack.

Differences between redirects and dispatchers

Comparing figure 7.1 to figure 7.5, you can see how the redirect result and the dispatcher result are very different. Redirects work by sending a 302 HTTP return code back to the browser along with the new location in the HTTP headers. The browser then issues an HTTP request to that location automatically. This is unlike the dispatcher result, which issues an internal request to the resource, giving the appearance to the browser that only one request has been made.

> **NOTE** Using a redirect causes some small performance penalties. That is the case because the browser now has to do two round-trip network calls rather than one (if a dispatcher was used). This effect is minor, but it should be noted.

The consequence is subtle but also very important. Imagine the following configuration:

```
<action name="checkout-order" class="com.acme.CheckoutOrder">
    <result name="success">order-confirmation.jsp</result>
</action>
```

If a user shopping for online books clicks the Checkout button—a link to /checkout-order.action—the order is processed and a confirmation page is displayed. The URL in the web browser stills points to checkout-order.action. This means that if the user clicks the Reload button, the order will be checked out again—not the most desirable behavior. Now, let's look at a slightly different configuration:

```
<action name="checkout-order" class="com.acme.CheckoutOrder">
    <result name="success" type="redirect">
        order-confirmation.jsp
    </result>
</action>
```

Using this configuration, when the user checks out, the final browser location is order-confirmation.jsp. This means that reloading the page won't cause the checkout action to be issued again—a much better behavior. But what if order-confirmation.jsp requires data that CheckoutOrder contains?

If the result needs data from the original action, redirection isn't much of an option: The new HTTP request will almost certainly be processed on a new thread in the servlet container, and all the state in the ActionContext (such as the value stack and the action itself) will be lost. Fortunately, there is a way to pass state across redirects. Suppose order-confirmation.jsp needs to display the confirmation number to the user. Assuming that the confirmation number is stored in a property in `CheckoutOrder` named `confirmationNumber`, you can modify the configuration as follows:

```
<action name="checkout-order" class="com.acme.CheckoutOrder">
    <result name="success" type="redirect">
        order-confirmation.jsp?confirmationNumber=
        ➡${confirmationNumber}
    </result>
</action>
```

The resulting location in the web browser is order-confirmation.jsp?confirmationNumber=123, where 123 is the confirmation number for that order. Now users can reload to their heart's content and a dynamic page will still be displayed, but orders won't be repeated.

Redirecting to another action

Suppose that the confirmation page is a bit more complex than just displaying the confirmation number. You could pass all the variables it needs through to the request the same way, but the URL could end up being very long. Another idea is to redirect to an action that takes the confirmation number as an input and then loads all the details of that order. The view for that action is a JSP that displays the confirmation screen.

To do a redirect to another action, you need to tweak your configuration only slightly. You must change the success result's location as well as add another action:

```
<action name="checkout-order" class="com.acme.CheckoutOrder">
    <result name="success" type="redirect">
        confirmation.action?confirmationNumber=
        ➡${confirmationNumber}
    </result>
</action>

<action name="confirmation" class="com.acme.Confirmation">
    <result name="success">order-confirmation.jsp</result>
</action>
```

Now the final URL is confirmation.action?confirmationNumber=123. Reloading won't cause any harm, because the confirmation action is a simple read-only action. This technique is highly recommended and can help you build many small-grained simple actions that can be loosely tied together to form complex application flows.

7.2.3 *Chaining to another action*

We just looked at a technique that allows you to build small-grained actions and then link them together by using the `redirect` result and passing the required parameter (`confirmationNumber`) through via a `GET` parameter. Sometimes you want to use fine-grained actions, but instead of redirecting between them, you'll execute one directly after another. This is called *action chaining*, and it's also a powerful technique for building complex dynamic web-based workflows using fine-grained actions.

The disadvantage of not using a redirect has already been pointed out: The browser location doesn't change, meaning a reload will cause the entire chain to be executed again. On the other hand, the advantage of action chaining is that you can easily share data between actions. This is the case because both actions are executing during the same request, meaning they share the same `ActionContext` and `OgnlValueStack`. The possibility for building detailed workflows is now wide open.

In figure 7.6, you can see how the `chain` result invokes another action, which in turn ends up at the dispatch result, bringing an end to an action chain. This diagram shows a short chain of only two actions; but depending on the granularity of your actions, you could easily have chains of five or six actions.

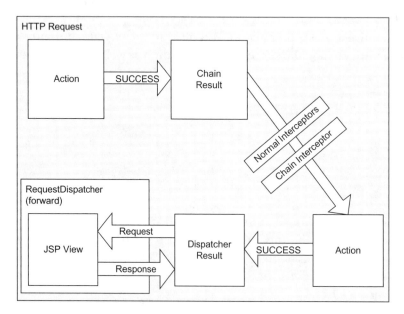

Figure 7.6 An action that chains to another action

NOTE Sometimes people think that dispatching to another action is the same as action chaining. They share some similar qualities—namely, that they execute in the same thread/request—but, they don't do exactly the same thing. An action chain executes both actions in the same action *invocation*, whereas dispatching to a second action causes two *invocations* to take place. Also, dispatching doesn't copy the parameters of the first action and set them on the second action. As a general rule, if you find yourself dispatching to another action, you probably should use action chaining.

Configuring an action chain

Like the dispatch and `redirect` results, using the `chain` result should require no or very few configuration changes as long as your action packages extend `webwork-default`. That is the case because a `chain` result is already defined in webwork-default.xml:

```
<result-type name="chain"
            class="com.opensymphony.xwork.ActionChainResult" />
```

Listing 7.6 shows how two actions might chain together to form a single request. The two actions, `Authenticate` and `Login`, might be split up because they serve different purposes and could be reused independently of each other. For example, during user registration, if the user created an account in the current session, you don't need to ask for authentication.

Listing 7.6 Two actions that chain together to form authentication and login

```
<package name="example3" extends="webwork-default">
    <action name="authenticate"
            class="examples.chap07.example3.Authenticate">
        <result name="success" type="chain">login</result>
        <result name="input">login.jsp</result>
    </action>

    <action name="login" class="examples.chap07.example3.Login">
        <result name="success">home.jsp</result>
    </action>
</package>
```

This `chain` result has two parameters: `namespace` and `actionName`. The default parameter is `actionName`, whereas the `namespace` parameter defaults to the current namespace. That is the case because more often than not, you'll find yourself chaining to actions in the same namespace; so, having to specify it all over the place would become tedious. In case you do need to chain beyond the current namespace, a complete example with two namespaces is given in listing 7.7.

Listing 7.7 Chaining between two namespaces

```xml
<package name="default" extends="webwork-default">
    <interceptors>
        <interceptor-stack name="myDefaultStack">
            <interceptor-ref name="chain"/>
            <interceptor-ref name="defaultStack"/>
        </interceptor-stack>
    </interceptors>

    <default-interceptor-ref name="myDefaultStack"/>
</package>

<package name="foo" extends="default" namespace="/foospace">
    <action name="foo" class="com.acme.Foo">
        <result name="success" type="chain">
            <param name="actionName" value="bar"/>
            <param name="namespace" value="/barspace"/>
        </result>
    </action>
</package>

<package name="bar" extends="default" namespace="/barspace">
    <action name="first-login" class="com.acme.Login">
        <result name="success">welcome.jsp</result>
    </action>
</package>
```

Unlike the other results we've looked at, the chain result requires one additional configuration element: An *interceptor* must be configured for any action that is being chained *to*. Actions that use the chain result don't need the interceptor unless they're just a link in a long chain and are therefore also an action being chained to.

As you learned in chapter 5, you can configure this interceptor on an individual basis for each action, or you can configure it for an entire package. Because this interceptor only does work when an action returns a result code that invokes a chain result, configuring it for every action is usually the simplest and easiest choice. Listings 7.7 and 7.8 show a complete xwork.xml file that demonstrates action chaining.

How action chaining works

Understanding what is going on under the hood with action chaining will enable you to maximize the full potential of this feature. The key thing to remember is that *every action executed is pushed onto the stack*. This is nothing new. In fact, this is the normal behavior you've been accustomed to. The only new aspect is that during action

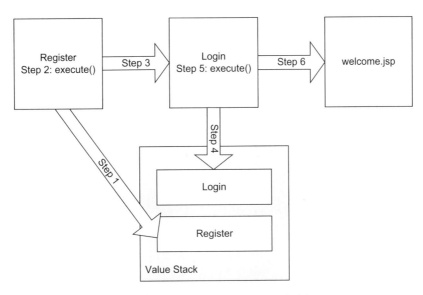

Figure 7.7 How actions are placed on the stack during chaining

chaining, multiple actions are executed, meaning that multiple actions are pushed onto the stack.

In the example in listing 7.8, the two different chains result in either welcome.jsp or home.jsp being displayed with the stack having a size of 2 and the stack configured with `Login` on top and `Register` or `Authenticate` on the bottom, respectively. An expression that requests a property that both actions have will result in the `Login` (top) action being used to retrieve the property value. Figure 7.7 illustrates the order in which actions are executed and placed in the value stack. Notice that the actions are first placed in the stack and then executed.

Listing 7.8 Login and registration configuration showing action chaining and reuse

```
<package name="default" extends="webwork-default">
    <interceptors>
        <interceptor-stack name="myDefaultStack">
            <interceptor-ref name="chain"/>
            <interceptor-ref name="defaultStack"/>
        </interceptor-stack>
    </interceptors>

    <default-interceptor-ref name="myDefaultStack"/>

    <action name="authenticate" class="com.acme.Authenticate">
        <result name="success" type="chain">login</result>
```

```
        <result name="input">login.jsp</result>
    </action>

    <action name="login" class="com.acme.Login">
        <result name="success">home.jsp</result>
    </action>
    <action name="register" class="com.acme.Register">
        <result name="success" type="chain">first-login</result>
        <result name="input">register.jsp</result>
    </action>
    <action name="first-login" class="com.acme.Login">
        <result name="success">welcome.jsp</result>
    </action>
</package>
```

To see how expressions are evaluated, look at figure 7.8. Note that the value for X is different in the first action and the second. As long as you're using the chain interceptor, as shown in listing 7.8 and illustrated in figure 7.6, all common values among actions in a chain are set to be the same. The only way for the values to differ is if the action modifies those values during execution. In figure 7.7, assume that the Login action also modifies the value of X by adding 3 to it. This means that when the Login action starts, the value is 1; but when it's finished and welcome.jsp begins to render, the value is now 4.

The chain interceptor works by copying common values from every object on the stack (all the previous actions in the chain) to the most recent action in the chain. The means that common properties between all actions in the chain, not just the contiguous ones, are copied. To use the login and registration example

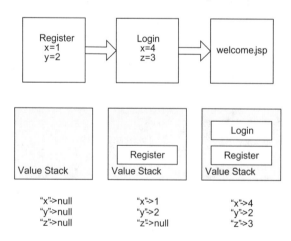

Figure 7.8
An illustration of how expressions evaluate to different values during the course of chaining

you've seen, this would be useful to pass around a `username` property among all the actions.

7.3 Other results

The three results you've seen so far—`dispatcher`, `redirect`, and `chain`—are the most common. But that doesn't mean they're the only results WebWork supports. Three other useful results also ship with WebWork. Two of these results are for template languages that can be used as an alternative to the heavier-weight JSP pages you've seen up until now. The other result is used to build reports in various formats, such as PDF and Excel.

7.3.1 Streaming Velocity templates directly to the output

Many developers feel that JSP is too heavy for their tastes. The ability to write *scriptlets* (essentially, Java code embedded in the JSP) is often a big turn-off. Although scriptlets are seen as a feature by some, advanced Java developers know that scriptlets always result in poorly designed code, especially when less experienced programmers use them. A few reasons often cited for using Velocity instead of JSP are as follows:

- Velocity is much faster than JSP in most servlet containers. Only the fastest servlet containers, such as Orion and Resin, can serve JSPs as fast as the Velocity templating engine can render Velocity templates.

- Scriptlets lead to a "code smell"—that is, if you give developers the option to write Java code in their pages, odds are they will use it when in a crunch, which is almost always considered a bad thing.

- Because Velocity has a simpler format (no angled brackets), it tends to integrate better with existing tools such as XML editors and HTML editors.

  NOTE　Because Velocity is a core part of WebWork (all the form tags are built using Velocity templates), chapter 10 is devoted to helping you understand the basics of Velocity. This section is here to help you understand the `velocity` result itself. Chapter 10 will bring you up to speed on the Velocity language before we begin to look at the form tags in chapter 11.

Velocity is part of the Apache Jakarta project and is released under the Apache license. You can find it freely available at http://jakarta.apache.org/velocity. Velocity currently comes included with WebWork versions 2.0 and 2.1; but in the future it may become optional, meaning that you'll need to download it and include it in your project's classpath to be able to utilize the Velocity features included with WebWork.

Velocity means speed

Recall that until now, we've been talking about `RequestDispatchers` (dispatcher result) and redirects as the two ways to render content to the browser. The `velocity` result introduces a new technique for rendering content: streaming the content directly to the response, *without* a need for an expensive `RequestDispatcher`. Figure 7.9 shows how a Velocity template is streamed directly to the HTTP response without the need for any of the overhead that the `dispatcher` result incurs or a more restrictive redirect.

One of Velocity's other speed improvements isn't in the form of execution speed but rather in compilation time. Unlike JSP, which must be compiled into Java and then into a .class file, Velocity is parsed and ready to be executed much more quickly (milliseconds instead of seconds). Although this difference may seem minor, when you're developing web applications, waiting one or two seconds after every change can become frustrating. Velocity helps with that aggravation.

Velocity for components, JSP for pages

`RequestDispatchers` are *expensive.* Of course, the magnitude of cost is different on each application server, but it's significant even on the fastest servers. This cost may not be noticeable if you're using a Front-controller style design (where there is one action and one page being rendered). It's much more noticeable if you're using a Page-controller style, where you've embedded many actions (and sub-pages, or views) in your main page.

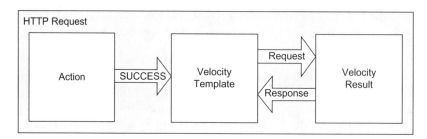

Figure 7.9   The `velocity` result streams output directly back to the browser without the need for a dispatcher.

NOTE   J2EE application servers have become much better recently, and the overhead of `RequestDispatchers` mentioned in this chapter is no longer as large as it used to be. However, the simplified code path, represented in figure 7.9, is much nicer to work with than that seen at the start of this chapter in figure 7.1.

Suppose you're building an application that includes portal-like behavior—including 20 or so components nested on a single page. The cost of 20 `Request-Dispatchers` would cripple the performance of your application. Instead, it's recommended that you make each of those embedded components use Velocity as the view technology. You can still use JSP for the view of the main page, meaning that one `RequestDispatcher` may still be occurring.

WebWork developers often use this technique: Velocity for embedded components, and JSP for pages that include those components. It's a balance between speed and familiarity. Of course, some prefer Velocity so much that they use it for everything, which makes their applications that much faster.

Configuring the velocity result

Just like with the other results you've seen, the `velocity` result is preconfigured as long as you include webwork-default.xml and extend the webwork-default package in xwork.xml. The name of the result is `velocity`. The result-type is configured in the `webwork-default` package as follows:

```
<result-type name="velocity"
            class="com.opensymphony.webwork.dispatcher.
         ➥VelocityResult" />
```

If you want to use Velocity as your primary view technology, you may wish to redefine the `velocity` result such that it's the default result instead of the `dispatcher` result. Chapter 10 includes much more information about various configuration elements that are specific to Velocity when used with WebWork.

The `velocity` result supports the same parameters that the `dispatcher` and `redirect` results support. That is, it supports the `location` parameter (default) as well as the `parse` parameter.

An example using Velocity

Now that you know what Velocity is, why it's useful, and how to configure it, let's look at a simple Velocity-based view. Given the action in listing 7.9 and the configuration in listing 7.10, listing 7.11 shows what the contents of the template would be if you wished to print out a member directory.

Listing 7.9   An action that retrieves a list of members

```java
package examples.chap07.example4;

import com.opensymphony.xwork.ActionSupport;

import java.util.List;
import java.util.ArrayList;

public class ListMembers extends ActionSupport
    implements MemberDAOAware {

    MemberDAO memberDAO;
    List members;

    public void setMemberDAO(MemberDAO memberDAO) {
        this.memberDAO = memberDAO;
    }

    public String execute() throws Exception {
        members = memberDAO.getAllMembers();

        return SUCCESS;
    }

    public List getMembers() {
        return members;
    }
}

public class Member {
    String email;
    String firstName;
    String lastName;

    public Member(String email, String firstName, String lastName) {
        this.email = email;
        this.firstName = firstName;
        this.lastName = lastName;
    }

    // getters and setters
    ...
}
```

This action delegates to an IoC component (see chapter 6) to retrieve all the members in the application. This is nice abstraction, and it also happens to make this example stay to the point. The members in the list are of type `Member`, which have bean properties for `firstName`, `lastName`, and `email`. This is the information you will display in your page.

```
<package name="example4" extends="webwork-default">
    <action name="list-members-vm"
            class="examples.chap07.example4.ListMembers">
        <result name="success" type="velocity">
            list-members.vm
        </result>
    </action>
</package>
```

This configuration maps a single action, `list-members-vm`, to a `velocity` result, using the file list-members.vm. Note that the type is `velocity`. Without this, the `dispatcher` result would be used instead, possibly causing undesired behavior.

```
<html>
    <head>
        <title>Members</title>
    </head>
    <body>

        <h1>Member Directory</h1>
        <hr/>

        #foreach ($member in $members)
            <li>$member.email -
                $member.firstName $member.lastName</li>
        #end

    </body>
</html>
```

The template you use to display the member directory is extremely simple. It's a combination of HTML, *directives*, and *variables*. Directives start with #, and variables start with $. (In chapter 10, you'll get a crash-course on Velocity and learn about all the other types of directives and variables available to you.) The key thing to note here is that $members is a variable referencing the members property in your action.

7.3.2 *FreeMarker: an alternative to Velocity*

Velocity isn't the only template engine on the block. Another popular choice is FreeMarker. Whereas Velocity strives to be strictly a template engine with no bells and whistles, FreeMarker provides many more features, such as the ability to use any JSP tag library. We'll take a brief look at a result that uses FreeMarker. If you'd like to learn more, the FreeMarker website has excellent documentation.

> **NOTE** *FreeMarker* is freely available at http://www.freemarker.org. WebWork currently provides optional support for FreeMarker, meaning that it doesn't ship with the required FreeMarker libraries. To use FreeMarker, you must download the library and include it in your classpath.
>
> *Velocity* doesn't support JSP tag libraries natively, but WebWork adds support for them as an extra feature that is specific to WebWork only.

Configuring the freemarker result

As you might have guessed, the FreeMarker result is also preconfigured as long as you include webwork-default.xml and extend the `webwork-default` package in xwork.xml. The name of the result is `freemarker`. The result-type is configured in the webwork-default package as follows:

```
<result-type name="freemarker"
              class="com.opensymphony.webwork.views.freemarker.
              ➥FreemarkerResult" />
```

You also need the optional FreeMarker libraries in your classpath in order to be able to use this result. Consult chapter 3, "Setting up WebWork," for a complete list of the required and optional dependencies for WebWork, including the JAR files necessary to use FreeMarker.

The `freemarker` result supports the same parameters as the `dispatcher`, `redirect`, and `velocity` results. That is, it supports the `location` parameter (default) as well as the `parse` parameter. In addition, it supports a `contentType` parameter that you can use to set the resulting content-type. This is useful if you'd like to output something other than `text/html`, such as a CSV file, plain text, or XML.

An example using FreeMarker

Listing 7.12 shows a very simple example of FreeMarker, which re-implements the Velocity example from listing 7.11. As you can see, it's similar to the Velocity example. The key differences is that *directives* are in the form of `<#directive>` ... `</#directive>` rather than Velocity's `#directive` ... `#end`. The other difference is that complex expressions, such as `member.firstName`, must be referenced using `${member.firstName}`, as opposed to Velocity's `$member.firstName`.

Listing 7.12 list-members.ftl, a FreeMarker template to display a member directory

```
<html>
    <head>
        <title>Members</title>
    </head>
    <body>

        <h1>Member Directory</h1>
        <hr/>

        <#list members as member>
            <li>${member.email} –
                ${member.firstName} ${member.lastName}</li>
        </#list>

    </body>
</html>
```

In this example, Velocity and FreeMarker share more in common than they differ. However, if you examine either template language in depth, you'll find unique characteristics for both projects. Depending on your needs and development style, one may be more suitable than the other. Fortunately, WebWork supports both. Switching from Velocity to FreeMarker (or vice versa) is trivially easy to do, in terms of both code and in configuration, as shown in listing 7.13.

Listing 7.13 Configuration for the member directory action and `freemarker` result

```
<package name="example5" extends="webwork-default">
    <action name="list-members-ftl"
            class="examples.chap07.example4.ListMembers">
        <result name="success" type="freemarker">
            list-members.ftl
        </result>
    </action>
</package>
```

Now let's look at a result supported natively by WebWork that lets you generate reports in many different formats.

7.3.3 Generating reports with JasperReports

Sometimes, you don't want to display a web page as the result of an action, but rather a PDF or Excel report. Fortunately, libraries are available that can help you create these types of graphics and reports. One such library is called JasperReports. Let's examine how a single report originally built using a JSP can be rendered in both HTML and PDF using this library.

NOTE   *JasperReports* is freely available under the LGPL license at http://jasperreports.sourceforge.net/. Because WebWork provides optional integration with JasperReports, it isn't included with the normal WebWork distribution; you'll need to download JasperReports separately.

Configuring the jasper result

Once again, the JasperReports result is preconfigured as long as you include webwork-default.xml and extend the webwork-default package in xwork.xml. The name of the result is `jasper`. The result-type is configured in the webwork-default package as follows:

```
<result-type name="jasper"
              class="com.opensymphony.webwork.views.jasperreports.
              ➥JasperReportsResult" />
```

You also need the optional JasperReports libraries in your classpath in order to be able to use this result. See chapter 3 for a complete list of the required and optional dependencies for WebWork, including the JAR files necessary to use JasperReports.

The `jasper` result supports the same parameters as the `dispatcher`, `redirect`, and `velocity` results: `location` and `parse`. In addition, it supports a `dataSource` parameter that indicates the property of the action that will be used to populate the results. A `format` parameter species what format the report should be generated in. Valid formats are PDF, HTML, XML, CSV (comma-separated value), and XLS (Excel). There is no default parameter, because the `jasper` result requires at a minimum that the `dataSource` and `location` parameters be specified.

In addition to the result configuration, the `jasper` result requires that a special 1 pixel by 1 pixel image be located in your web application at /images/px (note that there is no extension). This image is required for HTML reports and is used as a spacer. You can find this image included with the WebWork examples in the distribution.

An example: from JSP to JasperReports

Using the same member directory example you first saw when we introduced Velocity, let's write a JSP that displays an HTML table listing all the members' email addresses in your application along with their first and last names. The JSP is shown in listing 7.14.

Listing 7.14 A simple JSP result that displays users

```
<%@ taglib uri="webwork" prefix="ww" %>
<html>
    <head>
        <title>Members</title>
    </head>
    <body>
        <table border="1">
            <tr>
                <th>Username</th>
                <th>First Name</th>
                <th>Last Name</th>
            </tr>
        <ww:iterator value="members">
            <tr>
                <td><ww:property value="email"/></td>
                <td><ww:property value="firstName"/></td>
                <td><ww:property value="lastName"/></td>
            </tr>
        </ww:iterator>
        </table>
    </body>
</html>
```

Now suppose that management needs this report in several formats: PDF (for printing), HTML (for the Web), and Excel (for data manipulation). Rather than write an action and/or servlet for each different format, you can let JasperReports do all this work for you.

The first step is to set up a report definition file in XML. We won't go into detail about how these definition files are created—you can learn about them on the JasperReports website, which includes very good documentation. The report in listing 7.15 defines a simple table with rows 20 pixels high and columns 100 pixels wide.

Listing 7.15 A simple JasperReports definition

```
<?xml version="1.0"?>
<!DOCTYPE jasperReport PUBLIC
"-//JasperReports//DTD Report Design//EN" "http://
➥jasperreports.sourceforge.net/dtds/jasperreport.dtd">

<jasperReport name="members">
    <field name="email" class="java.lang.String">
        <fieldDescription>email</fieldDescription>
    </field>
```

```
<field name="firstName" class="java.lang.String">
    <fieldDescription>firstName</fieldDescription>
</field>
<field name="lastName" class="java.lang.String">
    <fieldDescription>lastName</fieldDescription>
</field>
<detail>
    <band height="20">
        <textField>
            <reportElement x="0" y="3" width="100" height="15"/>
            <textFieldExpression>$F{email}</textFieldExpression>
        </textField>
        <textField>
            <reportElement x="100" y="3" width="100"
                           height="15"/>
            <textFieldExpression>
                $F{firstName}
            </textFieldExpression>
        </textField>
        <textField>
            <reportElement x="200" y="3" width="100"
                           height="15"/>
            <textFieldExpression>
                $F{lastName}
            </textFieldExpression>
        </textField>
    </band>
</detail>
</jasperReport>
```

Next you need to compile the report. You can do so by using the class `com.open-symphony.webwork.views.jasperreports.CompileReport`. You'll need to run this class with webwork-2.0.jar and jasperreports.jar in the classpath. You must pass the XML definition file in as a program argument as well. This produces a members.jasper output file, which will be used to generate reports in PDF, Excel, HTML, CSV, and XML.

Listing 7.16 shows the configuration for the same action using three different results:

- A JSP-based HTML result, as shown in listing 7.14
- A JasperReports-based HTML result
- A JasperReports-based PDF result

Listing 7.16 Configuration showing JasperReports results and normal results for the same action

```
<package name="example6" extends="webwork-default">
    <action name="list-members-jsp"
            ⇒class="examples.chap07.example4.ListMembers">
        <result name="success">list-members.jsp</result>
    </action>

    <action name="list-members-pdf"
            ⇒class="examples.chap07.example4.ListMembers">
        <result name="success" type="jasper">
            <param name="location">members.jasper</param>
            <param name="dataSource">members</param>
            <param name="format">PDF</param>
        </result>
    </action>

    <action name="list-members-html"
            ⇒class="examples.chap07.example4.ListMembers">
        <result name="success" type="jasper">
            <param name="location">members.jasper</param>
            <param name="dataSource">members</param>
            <param name="format">HTML</param>
        </result>
    </action>
</package>
```

As you can see, the same action can be used for all three very different results. By changing the format parameter from PDF to HTML, you can display the same report in either format. With a bit more effort, you can easily create a beautiful report in multiple formats.

7.4 Summary

In this chapter, we looked at a variety of topics. The two most important concepts presented are pluggable result types and how redirects, chaining, and dispatching affect the workflow of your web application. When you're building complex web-based workflows, understanding the strengths and weaknesses of redirects, action chains, and dispatchers is extremely important. Generally, you can follow these rules of thumb:

- Dispatchers are good for serving JSP content but typically nothing else.

- Use the Velocity or FreeMarker result type when you're serving the respective templates, even if a dispatcher works.

- Action chaining is good when you have modular actions that you wish to combine to form unique behavior—but don't overuse it!

- Redirects should be used when the workflow is *finished* and you wish to send the user to a landing spot where clicking Reload won't cause the workflow to be re-executed.

In addition to these rules, knowing what view technology (JSP, Velocity, FreeMarker, JasperReports) to use is important. As you saw in the examples, switching between results isn't difficult if you're careful to keep the coupling between your view and your action very loose. We recommend that you do this not only to allow yourself room for change in the future, but also because loose coupling between views and actions tends to promote good, modular template design. We'll explore this type of modular design further in chapter 11, when we look at the UI components WebWork offers.

Getting data with the expression language

This chapter covers

- Accessing data in your actions
- Showing how the value stack interacts with WebWork's expression language
- Accessing elements in Maps and Lists
- Dynamically creating Maps and Lists expression scripts

A key feature of WebWork is that it provides read and write access to the data prepared by your actions. This is done through an *expression language*—a scripting language that allows for simple and concise access to JavaBeans, collections, and method calls. In this chapter, we'll explore all the power (and simplicity) that is offered by WebWork's expression language. At the end of this chapter we'll provide a quick reference table that will outline all the expression language features learned here.

In this chapter, we'll take a break from using examples from CaveatEmptor and add a little fun by replacing the mundane object User with a Muppet. But don't despair—both objects are very similar, and the lessons learned while working with Muppets can be applied when you go back to working with Users. Both have common properties like firstName, lastName, and age. And when you're using a loose-coupling technology like an expression language, the typing of the object matters much less than the properties that are available on that object. Let's start by defining an expression language.

8.1 What is an expression language?

Before we dig in to WebWork's expression language (EL), let's explore what an expression language is in general. We'll look at what constitutes an EL, and then we'll discuss why WebWork's EL—Object Graph Navigation Language (OGNL)—is the best choice for web page scripting. Finally, we'll take a quick look at other common expression languages, many of which can also be used in WebWork.

8.1.1 Why an expression language?

Expression languages are by their nature designed to help you write simple expressions that perform common tasks. Usually, ELs are included with particular frameworks with the intent to make your life easier. For example, the Hibernate project includes a special EL called Hibernate Query Language (HQL) that acts as a buffer between you and complex SQL statements.

In web frameworks, expression languages have similar goals. They exist to eliminate the repetitive code that you might otherwise write if you didn't have an EL. For example, without an EL, the act of getting a shopping cart from the session and then displaying its ID on the web page requires a few lines of Java code in a JSP:

```
<%
    ShoppingCart cart = (ShoppingCart) session.get("cart");
    int id = cart.getId();
%>
<%= id %>
```

You can condense the code down to a single line, as follows, but now the code looks ugly and is hard to read. In addition, the same parts of the original statements are still required, such as casting to `ShoppingCart`—you've moved three statements to a single statement, but the complexity remains the same:

```
<%= ((ShoppingCart) session.get("cart")).getId() %>
```

An expression language for a web framework buffers you from this kind of complexity. Rather than require you to use the Servlet APIs, cast an object, and then call a getter method, most ELs simplify this down to a much more readable expression similar to `#session.cart.id`.

The expression `#session.cart.id` has all the same keys, variables, and getters as the Java code. What it lacks, however, is all the Java language overheads such as calls to `get()` methods and casting. Because these kinds of operations are so common, using an EL makes perfect sense. You can use a much more loosely typed and dynamic language to act as a buffer between you and that nasty Java code you'd have to write otherwise.

8.1.2 Why OGNL?

If all ELs are designed to reduce the amount of tedious code you write, why is one better than another? *Better* is a subjective word, but some rational choice is involved in the decision of choosing an expression language. The key is to make an outline regarding the context in which the EL will be used. In the web environment, particularly programs built on the Servlet and JSP specifications, you can make the following assertions and conclusions:

- *Assertion*: All request parameters are type-agnostic, meaning they come in as `String`s or `String` arrays.

  Conclusion: There is a strong need to convert from `String`s and `String` arrays to other data types, such as `int`s, `boolean`s, `date`s, and possibly many others.

- *Assertion*: Because HTML doesn't do internationalization when displaying content, values must be converted to the correct localized `String` on the server side.

  Conclusion: The need to convert to a `String` is just as strong as the need to convert from `String`s.

- *Assertion*: During the course of a typical session on a web application, a piece of data may be converted many times back and forth between `String` and its native data type, such as 17 -> "17" -> 17.

Conclusion: The Web is a loosely typed platform, and some code must act as the buffer between it and a much more strictly typed Java platform.

- *Assertion*: Often you take a large, complex object such as a `Person` and wish to display parts of it, such as `first name` and `last name`, in multiple and different places on a single web page.

Conclusion: Accessing parts of an object in a granular manner is important.

You could derive many other assertions and conclusions; these are just a few of those that came into play when the WebWork developers choose WebWork's expression language: Object Graph Navigation Language (OGNL) (available for download at http://www.opensymphony.com/ognl). OGNL goes beyond "just" an expression language by providing many advanced but necessary features, particularly in the area of type conversion. As you'll learn later in this chapter (as well as in chapter 12, "Type conversion"), OGNL is a natural fit to act as a buffer between a loosely typed world (HTTP) and a strictly typed one (Java).

> **WARNING** OGNL also provides advanced expression features such as static or instance method execution, projection across collections, and dynamic lambda expression definition, so you never need to write Java code in your view. The hope is, however, that these advanced features won't be necessary very often. Although most developers claim that there should never be Java code in your JSPs, they generally mean that the JSPs shouldn't be complex. Switching from Java to scripting language *X* doesn't usually simplify much. In fact, it most likely complicates the situation, because the Java language is the most comfortable language for most JSP developers. Features such as lambda expressions are nice, but introducing them too often will have the same result as coding Java directly in your view layer. However, sometimes these advanced features come in handy, so we'll discuss them in this chapter.

8.1.3 *Other expression languages*

OGNL isn't the only kid on the block. In fact, there are more expression languages and scripting languages than we care to count. We'll quickly outline a few of the popular ones that could potentially work with WebWork:

- JSTL—Independently developed in the Java Community Process, JSP Standard Tag Library (JSTL) has since been integrated into JSP 2.0 as the standard scripting and expression language for JSP. Some WebWork users prefer JSTL because it's a standard. Using JSTL with WebWork involves almost no work. You can find out how to do so by consulting the WebWork documentation.

- *Groovy*—A fairly recent player in the space, Groovy builds on the Java syntax and adds a dash of Ruby. The end result is a loosely typed language that offers a lot of functionality with minimal typing. Groovy has been integrated into the Web (in a form called a Groovlet, similar to a JSP), and it isn't difficult to picture Groovy being used as a potential view for WebWork in the future.

- *Velocity*—Although Velocity isn't exactly an expression language, the syntax for writing Velocity templates is very similar to OGNL and other ELs. People who use Velocity as their view rarely need to use OGNL.

NOTE   Even if you use another EL, such as JSTL, OGNL will still be used for all the type-conversion functionality—a core feature in WebWork. Some ELs, such as JSTL, integrate with WebWork almost seamlessly. Other scripting languages, such as Groovy, may require creating your own result. Consult chapter 7, "Using results," as well as the documentation for the scripting language if you wish to use one of these other languages as the view technology.

8.1.4 Key OGNL concepts

Everything in OGNL is centralized around a *context* that contains one or more Java-Beans from which you evaluate your expressions. One of those JavaBeans is special because it's considered to be the *root* of the context. An object that is the root is assumed to be the object your expressions are concerned with if no other object from the context is specified.

What does this mean to you? Not much right now; but shortly we'll look at the concepts of the value stack and the related `ActionContext` and see how they related to these key concepts. In the meantime, know that when we give examples in this chapter, we'll indicate what the context contains as well as what object in the context is configured to be the root.

Now, let's explore some code samples using OGNL.

8.2 Basic expression language features

WebWork lets you write powerful expressions, but its greatest advantage is in the simplicity of basic features such as accessing bean properties and calling methods. Let's look at some examples of these basic features so you can get accustomed to OGNL as a language. After that, we'll examine intermediate and advanced features offered by OGNL and WebWork, all of which will help you write cleaner, simpler, more focused web applications.

8.2.1 *Accessing bean properties*

By far the most common expression you'll use in WebWork accesses bean properties. Accessing bean properties occurs whenever you want to get data from an action or set data on an action. Right off the bat in chapter 2, "HelloWorld, the WebWork way," you saw examples of accessing bean properties, and you've continued to see suggestions of it until this point. We'll now formally explain what is going on.

According to the JavaBeans specification, bean properties are a getter method and/or a setter method using a standard format such as getXxx(), setXxx(), isXxx(), or hasXxx(). The isXxx() and hasXxx() formats are used for boolean properties and are only provided to make the code more readable. In WebWork, accessing those properties (either setting or getting data) involves referencing the property as xxx. This probably isn't new to you, considering that we've been hinting about it throughout the book.

Let's look at a few simple examples that access a property from the root object. Suppose the context contains one object, Muppet, which is also set as the root (we won't concern ourselves with nonroot objects for the time being). Muppet is a class with a few properties, as indicated in listing 8.1.

> **Listing 8.1 Sample class Muppet, which is used to demonstrate expression language features**

```
package examples.chap08;

import java.util.List;
import java.util.Set;
import java.util.Map;

public class Muppet {
    public static final String OG_MUPPET = "Kermit";

    public static Muppet getOgMuppet() {
        Muppet og = new Muppet();
        og.setName(OG_MUPPET);
        return og;
    }

    private String name;
    private int age;
    private boolean lifesized;
    private Muppet father;
    private Muppet mother;
    private List children;
    private Set foods;
```

```
        private Map favorites;

        public int avgParentsAge() {
            return ((father.getAge() + mother.getAge()) / 2);
        }

        // getters and setters
        ...
    }
```

We'll use the `Muppet` class for all the examples in this chapter; as such, it contains many different types of properties and methods. Let's start with the simplest properties: `name` and `age`. The expression for accessing the values of these properties is as simple as the property names themselves. The expressions `name` and `age` retrieve the name and age of the muppet, respectively.

It's possible (and common) to chain properties together in order to navigate deep into the object graph. For example, the expression `father.age` retrieves the muppet's father's age. Likewise, `father.mother.age` gets the muppet's grandmother's age (on the father's side). This is equivalent to calling `muppet.getFather().getMother().getAge()` on the `Muppet` object. Table 8.1 contains some sample Java code snippets and compares them to their OGNL equivalents.

Table 8.1 Comparison of Java code and OGNL expressions for accessing bean properties

Java code	OGNL expression (Muppet is the root)
`muppet.getName()`	`name`
`muppet.getMother().getName()`	`mother.name`
`muppet.getFather().getFather().getAge()`	`father.father.age`

8.2.2 *Literals and operators*

Accessing data isn't useful if you can't do things to it. Fortunately, OGNL supports the same literals and mathematical operations found in Java. Table 8.2 lists the literals supported by OGNL and gives examples of their usage.

Notice that `String` literals in OGNL can be surrounded by either single or double quotes. This is designed to make embedding OGNL easier in languages like XML and JSP. Because characters are also identified by single quotes, `Strings` are only identified using single quotes when the `String` is more than one character. If you need to make a `String` literal that is one character long, you must use double

Table 8.2 All the literals supported by OGNL

Literal type	Example
char	'a'
String	'hello world' "hello world"
Boolean	true false
int	123
double	123.5
BigDecimal	123b
BigInteger	123h

quotes. If you're doing this in JSP, you'll most likely need to escape your double quotes, as shown here:

```
<ww:property value="\"a\""/>
is not the same as
<ww:property value="'a'"/>
```

In addition to literals, OGNL lets you use all the Java operations, such as addition (+) and division (/). Table 8.3 contains all the expressions that OGNL supports as well as an example of each one in use.

Table 8.3 Operators supported by OGNL

Operation	Example
add (+)	2 + 4 'hello' + 'world'
subtract (-)	5 - 3
multiply (*)	8 * 2
divide (/)	9 / 3
modulus (mod)	9 mod 2
increment (++)	++foo foo++
decrement (--)	bar-- --bar
equality (==)	foo == bar

Table 8.3 Operators supported by OGNL *(continued)*

Operation	Example
inequality (!=)	foo != bar
in	foo in someList
not in	foo not in someList
assignment (=)	foo = 123

8.2.3 *Calling methods*

Even though accessing properties is technically making method calls, OGNL also supports the ability to call any method. It does so because not all methods are in the form of getXxx(); sometimes you need to call non-property methods. The Muppet class includes an avgParentsAge() method that you might want to call; you can do so by evaluating the expression avgParentsAge().

You can also combine property expressions and method call expressions. For example, mother.avgParentsAge() evaluates to the average age of the muppet's grandparents' ages (on the mother's side). Table 8.4 contains sample expressions compared to their Java counterparts.

Table 8.4 Sample method and property OGNL expressions compared to their Java equivalents

Java code	OGNL expression (Muppet is the root)
muppet.avgParentsAge()	avgParentsAge()
muppet.avgParentsAge()—muppet.getAge()	avgParentsAge() - age
(muppet.getMother().getAge() + muppet.getFather().getAge()) / 2	(mother.age + father.age) / 2
muppet.getMother().getAge()	getMother().age or mother.getAge() or mother.age

NOTE For security reasons, method calls (nonstatic and static alike) aren't allowed during the part of the WebWork request lifecycle where POST and GET parameters are applied to your action (when the ParametersInterceptor is applied, as explained in chapter 5, "Adding functionality with interceptors"). Without this restriction, there would be no stopping an attacker from executing System.exit(0) or even more damaging code by submitting a request that includes a specially formatted parameter name.

8.2.4 Setting values and expression lists

OGNL lets you execute multiple expressions in a single statement by separating your expressions with a comma. The last expression is returned as the output of the entire statement. For example, if `foo` evaluates to 123 and `bar` evaluates to 789, then `foo, bar` calls both `getFoo()` and `getBar()`, but only 789 is returned.

Generally, you'll never need to do this. However, it will be necessary on a few occasions. For example, if you want to set the ages of Kermit's parents and then display their average age, you can do this: `father.age = 27, mother.age = 25,_avgParentsAge()`. The return value is the average age, 26.

8.2.5 Accessing static methods and fields

OGNL supports accessing static properties as well as static methods. In OGNL, you can call static fields and methods by using the notation `@[ClassName]@[FieldOr-Method]`. The class name must be referenced with the complete package, as well:

```
@examples.chap8.Muppet@OG_MUPPET
@examples.chap8.Muppet@getOgMuppet()
```

In addition to using the standard OGNL format for calling statics, WebWork lets you avoid having to specify the full package name and call static properties and methods of classes in the value stack using the `vs` prefix (where *vs* stands for Value Stack). Instead of `examples.chap8.Muppet`, you can use `vs` to tell WebWork to use the class of the object on the top of the stack:

```
@vs@OG_MUPPET
@vs@getOgMuppet()
```

You can also specify a number after `vs`, such as `vs1`, to indicate a selection of an object deeper in the stack. This is similar to the way accessing the value stack works, as we'll discuss in section 8.4.1. In general, using the `vs` notation is only good if you know what will be on the stack at all times. Otherwise, it's better to use the complete package and class name—especially because most modern refactoring tools know to rename `examples.chap8.Muppet` to `examples.chap9.Muppet` if you move the package, but they won't know that the `Muppet` object is now deeper in the stack and `vs` needs to be renamed `vs1`.

8.2.6 Accessing the OGNL context and the ActionContext

So far, you've only worked with the root object: `Muppet`. However, OGNL lets you access any element in its context map, called the `OgnlContext`. WebWork also has its own context called the `ActionContext`. One of the many ways WebWork is integrated with OGNL is that the two contexts, `OgnlContext` and `ActionContext`, are the same thing.

Many objects are often found in the `ActionContext`. Because these two contexts are the same, you can access those objects using OGNL's standard contextual access notation: the pound sign (#). Let's see how you might get access to some of those objects stored in the context. Table 8.5 provides a few examples using features of OGNL you've learned about thus far.

Table 8.5 Examples that access the `ActionContext` using OGNL

Java code	OGNL expression
`ActionContext().getContext().getParameters()`	`#parameters`
`ActionContext().getContext().getParameters().size()`	`#parameters.size`
`((Kermit) ActionContext.getContext().get("kermit")).getAge()`	`#kermit.age`

Many of the items in the `ActionContext` are identified by long and unique keys. For example, the key that is used to store the `HttpServletRequest` is `com.opensymphony.webwork.dispatcher.HttpServletRequest`. Obviously, you don't want to type that when you're using an otherwise simple expression language. To help you, WebWork identifies a few of the items in the context and aliases them with shorter identifiers:

- `Parameters`—A `Map` that contains all the `HttpServletRequest` *parameters* for the current request
- `Request`—A `Map` that contains all the `HttpServletRequest` *attributes* for the current request
- `Session`—A `Map` that contains all the `HttpSession` attributes for the current session
- `Application`—A `Map` that contains all the `ServletConfig` attributes for the current application
- `Attr`—A special `Map` that searches for attributes from the request, session, and application maps (in that order)

In the next section, you'll learn how to access collections, including `java.util.Map`, so that you can begin to get data from these five elements if you wish to.

8.3 *Working with collections*

One of OGNL's primary features as compared to other expression languages is its very good support for the Java Collections API. Creating and working with collections, lists, and maps is a fundamental feature in OGNL. We'll look at ways to dynamically access and create new collections as well as how you can filter and project based on their contents.

8.3.1 *Working with lists and arrays*

In OGNL, lists and arrays are generally treated the same. Thus *offset notation* that is normally reserved for arrays is also used to access list elements. Table 8.6 demonstrates some simple examples using array notation to work with lists and arrays.

Table 8.6   Examples of array and list notation

Java code	OGNL expression
`list.get(0)`	`list[0]`
`array[0]`	`array[0]`
`((Muppet) list.get(0)).getName();`	`list[0].name`
`array.length`	`array.legnth`
`list.size()`	`list.size`
`list.isEmpty()`	`list.isEmpty`

In addition to accessing the values of lists, OGNL lets you construct lists dynamically using curly braces with the elements inside separated by commas. Table 8.7 demonstrates how you can use a simple notation to quickly create lists. These lists (and maps, as you'll see shortly) are useful for presenting small pieces of data to a user or looping over a known set of items.

Table 8.7   Examples of constructing lists in the simplified notation

Java code	OGNL expression

`List list = new ArrayList(3);`
`list.add(new Integer(1));`
`list.add(new Integer(3));`
`list.add(new Integer(5));`
`return list;`
	`{1, 3, 5}`

Table 8.7 Examples of constructing lists in the simplified notation *(continued)*

Java code	OGNL expression

`List list = new ArrayList(2);`
`list.add("foo");`
`list.add("bar");`
`return list.get(1);`
	`{"foo", "bar"}[1]`

8.3.2 *Working with maps*

Maps are similar to lists, but instead of only being able to access elements by a numbered index, you can access elements with any object key. Their syntax for element access, however, is virtually identical. In the situation where primitives are used as keys, OGNL does *autoboxing* for you—this means it automatically converts a primitive `int` into an `Integer` object or a `boolean` into a `Boolean` object. Table 8.8 demonstrates how you can access maps as well as how OGNL automatically takes care of converting types for you, such as 1 (`int`) to 1 (`Integer`).

Table 8.8 Examples of map notation

Java code	OGNL expression
`map.get("foo")`	`map['foo']`
`map.get(new Integer(1))`	`map[1]`

`Muppet muppet = (Muppet)`
`map.get("Kermit");`
`return muppet.getAge();`
	`map['kermit'].age`

`map.put("foo", "bar");`	`map['foo'] = 'bar'`
`map.size()`	`map.size`
`map.isEmpty()`	`map.isEmpty`

As with lists, you can create maps dynamically. The syntax for doing so is slightly different: You must place a pound sign (#) before the opening curly brace. Table 8.9 contains a few examples of creating maps dynamically.

NOTE Chapter 11, "UI components," covers UI tags. Dynamic maps are especially useful for radio groups and select tags. For example, if you wanted to offer a true/false selection that displays as a Yes/No choice, `#{true : 'Yes', false : 'No'}` would be the value for the `list` attribute. The value for the `value` attribute would evaluate to either true or false.

Table 8.9 Creating maps dynamically

Java code	OGNL expression

```Map map = new HashMap(2);```
```map.put("foo", "bar");```
```map.put("baz", "whazzit");```
```return map;```
	```#{ "foo" : "bar",```
	```"baz" : "whazzit" }```

```Map map = new HashMap(3);```
```map.put(new Integer(1), "one");```
```map.put(new Integer(2), "two");```
```map.put(new Integer(3), "three");```
```return map;```
	```#{ 1 : "one",```
	```2 : "two",```
	```3 : "three" }```

```Map map = new HashMap(2);```
```map.put(kermit.getName(),```
```kermit.getMother().getName());```
```map.put(oscar.getName(),```
```oscar.getMother().getName());```
```return map;```
	```#{ #kermit.name :```
	```#kermit.mother.name,```
	```#oscar.name :```
	```#oscar.mother.name }```

```ActionContext.getContext().getParameters().get("id")```	```#parameters['id']```

```String name = muppet.getName();```
```Map map = ActionContext.getContext().getSession();```
```return map.get("muppet-" + name);```
	```#session["muppet-" + name]```

```session.put("mupper-kermit", muppet);```	```#session['muppet-kermit']``` ```= muppet```

OGNL also supports a shorthand notation for accessing elements. Rather than use the array-style notation, you can use bean property notation. This makes it especially easy to access parameters and request/session/application attributes. Table 8.10 provides several examples using this notation.

Table 8.10 Shorthand notation for accessing map values

Array-style notation	Shorthand notation
```#parameters['id']```	```#parameters.id```
```#request['id']```	```#request.id```
```#application["config"]```	```#application.config```

8.3.3 Filtering and projecting collections

OGNL has two interesting features when it comes to working with collections: filtering and projection. *Filtering* is the technique of taking a collection (a `List` or

`Set` or `Collection`) and producing a new collection with only objects that pass through the filter. The syntax for filtering is as follows:

```
collection.{? expression }
```

The expression is the actual filter that is evaluated for every object in the collection. The special variable `#this` is used to identify the object being evaluated. For example, the expression to filter for Kermit's children who are age 2 or younger is `#this.age <= 2`.

NOTE   In addition to using the `foo.{? bar }` syntax for filtering, you can also select just the first or last match by using the `foo.{^ bar}` and `foo.{$ bar}` syntaxes, respectively.

Whereas filtering takes a collection of size N and returns a potentially smaller collection of size between 0 and N, projecting always returns a collection of size N. However, whereas filtering returns the same objects that were in the original collection (provided they passed the filter), projection mutates the data according to the projection rule. The syntax for projection is as follows:

```
collection.{ expression }
```

The expression here is used to evaluate against the object currently being iterated over in the original collection. For example, if you want a list of the names of Kermit's children, you can project the children collection (`Muppets`) into a collection of names (`Strings`). The expression to do this is `name`. Table 8.11 shows several examples of filtering and projection.

Table 8.11   Examples of filtering and projection

OGNL expression	Description
`children.{name}`	Projects the names of all the children
`children.{?#this.age > 2}`	Filters for children who are more than 2 years old
`children.{?#this.age <= 2}.{name}`	Projects the names of a filtered list of all children who are 2 or younger
`children.{name + ' -> ' + mother.name}`	Projects a list of strings of the form `name -> motherName`

8.3.4   *The multiple uses of "#"*

You've now seen three different uses of the # operator. For the sake of clarity, we'll outline these uses here. You may see the # character in various OGNL expressions when

- Referring to values in the `ActionContext`
- Constructing `Maps` on the fly
- Filtering or projecting a collection

Remember, a simple expression that includes something like `#foo` is using the `#` character to refer to a value in the `ActionContext`. This is different than an expression that is creating a `Map` on the fly, because the `#` character isn't followed by curly braces (`{}`). Whereas `#foo` refers to an `ActionContext` variable, `#{1 : 'one', 2 : 'two'}` doesn't. Instead, that expression creates a new `Map`, as explained in section 8.3.2. Finally, you saw in section 8.3.3 a special case where `#this` doesn't refer to a variable in the `ActionContext` but is instead a special notation used to indicate how to do projection or filtering. In the next section, we'll look at advanced features of OGNL that also use the `#this` keyword, so it's important to understand now how these three uses of the pound sign (`#`) work and that they aren't related.

8.4 Advanced expression language features

OGNL and WebWork include advanced features in the expression language that we should mention. These features set WebWork apart from many other MVC frameworks available. The first one we'll discuss is accessing the value stack through the expression language. We'll then look at how data-type conversion happens when you're getting and setting values as well as what happens when you attempt to set a property on a null object. Finally, we'll show you a quick way to develop lambda expressions (functions) from within the expression language.

8.4.1 Linking the value stack to the expression language

The biggest addition that WebWork provides on top of OGNL is support for the value stack. OGNL operates under the assumption there is only one root object, but WebWork's value stack concept requires there to be many *virtual roots*.

In WebWork, the entire value stack is the root object in the context. But rather than have your expressions get the object you want from the stack and then get properties from that (for example, `stack[1].someProperty`), WebWork provides special integration with OGNL that automatically looks at all the entries in the stack (from the top down) until it finds an object with the property you're looking for.

For example, suppose the stack contains two objects: `Muppet` and `Person`. Both objects have a `name` property: `Muppet` has a `lifeSized` property, and `Person` has a `salary` property. `Muppet` is on the top of the stack, and `Person` is below it. This example is represented in Figure 8.1. Table 8.12 demonstrates how different expressions evaluate against different objects in the stack.

WebWork introduces a new keyword: the `top` keyword. It indicates that you would like to have the entire object on the top of the stack returned. This pseudo-property is especially useful when you're iterating over a collection of objects, such as `Strings`, and you wish to output the entire object rather than a property of the object. Table 8.12 also demonstrates an example of how you can use `top`.

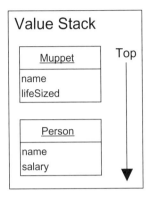

Figure 8.1 A sample value stack containing a Muppet and Person

Table 8.12 Examples of expressions accessing the value stack

OGNL expression	Description
`lifeSized`	Calls `muppet.isLifeSized()`
`salary`	Calls `person.getSalary()`
`name`	Calls `muppet.getName()` because `muppet` is on top of person in the stack
`[1].name`	Calls `person.getName()` because the `[1]` syntax indicates to WebWork that it should start looking down the stack at position 1 (instead of position 0)
`top`	Returns `Muppet`
`[1].top`	Returns `person` because first a smaller stack is returned, in which the expression `top` is requested, and `person` is the top of the new, smaller stack

WebWork's value stack will become increasingly important over time as you build more applications. The iterator tag you'll learn about in chapter 9, "Tag libraries," pushes the object it's currently iterating onto the stack. By doing that, an expression such as `name + '(' + [1].name + ')'` makes sense if you're iterating over the children of a particular person (or `Muppet`), because it would show the child's name and then the parent's name in parentheses.

Take special care to understand the array index notation when it's used in this manner. `[1]` doesn't mean "Get the object in the array index 1 on the stack." Instead, it means "Get a sliced version of the existing value stack." There is a difference. Suppose the stack has three objects, and object 0 and 2 both have the

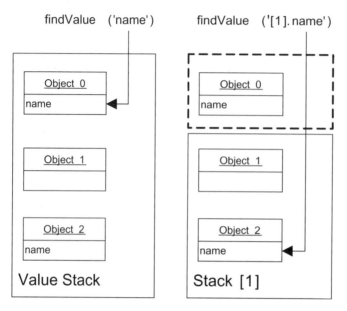

Figure 8.2 A value stack with three objects, indicating how the `[n]`
notation is used

property `name` (this example is represented in figure 8.2). The expression `name` is evaluated against object 0, because it's on top of the stack. The expression `[1].name` is evaluated against object 2, because `[1]` is a stack of objects 1 and 2, and in that stack, only object 2 has the property `name`.

8.4.2 *Data type conversion*

HTTP does nothing to ensure that parameters passed in from GET and POST requests have any data types associated with them. Looking at the Servlet APIs makes this obvious: `getParameter(String  name)` returns a `String` rather than a generic `Object`. Of course, most code isn't so lax when it comes to data types. We use primitives such as `int`, `boolean`, and `float`; simple objects such `String` and `Date`; and complex objects like `Muppet`. You often need to get the data submitted from a web page into these variables. Similarly, you often need to take that data and show it on another web page in its original `String` form. You need data type conversion.

OGNL natively supports conversion for properties being set as well as retrieved. For example, suppose you try to set `someInt` with `"5"` (note that `"5"` is different than `5`). In a type-agnostic world such as the Web, this is an important feature—so much so that we have devoted an entire chapter to type conversion: chapter 12.

We'll take an in-depth look at type conversion and explore building your own type converters. In the meantime, table 8.13 shows two simple cases of type conversion.

Table 8.13   Two examples of data type conversion

OGNL expression	Description
`#kermit.age = "25"`	Sets an int to a String value, which is then converted to 25
`#kermit.name = 25`	Sets a `String` to an int value, which is then converted to "25"

These examples are here to help you understand that one of WebWork's major goals is to ensure that you never get stuck having to write conversion code in your actions. Let's now look at a special kind of data type conversion: converting from null.

8.4.3 *Handling null property access*

As you become more familiar with writing WebWork applications, you'll often find yourself setting the values of properties using complex expressions. For instance, if you need to write a page that asks for Kermit's name, his father's name, and his grandfather's name, you can do one of two things:

- Set the properties `name`, `fatherName`, and `grandfatherName` in your action, and then write code that creates three `Muppet`s, sets their names, and reconnects their relationships.
- Set the properties `kermit.name`, `kermit.father.name`, and `kermit.father.father.name`, and include a single `Muppet` object, `kermit`, in your action.

Clearly, the second choice is simple: It involves only one property in your action instead of three, and it doesn't require you to reconstruct the objects. But how? Recall that there is no constructor in `Muppet` that places stubs for the `father` property, which means that attempting to set `kermit.father.name` with a value will result in a `NullPointerException`.

This is where OGNL steps in. It provides a way to swap in a null object with a real object whenever access to a property on a null object is detected. With WebWork's assistance, OGNL essentially constructs the object graph of the son-father-grandfather relationship automatically, reducing the code you need to write.

There is more to null property access, especially when it comes to `Lists` and `Maps`. We'll discuss these topics in detail in chapter 12.

8.4.4 Creating lambda expressions on the fly

In a few rare cases, it may be necessary (or at least easier to read) to declare a small function, or *lambda expression*, in your OGNL context that can be used by other expressions. The syntax for defining a lambda expression is :[...]. Lambda expressions can only take one argument, which can be referenced using the keyword #this. For example, to write a lambda expression that checks whether a muppet's name is Kermit, you can define the function as follows:

```
#isKermit = :[#this.name == @vs@OG_MUPPET ? true : false]
```

It can then be called as if it's a method that isn't part of any object but rather in the OGNL context itself. Table 8.14 gives three examples of calling the lambda expression.

Table 8.14 Examples of lambda expressions

OGNL expression	Description
#isKermit(top)	Determines whether the object at the top of the stack has Kermit's name.
#isKermit(#kermit)	Is kermit Kermit? We hope so.
#isKermit(#piggy)	This one won't be true.

The important thing to remember is that you shouldn't overuse lambda expressions. The few times you'll need them should be when the only other option is to use a series of conditional tags in your JSPs (if/else/then) multiple times, leading to code duplication. A good example of lambda expression usage is converting a status code (int) to a String that might be displayed several times on a page.

8.5 Summary

WebWork provides a rich language for accessing and updating data. The most important features, however, are the simplest ones. Complex expressions and accessing collections are by far the most common features of the expression language you'll be using. That isn't to say that advanced features like lambda expressions won't be used, but they shouldn't be over-emphasized.

In later chapters, we'll use the basics learned here to dive into some of WebWork's more interesting (and beneficial) use cases. Specific features to watch out for are type conversion and null property handling, both discussed in chapter 12. Similarly, chapters 9 and 11 cover JSP tags and explore 90 percent of the situations in which you'll need to write WebWork expressions.

The most important thing you can take away with this chapter is how the expression language interacts with the value stack. As we mentioned at the start of this chapter, we decided to use `Muppet` objects rather than CaveatEmptor's `User` objects for these examples. And yet, because we're going through an expression language (rather than writing native Java code to get and set various data elements), all that matters is that they share common properties and are available in the value stack. Take advantage of this loose coupling by not being afraid to utilize the value stack. In chapter 9, we'll discuss the `<ww:push>` tag. Once you understand the concept of pushing objects on to the stack, you'll soon find yourself embedding the same block of JSP on two pages that are rendered by different actions—all because the context in which those JSP blocks render is with the same object on the stack.

Tag libraries

9

This chapter covers

- The syntax used in WebWork tags
- Tags for manipulating data
- Tags for controlling the flow of execution
- Other miscellaneous non-UI tags

In chapter 7, "Using results," you learned how WebWork can support various view technologies, including JSP and Velocity. In chapter 8, "Getting data with the expression language," you learned how to use the expression language to access and manipulate data in the action context and value stack. Armed with this information, we can now explore the rich library of tags and components that WebWork provides. WebWork tags are split into two groups: non-UI tags and UI tags. Non-UI tags assist with control flow and data access. UI tags are used to let you build consistent user interfaces and forms. In this chapter, we'll cover non-UI tags. In chapter 11, "UI components," we'll look at WebWork's UI tags.

9.1 *Getting started*

The WebWork JAR file (webwork.jar) contains a tag library definition (TLD) file that describes all the tags that WebWork provides. Listing 9.1 provides a small sample of what that TLD looks like. We recommend that you look at the complete TLD sometime to get a review of every tag WebWork supports.

Listing 9.1 Snippet from WebWork's TLD file

```
<tag>
    <name>bean</name>
    <tagclass>com.opensymphony.webwork.views.jsp.BeanTag</tagclass>
    <bodycontent>JSP</bodycontent>
    <info>
        Create a JavaBean and instantiate its properties. It
        is then placed in the ActionContext for later use.
    </info>
    <attribute>
        <name>name</name>
        <required>true</required>
        <rtexprvalue>true</rtexprvalue>
    </attribute>
    <attribute>
        <name>id</name>
        <required>false</required>
        <rtexprvalue>true</rtexprvalue>
    </attribute>
</tag>
```

Listing 9.1 describes the `bean` tag. This particular tag has two attributes, `name` and `id`; the `name` attribute is required. In order to use this tag or any other tag described in the TLD, you must first register it with your web application by editing web.xml.[1] Here are the new elements you need to add to web.xml:

```
<taglib>
    <taglib-uri>webwork</taglib-uri>
    <taglib-location>/WEB-INF/lib/webwork.jar</taglib-location>
</taglib>
```

Once you've done this, you can use all the WebWork tags in your JSPs by adding a standard `taglib` directive at the beginning of your page: `<%@ taglib prefix="ww" uri="webwork"%>`. Note that all the JSP pages in the CaveatEmptor application start with this directive. Here's a very simple JSP that uses the `property` tag, one of the most commonly used tags in WebWork:

```
<%@ taglib prefix="ww" uri="webwork"%>
<html>
    <head>
        <title>A simple page</title>
    </head>
    <body>
        Hello, <ww:property value="name"/>!
    </body>
</html>
```

Now that you know how to set up your application to use WebWork's tags, let's explore the rich set of tags that are bundled with WebWork.

9.2 An overview of WebWork tags

WebWork comes with many different types of tags. They can be broken into four categories: data tags, control flow tags, UI tags, and miscellaneous tags. As already noted, we'll leave the UI tags for chapter 11; this chapter examines the other three categories. *Data tags* focus on ways to extract data from the value stack and/or set values in the value stack. *Control flow tags* give you the tools to alter the flow and/or output based on the state of the system. Miscellaneous tags, although hard to categorize, are no less useful and will be explored in depth. These tags include useful functionality such as rendering URLs and outputting internationalized text. However, before we can begin looking at any of WebWork's tags, we must first examine the general syntax that all tags adhere to.

---

[1] Depending on your Servlet container and the JSP specification it implements, this may not be necessary. JSP 1.2+ containers can automatically find taglib.tld files under the META-INF directory of tag library JAR files.

9.2.1 *The WebWork tag syntax*

In this book, we chose to take a forward-looking approach at documenting and teaching how to use WebWork. Instead of focusing on the default tag syntax that every version of WebWork has supported, we decided you'll be better served if we document the new tag syntax set to replace the existing syntax when WebWork 2.2 comes out (which should be shortly after this book is released).

This means we'll document the latest and greatest details of WebWork, but you must be aware that what we describe in this book is *not* the default behavior of WebWork 2.1.x (the version that CaveatEmptor is using). We'll document the default tag syntax as well as the new tag syntax, so you can identify the difference. We'll also show you how to instruct WebWork to use the new syntax and thereby utilize the examples given throughout this book.

The old syntax

In the original versions of WebWork, every tag attribute was evaluated against the value stack. This allowed for the most flexibility when developing JSP pages. For example, you'd render a URL that pointed to http://www.opensymphony.com using the URL tag, as follows:

```
<%@ taglib prefix="ww" uri="webwork"%>
<html>
    <head>
        <title>A simple page</title>
    </head>
    <body>
        Click <a href="<ww:url value="'http://www.opensymphony.com'"/>"/>
        ➥here</a>.
    </body>
</html>
```

As you can see, the value attribute is `'http://www.opensymphony.com'` (note the single quotes), because in the old syntax, every attribute was evaluated against the value stack. Thus if you wanted to set an attribute to have a string value, you had to create an Object Graph Navigation Language (OGNL) expression that was a string literal (as described in chapter 8). Setting the value to `http://www.opensymphony.com` would result in an OGNL parse error and an evaluation to null.

The advantage of this syntax was that everything was evaluated; users were never caught unable to set an attribute value to something dynamic from the value stack. The downside was that pages quickly began to have single quotes and double quotes everywhere, confusing page authors. So, for WebWork 2.2, the team decided it was time to change the syntax so it's easier for new users but also allows existing users to not have to upgrade all their pages right away. A migration path was created, and the new syntax was introduced in WebWork 2.1.4 as an optional setting.

The new syntax

The goal of the new syntax was to make tag attributes much easier to deal with, avoiding the single quote/double quote mess. This syntax instead assumes that generally, when users are filling out a tag attribute that's a string, they don't want it to evaluate against the value stack. However, to avoid losing any of the flexibility you previously had, you still have the ability to render expressions from the value stack.

The new syntax only changes for tag attributes that have a data type of `String`. If a tag attribute is meant to evaluate to a `List` or `Object`, then nothing changes—the entire attribute is evaluated from the value stack. This makes sense, given that the only value you can write inline in a JSP tag is a `String`. Tag attributes that are meant to evaluate to `Strings` are no longer evaluated but instead are *parsed*.

In the new syntax, *parsing* the attribute means that WebWork looks for the pattern `%{...}` and then evaluates the expression between the curly braces. This allows attributes to now be a mix of plain text and OGNL expressions, such as `hello, %{name}`. The previous example can be rewritten such that the attribute value is `http://www.opensymphony.com`—without any single quotes. Alternatively, if the value stack contains a URL you wish to display, you can still make the value attribute get its content dynamically, as shown here:

```
<%@ taglib prefix="ww" uri="webwork"%>
<html>
    <head>
        <title>A simple page</title>
    </head>
    <body>
        Click <a href="<ww:url value="%{url}"/>"/>here</a>.
    </body>
</html>
```

As you can see, the new syntax is much easier to work with.

Enabling the new syntax

Because WebWork 2.1.x doesn't have the new syntax enabled by default, you must enable it before you can use any of the examples in this book or in CaveatEmptor. This is easy to do—edit webwork.properties (located in WEB-INF/classes), and add the following entry:

```
webwork.tag.altSyntax = true
```

NOTE Remember that in the new syntax, any attribute that isn't listed as a string data type is automatically *evaluated* against the value stack. On the other hand, any attribute that is a string data type is *parsed*, with anything between %{ and } evaluated against the value stack. As we detail the tags in this chapter and in chapter 11, it's important to remember this difference.

9.3 Data tags

Data tags let you either get data out of the value stack or place variables and objects in the value stack. In this section, we'll discuss the `property` tag, `set` tag, `push` tag, `bean` tag, and `action` tag. The `property` tag is used to extract values from the value stack and display them to the user. The `set` tag is useful for defining temporary variables in your pages. The `push` tag is great for avoiding repetition. Finally, the `bean` and `action` tags are good for building reusable display-level components.

9.3.1 The property tag

The `property` tag is probably the most commonly used tag in WebWork. It's very simple in what it does: It lets users output the value of on OGNL expression. Table 9.1 shows the attributes (as well as the data types) the `property` tag supports.

Table 9.1 Property tag attributes

Attribute	Data type	Required	Description
value	Object	No	Expression to be evaluated.
default	String	No	A default value if no value is found in the value attribute.
escape	Boolean	No	Should the output be HTML escaped (& -> &)?

If the `value` attribute isn't specified, it's assumed to be `top`—which, as explained in chapter 8, returns the object from the top of the value stack. Note that because the `value` data type isn't a string, it's automatically parsed. You've already seen examples of the `property` tag. The `default` attribute is useful if you want a value to be displayed when the value can't be evaluated to a non-null value.

The `escape` attribute is useful if you want the output to be HTML escaped. By default, the values printed out by the `property` tag aren't escaped. This means that if a string contains the value `this & that`, it will be printed out exactly like that, which is technically invalid HTML. If you wish for the output to be `this &amp; that`, then you must set `escape` to `true`.

9.3.2 *The set tag*

The set tag is useful for evaluating an expression in the value stack and assigning it to a name in the specified scope. This is especially useful for placing temporary variables in your JSP, thereby making your code easier to read and slightly faster. Table 9.2 details the attributes that the set tag supports.

Table 9.2   Set tag attributes

Attribute	Data type	Required	Description
name	String	Yes	Reference name of the variable to be set in the specified scope
value	Object	Yes	Expression of the value you wish to set
scope	String	No	application, session, request, page, or default

To understand how you typically use the set tag, let's look at a simple example. The following example shows the property tag accessing several fields of a User object that is stored in the session:

```
<ww:property value="#session['user'].username" />
<ww:property value="#session['user'].age" />
<ww:property value="#session['user'].address" />
```

Repeating #session['user'] every time is not only tiresome, it's error prone. A better way to do this is to set up a temporary variable that points to the User object. Here's the set tag in action, making the overall code easier to read:

```
<ww:set name="user" value="#session['user']" />
<ww:property value="#user.username" />
<ww:property value="#user.age" />
<ww:property value="#user.address" />
```

The set tag makes your pages simpler because it lets you refactor your expressions to smaller, more manageable pieces. However, the set tag can be used for more than just refactoring. It can also set values in different scopes.

A note about scopes

The set tag supports five scopes: default (action context), application, session, request, and page. You've already seen the default scope in the previous example: It places objects in the action context, which can then be retrieved using the #foo notation you're already familiar with.

The other four scopes map directly to the four scopes that servlet applications provide. Typically, you won't need to set values into these scopes unless you're trying to integrate with a tag or servlet that doesn't know how to communicate with WebWork. We won't cover these scopes because they're most often used for legacy code. However, you should know their names.

9.3.3 *The push tag*

Whereas the set tag allows you to place values in the action context, the push tag allows you to push references onto the value stack. This is useful when you wish to do a lot of work revolving around a single object. Rather than having to prefix every expression with the object name, you can push the object down on the value stack and then operate on it directly. Table 9.3 provides the attribute for the push tag.

Table 9.3 Push tag attribute

Attribute	Data type	Required	Description
value	Object	Yes	The expression of the value to push on to the stack

Extending the previous example, here's how the push tag can be used to simplify the view even further:

```
<ww:set name="user" value="#session['user']" />
<ww:push value="#user" >
    <ww:property value="username" />
    <ww:property value="age" />
    <ww:property value="address" />
</ww:push>
```

As you can see, the push tag makes it easy to work with a single object. It can be especially useful when you're trying to include a common snippet of JSP even when the value stack has vastly different values. For example, suppose you have two pages being rendered. The contents of the value stack are very different when both pages are invoked, but you still want to display the contents of a user profile.

Suppose that in page 1, the user model can be accessed via the expression cart.user, and in page 2, the user model can be accessed via the expression order.user. Using the push tag and a static JSP include, you can easily render the same user details. The following examples provide a simple JSP for page 1:

```
<%@ taglib prefix="ww" uri="webwork"%>
<html>
    <head>
```

```
        <title><title>
    </head>
    <body>
        <ww:push value="cart.user">
        <%@ include file="/shared/jsp/user-details.jspf">
        </ww:push>
    </body>
</html>
```

and for page 2:

```
<%@ taglib prefix="ww" uri="webwork"%>
<html>
    <head>
        <title><title>
    </head>
    <body>
        <ww:push value="order.user">
        <%@ include file="/shared/jsp/user-details.jspf">
        </ww:push>
    </body>
</html>
```

Here's the common JSP fragment included by both pages:

```
<%@ taglib prefix="ww" uri="webwork"%>
<ul>
    <li>Username: <ww:property value="username"/></li>
    <li>Age: <ww:property value="age"/></li>
    <li>Address: <ww:property value="address"/></li>
</ul>
```

These three examples show how common JSP fragments can be shared through the power of the value stack. The value stack allows you to write views that make assumptions about the top of the stack without having to worry what might be lower in the stack. In the JSP for page 1 the stack may have very different values than it has in the JSP for page 2, but it doesn't matter because by the time the final fragment is included, the top of the stack is the same in both pages.

9.3.4 *The bean tag*

Sometimes you need to provide more complex logic or data processing than the basic WebWork JSP tags can provide. The bean tag lets you create a simple Java-Bean and push it on to the value stack. In addition to pushing the bean onto the stack between the opening and closing tags, you can also optionally assign a variable name for the bean to be accessible in the action context, just as the set tag lets you do. Table 9.4 details the attributes for the bean tag.

Table 9.4 Bean tag attributes

Attribute	Data type	Required	Description
name	String	Yes	Package and class name of the bean that is to be created
id	String	No	Reference name used if you want to reference the bean outside the scope of the closing bean tag

The bean tag is the first of a few tags we'll explore that are *parameterized*. That is, the tag is designed to surround the param tag, allowing you to customize the behavior of the tag by providing parameters. In the case of the bean tag, the parameters are used to set values on the properties of the bean. In order to understand the bean tag best, let's explore some of the beans that are included with WebWork and designed for use with the bean tag. We start with the Counter bean.

Counter bean

The Counter bean is good for tracking a count. It implements Iterator, meaning you can also loop over using the iterator tag (discussed later in this chapter). For example, to create a Counter bean that can be used to loop from 1 to 100, you can use the following code:

```
<%@ taglib prefix="ww" uri="webwork"%>
<ww:bean name="com.opensymphony.webwork.util.Counter" id="counter">
    <ww:param name="last" value="100"/>
</ww:bean>
<ww:iterator value="#counter">
    <li><ww:property/></li>
</ww:iterator>
```

In this example, the Counter bean is created, and setLast() is called with 100 as the argument. It's then looped over using the iterator tag, and the current value (a long) is printed out for each iteration.

DateFormatter bean

Recall that the bean tag pushes the bean onto the stack and then pops it off when the tag closes. The following example uses the included DateFormatter bean to print out a formatted date:

```
<%@ taglib prefix="ww" uri="webwork"%>
<ww:set name="user" value="#session['user']" />
<ww:bean name="com.opensymphony.webwork.util.DateFormatter" >
    <ww:param name="format" value="'MM/dd/yyyy'"/>
```

```
<ww:param name="date" value="#user.birthdate"/>
    The user's birthdate is: <ww:property value="formattedDate"/>
</ww:bean>
```

Note that this example not only sets parameters but also renders output within the body of the bean tag. This is possible because the bean tag pushes the JavaBean onto the stack, allowing you to access the properties on the bean without having to prefix the bean's ID as you did in the previous example. This is effectively the same as using the bean tag as you did earlier plus the push tag.

Although you can use this class to print out formatted dates, we recommend that you utilize *internationalization* (see chapter 14) to do your formatting. Not only is that approach generally easier, but you also get the added benefit of supporting multiple languages.

9.3.5　*The action tag*

Sometimes the bean tag isn't enough to implement complex or reusable views. Taking advantage of the existing WebWork infrastructure, you can use the action tag to add more advanced behavior to your pages. Rather than just putting Java-Beans into your action context, you can execute actions and then access the data in your JSP. Table 9.5 provides the attributes associated with the action tag.

Table 9.5　Action tag attributes

Attribute	Data type	Required	Description
name	String	Yes	The action name
namespace	String	No	The action namespace; defaults to the current page namespace
id	String	No	Reference name of the action bean for use later in the page
executeResult	Boolean	No	When set to true, executes the result of the action (default value: false)

Only the name attribute in the action tag is required. By default, the action tag won't execute the result of the action, making it safe to execute actions that might otherwise normally cause a different page to be rendered. Also, the namespace parameter is required only if the namespace of the action you're executing is different than the current namespace of the original action.

The action tag is great for creating simple reusable components without having to add scriptlets to your JSP pages. In CaveatEmptor, we wanted to display a tree selection of all the categories in many different places in the web application. Rather than make every action that might have a result that wants to display the category tree be responsible for getting the data needed to do so, we built a small action that got that data independently. Here's what the action definition looks like in xwork.xml:

```
<action name="categoryTree"
        class="org.hibernate.auction.web.actions.categories.CategoryPicker">
    <result name="success">/categoryTree.jsp</result>
</action>
```

Anywhere you want to display a category tree listing, you can invoke the `action` tag and tell it to execute its result. This will render the output of categoryTree.jsp directly inline in any of your pages. The following JSP displays the category listing:

```
<%@ taglib uri="webwork" prefix="ww"%>
<html>
  <head>
    <title>Dashboard</title>
  </head>

  <body>
    <hr/>
    <ww:action name="categoryTree" executeResult="true"/>
  </body>
</html>
```

Note that `executeResult` is set to true. This is necessary if you wish to tell Web-Work to invoke the typical output you would expect if you made an HTTP request directly to `categoryTree.action`. If `executeResult` weren't set, it would default to false; although the action would execute, nothing would be rendered.

The `action` tag, in essence, allows you to implement the Page-Controller pattern as discussed in chapter 1, "An overview of WebWork." Remember, typical action invocation until now has used the Front-Controller pattern. As you can see here, using both patterns together is possible and even encouraged.

Like the `bean` tag, the `action` tag may also be parameterized. However, unlike with the `bean` tag, the body of the action can't contain any content besides the `<ww:param>` tag. This is the case because action invocation isn't as simple as creating a bean and putting it on the value stack. Just like any other action, the set of interceptor stacks are invoked, the action is executed, and then (optionally) the result is rendered.

Instead, if you wish to access the `action` bean after it has been executed, you must provide an ID. You're then free to access it just as you can with the `bean` tag.

This is useful when you have a common set of logic you wish to execute but not necessarily a common result you wish to render.

9.4 Control tags

Now that you know how to manipulate and display data, it's time to learn how to navigate around it as well. Like every other language, the WebWork JSP tags have a set of tags that make it easy to control the flow of page execution. Using the iterator tag to loop over data and the if/else/elseif tags to make decisions, you can develop rich pages.

9.4.1 The iterator tag

Other than the property tag, the other most commonly used tag in WebWork is the iterator tag. The iterator tag allows you to loop over collections of objects easily. It's designed to know how to loop over any Collection, Map, Enumeration, Iterator, or array. It also provides the ability to define a variable in the action context that lets you determine certain basic information about the current loop state, such as whether you're looping over an odd or even row. Table 9.6 provides the attributes for the iterator tag.

Table 9.6   Iterator tag attributes

Attribute	Data type	Required	Description
value	Collection, Map, Enumeration, Iterator, or Array	Yes	The object to be looped over.
status	String	No	If provided, an IteratorStatus object is placed in the action context.

One of the nicest features about the iterator tag is that it can iterate over just about any data type that has a concept of iteration. When iterating over a Map, it iterates over the Set returned by Map.entrySet(), which is a set of Map.Entry objects, which in turn has the methods getKey() and getValue() to retrieve the associated key/value pairs.

The following example provides a simple way to iterate over the items made available by the Search action in CaveatEmptor:

```
<ww:iterator value="items">
  <li>
  <ww:property value="name"/>, <ww:property value="description"/>
```

```
      </li>
   </ww:iterator>
```

You could easily create a more advanced user interface. The expression items invoke `Search.getItems()`, which returns a `List` of `Item` objects. As each object is iterated over, it's temporarily pushed onto the value stack while the body of the `iterator` tag is invoked. After the body is complete, the value is popped off the stack and the process is repeated until no more items remain in the list.

Because the `Item` objects are pushed on the stack, the `property` tags can use the expressions `name` and `description` to invoke `getName()` and `getDescription()`, respectively. Once again, you see the power and simplicity of having a stack to evaluate expressions against.

Using IteratorStatus

Sometimes it's desirable to know status information about the iteration that's taking place. This is where the `status` attribute steps in. The `status` attribute, when defined, provides an `IteratorStatus` object available in the action context that can provide simple information such as the size, current index, and whether the current object is in the even or odd index in the list. Listing 9.2 provides the complete code for the `IteratorStatus` class as it is in WebWork.

Listing 9.2 IteratorStatus source code

```
package com.opensymphony.webwork.views.jsp;

/**
 * The iterator tag can export an IteratorStatus object so that
 * one can get information about the status of the iteration,
 * such as the size, current index, and whether any more items
 * are available.
 *
 * @author Rickard Öberg (rickard@dreambean.com)
 */
public class IteratorStatus {
    protected StatusState state;

    public IteratorStatus(StatusState aState) {
        state = aState;
    }

    public int getCount() {
        return state.index + 1;
    }

    public boolean isEven() {
```

```
        return ((state.index + 1) % 2) == 0;
    }

    public boolean isFirst() {
        return state.index == 0;
    }

    public int getIndex() {
        return state.index;
    }

    public boolean isLast() {
        return state.last;
    }

    public boolean isOdd() {
        return ((state.index + 1) % 2) == 1;
    }

    public int modulus(int operand) {
        return (state.index + 1) % operand;
    }

    public static class StatusState {
        boolean last = false;
        int index = 0;

        public void setLast(boolean isLast) {
            last = isLast;
        }

        public void next() {
            index++;
        }
    }
}
```

The most common use for the iterator status feature is to render a table of values and shade even-numbered rows one color and odd rows another color. You may find other uses for the tag; however, without knowing how to use if/else tags, you can't conditionally output HTML. So, let's take a moment to learn about these tags and then come back to the task of rendering a table with different shading for even and odd rows.

9.4.2 *The if and else tags*

The `if`, `else`, and `elseif` tags are required to do any sort of basic page flow and presentation. As in any other programming language, you can use the `if` tag alone, or with an `elseif` tag, or with an `else` tag. Not surprisingly, the `else` tag has no attributes. The `if` and `elseif` tags have a single attribute, which is outlined in table 9.7.

Table 9.7 If and `elseif` tag attribute

Attribute	Data type	Required	Description
test	Boolean	Yes	Boolean expression that is evaluated and tested for true or false

Looking at the iterator example we just discussed, let's now implement a table that has three shades: even, odd, and selected. Selected is a special shade used for only a single element in the entire list of objects. Listing 9.3 shows how you can use the `iterator` tag's status feature as well as the `if`, `else`, and `elseif` tags to create the table.

Listing 9.3 A table that has three shades for rows: even, odd, and selected

```
<table>
<thead>
  <tr>
    <th>Name</th>
    <th>Description</th>
  </tr>
</thead>
<tbody>
<ww:iterator value="items" status="status">
  <tr class="
      <ww:if test="id == itemId">row-selected</ww:if>
      <ww:elseif test="#status.even">row-even</ww:elseif>
      <ww:else>row-odd</ww:else>
      ">
    <td><ww:property value="name"/></td>
    <td><ww:property value="description"/></td>
  </tr>
</ww:iterator>
</tbody>
</table>
```

In this example, the `class` attribute (CSS) can have three possible values: row-selected, row-even, or row-odd. It's row-selected if the ID of the item is equal to the `itemID`. Remember, the value stack works this way: If `itemId` can't be found on the first item in the stack, each item lower down in the stack is searched until a property is found. The expression `id == itemId` causes the left side, `id`, to match against `Item.getId()`, whereas the right-hand side, `itemId`, matches against the action `Search.getItemId()` if it exists.

If the current item isn't the one that is requested to be selected, then the flow falls through to the `elseif` tag. In this example, the expression `#status.even` causes the `IteratorStatus` object to be queried. Note that the `status` attribute of the `iterator` tag is set to the value `status`. This is how you can access all those properties shown in listing 9.3.

NOTE   Although there is no requirement that `if` tags and `else` tags be directly next to each other, we highly recommend that you don't spread them too far apart. Your code can become very confusing if you place text or other logic in between `if` and `else` tags.

9.5 *Miscellaneous tags*

As we mentioned at the start of this chapter, WebWork includes a few different types of tags. You've already seen how the data tags and control tags work. Let's now look at the miscellaneous tags that, although very useful, can't be easily classified. In this section, we'll discuss WebWork's `include` tag (a slight variation of the `<jsp:include>` tag), the `URL` tag, and the `i18n` and `text` tags (both used for internationalization). Finally, we'll take another look at the `param` tag you've already seen and show how it can be used to its full power.

9.5.1 *The include tag*

Whereas JSP has its own include tag, `<jsp:include>`, WebWork provides a version that integrates with WebWork better and provides more advanced features. Like some of the other WebWork tags you've seen, the `include` tag can be parameterized. Table 9.8 provides the attribute for the `include` tag.

Table 9.8   Include tag attribute

Attribute	Data type	Required	Description
value	String	Yes	Name of the page, action, servlet, or any referenceable URL.

The include tag behaves very similarly to the JSP include tag. However, it's more useful when you're developing with WebWork, for two reasons: It integrates better with WebWork, and it provides native access to the value stack and a more extensible parameter model.

Let's start with the WebWork integration: The JSP include tag includes the output of any URL you give it, but WebWork's include tag is smarter. For example, you can determine that a page that will be included by evaluating against the value stack using the %{ ... } notation. Similarly, you give the include tag parameters with the <ww:param> tag (discussed in a moment). This tag also ties into the value stack, making it much easier to use than the <jsp:param> tag.

WebWork's include tag is also more user friendly. If you wish to include the URL ../index.jsp, you're free to do so even though some application servers don't support that type of URL when using the JSP include tag. That's the case because WebWork's include tag will rewrite ../index.jsp to an absolute URL based on the current URL where the JSP is located. To learn more about how includes work, look back at chapter 7.

9.5.2 *The URL tag*

When you're building web applications, it's extremely common to create URLs that link your various pages together. WebWork provides a URL tag to help you do this. The tag is simple: It renders relative or absolute URLs, handles parameters, and encodes the URL so it can be used with browsers that don't have cookies enabled. If you're planning to build a robust site that works with many different browsers and can be deployed in any application context, we highly recommend that you render all your URLs using the URL tag. Table 9.9 lists its attributes.

Table 9.9 URL tag attributes

Attribute	Data type	Required	Description
value	String	No	The base URL; defaults to the current URL the page is rendering from
includeParams	String	No	Selects parameters from all, get, or none; default is get
id	String	No	If specified, the URL isn't written out but rather is saved in the action context for future use
includeContext	Boolean	No	If true, then the URL that is generated must be prepended with the application's context; default is false

Table 9.9   URL tag attributes *(continued)*

Attribute	Data type	Required	Description
encode	Boolean	No	Adds the session ID to the URL if cookies aren't enabled for the visitor
scheme	String	No	Allows you to specify the protocol; defaults to the current scheme (http or https)

Let's begin by discussing each attribute. The `value` attribute is the most commonly used. When it's specified, the value is used as the basis for rendering the URL. When it isn't specified, the current URL, such as `search.action`, is used as the basis for rendering. For example, you can render a URL that points to http://www.opensymphony.com with `<ww:url value="http://www.opensymphony.com"/>`. You can render a URL that points back to the current URL with `<ww:url />`.

Like other WebWork tags, the URL tag can be parameterized. The parameters are used to construct the URL and make up the query string. The following example generates the URL string search.action?query=*XXX*, where *XXX* is the value the expression name evaluates to:

```
<ww:url value="search.action">
    <ww:param name="query" value="name"/>
</ww:url>
```

Often, when rendering URLs, you'll wish to include any parameters that are present in the current URL. For example, if you're looking at a list of auction items in a category in CaveatEmptor, and you want to display 20 items per page, the URL tag becomes handy. Because the current URL might be something like list-items.action?categoryId=123&page=0, rather than pass the `categoryId` and `page` attributes for the link associated with the Next Page link, you can do the following:

```
<a href="<ww:url>
    <ww:param name="page" value="page + 1"/>
</ww:url>">Next page</a>
```

Of course, this example isn't pretty. The `href` tag looks odd with all those line breaks in it. WebWork provides a way around this. If you provide a value for the `id` attribute in the URL tag, the URL isn't rendered out to the page. Rather, the URL is saved as a `String` in the action context, allowing you to access it later. This functionality is useful when you have complex logic for constructing a URL and don't want to embed it directly in your HTML tags. Rewriting the last example to take advantage of this feature produces the following:

```
<ww:url id="url">
    <ww:param name="page" value="page + 1"/>
</ww:url>
<a href="<ww:property value="#url"/>">Next Page</a>
```

By default, WebWork includes all params in the current page's query string. This is the same thing as specifying the `includeParams` attribute to `get`. If you don't want any parameters to be included, you can set this value to `none`. Alternatively, you can force all parameters, including those submitted via a `POST` request, by setting the value to `post`.

Building web applications that can be deployed under any context on a web server can be a pain. Typically, web developers solve this issue by putting the following in their JSPs:

```
<a href="<%= request.getContextPath() %>/search.action">Search</a>
```

You can achieve the same effect by using the `includeContext` attribute. By default, the value is `false`, meaning that if your application is in the context of `/auction` and you do `<ww:url value="/search.action"/>`, the link won't point to `/auction/search.action`. However, setting `includeContext` to `true` does this. Typically, you want to do this whenever you're using absolute URLs (those that start with `/`) and are linking to other places in your web application.

As you may already know, servlet containers keep track of session state by placing a session-level cookie in the browser. You may have seen the string *jsession* while browsing through web applications. This cookie holds the ID of the session object on the server side. If cookies aren't enabled, sessions aren't supported automatically. However, there is a way around this: Use the `encode` attribute when rendering URLs. Doing so causes the URL to be encoded such that even if cookies are disabled, the servlet container knows how to look up the proper session.

Also remember that URLs may use either the `http` scheme or the `https` scheme. By default, the URL tag renders URLs using the same scheme the current URL is using. That means if the page is rendered using HTTPS, then the URLs printed out use the `https` scheme. Likewise, they use `http` if the user isn't at an `https` URL. Sometimes you wish to render URLs that don't use the same scheme. For example, you might want to redirect the user from a nonsecure page to a secure page. You can do so by setting the `scheme` attribute to `https`.

Note that WebWork uses the default ports of 80 for HTTP and 443 for HTTPS. If for any reason your application uses different ports, you can redefine them in webwork.properties. Add the following entries:

```
webwork.url.http.port  = 8080
webwork.url.https.port = 8081
```

With these changes, WebWork will render URLs using your custom ports. Let's now look at the two tags WebWork provides to make writing internationalized applications much easier.

9.5.3 *The i18n and text tags*

Many applications need to work in multiple languages. The process of making this happen is called *internationalization*, or i18n for short. Chapter 14 discusses WebWork's internationalization support in detail, but we'd like to take a moment to detail the two tags that are central to this functionality: the i18n tag and the text tag.

The text tag is used to display language-specific text, such as English or Spanish, based on a key lookup. For example, the key title can map to a text value for each language. These mappings are specified in ResourceBundles, a standard class in the Java language. Table 9.10 lists the attributes that the text tag supports.

Table 9.10   Text tag attributes

Attribute	Data type	Required	Description
name	String	Yes	The key to look up in the ResourceBundle(s)
id	String	No	If specified, the text is stored in the action context under this name
value0	Object	No	Parameter 1 (deprecated)
value1	Object	No	Parameter 2 (deprecated)
value2	Object	No	Parameter 3 (deprecated)
value3	Object	No	Parameter 4 (deprecated)

Typical usage of the text tag is `<ww:text name="title"/>`. Like the URL tag, you can specify the id attribute, and nothing will be printed out immediately. Thus `<ww:text_id="title" name="title"/>` won't render anything, and the expression #title now references the language-specific title.

Also like the URL tag, the text tag is parameterized. However, unlike the action, bean, or URL tags, i18n parameters don't have names associated with them. That's because the standard message formatting supported by Java's MessageFormat class uses index parameters. For example, a resource bundle might specify that the key `searchResults` be equal to the English text *We searched {0} items in your database and found {1} matches.* You can parameterize that message like so:

```
<ww:text name="searchResults">
    <ww:param value="totalItems"/>
    <ww:param value="searchCount"/>
</ww:text>
```

We won't discuss the `text` tag in much more detail, because this topic is covered in depth in chapter 14. However, let's touch on the `i18n` tag. The `i18n` tag is useful when you have a resource bundle you wish to use in a certain part of your web page. The tag pushes that resource bundle on to the stack, allowing you to access the i18n resources associated with that bundle from within the body of the tag. Table 9.11 provides the `i18n` tag attribute.

Table 9.11   I18n tag attribute

Attribute	Data type	Required	Description
name	String	Yes	The name of the resource bundle

The `i18n` tag works much like the `bean` tag in that it pushes an object onto the stack during the body of the tag and then pops it off when the tag closes. If you have a resource bundle located at `org.hibernate.auction.myBundle`, you can push this bundle onto the stack by doing the following:

```
<ww:i18n name="org.hibernate.auction.myBundle">
    <ww:text name="someKey"/>
</ww:i18n>
```

In this example, `someKey` is looked up from `myBundle` rather than the typical resource bundles. This is described in chapter 14 as well.

NOTE In chapter 14, you'll learn that resource bundles can either be simple properties files or complex Java classes that look up key values from other locations, such as a database. The i18n tag works with either form of resource bundle. If the bundle you wish to push on the stack is a properties file, provide the name of the file (without .properties and any of the localization specifics, such as _en) and the package in which the file is located. If the bundle you wish to use is a class, provide the fully qualified class name.

9.5.4 *The param tag*

The last tag we'll discuss has been used throughout this chapter. The param tag does nothing by itself, but at the same time it's incredibly useful for many of the tags you've seen here. It's also useful when you're working with the UI tags, as you'll see in chapter 11. Table 9.12 lists the attributes you're now already familiar with.

Table 9.12 `Param` tag attributes

Attribute	Data type	Required	Description
name	String	No	all, get, or none
value	Object	No	Get the URL for the requested page

Note that neither the name nor value attribute is required for the param tag. This isn't to say that `<ww:param/>` does anything useful; rather, there are some param tag behaviors we haven't yet explored.

Remember that for all tags except the text tag, parameters are given in the form of a name/value pair. But because parameters are given in an indexed form for the text tag, you can't require that the name attribute be given.

Having an optional value may also seem a bit odd. That's only because we haven't looked at the alternative way to supply a value with the param tag: via the tag body content. Rather than provide an OGNL expression in the value attribute, you can instead place any content in the body of the parameter; it will be rendered and treated as a String parameter value. For example:

```
<ww:text name="searchResults">
    <ww:param>over 5 million</ww:param>
    <ww:param value="searchCount"/>
</ww:text>
```

Extending this example, you can internationalize the text over 5 million and then do the following:

```
<ww:text name="searchResults">
    <ww:param><ww:text name="fiveMillion"/></ww:param>
    <ww:param value="searchCount"/>
</ww:text>
```

With careful use of the param tag, you can do some incredibly powerful things. In chapter 14, we'll look at another example where using the body content of the param tag makes internationalization much easier.

9.6 *Summary*

This chapter has introduced you to the JSP tags that are included with WebWork. You've seen how each tag integrates with WebWork's value stack. We've also looked at the deprecated tag syntax and shown you why the new syntax is better and how to enable it. Remember, the examples in this book won't work until you turn on the newSyntax option or unless you're using WebWork 2.2.

Now that you have a grasp of the basic JSP tags WebWork offers, the next step is to look at the UI tags. However, before we can do that, you must understand the technology the UI tags are built on: Velocity. In chapter 10, we'll briefly explore the Velocity language and show how you can use all the JSP tags WebWork provides from within Velocity.

Don't be afraid to take advantage of the tags discussed in this chapter. If you find yourself putting too much logic in your JSPs, use the bean tag. If you start to see a lot of common code being placed in many different, unrelated actions, it might be a good time to break it out into a standalone action tag. Try to use the URL tag when you're generating links and image references; doing so will make your application much more portable. Finally, take advantage of the behavior of the param tag to integrate multiple tags, such as the text tag.

10

Velocity

This chapter covers

- The Velocity template language
- Static and dynamic languages used for view technologies
- Control statements in Velocity, such as loops and `if/else` blocks
- How to access utility objects in Velocity

As we explored in chapter 7, "Using results," WebWork supports many different technologies for displaying data. Those technologies include JSP, FreeMarker, JasperReports, XML, and Velocity. Velocity is a little more special to WebWork than the rest because it's not only a supported optional view technology, but it's also the default template language used for all the UI tag libraries supplied with Web-Work. This is why we devote a chapter to the basics of Velocity but not to any of the other technologies.

In this chapter, we'll cover Velocity from a high level and explore why it's used as a core technology in WebWork. We'll also compare it to JSP and explain the pros and cons of choosing Velocity as your view technology. By the end of this chapter, you'll understand how Velocity works, how WebWork integrates with it, and how to write your own Velocity templates. For more in-depth coverage, we recommend reading the excellent Velocity tutorial available on the Velocity web site: http://jakarta.apache.org/velocity.

NOTE As of version 2.1.7, WebWork supports other view technologies besides Velocity to render UI tag libraries. However, WebWork only ships templates written in Velocity; so, it's a good idea to learn Velocity even if you don't plan to use it directly.

10.1 Introduction to Velocity

Before you can get started with the nitty-gritty of how Velocity and WebWork integrate, we'll do a quick overview of what Velocity is. Then we can go over the simple steps required to set up Velocity in your environment. After that, we'll explore example templates, examine the language itself, and dive into WebWork integration.

10.1.1 What is Velocity?

Velocity is, in its most simplistic form, a template language. What does that mean? A *template* is text that is used as a basis for documents that all have a similar structure. Parts of the template are replaced with text specific to the document. For example, a Microsoft Word template for a Software License Agreement might have everything prewritten except the company name, which would be a blank space or highlighted text such as [COMPANY]. This way, a person could quickly replace the place-holding text with the actual company name, thereby having a license agreement that is customized for a particular company.

NOTE Although it was too late in the publishing process of this book, you should know that WebWork 2.2, which is scheduled to be released in Fall 2005, is deprecating Velocity in favor of FreeMarker. Velocity templates are still included in WebWork 2.2, but they will eventually be phased out in favor of FreeMarker templates. However, it's still a good idea to learn Velocity, because it's similar to FreeMarker and is still the basis for Web-Work 2.1—the latest stable release of WebWork at this point.

Templating languages

We've defined a template, but what is a template *language*? It's a standard format for defining where variables should be replaced in a document. For example, instead of the text [COMPANY], the Velocity language uses the dollar sign ($) to indicate a variable that needs replacement. So, you'd write $companyName.

As a template language, Velocity supports more than just variable replacements. It also allows for simple control structures, such as loops and if/else statements. This lends itself as a view technology in web-enabled MVC frameworks such as WebWork. Unlike JSP, which allows the full Java language to be embedded in HTML, Velocity provides only rudimentary access to data, forcing developers to separate presentation logic from business logic.

Runtime vs. compile-time

This isn't to say that Velocity is a perfect technology. Whereas JSP is a static, *compile-time language*, Velocity is a *runtime language*. This means tool support for Velocity is often bare bones or nonexistent. For example, if you have a JSP file that prints out the creator of a Document object, it's written using the expression <%= document.getCreator() %> (assuming you aren't using the JSP tags discussed in chapter 9, "Tag libraries"). In Velocity, the expression is $document.creator.

Now suppose you want to change the creator property in the Document class to author. If you aren't using an IDE with refactoring support, you can rename get-Creator() to getAuthor()—and the next time you access the JSP, you'll see a compile error. If you're using a refactoring IDE, the JSP is automatically updated.

However, the Velocity template won't automatically be updated to use $document.author, because no IDEs support refactoring of Velocity files. This is due to the fact that Velocity is runtime, and the *velocity context* (the area that determines what is available when using the dollar sign notation) can be modified by anyone during runtime. This is, in fact, how WebWork integrates into the Velocity language and provides access to the value stack. So, unless your IDE knows about WebWork, it will never know to change $document.creator to $document.author. When you access the Velocity template that is still using the old $document.creator expression, no error will occur. Rather, the output will include the string $document.creator. We'll discuss this more shortly.

NOTE There is great interest in WebWork plug-ins for both the IntelliJ IDEA and Eclipse IDEs. Although no fully working plug-in exists, it's expected that one of these IDEs will soon have support for the problem we've outlined. If you plan to use JSP and the WebWork tag libraries, you'll also face the issue of runtime versus compile-time: Tags like `<ww:property value="creator"/>` won't be rewritten to `<ww:property value="author"/>` even if you're using a refactoring IDE.

10.1.2 Getting ready to use Velocity

Before we delve too deep into how to use Velocity, let's examine how to configure Velocity. As we discussed earlier, Velocity is a template language. It reads a template file, merges the template with some data, and then renders a finished product. This means that at a minimum, you need to tell Velocity where it can find the templates and where it can find the data.

The data used to render the template comes from the WebWork value stack, as you saw in chapter 7. The template is based on the `<result/>` tag in your xwork.xml file. So, as long as you include webwork-default.xml when you're writing your xwork.xml file, there's nothing to configure when you're getting started with Velocity.

Sometimes, however, you'll need to do additional configuration. Velocity-related configuration can take place in three files: xwork.xml, webwork.properties, and velocity.properties.

xwork.xml

As you've already seen, the `velocity` result is automatically included as part of webwork-default.xml. However, if you aren't including this file as part of your configuration or you wish to create your own default configuration to extend, you need to add the following result type:

```
<result-type name="velocity"
             class="com.opensymphony.webwork.dispatcher.
             ➥VelocityResult" />
```

Once this result type is added, you can then refer to the `velocity` result type. And of course, you can make this result type the default if all your pages are `velocity` based, allowing you to avoid referencing the type for every action.

webwork.properties

WebWork's integration with Velocity can also be tuned. By default, the following entries are automatically assumed, meaning that if you don't need to change these values, you don't have to do anything. However, if you want to use a different velocity.properties file, configure additional Velocity contexts, or add support for other JSP tags, you must edit webwork.properties and override these values:

```
# Location of velocity.properties file.
webwork.velocity.configfile = velocity.properties

# Comma separated list of VelocityContext classnames
#  to chain to the WebWorkVelocityContext
webwork.velocity.contexts =

# JSP tag packages
webwork.velocity.tag.path =
    com.opensymphony.webwork.views.velocity.ui
```

Later in this chapter, we'll discuss more advanced WebWork-Velocity integration features, such as custom Velocity contexts and JSP tag support.

velocity.properties

Velocity's standard configuration takes place in velocity.properties. This configuration isn't WebWork-specific, and you can find in-depth configuration options in the Velocity documentation. Typically, you should specify your own configuration if you need to specify custom Velocity macros or override how Velocity templates are loaded.

> **NOTE** By default, WebWork loads resources from the file system as well as the classloader (`wwfile` and `wwclass`). Later in this chapter, we'll discuss how those resources are loaded and point you in the right direction if you wish to load resources from other sources, such as a database.

The following example shows sample velocity.properties content. This configuration is for products offered by Jive Software and overrides how Velocity does its logging, the template-loading options, and which macros are included by default (webwork.vm):

```
runtime.log.logsystem.class = com.jivesoftware.base.log.JiveLogImpl
resource.loader = wwfile, wwclass, jive
jive.resource.loader.public.name = Jive
jive.resource.loader.description = Jive Velocity Resource Loader
jive.resource.loader.class =
    com.jivesoftware.util.JiveVelocityResourceLoader
velocimacro.library = webwork.vm
```

These properties are all part of the standard Velocity configuration options. You can learn more about them in the Velocity documentation. However, we wish to call special attention to the inclusion of the webwork.vm `velocimacro` library. This file is included by default with WebWork and contains the following:

```
#macro(bean $bean_name $name)
   #set ($name = $webwork.bean($bean_name))
#end

#macro(includeservlet $name)
  $webwork.include($name,$req,$res)
#end

#macro(url $name)
   #set ($name =
      $webwork.bean("com.opensymphony.webwork.util.URLBean"))
   $name.setRequest($req)
   $name.setResponse($res)
#end

#macro(property $object $property)
$!{ognl.findValue($property, $object)}
#end
```

In section 10.3.2, we explain where $webwork comes from. In the meantime, know that webwork.vm provides a few helpful macros you can use in your Velocity templates. More important, know that you can make your own Velocity macro files modeled after this one and include them in velocity.properties. Once you do that, the macros are available for any Velocity template you write. And on that note, let's look at the basic syntax of Velocity so you can start writing templates.

10.2 Basic syntax and operations

Now that you know how to configure Velocity and you understand the issues involved when choosing a runtime or compile-time language, let's begin to explore Velocity's basic features. These include simple things such as printing data and calling methods. In addition to displaying data, you'll almost always need to use conditional logic and repeating loops. Finally, it's sometimes helpful to save the value of an expression in a variable so you can reuse it later without recomputing the entire expression.

> **NOTE** In all the examples in this chapter, we assume that the velocity result type is being used and that a simple action similar to those found in CaveatEmptor has been requested via a web browser.

10.2.1 Property access

Let's begin by displaying simple data elements. Here's what the JSP might look like for a simple page displaying an item up for bid. Note that the JSP code does *not* use the tag libraries you learned in chapter 9:

```
<% Item item = request.getAttribute("item"); %>
<h3><%= item.getName() %></h3>
Seller: <a href="mailto:<%= item.getSeller().getEmail() %>">
        <%= item.getSeller().getUsername() %>
        </a>
<br/>
Description: <%= item.getDescription() %>
<br/>
Date listed: <%= item.getStartDate() %>
```

Let's now rewrite the example using the JSP tags you learned in chapter 9:

```
<h3><ww:property value="item.name"/></h3>
Seller: <a href="mailto:<ww:property value="item.seller.email"/>">
        <ww:property value="item.seller.username"/>
        </a>
<br/>
Description: <ww:property value="item.description"/>
<br/>
Date listed: <ww:property value="item.startDate"/>
```

Finally, let's rewrite the example one more time, using Velocity:

```
<h3>$item.name</h3>
Seller: <a href="mailto:$item.seller.email">
        $item.seller.username
        </a>
<br/>
Description: $item.description
<br/>
Date listed: $item.startDate
```

Note that Velocity uses the familiar dot syntax that WebWork's expression language uses. Similarly, you can chain together properties, just as you did with $item.seller.email. This is all exactly like WebWork's expression language, explained in chapter 8, "Getting data with the expression language." However, remember that this language is *not* WebWork's expression language (EL); it's still Velocity. There are similarities but also differences, and using the two languages can get confusing.

You access these variables through a Velocity context (VelocityContext). This is an object that contains all the available objects Velocity can access for a given page. WebWork creates a special version of the VelocityContext that automatically maps calls in the form of $xxx to the WebWork expression xxx. However, $xxx.yyy is *not* the same as a WebWork expression xxx.yyy. Rather, it's the WebWork expression xxx; then Velocity takes the responsibility of finding the yyy property on the object returned by WebWork. It's a subtle but important difference.

If any Velocity expression returns null, Velocity writes the expression out directly: `$fakeObject`. This can be useful when you want to see where you aren't getting data that you thought you were. But other times, you'll wish to display nothing when the expression results in null. You can do this using the `$!` modifier rather than the `$` modifier. So now, if you have `$!fakeObject`, nothing is displayed.

10.2.2 Method calls

Sometimes, simple getters and setters aren't enough. Just as WebWork's EL provides a way to call methods, so does Velocity. Suppose you want to extend the previous example and display the number of bids an item has. Because `Collections` use the method `size()` rather than `getSize()`, you need to use a method call rather than a simple property:

```
<h3>$item.name</h3>
Seller: <a href="mailto:$item.seller.email">
        $item.seller.username
        </a>
<br/>
Description: $item.description
<br/>
Date listed: $item.startDate
<br/>
Bids: $item.bids.size()
```

Similarly, you could retrieve any of the properties using the `getXxx()` method syntax, such as `$item.getName()`. Typically you should avoid method calls, because the property syntax is easier to read and is less verbose.

10.2.3 Control statements: if/else and loops

Velocity also has simple control structure, just like the JSP tags from chapter 9. You can loop over collections as well as provide `if/else` blocks. Let's start with looping over data and then see how you can conditionally display data using the `if/else` directives.

Loops: the foreach directive

Continuing with our example, let's look at this page from the point of view of the item's owner. The owner wants to be able to view the bids on the item. This is easily done in Velocity by invoking a `#foreach` loop:

```
<h3>$item.name</h3>
Seller: <a href="mailto:$item.seller.email">
        $item.seller.username
        </a>
```

```
<br/>
Description: $item.description
<br/>
Date listed: $item.startDate
<br/>
Bids: $item.bids.size()
<br/>
<table>
<tr>
    <td>Bid Number</td>
    <td>Bidder</td>
    <td>Amount Bid</td>
    <td>Date Placed</td>
</tr>
#foreach( $bid in $item.bids )
    <tr>
        <td>$velocityCount</td>
        <td><a href="mailto:$bid.email">
                $bid.username
            </a>
        </td>
        <td>$bid.amount</td>
        <td>$bid.created</td>
    </tr>
#end
</table>
```

Here you create a simple table with one row for each bid. In Velocity, the *directives* are identified by the hash (#) character. This example uses the built-in directive foreach. It works by specifying a variable name that is available in the loop ($bid) as well as the values to loop over ($item.bids).

Now let's look inside the loop. You can see two variables that haven't been used before: $bid and $velocityCount. The $bid variable was defined in the foreach directive arguments; Velocity will use this variable name for each object in the iteration. The $velocityCount variable is created and populated for any foreach directive; this value represents the count of the current loop.

Velocity can iterate over Collections, Lists, Sets, Arrays, and even Maps. This is somewhat similar to how the iterator JSP tag works but not exactly the same. For example, when the iterator tag loops over a Map, the item in each loop is a Map.Entry object. In Velocity, the item is the value of map. If you wish to loop over the Map.Entry objects, you need to use $map.entrySet() rather than just $map as your values, as shown here:

```
The values stored in the map are:
#foreach ( $value in $map )
    <li>$value</li>#end<p/>
```

```
The actual mappings in the map are:
#foreach ( $entry in $map.entrySet() )
    <li>$entry.key -> $entry.value</li>
#end
```

In addition, there is another key difference between the `iterator` tag and the `foreach` directive: The `iterator` tag pushes each object onto the value stack, but the `foreach` directive doesn't. This is the case because Velocity has no concept of the value stack. However, you can emulate the behavior of the `iterator` tag by pushing the object directly on the stack yourself. The following example shows both ways to loop over a list of bids:

```
Without pushing the bids on to the stack:
#foreach( $bid in $item.bids )
    <tr>
        <td>$velocityCount</td>
        <td><a href="mailto:$item.bidder.email">
                $item.bidder.username
            </a>
        </td>
        <td>$bid.amount</td>
        <td>$bid.created</td>
    </tr>
#end

With pushing the bids on to the stack:
#foreach( $bid in $item.bids )
    $stack.push($bid)
    <tr>
        <td>$velocityCount</td>
        <td><a href="mailto:$bidder.email">
                $bidder.username
            </a>
        </td>
        <td>$amount</td>
        <td>$created</td>
    </tr>
    #set ($trash = $stack.pop())
#end
```

In the first example, the contents of the loop refer to the values by prepending every expression with $bid. In the second example, this is no longer needed because the Bid object is pushed onto the value stack. Recall that $xxx maps to a WebWork EL expression of xxx; inside the loop, $amount asks WebWork for the output of the expression amount, which in turn accesses the Bid object before the other items in the value stack.

This example introduces two new concepts: the $stack variable and the set directive. We'll discuss those shortly.

> **NOTE** Velocity doesn't have a concept of *scopes* like the Java language does. That is, variables defined in loops and if/else blocks are still accessible after those blocks have finished executing. For example, after the list of bids is displayed, you can still reference $bid and get access to the most recent bid. This often confuses new Velocity users, so you should remember it. Consult the Velocity documentation for more information about the consequences of this behavior.

Conditional logic using the if/else directives

Suppose you want to modify the working example such that a table is displayed only if the user has one or more bids. Otherwise, the text *No bids have been placed* should be displayed. Here's how you can do this:

```
<h3>$item.name</h3>
Seller: <a href="mailto:$item.seller.email">
        $item.seller.username
        </a>
<br/>
Description: $item.description
<br/>
Date listed: $item.startDate
<br/>
Bids: $item.bids.size()
<br/>
#if( $item.bids.size() > 0 )
<table>
<tr>
    <td>Bid Number</td>
    <td>Bidder</td>
    <td>Amount Bid</td>
    <td>Date Placed</td>
</tr>
#foreach( $bid in $item.bids )
    <tr>
        <td>$velocityCount</td>
        <td><a href="mailto:$item.bidder.email">
                $item.bidder.username
            </a>
        </td>
        <td>$bid.amount</td>
        <td>$bid.created</td>
    </tr>
#end
</table>
#else
```

```
    No bids have been placed.
#end
```

In addition to the `if` and `else` directives, an `elseif` directive is also available. Let's now look at the `set` directive you briefly saw earlier.

10.2.4 Assigning variables

From time to time, you'll want to create your own Velocity variables. This is most often done to simplify your templates. For example, rather than access `$some.long.expression` all over the place, you may wish to alias it as `$sle`. This can be accomplished with the `set` directive:

```
#set( $seller = $item.seller )
```

Once you've done this, for the rest of the page you can reference the object `$seller` directly. Not only is this easier on your fingers, but it also keeps the full expression from being evaluated multiple times. You may see a performance gain as well, depending on what your object graph looks like and whether any complex operations are happening in the background when the expression evaluates.

In the previous example, you saw the following:

```
#set ($trash = $stack.pop())
```

This line sets a variable `$trash` to the value of the item being popped off the value stack. In that example, you did this (and called the variable `trash`) because you needed to pop the value off the stack but not display it. If you used `$stack.pop()`, the object would be written out.

10.3 Advanced techniques

In addition to the simple things you've already seen, Velocity has a few more tricks up its sleeve. We won't go through all the features and built-in directives it supports, because an entire book could be devoted to the topic. However, with the information you learned in the last section, you should be able to produce complete Velocity templates by now.

Certain advanced topics aren't Velocity-specific but rather are related to how WebWork integrates with Velocity. In this section, we'll go over these topics.

10.3.1 The VelocityContext

As we've mentioned, Velocity gets all its variables via a `VelocityContext`. The `VelocityContext` is similar to the `ActionContext` in WebWork: It's a simple map where variables can be stored. When WebWork and Velocity are integrated together, the difference is that WebWork provides a custom implementation called the `WebWorkVelocityContext`. It checks local variables first; then, if nothing can be found, it evaluates a WebWork expression against the value stack using the requested variable as the expression.

This is how $xxx turns into a WebWork expression of xxx, and why $xxx.yyy doesn't invoke an expression of xxx.yyy. The `VelocityContext` is asked to find xxx first; once an object is found (via a request for the WebWork expression xxx), Velocity calls `getYyy()` on the object returned.

10.3.2 *WebWork-supplied objects in the context*

WebWork automatically provides a set of objects in the value stack. These variables aren't evaluated against the value stack, because the stack is called only if nothing is found in the base context. These variables are listed in table 10.1.

Table 10.1   Default objects in the `WebWorkVelocityContext`

Variable	Class	Description
req	`javax.servlet.http.HttpServletRequest`	The HTTP request object
res	`javax.servlet.http.HttpServletResponse`	The HTTP response object
stack	`com.opensymphony.xwork.util.OgnlValueStack`	The value stack
webwork	`com.opensymphony.webwork.util.VelocityWebWorkUtil`	Simple utility object
action	`com.opensymphony.xwork.Action` (your action class)	The action executed; useful if you don't wish to use the value stack

The `req` and `res` variables are straightforward—if you require access to the request/response objects, they're easily available. The `stack` variable is also pretty straightforward: Methods such as `push()`, `pop()`, and `findValue()` are the most often used. Consult the JavaDocs for `OgnlValueStack` for more details.

The `action` variable may be useful if you wish to access your action class directly. Typically, doing so is discouraged because it ties you down too tightly to your action classes. However, sometimes direct access to the class (as opposed to indirection via the value stack) is required.

The `webwork` variable provides many utility functions, such as parsing numbers, encoding strings as HTML, converting plain text to HTML, and including other pages. Consult the JavaDocs for the `VelocityWebWorkUtil` and `WebWorkUtil` classes for more information.

10.3.3 *Customizing the Velocity context*

Sometimes, the default variables provided by WebWork aren't enough. For example, you may have a certain utility object you want to be available in all your Velocity templates. You can accomplish this by creating your own `VelocityContext` class. The default `WebWorkVelocityContext` is designed to *chain* together multiple contexts, allowing you to use WebWork's context but also include additional variables.

For example, Velocity doesn't provide a simple way to access math functions from your template. Because the `Math` class uses static methods, you can't easily access those functions. Instead, you can create a wrapper class and then make sure that object is available using the math variable in your templates. Here's a complete example:

```
public class MathVelocityContext extends VelocityContext {
    public static final String MATH = "math";

    private static final MathUtil O_MATH = new MathUtil();


    public Object internalGet(String key) {
        if (MATH.equals(key)) {
            return O_MATH;
        } else {
            return super.internalGet(key);
        }
    }

    public boolean containsKey(Object o) {
        return MATH.equals(o) || super.containsKey(o);
    }

    public static class MathUtil {
        public long round(double a) {
            return Math.round(a);
        }

        public double ceil(double a) {
            return Math.ceil(a);
        }
    }
}
```

Configuring WebWork to chain with this Velocity context requires you to edit web-work.properties. As you saw previously, the `webwork.velocity.contexts` key can be configured as a comma-separated list of contexts. Adding the following to web-work.properties configures the `velocity` context and guarantees that $math always references to a single instance of the `MathUtil` class:

```
# Comma separated list of VelocityContext classnames
#  to chain to the WebWorkVelocityContext
webwork.velocity.contexts = com.acme.MathVelocityContext
```

That's all there is to WebWork-specific configuration related to Velocity. We highly recommend that you consult the Velocity documentation to get a better grasp of the overall language. In the meantime, let's go over two more features that are unique to WebWork's Velocity integration: JSP tag support and resource loading.

10.4 Using JSP tags in Velocity

WebWork provides limited support for using JSP tags in Velocity. Unfortunately, the implementation is far from perfect and isn't guaranteed to behave correctly on all application servers. The general idea is that WebWork provides three new directives: tag, bodytag, and param. Here are a few examples of using JSP tags in a Velocity template:

```
Generate a query URL for Google:
#bodytag( URL "value=http://www.google.com" )
    #param( "name=q" "value=OpenSymphony" )
#end

Generate a URL for the current page:
#tag ( URL )
```

You specify tags by name ("URL") based on the classname of the tag implementation. Because the url tag is implemented as the class com.opensymphony.webwork.views.jsp.URLTag, the string "URL" maps to this class. Remember, webwork.properties by default contains the following value:

```
# JSP tag packages
webwork.velocity.tag.path =
    com.opensymphony.webwork.views.velocity.ui
```

If you wish to use other JSP tags, you can add the packages of those tags to webwork.properties. The tags' classes may be in the form XxxTag or Xxx—WebWork will search for both classes.

> **NOTE**   Although the WebWork JSP tags, including the UI tags, have been tested and verified to work inside Velocity, other tags may not work so well. Several critical bugs have been reported with JSP tag support, most relating to how buffered content is handled. It's highly recommended that you not try to depend on this functionality. If you wish for a non-JSP template

language that supports JSP tags, we recommend the much more robust FreeMarker template library. Future versions of WebWork may switch all internal templates to FreeMarker due to its superior feature set.

10.5 *Loading Velocity templates*

Velocity supports the concept of *resource loaders*: pluggable classes that can load templates from any location. Typically, templates are loaded from files on disk, although sometimes they're loaded from a database or even a URL. WebWork provides two default resource loaders: wwfile and wwclass, in that order.

The wwfile resource loads templates from your web application using the Servlet API to access actual java.io.File objects (rather than access resource streams through the class loader). That is, if your WAR file or expanded WAR has a file located in /template/test.vm, and you have an action-result mapping of <result name="success" type="velocity">/template/test.vm</result>, the wwfile resource loader finds test.vm. Note that the root of the wwfile resource loader (/) is relative to your web application, not your server's file system.

The wwclass resource loader loads templates from the classpath, including any JAR in WEB-INF/lib as well as any resources in WEB-INF/classes. This is useful if you want to package templates in your binary JAR files. Because the wwclass resource loader comes *after* the wwfile resource loader, files take priority. So, you can provide default templates in a JAR or in WEB-INF/classes but then override some of them by providing them in your web application/WAR contextbase. This ability becomes useful when you're customizing the UI taglibs, as discussed in chapter 15 ("Best practices").

Sometimes, you may also wish to provide your own resource loader implementation. For example, you might want to store templates in a database and load from there. You can do so by editing velocity.properties, as shown at the start of this chapter. You'll probably also want to keep the wwfile and wwclass resource loaders as well. See the first code snippet in this chapter for a real-world example of an additional resource loader being used. Consult the Velocity documentation, including the ResourceLoader interface, for more information.

10.6 *Summary*

This chapter provided a high-level introduction to Velocity as the template framework as well as a low-level detailing of all the unique WebWork-Velocity integration points you should be aware of. However, it's by no means meant to serve as a complete guide to Velocity. We recommend that you check out the tutorials available on the Internet to learn more about Velocity if you're going to get serious about using alternatives to JSP.

Velocity is extremely important to WebWork because all the default UI tags are written in Velocity. They may change to another template language like FreeMarker, but the fundamentals are essentially the same. The UI tags are a huge part of WebWork's functionality; in order to fully take advantage of them, knowing Velocity is a must. We highly recommend that you consult the Velocity documentation if you're having any trouble—it's an excellent resource and will introduce you to other built-in directives not covered in this chapter.

UI components

This chapter covers

- Why WebWork's UI tags are useful, even for advanced HTML designers
- Built-in UI tags, such as `form`, `textfield`, and `select`
- How to build your own themes by extending existing ones
- How to create your own templates using the `Component` tag

271

Professional web sites have a consistent look and feel. This standard look and feel is typically achieved through many means, including standard colors and fonts, layout, and page flow. Technologies like HTML, CSS, and Java can help address these different requirements. WebWork goes one step further and provides a framework in which all these technologies are integrated together, allowing you to build rich, standardized web applications. Specifically, WebWork provides a great set of tags that assist with building forms for users to use to interact with your web site. These tags are different than those discussed in chapter 9 ("Tag libraries") in that they focus on producing HTML, especially for building HTML forms. These tags are referred to as UI *tags* because they're used to build up rich user interfaces.

In this chapter, we'll look at the pain that developers face when building forms without frameworks like WebWork. We'll then show you what the same forms look like when they're built using UI tags, and we'll explain what each of those tags does. This chapter includes a complete reference for every UI tag and shows you how to customize the UI tags and build components that can be reused by content developers. Chapter 15 will explore advanced WebWork topics, including building up your own theme library and other UI tag best practices.

11.1 Why bother with UI tags?

Many developers (especially those who come from a background of producing HTML) complain that tags such as WebWork's UI tags take away their ability to build web applications that meet their specific needs. We're going to show that this initial reaction is incorrect and why UI tags are the only way to build large-scale sites with a consistent look and feel while minimizing potential bugs.

> **NOTE** WebWork's UI tags are just one of many solutions that can help with a consistent look and feel. Another project often used along side WebWork is SiteMesh, which is used in the CaveatEmptor application, although it isn't detailed in this book. SiteMesh uses the Decorator pattern to apply a common style to all your pages without your having to make any changes to them. You can learn more about SiteMesh at http://www.opensymphony.com/sitemesh.

11.1.1 Eliminating the pain

Before we explain what the UI tags are, let's first look at the problem that thousands of Java developers face every day when building web applications. In this chapter, we'll focus on CaveatEmptor's Update Profile screen, shown in figure 11.1.

**Figure 11.1
Update Profile form**

This is a typical form that every HTML developer is familiar with. It includes text fields, radio buttons, drop-down selections, and checkboxes. We'll now look at the evolution of how this example turned from an ugly JSP-only implementation into a clean implementation using WebWork's UI tags.

Example: pure JSP

In order for you to understand why UI tags are necessary, we need to explore what life is like without tags or components to assist with building HTML forms. The JSP code in listing 11.1 is a simple implementation of the form in figure 11.1.

Listing 11.1 A simple JSP-only implementation

```
<%
  User user = ActionContext.getContext()
%>
<form action="updateProfile.action" method="post">
<table>
<tr>
  <td align="right"><label>First name:</label></td>
  <td><input type="text" name="user.firstname"
          value="<%= user.getFirstname() %>"/></td>
</tr>
<tr>
  <td align="right"><label>Last name:</label></td>
  <td><input type="text" name="user.lastname"
          value="<%= user.getLastname() %>"/></td>
</tr>
<tr>
  <td align="right"><label>Email:</label></td>
  <td><input type="text" name="user.email"
          value="<%= user.getEmail() %>"/></td>
```

**❶ Simple
text field**

```
    </tr>
    <tr>
      <td align="right"><label>Gender:</label></td>
      <td>
      <input type="radio" name="user.gender" value="0" id="user.gender0"
           <% if (user.getGender() == 0) { %>
           checked="checked"
           <% } %> />                                Two radio buttons     ❷
      <label for="user.gender0">Male</label>

      <input type="radio" name="user.gender" value="1" id="user.gender1"
           <% if (user.getGender() == 1) { %>
           checked="checked"
           <% } %> />
      <label for="user.gender1">Female</label>
      </td>
    </tr>
<%
    Address address = user.getAddress();
    boolean nullAddress = address == null;
%>
    <tr>
      <td align="right"><label>Street Address:</label></td>
      <td><input type="text" name="user.address.street"
               value="<%= !nullAddress ?
                         address.getStreet() : ""%>"/></td>
    </tr>                                       Simple text field     ❸
    <tr>                                        with null check
      <td align="right"><label>Zip Code:</label></td>
      <td><input type="text" name="user.address.zipcode"
               value="<%= !nullAddress ?
                         address.getZipcode() : ""%>"/></td>
    </tr>
    <tr>
      <td align="right"><label>City:</label></td>
      <td><input type="text" name="user.address.city"
               value="<%= !nullAddress ?
                         address.getCity() : ""%>"/></td>
    </tr>
    <tr>
      <td align="right"><label>State:</label></td>
      <td><select name="user.address.state">        Drop-down     ❹
          <option value="California"                selection field
            <% if (!nullAddress &&
                   "California".equals(address.getState())) { %>
            selected="selected"
            <% } %>>California</option>
          <option value="Oregon"
            <% if (!nullAddress &&
                   "Oregon".equals(address.getState())) { %>
            selected="selected"
```

```
              <% } %>>Oregon</option>
        </select></td>
</tr>
<tr>
  <td align="right"><label>Country:</label></td>
  <td><select name="user.address.country">
        <option value="USA"
          <% if (!nullAddress &&
                 "USA".equals(address.getCountry())) { %>
          selected="selected"
          <% } %>>USA</option>
        <option value="Canada"
          <% if (!nullAddress &&
                 "Canada".equals(address.getCountry())) { %>
          selected="selected"
          <% } %>>Canada</option>
        <option value="Mexico"
          <% if (!nullAddress &&
                 "Mexico".equals(address.getCountry())) { %>
          selected="selected"
          <% } %>>Mexico</option>
        <option value="Other"
          <% if (!nullAddress &&
                 "Other".equals(address.getCountry())) { %>
          selected="selected"
          <% } %>>Other</option>
      </select></td>
</tr>
<tr>
  <td colspan="2">
    <table>
    <tr>
      <td valign="middle">
        <input type="checkbox" name="user.address.poBox"
               value="true"
               <% if (!nullAddress && address.isPoBox()) { %>
               checked="checked"
               <% } %>/>
      </td>
      <td valign="middle" width="100%">
        <label>P.O. Box</label>
      </td>
    </tr>
    </table>
  </td>
</tr>
<tr>
  <td colspan="2"><div align="'right'">
    <input value="Update Profile" type="submit"/>
  </div></td>
</tr>
```

④ **Drop-down selection field**

⑤ **Simple checkbox**

```
</table>
</form>
```

■

❶ This is a typical input field. Note that the name is user.firstname, which matches the expression language graph for that action: getUser().setFirstname(...). This is the least complex type of form element and is considered the base for other form elements to build on. All elements in this example use the same naming convention.

❷ The radio buttons associated with the Male/Female choice are another common form element. This type is a bit more complicated for two reasons:

- The labels for the radio buttons must be associated with the radio element, so that clicking the label selects the element. This is done with the id attribute in the input element and the for attribute in the label element.

- In order to make an element be checked, the checked attribute must be set. The code here must compare the real value to the different options and determine which radio button should be preselected.

❸ This is another typical input field, but with a twist. Because the Address object may be null, you have to check it to avoid a NullPointerException. If the object is null, you set the initial value to an empty string.

❹ This select box is almost exactly like the radio buttons. Select boxes and radio buttons are, at least conceptually, pretty much the same thing. The only difference is the layout and interface behavior.

❺ Looking at figure 11.1 again, you can see that the checkbox element differs from the rest because the label is to the *right* of the form element rather than to the left. This is a common requirement because many users feel that it just makes sense. To ensure that the checkbox row isn't affected by the labels and form elements in the rest of the table, you create a table inside the cell to allow the element to be independent.

Whew! That's a lot of code, and it's painful to look at. The main thing to notice is that the listing contains well over 100 lines of code, and all it does is display a basic form. Toss in styling, error reporting, and internationalization, and the number of lines will grow even more.

Example: using simple tags

Let's make the next evolution in form layout and address some of the pain that each form element causes. Notice that every form element is responsible for either setting a value attribute or ensuring that the correct value is preselected (radio, checkbox, and select). We'll look at an *imaginary* tag library that addresses this pain and makes the JSP a little more readable. We won't reprint the entire example, because it's still unnecessarily long, but listing 11.2 addresses the five examples called out in listing 11.1.

Listing 11.2 A simple implementation using imaginary JSP tags

```
<tr>
  <td align="right"><label>First name:</label></td>          1  Same simple
  <td><form:textfield name="user.firstname"/></td>              text element
</tr>
...
<tr>                                                 Much    2
  <td align="right"><label>Gender:</label></td>   simpler radio
  <td>                                            implementation
    <form:radio name="user.gender" value="0" id="user.gender0"/>
    <label for="user.gender0">Male</label>
    <form:radio name="user.gender" value="1" id="user.gender1"/>
    <label for="user.gender1">Female</label>
  </td>
</tr>
...
<tr>
  <td align="right"><label>Street Address:</label></td>
  <td><form:textfield name="user.address.street "/></td>     3  No more
</tr>                                                            null checks
...
<tr>
  <td align="right"><label>State:</label></td>
  <td>
    <form:select name="user.address.state">
      <form:option value="California"/>        4  Much simpler select
      <form:option value="Oregon"/>               implementation
    </form:select>
  </td>
</tr>
...
<tr>
  <td colspan="2">
    <table>                          Much simpler checkbox  5
    <tr>                                implementation
      <td valign="middle">
        <form:checkbox name="user.address.poBox" value="true"/>
      </td>
      <td valign="middle" width="100%">
        <label>P.O. Box</label>
      </td>
    </tr>
```

```
    </table>
   </td>
  </tr>
```

❺ Much simpler checkbox
implementation

❶ The base element, the text field, is slightly simpler. The value is determined based on the name of the element, and the value is looked up using WebWork's expression language. *Keep in mind that these tags are made up for the purpose of this example and do not exist!*

❷ The radio implementation is simpler now, too. You no longer have to include a bunch of if statements to fill out the selected attribute. The tag handles this task, leaving you to focus on the layout of the labels and form elements.

❸ This field is exactly like the other text field. You no longer have to worry about null checks—the tag takes care of that.

❹ Like the radio selection, these new tags let you avoid worrying about the selected attribute.

❺ The checkbox still has the complicated table within a table layout, but at least you don't have to worry about setting the checked attribute.

This code looks nicer, but it still contains a lot of repetition. With these imaginary tags, you avoid having to set the value of elements or indicate them as checked or selected. You also avoid having to do any null checks. However, you're left with the problem of having to repeat the layout (table structure, in this example) over and over again.

> **NOTE** The Struts framework provides tags that are very similar to the imaginary ones presented here. They work nicely, but we think the tags included with WebWork go that extra mile in helping you reuse HTML and code, thereby decreasing your development time as well as decreasing the number of bugs that might occur due to long copy-and-paste exercises.

Example: WebWork UI tags

Let's now examine the code that creates this form using the UI tags that are part of WebWork. The tags build on the conceptual ideas represented by the imaginary tag library, but they go even further: They let you build forms using much larger building blocks, and you don't have to worry about ensuring that your HTML is standardized. Listing 11.3 demonstrates how much easier UI tags are to work with.

NOTE   Unlike the example in listing 11.2, the example code in listing 11.3 is real and is available for you to try out immediately.

Listing 11.3 A much simpler implementation using WebWork's UI tags

```
<ww:form action="updateProfile" method="post">
<ww:textfield label="First name" name="user.firstname"/>    ←——①
<ww:textfield label="Last name" name="user.lastname"/>
<ww:textfield label="Email" name="user.email"/>
<ww:radio label="Gender" name="user.gender"
       list="#{0 : 'Male', 1 : 'Female'}"/>
<ww:textfield label="Street" name="user.address.street"/>    ←——③
<ww:textfield label="Zip Code" name="user.address.zipcode"/>
<ww:textfield label="City" name="user.address.city"/>
<ww:select label="State" name="user.address.state"
       list="{'California', 'Oregon'}"/>
<ww:select label="Country" name="user.address.country"
       list="{'USA', 'Canada', 'Mexico', 'Other'}"/>
<ww:checkbox label="P.O. Box" name="user.address.poBox"
          fieldValue="true"/>
<ww:submit value="Update Profile"/>
</ww:form>
```

② **Outputs multiple form elements**

④ **Outputs select and option elements**

⑤ **Handles all complex layout**

① This time, you don't even output the table rows and cells. Rather, the UI tag takes care of the entire row. In section 11.2.2, you'll see where the HTML came from.

② Notice that there is no longer any HTML, including the HTML for the select and option tags required to display a drop-down selection list. Instead, you specify the name of the element (which, in turn, gets the value based on the assumption that the name is the expression to retrieve the value) as well as a list of the possible selection choices.

Notice that the list attribute is actually a Map represented in the expression language (see chapter 8 for a review). The Map contains two entries: a key of 0 (zero) mapping to Male, and a key of 1 (one) mapping to Female. The tag looks at the value of the expression user.gender and determines which should be selected.

③ Once again, you don't have to do any null checking. This example is now exactly like ①.

④ Because radio buttons and select boxes are so similar, it isn't surprising that the tags to produce those elements are almost exactly the same. The only difference from ② is that the list attribute is a List rather than a Map.

❺ The checkbox is like the other tags, except for the additional attribute `field-Value`. This tells the UI tag what the value of the parameter should be if the form is submitted with the checkbox checked.

The code is much simpler now. Instead of the original 120+ lines of code, you have fewer than 20 lines of code when the UI tags are used. That means you avoid writing at least 85 percent of the code you would have if you hadn't use the UI tags. But what happened to the HTML? It must be somewhere! In the next section, we'll take a detailed look at the UI tags and how they control layout and much more.

11.1.2 More than just form elements

As you saw in the last section, WebWork's UI tags do a lot more than output the HTML form elements. They also ensure that a common layout is followed and that a consistent style is used. On top of that, the tags also take care of error reporting and integrate seamlessly with the rest of the WebWork framework. In this section, we'll examine the individual features of the UI tags and go over the benefits they bring to the table.

Layout

As you've seen, most forms use tables to align labels and form elements. WebWork uses this assumption and automatically handles the entire form layout for you. This means when you're using the UI tags, you don't need to write a single table, row, or cell element in HTML: WebWork takes care of all that. Figure 11.2 shows figure 11.1 again, but this time with the table cells clearly outlined.

The `ww:form` tag is responsible for creating the `form` element as well as the surrounding table. The rest of the tags are responsible for creating one row in the table. Some tags, such as the checkbox and submit button, don't follow the standard two-column approach. Rather, they output a single table cell that spans both columns so they can do special formatting.

Errors

In addition to being responsible for creating a single row, each tag is also responsible for displaying any errors that may be associated with that field. For example, if you try to submit the Update Profile

Figure 11.2   Figure 11.1 redrawn with the table clearly outlined

form with a blank first name, WebWork's validation framework will kick into place and return an
error indicating that the field is required.

Displaying the actual error is up to the UI tags.
Figure 11.3 shows a form that has just been submitted and on which an error occurred. The
error is displayed above the row the tag renders,
and both the label and the error message are col-
ored red to gain the user's attention.

Suppose you want every field in the form to be
able to display errors. If you were using pure JSP,
the code for a single field would have to be
updated to check for any error messages and, if
there were any, to display another row for each
error immediately above the field. Here's an
example of such code:

Figure 11.3 A form with an error

```
<%
  User user = (User) request.getAttribute("user");
  Map fieldErrors = (Map) request.getAttribute("fieldErrors");
  if (fieldErrors == null) {
    fieldErrors = Collections.EMPTY_MAP;
  }
%>
...
<%
  if (fieldErrors.containsKey("user.firstname"))  {
    List errors = (List) fieldErrors.get("user.firstname");
    for (Iterator iterator = errors.iterator();
         iterator.hasNext();) {
      String error = (String) iterator.next();
%>
<tr>
  <td align="center" valign="top" colspan="2">
  <span class="errorMessage"><%= error %></span>
  </td>
</tr>
<%
    }
  }
%>
<tr>
  <td align="right"><label>First name:</label></td>
  <td><input type="text" name="user.firstname"
```

```
            value="<%= user.getFirstname() %>"/></td>
    </tr>
    ...
```

Recall that the `ActionSupport` base class exposes a `Map` for field-level errors via the `getFieldErrors()` method. Also recall that the keys in that `Map` are the field names, whereas the values in the `Map` are `List` objects, with each `List` containing one or more errors associated with the field. This example shows how you could manually display the field errors. Rather than go through all that hassle, the UI tags do this for you automatically.

Styles

In addition to handling layout and error reporting, the UI tags also reference a set of styles that you can define in your Cascading Style Sheets (CSS), thereby further customizing the look and feel. The CSS classes referenced in the HTML produced by the UI tags are identified in table 11.1.

Table 11.1   CSS classes referenced by the UI tags

Class name	Description
wwFormTable	Surrounding table produced by the `ww:form` tag
label	Label associated with all UI tags except `checkbox`
checkboxLabel	The label associated with the `checkbox` tag
errorLabel	Used when an error is associated with that field
checkboxErrorLabel	Just like `errorLabel`, except for `checkboxes`
errorMessage	Error message being displayed
required	Required notification: * (more on this later)

The recommended values for those styles are included in the WebWork distribution, but typically developers wish to provide their own values. The default set is shown here:

```
.wwFormTable {}
.label {font-style:italic; }
.errorLabel {font-style:italic; color:red; }
.errorMessage {font-weight:bold; text-align: center; color:red; }
.checkboxLabel {}
.checkboxErrorLabel {color:red; }
.required {color:red;}
```

These style definitions are very basic and aren't intended to be the final styles you use for your application. Rather, they're meant to be a starting point from which you can further customize the look of the form such that it fits with the rest of your application.

Seamless integration

You've seen how the UI tags do much more than render HTML form elements. It's now time to understand how they work and how they integrate with WebWork. For example, the `ww:select` and `ww:radio` tags are interesting because a single tag is outputting not only layout HTML but also multiple HTML form elements, such as `select` and `option`, based entirely on the contents of the value stack and the evaluation of an expression.

The UI tags are more than just simple tags to render HTML form elements. We've shown how they integrate with `ActionSupport` to provide seamless error reporting. To take full advantage of the benefits of the UI tags, it's recommend that you utilize all the other features of WebWork, including validation, internationalization, the expression language, and the value stack.

During the rest of this chapter you'll see more examples of how the UI tags integrate nicely with many of the other features WebWork provides. Let's now begin our examination of the UI tags offered by WebWork.

11.2 UI tag overview

Until now, you've seen the code you'd need to write if you didn't use the UI tags. Because there's no such thing as magic in programming, we need to explain how we were able to avoid writing all that code. More specifically, we'll examine the templates that WebWork uses to render the various UI components you've seen thus far.

We've also only looked at form layouts using the traditional two-column approach. Obviously, this won't work for everyone. In this section we'll also discuss the concept of *themes* and how you can use them to build up distinct sets of templates for use in your application. Using themes and customized templates, you can get all the benefits of the UI tags without compromising your site's layout and design.

11.2.1 Templates

As we explained in chapter 7, WebWork is a view-agnostic framework. That means you're free to write your user interface in JSP, Velocity, FreeMarker, or any other supported technology. The UI tags are no exception. By default, WebWork only supports JSP tags as the method for invoking the UI tags. This generally isn't a problem, because FreeMarker supports JSP tag calls natively and Velocity has integration provided by WebWork, as explained in chapter 10. Although we don't discuss them in this book, recent features in WebWork allow for native invocation (no JSP tag invocation) to be created. It's expected that native support for the UI tags will be provided in WebWork 2.2 or later.

WebWork UI tags can also be written in any template language, including JSP and Velocity. However, only one language is provided out of the box: Velocity. That is the case because Velocity is commonly used and extremely fast. As such, in this chapter we'll only review the most typical usage of calling the UI tags: tag calls from JSP views with Velocity-backed templates.

> **NOTE** To help clear up any confusion between the terms *template*, *theme*, and *tag*, we provide the following descriptions. A *template* is a file written in Velocity, JSP, or FreeMarker that renders HTML markup. A *theme* is a collection of *templates* that, when combined together, form a common look and feel. A *tag* is a JSP tag that reads in attributes and renders a *template* using those values.

Template lookup

Templates are looked up the same way as all other Velocity templates: through both the web application server's `ClassLoader` and the web application's file path. Consult chapter 10 for more details about how this works.

Velocity integration

Using Velocity as a view for your action provides a few default variables in the `VelocityContext`, such as `$stack`, `$req`, and others. The templates that back up the UI tags and dictate the HTML that gets rendered are no exception. However, in addition to those variables, templates invoked by the UI tags also have access to one more variable: `$parameters`. This variable is a `Map` of all the parameters provided by you when invoking each UI tag. For example, `$parameters.label` references the label specified in the tag.

Let's look at the contents of these templates and explain what they're doing. Listing 11.4 shows a simplified version of the Velocity template for the `textfield` tag.

Listing 11.4 A simplified Velocity template for the `textfield` tag

```
#parse("/template/xhtml/controlheader.vm")
<input type="text"
       name="$parameters.name"/>
#parse("/template/xhtml/controlfooter.vm")
```

The controlheader.vm template takes care of opening a new table row, printing out the label and any errors associated with this input, and positioning the layout according to the attributes given in the UI tag. Next comes the actual form element that is being rendered: This element is included in the right-hand column of the surrounding table. In this example, the template is much more simplified than in reality. (You'll see a complete example shortly.) For now, it's important to notice the use of `$parameters.name`, which prints out the name attribute of the UI tag. The controlfooter.vm template is responsible for closing the right-hand column cells as well as the enclosing table row. As you'll see shortly, this template is much simpler than controlheader.vm.

This example demonstrates how a typical UI tag utilizes the same header and footer components. In the most common case, the header is responsible for printing out the table row and other common features you've seen in the form examples so far. However, as we've mentioned, this two-column layout is far from the only one you can use. In the next section, we'll explore the concept of themes and see how customized layouts can quickly be created.

11.2.2 Themes

Up to now, you've seen form layouts that use the typical two-column approach. This approach works for most usages; but when it doesn't, it can be very frustrating to try to work around. Some engineers, not knowing they could use alternative themes, have gone so far as to create surrounding tables for every UI tag just to ensure that proper HTML is rendered.

Themes define layout and style. WebWork ships with two themes, both of which you can extend or copy for your own customized themes. We'll first look at the default theme, XHTML, which we've been using in all our examples thus far. Then we'll look at the simple theme the XHTML theme builds on. Later in this chapter, we'll explore the process of creating your own themes.

XHTML theme

The XHTML theme is named that way because it's the default theme and renders XHTML-compatible HTML. However, it does much more than the name suggests. As you've seen, this theme is responsible for rendering UI tags using the two-column form layout. The left column is used for the label, and the right column is used for the actual `form` element, as shown in figure 11.4.

This theme also provides an alternative way to render the labels and `form` elements. Figure 11.5 shows the same form as figure 11.4, using the alternate label position.

Let's explore how these two different layouts can be rendered by the same theme. The answer lies in how the header of each template, control-header.vm, renders the table row. The template is shown in listing 11.5.

Figure 11.4 A simple form using the default label position

Figure 11.5 A simple form using the top label position

```
## Only show message if errors are available.
## This will be done if ActionSupport is used.
#if( $fieldErrors.get($parameters.name) )
  #set ($hasFieldErrors = $fieldErrors.get($parameters.name))
  #foreach ($error in $fieldErrors.get($parameters.name))
    <tr>
        #if ($parameters.labelposition == 'top')
            <td align="left" valign="top" colspan="2">
        #else
            <td align="center" valign="top" colspan="2">
        #end
        <span class="errorMessage">
        $!webwork.htmlEncode($error)
        </span>
        </td>
    </tr>
  #end
#end
## if the label position is top,
## then give the label its own row in the table
<tr>
#if ($parameters.labelposition == 'top')
    <td align="left" valign="top" colspan="2">
```

Preceding row(s) that ❶ **display field errors**

❷ **Label position**

❷ **Label position**

```
#else
    <td align="right" valign="top">
#end

#if ($parameters.label)
    <label
        #if ($parameters.id)
            for="$!webwork.htmlEncode($parameters.id)"
        #end
        #if ($hasFieldErrors)
            class="errorLabel"
        #else
            class="label"
        #end>
        #if ($parameters.required)
            <span class="required">*</span>
        #end
            $!webwork.htmlEncode($parameters.label):</label>
#end

</td>

## add the extra row
#if ($parameters.labelposition == 'top')
</tr>
<tr>
#end
            <td>
```

❷ Label position

Actual label ❸

❷ Label position

❹ Opening cell for form element

❶ If any field errors are associated with the name of the UI tag, each error is displayed as its own row that precedes the label and `form` element. Note that the error is HTML-encoded using the `$webwork.htmlEncode()` utility method. This ensures that characters like & are converted to HTML-compatible strings such as &.

❷ This is the logic that determines how the table row is laid out. Note that this logic is required in a few places in the header to provide a good look and feel. Some of the adjustments are subtle, such as alignment of the error messages, but all are required in order to give a consistent form layout.

❸ The label is rendered here. Notice that the label is rendered differently, including an alternative CSS class, depending on whether any errors are associated with the field.

❹   This is where the right-hand column (or the second row, if you're using a `label-position` of `top`) is opened. The contents in this cell are the `form` element itself and are determined by the template that included controlheader.vm.

The contents of controlheader.vm are fairly complicated but provide some powerful features. The most obvious features to note are as follows:

- Controlheader.vm automatically displays field errors and provides a different CSS style for fields that have errors.

- It allows for a horizontal (two-column) and vertical (two-row) approach to laying out HTML forms.

- It provides for a feature-rich label, including a `required` marker (which does *not* currently tie in with the validation framework—it's merely a visual indicator), HTML character escaping, and a link from the label to the `form` element using the `for` attribute.

NOTE   In HTML, the `for` attribute on the `label` tag allows you to link a label to a `form` element. The value given for the `for` attribute must be the ID of the `form` element. When they're properly linked, clicking the label causes the cursor to focus on the `form` element specified.

Fortunately, the footer is much simpler than the header. Listing 11.6 shows the complete contents of controlfooter.vm. As you can see, it merely closes the table cell (for both two-column and two-row label positions) and the table row.

Listing 11.6   Contents of controlfooter.vm

```
    </td>
</tr>
```

That's all there is to the XHTML theme. It's the default theme in WebWork and tends to work well 90 percent of the time. As we mentioned previously, the XHTML theme extends the `simple` theme. Let's now look at the `simple` theme and see why it's called *simple*.

The Simple theme

Sometimes, a two-column or two-row approach doesn't work. And sometimes, you need to use something other than the XHTML theme only once. Rather than make a new template or theme that won't be reused, you may want to render the `form` element independently of layouts, labels, and field errors. You can do so using the `simple` theme.

In listing 11.4, you saw an example of a simplified Velocity template for the `textfield` tag. Listing 11.7 shows the contents of the `textfield` template for the XHTML theme.

Listing 11.7 Template for the XHTML `textfield` template

```
#parse("/template/xhtml/controlheader.vm")
#parse("/template/simple/text.vm")
#parse("/template/xhtml/controlfooter.vm")
```

Notice that the XHTML template wraps a header and footer around the `simple` template. This is how the XHTML theme extends the `simple` theme—they both use the same core templates to render the form elements.

Let's now look at the contents of the simple theme's `textfield` template. Listing 11.4 only displayed a simple template that rendered an `input` element with the `type` and `name` attributes populated. Listing 11.8 shows the complete template, including all the optional parameters you haven't seen before.

Listing 11.8 Template for the simple `textfield` template

```
<input type="text"
       name="$!webwork.htmlEncode($parameters.name)"          ⟵┐  Most parameters
#if ($parameters.size)                                    ⟵     └─ are HTML encoded
       size="$!webwork.htmlEncode($parameters.size)" #end
#if ($parameters.maxlength)
       maxlength="$!webwork.htmlEncode($parameters.maxlength)" #end
#if ($parameters.nameValue)
       value="$!webwork.htmlEncode($parameters.nameValue)" #end
#if ($parameters.disabled == true)                                Optional
       disabled="disabled" #end                                   parameters are
#if ($parameters.readonly)                                        checked with an
       readonly="readonly" #end                                   if statement
#if ($parameters.tabindex)
       tabindex="$!webwork.htmlEncode($parameters.tabindex)" #end
#if ($parameters.id)
       id="$!webwork.htmlEncode($parameters.id)" #end
#if ($parameters.cssClass)
       class="$!webwork.htmlEncode($parameters.cssClass)" #end
#if ($parameters.cssStyle)
       style="$!webwork.htmlEncode($parameters.cssStyle)" #end
#parse("/template/simple/scripting-events.vm")   ⟵┐  Common set of
    />                                             │  JavaScript events
```

Most of listing 11.8 is straightforward. Optional attributes are printed out only if specified, and almost all attributes are encoded using the `htmlEncode()` helper method. The only interesting part of this template is the inclusion of the scripting-events.vm template. This template is responsible for rendering all the supported JavaScript event handlers. Because every UI tag supports the same events, the code is shared among all the simple UI tag templates. Here's part of scripting-events.vm, to give you an idea of how WebWork renders the event handlers:

```
#if ($parameters.onclick)
        onclick="$!webwork.htmlEncode($parameters.onclick)" #end
#if ($parameters.ondblclick)
        ondblclick="$!webwork.htmlEncode($parameters.ondblclick)"#end
...
```

Once again, the template is simple. All scripting events are handled the same way: An optional check occurs, and then, if required, the attribute is printed out with the value escaped for special HTML characters.

That's all there is to the `simple` theme. A complete XHTML UI tag may be a lot to take in all at once, but it isn't that bad once all the various templates are broken down. In figure 11.6, the XHTML `textfield` template is represented graphically in two-column mode. You can see how the header is responsible for the error messages (the top row or rows) and the label (the left-hand column). The XHTML `textfield` template then includes the simple `textfield` template to render the `form` element, which in turn calls out to the common scripting events template. Finally, the footer is included, which closes the row.

Now that we've explored the basics of UI tags, it's almost time to look at the UI tags that are available and how to make your own components and themes. But before you can do any of that, let's take a quick refresher look at how tag attributes are evaluated in WebWork; this will affect how you read the UI tag reference in section 11.3.

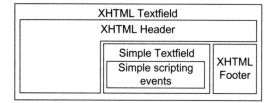

Figure 11.6
Graphical representation of the relationship between the `simple` and `XHTML` themes

11.2.3 *Tag attributes*

Recall in chapter 9 how tag attributes are parsed. The same applies for the UI tags discussed in this chapter as well. As we mentioned in that chapter, it's extremely important that you understand that this book doesn't document or cover the normal syntax that the tags use in WebWork 2.1.x. Rather we decided to focus on the default syntax that will be used when WebWork 2.2 comes out in the fall of 2005. We feel that the new syntax is easier to read and new users can get up to speed much quicker.

As a reminder, if you're using WebWork 2.1.4 or higher, you must remember to enable the alternative syntax order to use the examples in this book. You can do that by adding the line `webwork.tag.altSyntax = true` in webwork.properties.

Please refer to chapter 9 for more detail on how the tag attributes behave. Specifically, it's important to understand which attributes are parsed for the `%{...}` notation and which are evaluated completely. As a general rule, attributes that are designated as a `String` type are parsed for the `%{...}` notation, while non-`String` attributes are automatically evaluated. While this may seem like you're required to remember the data type for each attribute, it's actually very easy to work with. Specifically, almost all attributes are of type `String` except for the very few that are always going to be evaluated (such as the list attribute for `Collection`-based tags).

Now that you know how the UI tags work in general, it's time to look at each tag offered by WebWork.

11.3 UI tag reference

We'll now explore several classes of UI tags, ranging from the simple tags you've already seen—such as `form` and `textfield`—all the way to `Collection`-based and advanced tags. `Collection`-based tags offer the user a choice of values to select and/or allow users to select multiple values for a single field. Advanced tags include custom templates and tags that offer more interactive functionality through JavaScript.

11.3.1 *Common attributes*

Every UI tag has a common set of attributes. Before we examine the simple UI tags, let's take a moment to discuss the common attributes that all tags support (although some may choose to ignore certain attributes, depending on the type of tag). All the attributes except those that deal with labels work for both the simple and XHTML themes. Table 11.2 lists all the common attributes for the UI tags, the theme they work with (the `simple` theme implies XHTML by extension), the data type of that attribute, and the attribute description.

Table 11.2 Common attributes for all UI tags

Attribute	Theme	Data type	Description
name	simple	String	Field name the `form` element maps to.
value	simple	Object	Value of the `form` element.
label	XHTML	String	Label used by the XHTML theme (ignored by the `simple` theme).
labelposi- tion	XHTML	String	Location of the element label. By default, the label is to the left of the element; but specifying `top` indicates that the label should be in its own row above the element.
required	XHTML	Boolean	If `true`, an asterisk appears next to the label indicating the field is required. By default, the value is `true` if a field-level validator is mapped to the field indicated in the `name` attribute.
id	simple	String	HTML `id` attribute, allowing for easy JavaScript integration.
cssClass	simple	String	`class` attribute of the `form` element.
cssStyle	simple	String	`style` attribute of the `form` element.
disabled	simple	Boolean	`disabled` attribute of the `form` element.
tabindex	simple	String	`tabindex` attribute of the `form` element.
theme	N/A	String	Theme in which the template should be looked up. By default, this is either the theme specified in webwork.properties or the XHTML theme.
template	N/A	String	Template to look up to render the UI tag. All UI tags have a default template (except the `component` tag), but the template can be overridden.

It's important to underscore the relationship between the tag attributes and the parameters available to the Velocity templates. Recall from previous code listings that attributes are available through the `$parameters` map. That is, the `foo` attribute can be retrieved by using the expression `$parameters.foo`.

There are a few exceptions to this rule, namely the theme and template attributes. Because these attributes are used to help determine which template to load, they aren't useful as parameters inside the template itself.

The nameValue parameter

The other exception to that rule is much more important. Rather than the `value` attribute being available with the expression `$parameters.value`, it's available as `$parameters.nameValue`. This is the case because the `name` and `value` attributes have an intertwined relationship. To understand their relationship, look at this simple form:

```
<ww:form action="updateProfile">
    <ww:textfield name="user.firstName" value="%{user.firstName}"/>
</ww:form>
```

As you can see, the `value` attribute is the evaluation of the `name` attribute. This is almost always what you want when building a form, because 99 percent of the time the field on which you set form data (determined by the `name` attribute) is also the field you wish to get data from and display in the form (determined by the `value` attribute).

Rather than enter redundant data for every UI tag, you can define the name of the field, and WebWork automatically assumes the value for you. Here you can see what the same tag looks like when the value is implicitly assumed:

```
<ww:form action="updateProfile">
    <ww:textfield name="user.firstName"/>
</ww:form>
```

Of course, sometimes you may not want the default value displayed in the form to be the value of the field. For example, if you were asking a user to pick a screen name and that screen name had already been selected by a different user, you might wish to suggest an alternative. You could do so by using a value of `%{suggestedUsername}`.

The id attribute

Except for the `form` tag (discussed in section 11.3.2), all UI tags have a default value for their `id` attribute. Having a value for the `id` attribute is nice for a couple of reasons. First, it makes the form labels more tightly integrated into your form because they specify the `for` attribute. Second, knowing that every `form` element has an ID allows for easy JavaScript integration. You're always free to specify your own `id` attribute, but by default the value is `[formName]_[elementName]`. Thus if you have a form named `updateProfile` and a field named `user.firstname`, the `id` attribute is `updateProfile_user.firstname`.

JavaScript events

In addition to the common attributes in table 11.2, all the UI tags in the `simple` theme (and, thus, the XHTML theme) support the common setup JavaScript event attributes as well (see table 11.3). These allow for easy JavaScript integration and let you make your forms much more interactive.

Table 11.3 Common JavaScript event attributes for all UI tags

Attribute	Theme	Data type
onclick	simple	String
ondblclick	simple	String
onmousedown	simple	String
onmouseup	simple	String
onmouseover	simple	String
onmousemove	simple	String
onmouseout	simple	String
onfocus	simple	String
onblur	simple	String
onkeypress	simple	String
onkeydown	simple	String
onkeyup	simple	String
onselect	simple	String
onchange	simple	String

Now that you're familiar with the common set of attributes, let's dive into the basic UI tags.

11.3.2 Simple tags

Simple tags are UI tags that are bound to a single element (rather than `Collection`-based tags, which we'll discuss in section 11.3.3). In addition to these tags, we'll also discuss the `form` tag, which acts as a container for all the tags in this chapter. The simple tags we'll discuss are `textfield`, `password`, `textarea`, and `checkbox`. These, alone with the `form` tag, make up the basic elements necessary to get started with any web-based form. Once you've mastered how these tags work, moving on to the `Collection`-based and advanced tags should be no problem.

The form tag

The form tag is unique among all the UI tags because it acts as a container. That is, it has a start (`<ww:form>`) and an end (`</ww:form>`). In the simple theme, it renders the opening and closing form elements. In the XHTML theme, it renders the surrounding table in addition to the form elements.

As such, the form tag maps to two templates: form.vm and form-close.vm. The common attribute template is mapped to form-close.vm by default. In table 11.4, you can see another attribute, openTemplate, which by default maps to form.vm. The other attributes the form tag supports are also listed in table 11.4.

Table 11.4 The form tag attributes

Attribute	Data type	Description
action	String	Name of the action to submit to.
namespace	String	Namespace of the action; defaults to the namespace based on the current request.
method	String	POST or GET.
target	String	Target to which the form submits. Typically a frame name, _blank, _top, or any of the other special target values.
enctype	String	Set to multipart/form-data when you're doing file uploads.
openTemplate	String	Maps to form.vm by default.
validate	Boolean	Used for client-side validation.

> **NOTE** Some of the common attributes previously listed aren't applicable to the form tag. For example, the label attributes don't affect the form tag's behavior.

The two most important attributes to note are action and namespace. When combined, they're used to link your form to a particular action. For example, `<ww:form action="updateProfile" namespace="/secure">` submits to /secure/updateProfile.action. Often, the request that is rendering the current form is in the same namespace to which you're submitting, so you can leave out the namespace. For example, if the form is rendered because of a call to /secure/updateProfile!default.action, then the namespace is assumed to already be /secure, and you can use `<ww:form action="updateProfile">`.

> **NOTE** Notice that the action extension, .action, is used in this example. Recall that you can change this extension to any value you'd like by editing the servlet-mapping in web.xml *and* editing the extension value in

webwork.properties. The value in webwork.properties must be the same as the `servlet-mapping`, because it's used to generate the URL used by the `form` tag in this example.

This works great when you're submitting a form to a WebWork action that is part of your web application. But sometimes you may want to submit to a location that isn't a WebWork action or is otherwise unknown by WebWork. Doing so is simple enough: Provide the URL (complete or relative, it doesn't matter) in the `action` attribute. The `form` tag can recognize the difference between an action name that is a WebWork action and one that isn't, so it automatically does the right thing. Submitting a form to Google's search engine is as simple as `<ww:form action="http://www.google.com/search">`.

TIP   The URL `/secure/updateProfile!default.action` may look new to you. It's a little-known feature in WebWork that lets you execute a method other than `execute()`. The text after the `!` indicates the method Web-Work will call. In this example, WebWork tries to execute both `default()` and `doDefault()`. This is just like copying the `updateProfile` action definition in xwork.xml and adding a `method` attribute equal to `default`. As you'll see again in chapter 15, "Best Practices," this feature is useful for adding multiple behaviors in a single action.

The `method` and `enctype` attributes are passed directly in to the same attributes in the `form` tag. These are your standard HTML attributes, and nothing is different about them here. Keep in mind that if you're trying to do file uploads, you must set enctype to the value `multipart/form-data`. The `method` attribute can be either GET or POST, just like any other HTML form.

The final attribute in table 11.4 is `validate`. It's used to tell WebWork that you would like the form to do some limited client-side JavaScript validation. Unfortunately, this feature is just getting off the ground and isn't fully working or fully documented. By the time this book comes out, we hope to have a very robust client-side validation implementation in WebWork. In the meantime, if you wish to get client-side validation working, set this attribute to `true` and consult the latest WebWork documentation for more details.

NOTE   Even when you're using the `simple` theme, we highly recommend using the `form` tag rather than printing out your own `<form>` HTML tag. There are several reasons, including better linking to your WebWork actions and template reusability. But the most important reason for using the `form` tag is that it acts as a smart container for the other UI tags. Currently, this provides for limited client-side validation; but in the future, it can be used for added security, better validation, and richer client-side behavior.

It's worth noting that the `name` attribute is, by default, the name of the action you're submitting to. This is useful for easy JavaScript integration. For example, if your form is `<ww:form action="updateProfile">`, then it's safe to assume that the Java-Script `document.updateProfile` or `document.forms['updateProfile']` will get you a reference to the form. Similarly, the `id` attribute is also, by default, the value of the action. You're free to override either of these defaults to whatever value you choose.

The textfield tag

You've already seen quite a bit of the `textfield` tag, so nothing should be new here. Table 11.5 provides all the attributes that are unique to this tag, in addition to all the common attributes already discussed.

Table 11.5   The `textfield` tag attributes

Attribute	Data type	Description
maxlength	String	Maximum length that can be entered in this field.
readonly	Boolean	When set to true, the user is unable to set a value in the `form` element.
size	String	Visible size of the field.

Note that these three attributes are all standard HTML attributes for textfields.

The password tag

The `password` tag is similar to the `textfield` tag, with one small exception: The value isn't displayed by default unless the `show` attribute is set to `true`. Typically, forms shouldn't prepopulate password fields for users, so this value is normally `false`. However, sometimes you may which to change this behavior, so setting the `show` attribute to `true` ensures that the value is prepopulated.

The other three attributes are exactly like those of the `textfield` tag. In terms of class hierarchies, the `password` tag (`PasswordTag` class) extends the `textfield` tag (`TextfieldTag` class). Table 11.6 lists the three attributes the `textfield` tag supports as well as the additional `show` attribute.

Table 11.6 The password tag attributes

Attribute	Data type	Description
show	Boolean	False by default; when set to true, the value is set and the password field is prepopulated.
maxlength	String	Maximum length that can be entered in this field.
readonly	Boolean	When set to true, the user is unable to set a value in the form element.
size	String	Visible size of the field.

The textarea tag

The textarea tag is used for gathering larger amounts of text (including line breaks) than the textfield tag can. Rather than rendering an <input> tag like the textfield and password tags do, this tag renders out the HTML tag <textarea>. Not surprisingly, it also supports all the HTML attributes the <textarea> tag does, as listed in table 11.7.

Table 11.7 The textarea tag attributes

Attribute	Data type	Description
cols	String	Number of columns in the text area.
rows	String	Number of rows in the text area.
readonly	Boolean	When set to true, the user is unable to set a value in the form element.
wrap	String	Specifies whether the content in the text area should wrap to the next line or not.

The checkbox tag

Unlike the other tags you've seen, the checkbox tag doesn't treat the value of the field as type String. Rather, checkboxes must have a field value that either evaluates to Boolean or can be converted to a Boolean. Because a checkbox has only two states, a boolean field works perfectly. Here's the checkbox tag that was first used in listing 11.3:

```
<ww:checkbox label="P.O. Box" name="user.address.poBox"
            fieldValue="true"/>
```

Recall that the User object contains an Address field, which in turn has a Boolean field poBox. The tag shown here maps to that Boolean and indicates that the fieldValue should be true. This means that if the box is checked, the value true is submitted to the action, which in turn is converted to a Boolean. As indicated in table 11.8, only one attribute is unique to the checkbox tag.

Table 11.8 The checkbox tag attribute

Attribute	Data type	Description
fieldValue	String	Value to submit to your action if the box is checked

Checkboxes are a little different than other tags. The way the HTML specification works requires that the value (indicated by the fieldValue attribute) be submitted only if the box is checked. If the box isn't checked, then no name or value is submitted. Thus, if the Boolean field in your action or model is false by default, you should set fieldValue to true. Similarly, if the Boolean field is true by default, you should set the fieldValue to false. Doing so ensures that regardless of the state of the checkbox when the form is submitted, the Boolean field will have the expected state.

11.3.3 *Collection-based tags*

Now that we've gone over the simple UI tags, it's time to discuss the more complex ones. Often, you want users to select from a list of options. So far, all the tags you've seen allow users to input free-form text or select from only two choices: on or off. In order to provide a rich web experience, you need to offer select boxes, radio buttons, and choices of multiple checkboxes. In this section, we'll look at the three tags you can use to do that.

The select tag

Early in this chapter, you saw a small sample usage of the select tag. Now we'll detail all the ways it can be used and also explain how it relates to your action or model fields for both setting and getting data. Table 11.9 shows all the attributes the select tag supports in addition to the common attributes.

Table 11.9 The select tag attributes

Attribute	Data type	Description
list	Collection, Map, Array, or Iterator	Expression that evaluates to the list of options the user will select from.
listKey	String	Expression for the list key; key by default.

Table 11.9 The `select` tag attributes *(continued)*

Attribute	Data type	Description
listValue	String	Expression for the list value; `value` by default.
headerKey	String	Value to be submitted if the user selects the header option.
headerValue	String	What the user sees for the header option.
emptyOption	Boolean	When set to `true`, an empty option is placed between the header option and the choices from the list attribute.
multiple	Boolean	When set to `true`, the select box allows users to select more than one value.
size	String	When included, specifies the size (in terms of number of visible options at one time) of the select box.

The most important attribute is `list`, which tells the tag what the selection's options are. In the simplest form, the list is presented to the user, and the value selected is then submitted to the form and mapped to the field specified in the `name` attribute. If a value is prepopulated, then the option in the list that has the same value as the field is selected automatically. For example, look at the following code, which was originally shown in listing 11.3:

```
<ww:select label="State" name="user.address.state"
           list="{'California', 'Oregon'}"/>
```

In this example, the value of the expression `user.address.state` will be set to either California or Oregon. If the value is currently one of those two values, then the `select` tag will mark that value as selected, thereby prepopulating the form as you would expect. The HTML printed out might be as follows:

```
<option>California</option>
<option selected="selected">Oregon</option>
```

Sometimes a simple list of `Strings` isn't what you want to display to the user, nor is it what you want to store in your model objects. Instead, it's ideal to have a key and a value, where the key is used as the actual value stored in your model (the value submitted to the action) and the value is displayed to the user. In HTML, this is done by done by specifying the `value` attribute for the `<option>` tag.

For example, suppose you have a list of objects, each of which has an `id` attribute and a `name` attribute. You may expect this HTML for the `option` tags:

```
<option value="1">California</option>
<option value="2">Oregon</option>
```

This shows *Oregon* to the user but submits 2 to the action. This is easy to do with the `select` tag by providing the `listKey` and `listValue` attributes. Assuming you now have a list of `State` objects, and each object has `getId()` and `getName()`, then you use `select` in the following way: `<ww:select name="user.address.stateId" list="stateList" listKey="id" listValue="name"/>`. This tells the `select` tag to use the expressions `id` and `name` for the option's value and label, respectively.

The `listKey` and `listValue` features work by iterating over the list and pushing the object on the top of the stack for each loop. This is the same behavior the `Iterator` tag uses, as explained in chapter 9. Then the expressions specified in the `listKey` and `listValue` attributes are executed against the value stack.

If you're using a `Map` as the list to iterate over in the `select` tag, the object being iterated over is `Map.Entry`, just like the `Iterator` tag does. Because `Map.Entry` provides `getKey()` and `getValue()` methods, these are typically used as `listKey` and `listValue` values. Using a `Map` is so common that the `select` tag makes the `listKey` and `listValue` attributes equal to `key` and `value`, respectively, by default. Here, you see the state select box redone using a `Map`-based approach:

```
<ww:select label="State" name="user.address.stateId"
           list="#{1 : 'California', 2 : 'Oregon'}"/>
```

Often, especially in situations where the select box is a drop-down selection (`size` attribute not specified), having a value at the top of the list such as "Select a state" helps indicate to users what you expect them to do. Rather than try to make your list of selections include a dummy header option at the start of the list, you can use the `select` tag's simple mechanism to do this. The `headerKey` and `headerValue` attributes can be used to populate a complete `<option>` tag before the list is iterated over.

Similarly, sometimes people wish to have an empty selection choice between the header and the list of choices. This helps separate the instructions, such as "Select a state," from the data to be picked. If the `empty-Option` attribute is set to `true`, the text `<option value=""></option>` is printed between the header and the list of options. Continuing with the state example, the following code and figure 11.7 show how the `headerKey`, `headerValue`, and `emptyOption` attributes can be used to make a select box more user-friendly:

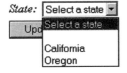

Figure 11.7 A simple form utilizing the headerKey, headerValue, and emptyOption attributes

```
<ww:select label="State" name="user.address.stateId"
        list="#{1 : 'California', 2 : 'Oregon'}"
        headerKey="-1" headerValue="Select a state"
        emptyOption="true"/>
```

The `select` tag supports two final attributes: `multiple` and `size`. `multiple` allows the user to select multiple values; by default, it's set to false. `size` tells the browser to render the `select` tag using a scrollable select list rather than a drop-down select list. The value of `size` is the number of items that should be shown at any time. Here's how you can let the user select multiple countries and make the size large enough to show all the countries without the user having to scroll up or down:

```
<ww:select label="Countries" name="user.address.countries"
        list="countryList" multiple="true"
        size="%{countryList.size()}"/>
```

NOTE   Multiple selections are trickier than they appear here. Because lists of checkboxes are always multiple selections, we'll leave that discussion alone for now. After we look at the `checkboxlist` tag, we'll explain in detail how multiple selections work.

The radio tag

The `radio` tag works similarly to the `select` tag but is even simpler. It has only three unique attributes, all which we've already discussed in detail (see table 11.10). Radio buttons, by definition, are a single-select tag. Therefore, there is no `multiple` attribute. Similarly, radio buttons need no headers.

Table 11.10   The `radio` tag attributes

Attribute	Data type	Description
list	Collection, Map, Array, or Iterator	Expression that evaluates to the list of options the user will be selecting from
listKey	String	Expression for the list key; key by default
listValue	String	Expression for the list value; value by default

The checkboxlist tag

The `checkboxlist` tag is almost exactly like the `radio` tag except that instead of being a single-select tag, it's a multiselect tag. That is, users are free to select one or more checkboxes. The end result is effectively the same as the `select` tag when its `multiple` attribute is set to `true`. Table 11.11 shows the attributes the `checkbox-list` tag supports.

Table 11.11 The checkboxlist tag attributes

Attribute	Data type	Description
list	Collection, Map, Array, or Iterator	Expression that evaluates to the list of options the user will be selecting from
listKey	String	Expression for the list key; key by default
listValue	String	Expression for the list value; value by default

Multiselect tags

As previously mentioned, multiselect tags such as checkboxlist and select tag aren't totally straightforward. We'll now explain why they're different and how they work. In single-select tags, the value (which is assumed based on the name attribute if not specified) is compared to every key in the list specified.

Looking back at the earlier State example, the list was defined to be a Map. The *key* for the list is the state ID, and the *value* is the name of the state. Because the name of the tag is user.address.stateId, you know that the value is also a state ID. The Collection-based tags compare each key in the list with the value of the stack and decide whether the option should be selected. In the case where there is no key, the value itself is used.

But what happens when your value isn't just a single state ID, but a collection of state IDs? Let's look at the following example of a multiselect tag:

```
<ww:select label="State" name="user.address.stateIds"
           list="#{1 : 'California', 2 : 'Oregon'}"
           headerKey="-1" headerValue="Select a state"
           emptyOption="true" multiple="true"/>
```

Now let's assume that user.address.stateIds returns a List of Integers (or an array of ints). The select tag tries to compare a List of Integers to an Integer (the key of the list attribute). Obviously, these aren't equal. However, the select tag doesn't just compare the value with the list key. Rather, it checks to see whether the value is a Collection, Map, or array. If it's any of those, it determines whether the list key is contained in any of those collections. If the value isn't a Collection, Map, or array, the select tag finally compares the values directly using equals(), which is the behavior you want when you're using a single-select tag. To better understand how this works, let's look at the utility method that performs all the comparisons in the tag. The class is called ContainUtil, and it's shown in its entirety in listing 11.9.

Listing 11.9 ContainUtil source code

```java
package com.opensymphony.webwork.util;

import java.lang.reflect.Array;
import java.util.Collection;
import java.util.Map;

public class ContainUtil {
    public static boolean contains(Object obj1, Object obj2) {
        if ((obj1 == null) || (obj2 == null)) {
            return false;
        }

        if (obj1 instanceof Map) {
            if (((Map) obj1).containsValue(obj2)) {
                return true;
            }
        } else if (obj1 instanceof Collection) {
            if (((Collection) obj1).contains(obj2)) {
                return true;
            }
        } else if (obj1.getClass().isArray()) {
            for (int i = 0; i < Array.getLength(obj1); i++) {
                Object value = null;
                value = Array.get(obj1, i);

                if (value.equals(obj2)) {
                    return true;
                }
            }
        } else if (obj1.equals(obj2)) {
            return true;
        }

        return false;
    }
}
```

The contains() method takes two arguments: obj1 and obj2. In Collection-based tags, this method is called to compare the value for the tag and the key values in the list, which determines whether checkboxes, radio buttons, and select options will be preselected. The first argument, obj1, is the value specified by the tag. In the earlier example of a multiselect tag, this is a List of Integers; in the listing prior to that, it's a single Integer. In both examples, obj2 is an Integer representing a key from the Map specified in the list attribute.

WARNING! Because of the way ContainUtil works, some people get into trouble when their data types don't match up properly. For example, if you have a list attribute specified as #{'1' : 'California', '2'_: 'Oregon'}, and your value is an int or Integer, no values will be selected. That is the case because the keys in the map are no longer Integers but Characters (note the single quotes around 1 and 2). You have to be very careful to ensure that when the keys are compared, the equals() method does what you expect. Character.equals(Integer) obviously always returns false.

11.3.4 Advanced tags

In this section, we'll discuss alternative and advanced tags. They include simple tags such as hidden tags and labels, as well as more complex collection tags such as doubleselect and combobox. Finally, we'll begin to look at the component tag and how you can easily create custom tags. We discuss customizing your components and themes further in chapter 15.

The label tag

Among all the UI tags in this chapter, the label tag is unique, because it doesn't render any form elements. Rather, it's a way to print out values as labels. For example, a common use involves displaying a read-only parameter in a form, such as username. Here's an example of the label tag:

```
<ww:label label="Username" name="username"/>
```

The label tag can be confusing when you first look at this example. The label tag has a label attribute, but that doesn't correspond to the value of the label you're printing out. Put another way, the label attribute here works exactly like it does in the other XHTML UI tags: It's the label on the left-hand side of the table (or above the form element if you're using the top label positioning). On the right-hand side, a *second* label is rendered, which corresponds to the name attribute. Here's how the XHTML label tag renders:

```
<tr>
<td align="right" valign="top">
    <label for="form_username" class="label">Username:</label>
</td>
<td>
    <label id="form_username">plightbo</label>
</td>
</tr>
```

The hidden tag

The `hidden` tag is also unique. Unlike every other UI tag in the XHTML theme, it doesn't render a table row. The XHTML `hidden` tag is the exact same thing as the `simple` `hidden` tag. This is expected because you don't want hidden values causing any of the UI to change (such as having a blank table row). The `hidden` tag works almost exactly like the other `simple` tags, such as the `textfield` tag. Although the `hidden` tag doesn't do as much as some of the other tags, it's provided for consistency.

The doubleselect tag

The `doubleselect` tag is an extension of the `select` tag. It's useful when you have a large list of items for the user to choose from and you'd like to break the choices into groups. Instead of a single `select` tag, the `doubleselect` renders two `select` tags that are tied together. The first select box is a list of the groupings and is specified by the `list` attribute. The second select box changes, using JavaScript, based on the group selected in the first select box. The `doubleList` attribute determines the contents of the second select box. Table 11.12 shows the attributes available in addition to the common attributes for every UI tag.

Table 11.12 The `doubleselect` tag attributes

Attribute	Data type	Description
List	Collection, Map, Array, or Iterator	Expression that evaluates to the list of options from which the user selects in the first select box.
listKey	String	Expression for the list key; key by default.
listValue	String	Expression for the list value; value by default.
doubleList	Collection, Map, Array, or Iterator	Expression that evaluates to the list of options from which the user selects. This expression is evaluated for each element in the list attribute and is expected to return a different list due to the contents of the value stack.
doubleListKey	String	Expression for the list key; key by default.
doubleListValue	String	Expression for the list value; value by default.
doubleName	String	Field name that the form element maps to for the second select box. Because of the nature of the doubleselect tag, this is typically the field you're more concerned with.
doubleValue	Object*	Value of the form element for the second select box.
headerKey	String	Value that is submitted if the user selects the header option. Applies only to the first select box.

Table 11.12 **The doubleselect tag attributes** *(continued)*

Attribute	Data type	Description
headerValue	String	What the user sees for the header option. Applies only to the first select box.
emptyOption	Boolean	When set to true, an empty option is placed between the header option and the actual choices from the list attribute. Applies only to the first select box.
multiple	Boolean	When set to true, both select boxes let users select more than one value.
size	String	When given, specifies the size (in terms of number of visible options at one time) of the both select boxes.

As you can see, the doubleselect tag is similar to the select tag, except it has the additional attributes doubleList, doubleListKey, doubleListValue, doubleName, and doubleValue. These are all exactly like their nondouble counterparts. The only difference between doubleList and list is when they're evaluated. Because doubleList should return a different list depending on the group selected, doubleList is evaluated once for every item in list. Each item (or item key) in list is pushed onto the stack, and then doubleList is evaluated.

The following example shows how states can be grouped into areas, such as North and South:

```
<ww:doubleselect label="State" name="region"
                 doubleName="stateID"
                 list="{'North', 'South'}"
                 doubleList="top == 'North' ?
                             {'Oregon', 'Washington'} :
                             {'Texas', 'Florida'}"/>
```

The doubleList expression uses the top variable to decide which list should be returned. This could also be a method such as getDoubleList(Object itemKey) in your action. Figure 11.8 shows what this simple example looks like when rendered in the browser.

Remember that the doubleselect tag uses JavaScript to function correctly. In figure 11.8, if the user selects South from the first select box, the options in the second select box automatically change to Texas and Florida. If JavaScript is disabled, this feature doesn't work properly.

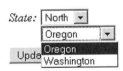

Figure 11.8 The doubleselect tag rendered in a browser

Combo box

A combo box is a small extension of the `textfield` UI tag. Instead of requiring users to type values by hand, a select box is offered to allow users to choose a pre-existing entry. However, they're free to enter their own value or change the existing choices as well. A perfect example of a combo box is an online voting form. The select box lists the nominated candidates' names, but the voter still has the choice of providing a write-in candidate.

Table 11.13 outlines the attributes supported by the `combobox` tag in addition to the common attributes. Note that it's almost exactly like the `textfield` tag, with the addition of the `list` attribute. Also note that the list behaviors of this tag aren't as complex as those in the other `Collection`-based tags. That is the case because there is no need to differentiate between keys and values given the behavior of the combo box and the fact that the only value submitted is the one entered in the textfield.

Table 11.13   The combobox tag attributes

Attribute	Data type	Description
list	Collection, Map, Array, or Iterator	Expression that evaluates to the list of options from which the user selects.
maxlength	String	Maximum length that can be entered in this field.
readonly	Boolean	When set to `true`, the user is unable to set a value in the `form` element.
size	String	Visible size of the field.

Here's a simple example of the combo box; figure 11.9 shows the example rendered in the browser:

```
<ww:combobox label="State" name="state"
              list="{'California', 'Oregon'}"/>
```

Just like the `doubleselect` tag, the `combobox` tag requires JavaScript to function correctly. If you're building forms that must work for browsers that don't have JavaScript enabled, neither of these tags is an option for you.

Figure 11.9   The combobox tag rendered in a browser

The component tag

The final tag that WebWork offers out of the box isn't much of a UI tag at all. Rather, the `component` tag offers a way for you to build custom UI tags. For example, suppose you want a three-way checkbox to represent explicitly on, explicitly off, and not specified. You can write one in HTML using JavaScript and some custom images that represent the three states.

If you want to reuse this type of checkbox and integrate it with WebWork, all you need to do is write a custom template (in Velocity, for example) that is similar to the other templates that make up the `simple` and XHTML themes. The following code renders a three-way checkbox:

```
<ww:component label="Permission" name="permission"
              template="threewaycheckbox"/>
```

The `component` tag looks up threewaycheckbox.vm and passes in the same variables in the `$parameters` Map that you've seen throughout this chapter. The tag looks up threewaycheckbox.vm in /template/xhtml (assuming you're using the XHTML theme) in either the classpath or in your web application. Refer to chapter 10 for more information about how Velocity templates are retrieved.

Recall that in section 11.3.1, we discussed common attributes for all tags. The `template` attribute is one of those common attributes. This means that if you wish to extend the `textfield` tag to include a date picker, you can write your own datepicker.vm tag and then use the following JSP:

```
<ww:textfield label="Birthday" name="birthday"
              template="datepicker"/>
```

The advantage of using the `textfield` tag rather than the `component` tag is that all the parameters available in the default `textfield` tag are available in datepicker.vm. The `component` tag is more useful for when you're building a UI tag from scratch. In chapter 15, we'll give much more detailed examples showing how you can extend existing UI tags, build your own UI tags, and even create your own themes.

11.4 Summary

This chapter introduced the notion of building reusable HTML components that tie in with WebWork. We discussed the concept of themes and templates, showed how you can build up standard forms, and detailed all the UI tags included in WebWork. We also explored how the templates and the UI tags integrate together and how parameters are passed through the `$parameters` map. Now you can begin to build complex forms using a library of rich tags. In chapter 15, we'll use this knowledge to explore how you can create your own application-specific library of rich tags.

We recommend that you spend some time putting together some sample forms and even explore writing your own templates or overriding the existing ones. Learning how to extend the UI framework is the best way to get the most use out of the framework and make your applications easy to develop and modify.

Part 4

Advanced topics

The last part of the book presents advanced topics. Chapter 12 covers advanced type conversion and shows why data-type support is an important part of WebWork. Chapter 13 shows you how to decouple the validation rules from your core business logic and how you can reuse those validation rules. Chapter 14 examines the incredibly complex topic of internationalization (i18n) and how WebWork breaks it into pieces that are easy to understand.

Finally, in chapter 15, we offer a series of best practices. Everything from testing techniques to common challenges in web-based applications is covered here. This chapter doesn't show every best practice that WebWork helps with (to do so would require a book by itself), but it gives you a taste for what is possible.

Type conversion

12

This chapter covers

- Examples of different types of type conversion
- Examples with and without type conversion
- Type conversion on a global or local basis
- Advanced type conversion

The Web—or, more specifically, the HTTP protocol—doesn't deal with the concept of data types. No data types are specified in HTTP, HTML, or even the Servlet specification. Rather, everything is transferred as a String or array of Strings. This approach makes the specification simpler, but it usually leaves the work of converting input Strings to a proper data type up to the developer. In this chapter, we'll look at how WebWork removes all the pain usually associated with this task, allowing you to focus on the things that really matter: business logic and speedy development.

12.1 Why type conversion?

In order for us to underscore why type conversion is necessary, you need to understand the pain associated with writing web application UIs without any type conversion support. Let's start by taking a peek at the Servlet specification to see where this problem begins. Then we'll look at what both an action and a view might look like without type conversion.

12.1.1 The Servlet specification

Remember that the HTTP and HTML specifications make no effort to handle data types. When a form is submitted, such as the one in listing 12.1, the HTTP POST request sent from the browser has no information about the type of data each input.

Listing 12.1 A simple HTML form used to create a new user

```
<%@ taglib uri="webwork" prefix="ww" %>
<html>
    <head>
        <title>New User Form</title>
    </head>
    <body>
        <form method="POST" action="createUser.action">
            Username: <input name="username"/><br/>
            Password: <input type="password" name="password"/><br/>
            First name: <input name="firstName"/><br/>
            Last name: <input name="lastName"/><br/>
            Age: <input name="age"/><br/>
            Birth date: <input name="birthDate"/><br/>
            Email: <input name="email"/><br/>
            <input type="submit" value="Create User"/>
        </form>
    </body>
</html>
```

The first four inputs—username, password, firstName, and lastName—will end up as String data types, so this isn't much cause for concern. However, the other inputs—age, birthDate, and email—will eventually be turned into an int (or Integer), a Date data type, and an Email data type, respectively. So, at some point, your code must remember to take care of calling Integer.parseInt(), Simple-DataFormat.parse(), and Email.parse(), as well as figure out what to do if the value entered can't be converted properly.

NOTE   The Email class is a simple compound object used to represent the different parts of an email address. It provides an example how you often would like to deal with objects in their pure state (such as an Email instance); but often in web applications you deal with them in their unpure state—specifically, as a String. This class breaks an email address string into two parts: username and domain. You reconstruct the email address string with username + '@' + domain.

The only thing you have to work with when building J2EE web applications is the simplified access to HTTP request parameters via HttpServletRequest's methods:

- getParameter(String name)—Returns a single value for a GET or POST named parameter. This is the most commonly used method when writing web applications.

- getParameterValues(String name)—Returns an array of values in the form of String[] for a GET or POST named parameter. This is used when many values are mapped to the same parameter name in the request.

- getParameterNames()—Returns an Enumeration of all the parameter names in the request.

- getParameterMap()—Returns a Map of type String -> String[] where the key is every named parameter and the value is a String array representing one or more values in the request for that parameter name.

As you've already seen, WebWork maps request parameters to your action's fields automatically. Let's see what an action would look like if all its fields were of type String.

12.1.2 *An action without type conversion*

In listing 12.2, a version (but not the final version) of CaveatEmptor's CreateUser action is defined with all its fields of type String. Then, in the execute() method, the action must convert the age, birthDate, and email fields to their proper type.

Finally, you can create a User object and create the user by calling the UserDAO component that's provided to the action via Inversion of Control (see chapter 6).

Listing 12.2   An action that doesn't take advantage of automatic type conversion

```
package org.hibernate.auction.web.actions.users;

import com.opensymphony.xwork.ActionSupport;
import org.hibernate.auction.dao.UserDAO;
import org.hibernate.auction.dao.UserDAOAware;
import org.hibernate.auction.model.User;
import org.hibernate.auction.model.Email;

import java.text.DateFormat;
import java.util.Date;

public class CreateUser extends ActionSupport
    implements UserDAOAware {

    String username;
    String password;
    String firstName;
    String lastName;
    String age;
    String birthDate;
    String email;
    User user;
    UserDAO userDAO;

    public String execute() throws Exception {
        int realAge = Integer.parseInt(age);
        DateFormat df = DateFormat.getDateInstance(DateFormat.SHORT);
        Date realBirthDate = df.parse(birthDate);
        Email realEmail = Email.parse(email);
        user = new User(username, password,
                firstName, lastName, realAge,
                realBirthDate, realEmail);

        userDAO.makePersistent(user);
        return SUCCESS;
    }

    // setters and getters
    ...
}
```

Notice that four of the eight lines in the execute() method are spent converting Strings to the proper data type. In addition, notice that you must have similar getters and setters, such as `getFirstName()`, in the `CreateUser` class and also in the `User` class (not shown). That's because you're choosing to set the values in a *flat* manner rather than in a *deep* manner. *Flat* means the action always has all the fields needed to construct the entire request. *Deep* means the action only has the objects it works with, such as `User`.

Although deep is almost always preferred, it isn't possible without type conversion. That is the case because the `User` class has fields of type `int`, `Date`, and `Email`, which aren't (yet) automatically converted. Likewise, because the action uses a flat structure, you also need another line constructing the `User` object once the types have all been converted. If you think about the role of the `CreateUser` at a high level, it shouldn't even be responsible for initializing the `User` object—the only thing it should be responsible for is creating a user (by calling the `UserDAO`) and indicating whether the action successfully completed (`return SUCCESS`). Thus six of the eight lines, or 75 percent, are used to prepare to do the work you actually want to do.

Can't you do better?

12.1.3 *A view without type conversion*

Before we look at the better way of handling type conversion, let's examine the other side of conversion. You've seen how you need to convert from `String` to various data types, but what about converting from other data types to `Strings`? You need to do this whenever you wish to display a web page, because HTML is 100 percent text. In listing 12.3, you can see what a JSP might look like if type conversion weren't available.

Listing 12.3   A JSP indicating success without using type conversion

```
<%@ taglib uri="webwork" prefix="ww" %>
<%@ page import="com.opensymphony.xwork.ActionContext,
                java.util.Date,
                java.text.DateFormat"%>
<html>
    <head>
        <title>New User Created</title>
    </head>
    <body>
        A new user was created!
        <p/>

        Username: <ww:property value="user.username"/><br/>
        Password: [Not shown]<br/>
        First name: <ww:property value="user.firstName"/><br/>
```

```
Last name: <ww:property value="user.lastName"/><br/>
Age: <ww:property value="user.age"/><br/>
Email: <ww:property value="user.email"/><br/>
<%
    Date birthDate = (Date)
        ActionContext.getContext().getValueStack().
        findValue("user.birthDate");
    DateFormat df =
            DateFormat.getDateInstance(DateFormat.SHORT);
%>
    Birth Date: <%= df.format(birthDate) %><br/>
</body>
</html>
```

The first thing to notice is that you're able to afford using deep notation in this JSP, because the User object is now created and can be accessed (as explained in chapter 8, "Getting data with the expression language") using complex expressions. The first three fields—username, firstName, and lastName—aren't a concern, because they're already in the correct format.

The next field, age, is more complicated but not much of a problem. This prints out correctly because the process of converting an int to a String is trivial and is handled automatically.

The situation gets more involved when you try to print out the email address. The expression user.email returns an Email object, which must then be converted to a String. WebWork first attempts to find a type converter to do this, but if it can't find one, it uses the object's toString() method. In this case, let's assume that Email's toString() method has been correctly implemented to do the right thing.

The final field, birthDate, is the most complicated. So much more code is required to print out this field because the toString() method for Date isn't your desired format. When you first enter the birth date, you enter it in SHORT notation (in the United States, this is the form MM/dd/yyyy). However, Date's toString() method tries to return the date in LONG notation. This would be confusing for users of the web application, especially if they needed to re-enter any data that was marked invalid for another reason. Can you imagine how annoying it would be if you typed in 02/12/1982 and got back February 12, 1982 00:00:00 PST?

The code in listing 12.3 gets the raw Date object using WebWork's internal APIs. It creates a date formatter object, specifying a SHORT format, and then uses that object to format the date back to the format you'd like. This is effectively the opposite of what happens in the CreateUser action in listing 12.2.

12.1.4 *What WebWork's type conversion gives you*

Recall that 75 percent of the code in the execute() method in listing 12.2 is spent preparing for the actual work taking place. Now it's time to look at a better way. Let's rewrite the CreateUser action but this time not spend any time preparing the data. The action is show in listing 12.4.

Listing 12.4 An action that takes advantage of automatic type conversion

```
package org.hibernate.auction.web.actions.users;

import com.opensymphony.xwork.ActionSupport;
import org.hibernate.auction.dao.UserDAO;
import org.hibernate.auction.dao.UserDAOAware;
import org.hibernate.auction.model.User;
import org.hibernate.auction.model.Email;

import java.text.DateFormat;
import java.util.Date;

public class CreateUser extends ActionSupport
    implements UserDAOAware {

    User user;
    UserDAO userDAO;

    public String execute() throws Exception {
        userDAO.makePersistent(user);
        return SUCCESS;
    }

    // setters and getters
    ...
}
```

As you can see, there are now only two lines in the execute() method, both of which are definitely required. Where did all those other lines go? What about all the fields you had before? We'll discuss how this is possible in section 12.3; for now, recall that accessing fields in a deep manner tends to reduce code duplication and allows the WebWork framework to do as much work as possible on your behalf.

Now let's look at the success page in listing 12.5 and compare it to the one previously shown in listing 12.3.

Listing 12.5 A JSP indicating success using type conversion

```
<%@ taglib uri="webwork" prefix="ww" %>
<html>
    <head>
        <title>New User Created</title>
    </head>
    <body>
        A new user was created!
        <p/>

        Username: <ww:property value="user.username"/><br/>
        Password: [Not shown]<br/>

        First name: <ww:property value="user.firstName"/><br/>
        Last name: <ww:property value="user.lastName"/><br/>
        Age: <ww:property value="user.age"/><br/>
        Email: <ww:property value="user.email"/><br/>
        Birth Date: <ww:property value="user.birthDate"/><br/>
    </body>
</html>
```

Notice that you no longer do anything different for dates than you do for the
other fields. With type conversion in place, you can avoid worrying about the LONG
format that toString() returns. How is this happening? To find out, let's look at
how to configure and build your own type converter.

12.2 Configuration

Type converters by themselves aren't very interesting. However, the style of development they enable you to pursue, although not revolutionary, isn't easily dismissed. You did, after all, save 75 percent in your previous example. When you're
using WebWork to its full capacity, including full use of type conversion, you may
find yourself writing painfully simple actions because you no longer need to
spend time on the tedious stuff.

Not only does this make your overall code simpler, it makes it easier to test.
Now you aren't working with just data—you're working with objects directly. Let's
examine what type converters do and then explore the two possible ways to configure them.

12.2.1 *Role of a type converter*

In WebWork, type converters can be used to convert between any two types. However, practically speaking, there are only two classes of types you care about when building web applications: `Strings` and non-`Strings`. The best way to understand what a type converter looks like as well as what it does is to dive right into one. Listing 12.6 shows a type converter that converts between the types `Email` and `String`.

Listing 12.6 A type converter that takes advantage of the prebuilt functions in `Email`

```
package org.hibernate.auction.web.typeconverters;

import ognl.DefaultTypeConverter;

import java.util.Map;

import org.hibernate.auction.model.Email;

public class EmailConverter extends DefaultTypeConverter {
    public Object convertValue(Map ctx, Object o, Class toType) {
        if (toType == Email.class) {
            String email = ((String[]) o)[0];
            return Email.parse(email);
        } else if (toType == String.class) {
            Email email = (Email) o;
            return email.toString();
        }

        return null;
    }
}
```

The `EmailConverter` is simple, because most of the work is delegated to already-implemented methods (not shown) such as `Email.parse()` and `Email.toString()`. However, let's take this small class apart to fully understand it.

First, notice that all type converters must implement the interface `ognl.Type-Converter`. A utility class, `ognl.DefaultTypeConverter`, provides a simpler `convertValue()` method to override. This example extends `DefaultTypeConverter`. Consult the Object Graph Navigation Language (OGNL) docs at http://www.opensymphony.com/ognl for more information.

Next, you override the `convertValue()` method, providing an implementation that knows how to convert to the types `String` and `Email`. The arguments provide assistance with the work of converting the values:

- context—A Map that represents the ActionContext
- o—The object that needs converting
- toType—The type that WebWork is requesting the type converter to convert o to.

Most of the code is straightforward. However, notice that you convert from Email to String and from String[] to Email. That doesn't immediately make sense (this is the most common mistake made when writing type converters). Let's explore why you're dealing with String[] and not String.

Recall that HttpServletRequest's getParameterMap() method returns a map of String -> String[]. Well, WebWork takes this Map and attempts to apply the values onto the action. If a particular key is a complex expression, such as user.email, it then tries to apply the String[] onto the email field in the User object. At this point, WebWork realizes the types don't match up, and it enlists the help of a type converter.

And how does WebWork know which type converter to call? You must configure it, as shown in the next two sections.

12.2.2 *Global type converters*

There are two ways to configure a type converter in WebWork: You can either specify a type converter on a per-class basis or you may specify it on a per-field basis for an individual class. To specify a type converter globally, you need to create a file called xwork-conversion.properties and place it in the root of your classpath. This is generally found in WEB-INF/classes or in the base of your project's JAR file.

Listing 12.7 is a simple yet complete example of what this file might look like.

> **Listing 12.7 A complete xwork-conversion.properties file with global type converters**

```
org.hibernate.auction.model.Email =
    org.hibernate.auction.web.typeconverters.EmailConverter
```

On the left side, you specify the type for which you want WebWork to invoke the type converter. On the right side, you specify the type converter class. That's all there is to it. Now, let's see how you can configure a type converter for a specific class.

12.2.3 *Class-level type converters*

The other way to specify a type converter is on a per-class basis. This approach is especially useful if you want to specify a converter for a common field type (such as

String or Date) and don't wish to make a global change. You do so by creating a file in the form of *ClassName*-conversion.properties and placing it in the same package as the class. For example, if you want to specify type converters for the User class, you'll create a file named User-conversion.properties and place it in the org/hibernate/auction/model directory—the same place the class is. Listing 12.8 shows what this file looks like.

Listing 12.8 A complete User-conversion.properties file with field-level type converters

```
email = org.hibernate.auction.web.typeconverters.EmailConverter
```

This file is a little different than the global configuration. The right side remains the same, but instead of specifying a type, you specify a field. This corresponds to User's getEmail() and setEmail() JavaBean-style methods.

The class-level type converter configuration follows the same rules as normal class and interface hierarchies. That is, if User were to extend Person, then you could have a Person-conversion.properties file that would also be read. You can do the same for any interfaces. This allows you to specify base-level conversion rules for a base object in a single place, saving duplicate configuration lines.

12.3 Simple type conversion

Now that you've seen a type converter and know how to configure it, let's examine the rules of how and when type converters are called and look at the built-in type converters that come with WebWork.

12.3.1 Basic type conversion

As we've already discussed, type conversion occurs whenever WebWork attempts to apply a value to a type that it can't convert. Obvious conversions, such as String -> int or vice versa, are handled automatically. But let's look at the inputs for the previous two examples: one where you did the type conversion yourself and one where it was handled for you. Listing 12.9 shows the flat input scheme, which submits to the action shown in listing 12.2.

Listing 12.9 An example of a flat input scheme

```
<%@ taglib uri="webwork" prefix="ww" %>
<html>
    <head>
```

```
            <title>New User Form</title>
    </head>
    <body>
        <form method="POST" action="createUser.action">
            Username: <input name="username"/><br/>
            Password: <input type="password" name="password"/><br/>
            First name: <input name="firstName"/><br/>
            Last name: <input name="lastName"/><br/>
            Age: <input name="age"/><br/>
            Birth date: <input name="birthDate"/><br/>
            Email: <input name="email"/><br/>
            <input type="submit" value="Create User"/>
        </form>
    </body>
</html>
```

In listing 12.10, the deep input scheme is used to submit to the action in listing 12.4. Notice that the only difference in this file is that the names of the fields all include the prefix user.

NOTE Listings 12.9 and 12.10 don't use the WebWork UI tags, for a specific purpose: to show how the tags have no relationship to type conversion or the actual HTTP request. As you can see in these examples, the parameter naming conventions themselves determine the type conversion behavior. However, we generally recommend you use the UI tags as often as possible.

Listing 12.10 An example of a deep input scheme

```
<%@ taglib uri="webwork" prefix="ww" %>
<html>
    <head>
        <title>New User Form</title>
    </head>
    <body>
        <form method="POST" action="createUser.action">
            Username: <input name="user.username"/><br/>
            Password: <input type="password"
                            name="user.password"/><br/>
            First name: <input name="user.firstName"/><br/>
            Last name: <input name="user.lastName"/><br/>
            Age: <input name="user.age"/><br/>
            Birth date: <input name="user.birthDate"/><br/>
            Email: <input name="user.email"/><br/>
            <input type="submit" value="Create User"/>
```

```
            </form>
        </body>
    </html>
```

By changing the input names to all have a `user` prefix, you tell WebWork that these inputs should be applied to the `user` field in the action to which you're submitting. Making this small change gets rid of all the fields in the `CreateUser` action.

12.3.2 *Built-in type conversion*

For the `email` field, you build a type converter to do the right conversion. But for the other fields, such as `age` and `birthDate`, you don't need to do anything, because WebWork supplies a few built-in type converters, as follows:

- `String`—This is the simplest form of type conversion. `String` arrays are converted to `String`s by pulling the first element in the array. Although this is the simplest conversion, it happens for every `String` being set, because all values from the Web start as `String` arrays.

- Primitives (`int`, `boolean`, `double`, and so on)—Primitives are handled automatically, although locale-specific features aren't supported. Thus a `String` of `"123,456"` isn't converted to a proper `int`. If you wish to support these kinds of numbers, you must write your own type converter.

- `Date`—Dates are handled by WebWork for both input and output using the `SHORT` format. In the United States, this is the format MM/dd/yyyy. The locale used to determine this is the one specified by the browser and/or the WebWork configuration. More on internationalization can be found in chapter 14.

- `List`—Conversion to a `List` is done automatically. WebWork takes all the `String` array values and creates a `List` of the same size, placing all those values in the `List`. The resulting `List` contains `String` objects.

- `Set`—Similar to the `List` conversion, WebWork handles `Set`s for you. Duplicates, by the nature of `Set`s, are discarded.

- `Collection`—`Collection`s follow the same rules as `List`.

- Any array—Because arrays inherently describe their type, WebWork uses the type converter for the array type (for instance, `Date`, if you're converting to a `Date[]`). It loops over each value being set, constructs an array of the new type, and then sets the value.

In section 12.4, we'll discuss how to do advanced conversion for `Collections` that don't describe the object type they contain. In the meantime, know that unless otherwise specified, all `Lists`, `Sets`, and `Collections` contain values of type `String`.

12.3.3 Handling null property access

Before we look at the advanced topics, let's examine listing 12.10 again. Recall that you removed 75 percent of the code in the `CreateUser` action by adding the user prefix to all the field names. However, if you look back at listing 12.4, you'll see that the `user` field is null initially. How does it get instantiated?

WebWork does this for you when it detects null property access. That is, when the expression `user.username` is being evaluated, WebWork sees that `user` is null and realizes that it needs to create a `User` object. WebWork can do this only if the object has a zero-arg constructor, as specified by the JavaBean specification. Once WebWork creates the object, it needs to set the object back into the action. WebWork can do this only if the action has a setter method for the `user` field.

Without these two features, the `user` field would continue to be null, and none of the values from the form would be captured.

12.4 Advanced topics

Now that you've seen the simple stuff, let's explore some of the more advanced features of type conversion. Although they're considered advanced for organizational sake, you'll often find that these features are the ones that save you from pain when you're building anything but the simplest web interfaces.

12.4.1 Handling null Collection access

One of the biggest pains with the Java language is the fact that `Collections` aren't type-specific. Java 1.5 fixed this, but many developers still are forced to deploy using Java 1.3 and 1.4. The addition of generics to the Java language is welcome, but most developers won't have the opportunity to use them for some time. For now, you're stuck with casting your objects and hoping you remember the type of a particular collection's contents.

Automatic processing, like the type conversion in WebWork, makes life even trickier. Should that `List` contain `Strings` or `Emails`? Ideally, you always want your actions to do as little of this dirty work as possible. Listing 12.11 shows an action that creates a list of users without doing any of the conversion shenanigans.

Listing 12.11 An action that creates multiple users

```
package org.hibernate.auction.web.actions.users;

import com.opensymphony.xwork.ActionSupport;
import org.hibernate.auction.dao.UserDAOAware;
import org.hibernate.auction.dao.UserDAO;
import org.hibernate.auction.model.User;

import java.util.List;
import java.util.Iterator;

public class CreateUsers extends ActionSupport
    implements UserDAOAware {

    List users;
    UserDAO userDAO;

    public void validate() {
        // see if the name already exists
        if (users != null) {
            int i = 0;
            for (Iterator iterator = users.iterator();
                 iterator.hasNext();) {
                User user = (User) iterator.next();
                User existing =
                    userDAO.findByUsername(user.getUsername());
                if (existing != null) {
                    addFieldError("users[" + i + "].username",
                                  getText("user.exists"));
                }
                i++;
            }
        }
    }

    public String execute() throws Exception {
        if (users != null) {
            for (Iterator iterator = users.iterator();
                 iterator.hasNext();) {
                User user = (User) iterator.next();
                userDAO.makePersistent(user);
            }
        }

        return SUCCESS;
    }

    public String doDefault() throws Exception {
        return INPUT;
    }
```

```
    public List getUsers() {
        return users;
    }

    public void setUsers(List users) {
        this.users = users;
    }

    public void setUserDAO(UserDAO dao) {
        this.userDAO = dao;
    }
}
```

Nowhere in this class is anything that indicates that the users field is a List of User objects. So, you need to tell WebWork that this is the case. You can do so by creating a class-specific conversion configuration for the action itself. Listing 12.12 shows the contents of CreateUsers-conversion.properties.

Listing 12.12   CreateUsers-conversion.properties

```
Collection_users = org.hibernate.auction.model.User
```

The prefix Collection_ before the field name tells WebWork that you aren't specifying a type converter, but rather you're telling it that the users field should contain objects of the type User. Regardless of the type of your collection (Map, List, or Collection), the prefix is always Collection_.

This information is used only when the collection field is null. Notice in CreateUser that the list is never initialized. This is important because WebWork can then provide a special List implementation designed to grow the list with empty User objects as needed. This special implementation then creates an empty object (using the zero-arg constructor, of course) and returns it whenever users.get() is called.

Thus you can name fields in your HTML forms like users[0].firstName and users[1].email, as you'll see in a minute when we pull together all the concepts in this chapter. For Maps, valid field names can be in the form of someMap['someKey'].foo or someMap.someKey.foo, as indicated in chapter 8.

> **NOTE**   As of WebWork 2.1, there is one small piece of functionality you can't do when it comes to Collections and type conversion: non-JavaBeans can't be automatically created in Lists, Maps, and Collections. This means you can't, for example, have a List of Dates automatically be converted

for you. You can, however, use `Date[]` to work around this limitation. The reason is that WebWork needs to create the object, such as `User`, and then it assumes you'll be modifying various properties, such as `birth-Date`. It doesn't know what to do if you attempt to modify the base object, meaning that expressions such as `dates[0]` aren't valid. To get an array of dates, name all your fields the same—such as `dates`—and WebWork will take care of the rest.

12.4.2 *Handling conversion errors*

An important aspect of type conversion that we have yet to discuss is the task of reporting conversion errors. If a user enters the value `abc` for an `int`, you need a way to report the mistake. One way to do this is to use the validation framework, discussed in chapter 13 ("Validating form data"), to see whether the `int` is still zero, but that approach presents two problems:

- What if zero is an acceptable value?
- What if you want to display a different error message if the value was incorrectly entered than you do when the value converted fine but isn't an acceptable value?

Whenever WebWork is unable to convert a value, it places that failure in a special place in the `ActionContext`. Adding the `conversionError` interceptor to the action stack causes those errors to be reported as field errors. Like all other interceptor stacks, this can be configured on a per-package or per-action basis. If you're using the `completeStack`, this interceptor is included by default.

Now, if a conversion fails, an error message will be attributed to that field. By default, the text will be *Invalid field value for field 'xxx'*—not exactly the most user-friendly message. As you'll see in chapter 14, you can specify an internationalization key named `invalid.fieldValue.xxx` to provide a better error message.

In addition to adding a field-level error message, the conversion interceptor also makes it possible to show the original value a user entered. For example, if someone typed in `02/1`2/82` for a date field, the value wouldn't be converted properly. However, it's clear that the submitted value is a typo; to provide a good user experience, you should return the user to the same form with this original value in the textfield.

Knowing how the UI tags work, this normally wouldn't be possible. A field named `user.birthDate` would normally invoke `getUser().getBirthdate()`, which would return null because the value was never set in the first place. In order to allow the original value to be seen, WebWork needs to intercept the expression `user.birthDate` and short-circuit the evaluation to return the original value (02/1`2/82) rather than evaluate the real expression. This is automatically done for you when you're using the `conversionError` interceptor.

Sometimes you don't want to report all conversion failures. In chapter 13, you'll see how you can use the `ConversionErrorFieldValidator` to check for conversion failures only on particular fields.

12.4.3 *An example that puts it all together*

Now that you've seen the `CreateUser` action as well as the configuration for the action (including the interceptor that reports conversion errors), the final piece of the puzzle is the JSP that prompts for inputs: createUsers.jsp. Listing 12.13 shows what this looks like.

> **Listing 12.13 A form to create three users at once**

```
<%@ taglib uri="webwork" prefix="ww"%>
<html>
  <head>
    <title>Create three users</title>
  </head>

  <body>
    <ww:form action="createUsers">
      <ww:token/>

      <ww:textfield label="%{getText('username')}"
                    name="users[0].username"/>
      <ww:password  label="%{getText('password')}"
                    name="users[0].password"/>
      <ww:textfield label="%{getText('firstname')}"
                    name="users[0].firstname"/>
      <ww:textfield label="%{getText('lastname')}"
                    name="users[0].lastname"/>
      <ww:textfield label="%{getText('email')}"
                    name="users[0].email"/>

      <tr><td colspan="2"><hr/></td></tr>

      <ww:textfield label="%{getText('username')}"
                    name="users[1].username"/>
      <ww:password  label="%{getText('password')}"
                    name="users[1].password"/>
      <ww:textfield label="%{getText('firstname')}"
                    name="users[1].firstname"/>
      <ww:textfield label="%{getText('lastname')}"
                    name="users[1].lastname"/>
      <ww:textfield label="%{getText('email')}"
```

```
                              name="users[1].email"/>

        <tr><td colspan="2"><hr/></td></tr>

        <ww:textfield label="%{getText('username')}"
                      name="users[2].username"/>
        <ww:password  label="%{getText('password')}"
                      name="users[2].password"/>
        <ww:textfield label="%{getText('firstname')}"
                      name="users[2].firstname"/>
        <ww:textfield label="%{getText('lastname')}"
                      name="users[2].lastname"/>
        <ww:textfield label="%{getText('email')}"
                      name="users[2].email"/>

        <tr><td colspan="2"><hr/></td></tr>

        <ww:submit value="Submit"/>
      </ww:form>
    </body>
  </html>
```

This JSP prompts the user to enter exactly three users. Using a bit of DHTML and some smarter server-side code that iterates through all the users submitted, you could turn this into a nice UI. Disregarding the potential for a better UI, you should take away two main lessons:

- Naming elements in the array-index format of `users[x]` lets you avoid reconstructing the list of `User` objects in the action code in listing 12.11.

- Using the UI tag library, as discussed in chapter 11, displays conversion error messages (and other field-level error messages) automatically.

12.5 *Summary*

In this chapter, you learned how to remove up to 75 percent of the code in your action classes. You saw that a deep tree structure can be used when combined with good type conversion. You learned that WebWork allows you to simplify your actions by removing all the plumbing you might normally put in your actions and instead letting WebWork's type-conversion framework do that work for you.

More important, however, you saw how all the parts of WebWork are coming together. You can use interceptors and validators to place conversion errors into field-level errors. UI components can be used to display those field-level errors. The expression language can be used to name HTML fields with deep expressions.

This is the power of type conversion—it's a *binding* technology. That is, it doesn't do much by itself, but when combined with other supporting technologies, it can radically change how you develop web applications. You can finally focus on working with your objects instead of wrestling with swapping data in and out of a particular format.

Validating form data

13

This chapter covers

- Manual validation and the `Validateable` interface
- Automatic validation using external XML files and the Validation Framework
- Validation-related workflow
- Advanced validation features

333

Validating form data is essential to preventing incorrect data from getting into your applications. The back-end services that your web applications often call aren't usually forgiving of invalid data; so, unless you like showing stack traces to your users, it's a good idea to catch problems with what they've entered as soon as possible. It's a hallmark of user-friendly systems to show users where they've made a mistake and what they need to do to correct it. Validating form data and providing meaningful error messages is one of the keys to providing feedback to the user. It's important to note here that we separate the idea of data validation from type conversion. If the user enters data that is incorrectly formatted and can't be converted to the correct type for the property, this problem will be caught and handled by the type conversion framework discussed in chapter 12.

Throughout this chapter, you'll work with the User domain object from the CaveatEmptor application, using the User instance to directly back the form. This User class is simple, as you can see in listing 13.1.

> **Listing 13.1   The User class: a domain object with properties and associations with other domain objects**

```
public class User implements Serializable, Comparable {
    protected Long id = null;
    private int version;
    private String firstname;
    private String lastname;
    private String username;
    private String password;
    private String email;
    private int ranking = 0;
    private Date created = new Date();
    private Address address;
    private Set items = new HashSet();
    private Set billingDetails = new HashSet();
    private BillingDetails defaultBillingDetails;
    private boolean admin = false;

    //getters and setters omitted...
}
```

The CreateUser action class is also simple; it provides a User object and a way to save it, as shown in listing 13.2.

Listing 13.2 **CreateUser action, which provides a User object via the getUser() method**

```
public class CreateUser extends ActionSupport
                        implements UserDAOAware {
  User user;
  private UserDAO userDAO;

  public String execute() throws Exception {
    if (hasErrors()) {
      return INPUT;
    }

    userDAO.makePersistent(user);
    return SUCCESS;
  }

  public User getUser() {
    return user;
  }
  ...
}
```

We'll look at more of the details of the CreateUser action in a bit; but for now, the important part is the User object and the getUser() method.

You'll use the same form to enter data to be validated for all the examples; you can see it in listing 13.3.

Listing 13.3 **The form in createUser.jsp, used to enter data for all the examples in this chapter**

```
<ww:form action="createUser">
  <ww:token/>
  <ww:textfield label="%{getText('username')}"
                name="user.username"/>
  <ww:password label="%{getText('password')}" name="user.password"/>
  <ww:textfield label="%{getText('firstname')}"
                name="user.firstname"/>
  <ww:textfield label="%{getText('lastname')}"
                name="user.lastname"/>
  <ww:textfield label="%{getText('email')}" name="user.email"/>
  <ww:submit value="Submit"/>
</ww:form>
```

The action provides the User object through a getUser() method, and you bind the properties of the User object to your form fields. Your validations are applied to the User object in each case, showing the differences between the different validation strategies.

13.1 Manually validating data

Now that you know what use case you're implementing (creating a user), let's move to the topic of this chapter, validating form data. The most direct method of validating form data is often to code the validations in your action. With this approach, there is the issue of limiting reuse, because validations are locked up in action classes and aren't easily reused between actions or in other parts of your application. However, in some cases complex business rules must be validated that can't easily be expressed in any other way than code; so, coding validations in your action has its place.

13.1.1 Validating in the execute() method

It's simple to put your validations in the execute() method. After all, you're coding the execute() method to do something anyway, so why not check the values in the same method as the code that uses them? Listing 13.4 shows what the execute() method of the CreateUser class looks like using this strategy.

Listing 13.4 execute() method of the CreateUser action, with validatation

```
public String execute() throws Exception {
  User user = getUser();
  String firstname = user.getFirstname();
  if ((firstname == null) || (firstname.trim().equals(""))) {
    addFieldError("user.firstName", "You must enter a first name.");
  }
  String lastname = user.getLastname();
  if ((lastname == null) || (lastname.trim().equals(""))) {
    addFieldError("user.lastname", "You must enter a last name.");
  }
  String username = user.getUsername();
  if ((username == null) || (username.trim().equals(""))) {
    addFieldError("user.username", "You must enter a user name.");
  }
  String email = user.getEmail();
  if ((email == null) || (email.trim().equals(""))) {
    addFieldError("user.email",
                  "You must enter an email address.");
  }
  if (hasErrors()) {
```

```
      return INPUT;
   }
   userDAO.makePersistent(user);
   return SUCCESS;
 }
```

Here you see that you get the `User` object; then check `firstname`, `lastname`, `username`, and `email` to see if any of them are `null` or empty; and add a field-level error message if they are. This process makes those properties required (note that with HTML forms, if the properties are displayed as textfields, they come in on the request as empty strings if nothing is put in by the user, so checking for `null` isn't enough). Finally, the code checks to see whether any error messages have been added to the action (remember from chapter 12 that this could include a type-conversion error message if the `conversionErrors` interceptor is applied). If there are any errors, it returns `Action.INPUT`, otherwise it saves the `User` and returns `Action.SUCCESS`. As you've seen in earlier chapters, these return codes are mapped to results by the framework. In this case, `INPUT` returns you to the same page to re-edit your form, whereas `SUCCESS` redirects you to the main dashboard page.

13.1.2 *Implementing the Validateable interface*

Although implementing validations in the `execute()` method is workable, it adds a lot of code to `execute()`. The previous example included some simple validations for a few fields. Multiply this by dozens of fields and multiple validations per field for a complex form, and you'll see that the business function your action implements can quickly become obscured beneath many lines of code devoted to validating the form data before doing any real processing.

Moreover, you might want to have several methods on your action class that could each be mapped to a separate action alias, as you saw in chapter 3 ("Setting up WebWork") when we talked about aliasing action methods. Each of these methods would deal with the same objects but have different business functions. If you put your validation code in the methods, your validations would need to be cut-and-pasted into each method, rather than being reused. If you were faced with this situation, you would probably pull this functionality out into a separate method that could be reused across action aliases, which is what you'll do in a moment.

Finally, checking for error messages in the action and returning `Action.INPUT` as the result to look up from the action configuration if there are errors should seem familiar. In chapter 5, "Adding functionality with interceptors," the `DefaultWork-FlowInterceptor` did this (mapped as `workflow`). The `DefaultWorkFlowInterceptor` also checks whether the action implements the com.opensymphony.xwork.Validateable interface. As you may remember, this interface declares one method and is implemented by ActionSupport:

```
void validate()
```

To separate your validation code from your business logic, you'll refactor your action class to implement the Validateable interface and pull your validation code out of your execute() method and into the validate() method. Listing 13.5 shows the CreateUser execute() and validate() methods when implementing the Validateable interface.

Listing 13.5 Validation code in the `validate()` method from the `Validateable` interface

```java
public void validate() {
  User user = getUser();
  String firstname = user.getFirstname();
  if ((firstname == null) || (firstname.trim().equals(""))) {
    addFieldError("user.firstName",
                  "You must enter a first name.");
  }
  String lastname = user.getLastname();
  if ((lastname == null) || (lastname.trim().equals(""))) {
    addFieldError("user.lastname", "You must enter a last name.");
  }
  String username = user.getUsername();
  if ((username == null) || (username.trim().equals(""))) {
    addFieldError("user.username", "You must enter a user name.");
  }
  String email = user.getEmail();
  if ((email == null) || (email.trim().equals(""))) {
    addFieldError("user.email",
                  "You must enter an email address.");
  }
}

public String execute() throws Exception {
  userDAO.makePersistent(user);
  return SUCCESS;
}
```

Not only is this code smaller and clearer, because you can easily see which code is involved in validation and which implements your business logic, but it can also make your actions more testable! When you're unit testing, it's important to be able to get to small units of code to test, because you can individually test your business functionality and your validations. In this case, you have only the saving of the User for business logic; but in more complex applications, testing the business logic is critical. We'll look in depth at the issue of testing WebWork apps in chapter 15.

In addition, in some use cases you may want to apply validations, whereas in others you don't. This is simple now, because you can customize your interceptor set per action alias and leave out the workflow interceptor if you don't want to use the validate() method.[1]

In general, it's preferable to implement the Validateable interface if you're going to do field validation in your action class. One exception to this rule is when your action has multiple action aliases that are mapped to different methods in your action, and you want a different validation for each method. In this case, it wouldn't make sense to implement Validateable, even to group common validations. The reason is the lifecycle the workflow interceptor puts around your action, as you see in figure 13.1.

If any errors occur after executing the validate() method, processing stops, and the action execute() isn't called. Thus any custom validations for this execute() method (or other equivalent method, as mapped in the xwork.xml file) aren't run. The user is sent back to the form to fix the form field problems shown (those generated from the common validations in validate()) and repost the form. After the user corrects the errors and resubmits, if problems with the field

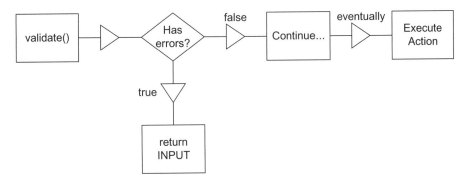

Figure 13.1   The workflow provided by the DefaultWorkflowInterceptor

---

[1] This would also leave out the error checking done in the workflow interceptor that can catch type-conversion errors. If you need to have this error checking and want to be able to turn validation on and off, it should take you about 5 minutes to build an interceptor that can just do the error checking. See chapter 5 for details on creating your own interceptor classes.

data are caught in the validations in the `execute()` method, the user is sent back
to the form to fix the input *again*, which is quite frustrating. In the case of multiple action aliases, it's a better idea to pull your common validations into a method
and then call that method from each of your `execute()` equivalent methods, or to
use the Validation Framework, which we'll discuss next.

13.2 Using the Validation Framework

As you saw in section 13.1, validations can be performed in code in your action
class. As you also saw, this approach can clutter your code and become complicated when you want different validations in different use cases. These concerns
led to the development of the XWork Validation Framework, which is part of
XWork (and therefore included in WebWork). The Validation Framework uses
external metadata in the form of XML files to describe what validations should be
performed on your action.

13.2.1 Building your first *-validation.xml file

Validations to be applied by the Validation Framework are defined in XML files
named *ClassName*-validation.xml. These files go alongside your action classes in
the same packages, so they're easier to manage. As an example, let's look at the
validation XML file for the `CreateUser` example that would accomplish the same
thing you've been doing. Listing 13.6 shows the CreateUser-validation.xml file.

Listing 13.6   CreateUser-validation.xml

```
<!DOCTYPE validators PUBLIC
    "-//OpenSymphony Group//XWork Validator 1.0//EN"
    "http://www.opensymphony.com/xwork/xwork-validator-1.0.2.dtd">
<validators>
    <field name="user.firstname">
        <field-validator type="requiredstring">
            <message>First name is required!</message>
        </field-validator>
    </field>
    <field name="user.lastname">
        <field-validator type="requiredstring">
            <message>Last name is required!</message>
        </field-validator>
    </field>
    <field name="user.username">
        <field-validator type="requiredstring">
            <message>Username is required!</message>
        </field-validator>
```

```
      </field>
      <field name="user.password">
         <field-validator type="requiredstring">
            <message>Password is required!</message>
         </field-validator>
      </field>
      <field name="user.email">
         <field-validator type="requiredstring">
            <message>Email name is required!</message>
         </field-validator>
      </field>
   </validators>
```

Looking at the structure of this file, you see that it starts with a DOCTYPE declaration; this allows the parser to associate this file with the DTD for validating the file structure. Next, you group all the validations inside one `<validators>` root element. Then, you apply one field validator each to the user.firstname, user.lastname, user.username, user.password, and user.email fields. These field validators are requiredstring validators, which do the null and empty String checks you've been doing.

Each validator also includes a `<message>` element that provides the error message to be added to the action if the validator fails. The text between the `<message>` and `</message>` is the default message text. If you want to use a localized message looked up from a resource bundle, you can add a key attribute to the message element, like this:

```
<message key="invalid.email">
```

If the message key isn't found in the resource bundles, the default text is used.

Next, let's look at what validators are available and how you register them.

13.2.2 *Registering validators*

Validators can be any class that implements the com.opensymphony.xwork.validator.Validator interface. Validators are called by the framework to validate an object and are passed the object to access its properties. Validators are mapped from a name to a class that implements the Validator interface. They must be registered with the com.opensymphony.xwork.validator.ValidatorFactory to do this mapping. This may either be done programmatically, using the registerValidator(String name, Class clazz) static method of the ValidatorFactory, or by putting a file named validators.xml in the root of the classpath, which is the usual method. Listing 13.7 shows a validators.xml file that includes all the bundled validators.

Listing 13.7 validators.xml[2]

```
<validators>
    <validator name="required" class="...RequiredFieldValidator"/>
    <validator name="requiredstring"
               class="...RequiredStringValidator"/>
    <validator name="int" class="...IntRangeFieldValidator"/>
    <validator name="date" class="...DateRangeFieldValidator"/>
    <validator name="expression" class="...ExpressionValidator"/>
    <validator name="fieldexpression"
               class="...FieldExpressionValidator"/>
    <validator name="email" class="...EmailValidator"/>
    <validator name="url" class="...URLValidator"/>
    <validator name="visitor" class="...VisitorFieldValidator"/>
    <validator name="conversion"
               class="...ConversionErrorFieldValidator"/>
    <validator name="stringlength"
               class="...StringLengthFieldValidator"/>
</validators>
```

Table 13.1 shows the bundled validators using the names shown and gives a description of each. All validators have the properties defaultMessage, messageKey, and shortCircuit, which are configured using built-in attributes in the XML file. In addition, all validators except the expression validator support a fieldName property that is normally set by the field validators being inside a <field> element. Additional properties are discussed in the table.

Most of the validators listed in table 13.1 are relatively simple. They do things like check for null, check for a range of values, or check that a String is in some defined format for an email or a URL. Two of the validators stick out as more advanced, however: VisitorFieldValidator and Expression/FieldExpressionValidator. We look at these in detail in the advanced Validation Framework section later in this chapter.

---

[2] All of the bundled validators listed here are in the package com.opensymphony.xwork.validator.validators. The package name is omitted for readability.

Table 13.1 The bundled validators as mapped in a validators.xml file from their common name to the class implementing the validation

Validator name	Function
`required`	Field validator that checks whether the field is null and adds a field error if it is.
`requiredstring`	Field validator that checks whether the `String` is null or empty. This is necessary because web request parameters naturally come in as strings, and even if nothing is typed into a textfield, an empty `String` will be passed to the property. **Extra parameters** `trim` — `boolean` property that tells the validator whether to call `trim()` to remove extra whitespace before checking if the `String` value is empt Defaults to `true`.
`stringlength`	Field validator that checks to be sure the length of a `String` property's value is within a certain range. **Extra parameters** `trim` — `boolean` property that tells the validator whether to call `trim()` to remove extra whitespace before checking the String's value. `minLength` — `int` property that represents the minimum allowable `String` length. Defaults to `-1`, which is ignored. `maxLength` — `int` property that represents the maximum allowable `String` length. Defaults to `-1`, which is ignored.
`int`	Field validator that checks to be sure the `integer` (or `Integer`) field value is in a given range of numbers. **Extra parameters** `min` — `iInteger` property that represents the minimum allowable value. Defaults to null, which doesn't check the minimum. `max` — `Integer` property that represents the maximum allowable value. Defaults to null, which doesn't check the maximum.
`date`	Field validator that checks to be sure the `Date` field value is in a given range of dates. **Extra parameters** `min` — `iDate` property that represents the minimum allowable value. Defaults to null, which doesn't check the minimum. `max` — `Date` property that represents the maximum allowable value Defaults to null, which doesn't check the maximum.
`email`	Field validator that checks for a valid email address format.
`url`	Field validator that checks for a valid URL format.

Table 13.1 The bundled validators as mapped in a validators.xml file from their common name to the class implementing the validation *(continued)*

Validator name	Function
conversion	Field validator that implements the same functionality as the `conversionError` interceptor you saw in chapter 12, but only for the fields to which it's applied. The `conversion` field validator checks whether a type-conversion error occurred when setting the value on this field and uses the type-conversion framework to create the correct field error message to be added for this field. This field validator should only be used if the `conversionError` interceptor isn't applied and you want to handle setting conversion error messages on a per-field basis.
expression / fieldexpression	Validators that evaluate any OGNL expression that evaluates to a `boolean` (or Boolean). For example: `user.name != "fred"` These validators allow you to create powerful validations using just XML and your existing model. The `expression` validator should be applied when the validation isn't specific to one field, because it adds action-level error messages. The `fieldexpression` validator is a field validator that adds error messages specific to that particular field. Except for the location where error messages are stored, these two validators are the same. **Extra parameters** <table><tr><td>expression</td><td>An OGNL expression that evaluates to a boolean or Boolean value. A value of `true` means the object or field is valid. A value of `false` or a `non-boolean/Boolean` value means the object or field is invalid and causes an error message to be added.</td></tr></table>
visitor	Field validator that allows validation to be run against the value of the field to which this validator is applied. For example, if a `visitor` field validator is applied to the user object of the `CreateUser` action, it applies the validations mapped for the `User` class. The framework uses the validations defined in *-validation.xml files for the `Object` types of the property value. We'll discuss this more in section 13.3.5. **Extra parameters** <table><tr><td>context</td><td>Allows you to specify a different context under which to validate this object. By default, the context is the name of the action alias the `visitor` field validation came from.</td></tr><tr><td>append- Prefix</td><td>Tells the `visitor` field validator whether to append the name of this property to the full property name when adding error messages. For example, if the `visitor` field validator is added to the `user` property, and `appendPrefix` is set to `true`, then field error messages for the `firstName` property of the `User` add field error messages for `user.firstName` to the action. By default, this is `true`. For `ModelDriven` actions where the visitor field validator is applied to the model property, this should be set to `false`.</td></tr></table>

13.2.3 *Applying the validation interceptor*

The Validation Framework can be set up to automatically use your *ClassActionName-* validation.xml files by adding the `validation` interceptor. As you saw in chapters 3 and 5, you can apply interceptors to an action by adding `<interceptor-ref>` elements to your action configuration in xwork.xml. Here's the configuration for the `CreateUser` action before you apply the `validation` interceptor:

```
<action name="createUser"
  class="org.hibernate.auction.web.actions.users.CreateUser">
    <interceptor-ref name="defaultStack"/>
    <interceptor-ref name="workflow"/>
    <interceptor-ref name="token-session"/>
    <result name="input">createUser.jsp</result>
    <result name="success" type="chain">login</result>
</action>
```

After you apply the `validation` interceptor, this configuration looks like this:

```
<action name="createUser"
  class="org.hibernate.auction.web.actions.users.CreateUser">
    <interceptor-ref name="defaultStack"/>
    <interceptor-ref name="validation"/>
    <interceptor-ref name="workflow"/>
    <interceptor-ref name="token-session"/>
    <result name="input">createUser.jsp</result>
    <result name="success" type="chain">login</result>
</action>
```

Because you had already added the `workflow` interceptor to call the `validate()` method and check for error messages, the interceptors include the default stack and the `workflow` interceptor. Because it's a common set of interceptors, the default stack + `workflow` + `validation` are also grouped together as a named interceptor stack (validationWorkflowStack) in the webwork-default.xml file. Your application also uses the component manager and other services, so you use the `completeStack`, which includes all of those in the validationWorkflowStack and more, as shown in listing 13.8.

> **Listing 13.8 The definition of completeStack in webwork-default.xml**

```
<interceptor-stack name="completeStack">
  <interceptor-ref name="prepare"/>
  <interceptor-ref name="servlet-config"/>
  <interceptor-ref name="chain"/>
  <interceptor-ref name="model-driven"/>
  <interceptor-ref name="component"/>
  <interceptor-ref name="fileUpload"/>
  <interceptor-ref name="static-params"/>
```

```
    <interceptor-ref name="params"/>
    <interceptor-ref name="conversionError"/>
    <interceptor-ref name="validation"/>
    <interceptor-ref name="workflow"/>
</interceptor-stack>
```

Because of this, you can easily make this one interceptor stack the main interceptor reference in your action configuration, as you see here:

```
<action name="createUser"
  class="org.hibernate.auction.web.actions.users.CreateUser">
    <interceptor-ref name="completeStack"/>
    <interceptor-ref name="token-session"/>
    <result name="input">createUser.jsp</result>
    <result name="success" type="chain">login</result>
  </action>
</package>
```

You also add the `token-session` interceptor to prevent duplicate posts and to take the user to the correct page after processing without seeing an error. See chapters 5 and 15 for details on the token interceptors.

13.2.4 *Pulling it all together*

Now you've defined your first validation file, CreateUser-validation.xml, which you built in section 13.2.1. This file sits in the same package as your `CreateUser` action class. In section 13.2.2, we looked at how to define the validators you're using (probably just copying over the validators.xml file from the WebWork example app) so they're registered and can be used in your validation xml files. In section 13.2.3, we explained how to apply the `validation` interceptor to your action configuration so that the validation is done for you automatically. Finally, let's look at what this means for your action class. Listing 13.9 shows the important parts of the action code before applying the Validation Framework.

Listing 13.9 CreateUser action before using the Validation Framework

```
public class CreateUser extends ActionSupport {
  private User user = new User();

  public User getUser() {
    return user;
  }

  public void validate() {
    User user = getUser();
```

```
    String firstname = user.getFirstname();
    if ((firstname == null) || (firstname.trim().equals(""))) {
      addFieldError("user.firstName",
                    "You must enter a first name.");
    }
    String lastname = user.getLastname();
    if ((lastname == null) || (lastname.trim().equals(""))) {
      addFieldError("user.lastname",
                    "You must enter a last name.");
    }
    String username = user.getUsername();
    if ((username == null) || (username.trim().equals(""))) {
      addFieldError("user.username",
                    "You must enter a user name.");
    }
    String email = user.getEmail();
    if ((email == null) || (email.trim().equals(""))) {
      addFieldError("user.email",
                    "You must enter an email address.");
    }
  }

  public String execute() throws Exception {
    userDAO.makePersistent(user);
    return SUCCESS;
  }
}
```

Applying the Validation Framework makes this code *much* easier. Listing 13.10 shows the action class after applying the Validation Framework.

Listing 13.10 Simplified action code that results from applying the validation interceptor

```
public class CreateUser extends ActionSupport
                        implements UserDAOAware {
    User user;
    private UserDAO userDAO;

    public String execute() throws Exception {
        userDAO.makePersistent(user);
        return SUCCESS;
    }

    public String doDefault() throws Exception {
        return INPUT;
    }
```

```
public User getUser() {
    return user;
}

public void setUser(User user) {
    this.user = user;
}

public void setUserDAO(UserDAO dao) {
    this.userDAO = dao;
}
}
```

As you can see, after you apply the `validation` interceptor, the code becomes smaller and simpler because you don't need to override `validate()` to implement the validations in code. Now, between the `validation` interceptor validating your action and the `workflow` interceptor checking for errors, all your action's `execute()` method has to do is return `SUCCESS`: The rest of the work is done before you get to the `execute()` method. The validations are applied, reading which validations you've applied from your CreateUser-validation.xml file; then the action is checked for any errors, and it returns `INPUT` if there are any. By the time the `execute()` method is called, you know your data has been validated and is acceptable, so your action code can contain just the business logic (in this case, saving the `User`). Other times, you may have validations that work better in code than declared in a validation XML file. In such cases, you could leave those validations in the `validate()` method and separate the other validations to an XML file.

Before we move on, let's look at some example validation xml file snippets to see how these validations can be applied.

13.2.5 *Looking at some validation XML examples*

You've seen the basics of setting up the Validation Framework, so now let's look at some examples that show how you'd *use* it. Let's start with a simple example that shows the use of the `stringLength` field validator. Here's the configuration for the field validator:

```
<field name="username">
  <field-validator type="stringlength">
    <param name="trim">true</param>
    <param name="minLength">5</param>
    <param name="maxLength">10</param>
    <message>trim-min5-max10</message>
  </field-validator>
</field>
```

Here you configure a field validator for the username field to check the length of the String put into that field to make sure it's between 5 and 10 characters. With trim set to true, the validator calls trim() on the String to remove any extra whitespace before checking the String length.

Next, let's look at a similar example that uses the date field validator. Here's a field validator that prevents birthdates earlier than 1970:

```
<field name="birth">
  <field-validator type="date">
    <param name="min">01/01/1970</param>
    <message>You must have been born after 1970.</message>
  </field-validator>
</field>
```

As you can see, the min property is set by putting a String representation of the date inside the <param> element. The type conversion framework is used to set the validator configuration parameters onto the validator instances, so this is set as a java.util.Date converted from the String 01/01/1970. It's also interesting to notice that when you only want to check that a value is greater than a certain value, you can set the min parameter. Likewise, if you're just interested in setting a maximum value, you can set the max parameter.

Finally, let's look at a more interesting example that shows the use of the int range validator and how you can use the values from the action and the validator to parameterize the message. Following are the validators for a field named count:

```
<field name="count">
  <field-validator type="required">
    <message>You must enter a value for count.</message>
  </field-validator>
  <field-validator type="int">
    <param name="min">0</param>
    <param name="max">5</param>
    <message>count must be between ${min} and ${max},
            current value is ${count}.</message>
  </field-validator>
</field>
```

As you can see, two field validators are applied to the count property: a required validator, and an int validator that checks whether the count value is within a given range. At first look, it might seem that a null value would add two error messages, but this isn't the case. The int field validator, like the other field validators other than required and requiredstring, is designed to ignore null values. The reason for this is to remain orthogonal to the other validators. As you see in this example, if you want to ensure that a null value adds an error message for the

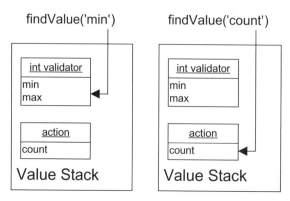

Figure 13.2
The expression blocks from the error message are evaluated against the value stack with the validator instance pushed on.

field, then you should add a `required` validator. Keeping the validators orthogonal is important and should be maintained in your own custom validators if at all possible because it simplifies composition and reuse of validators.

The second important point in this example is the parameterization of the error message for the `int` validator. As you saw, the range validators (`int` and `date` field validators) take `min` and `max` parameters to set the boundaries of the range. In this case, the `count` value has to be an integer between 0 and 5. If the value is outside this range, the error message is created and put into the field error map for the `count` field.

As the previous code shows, error messages can be parameterized using OGNL expressions to get values. Expressions wrapped in `${...}` are evaluated to get the text to put into that spot in the error message. The expressions are evaluated against the value stack with the validator instance pushed onto the stack. Figure 13.2 shows the evaluation of the `${min}` and `${count}` parameter placeholders.

Now that you've seen how the basic validation system works, let's look at the more advanced validation features WebWork provides.

13.3 Exploring the advanced features of the Validation Framework

In the previous section, you saw the simplest usage of the Validation Framework. For larger and more complex applications, you'll want to use the advanced features discussed in this section to reuse validations, build custom validators, or build up powerful validations using the OGNL expression language without needing to write Java code.

13.3.1 *Implementing a custom validator*

The Validation Framework allows for custom validators to be built and applied in the same declarative fashion as the prebuilt validators. Implementing a custom validator is as simple as creating a class that implements the com.opensymphony.xwork.validator.Validator interface, which is shown in listing 13.11.

Listing 13.11 com.opensymphony.xwork.validator.Validator interface

```
public interface Validator {
    void setDefaultMessage(String message);

    String getDefaultMessage();

    String getMessage(Object object);

    void setMessageKey(String key);

    String getMessageKey();

    /**
     * This method will be called before validate() with a non-null
     * ValidatorContext.
     * @param validatorContext
     */
    void setValidatorContext(ValidatorContext validatorContext);

    ValidatorContext getValidatorContext();

    /**
     * The validation implementation must guarantee that setValidatorContext
     * will be called with a non-null ValidatorContext before validate is
     * called.
     * @param object
     * @throws ValidationException
     */
    void validate(Object object) throws ValidationException;
}
```

As you can see, the com.opensymphony.xwork.validator.Validator interface has a few methods for setting up the message to add if the validation fails. You can set the default message and/or the message key to look up, and getMessage() handles figuring out what the final message should be. The interface also provides a getter and setter for a ValidatorContext object. ValidatorContext is an interface that provides methods for getting localized message texts, setting error messages, and getting the locale.

The good news is that you don't have to implement the `Validator` interface from scratch. `com.opensymphony.xwork.validator.validators.ValidatorSupport` is an abstract class that implements the `Validator` interface, leaving the `validate()` method for subclasses to implement, and adds some helpful methods such as `add-ActionError()`, `addFieldError()`, and `getFieldValue()`. The `FieldValidator` interface, which adds a getter and setter for a property named `fieldName`, likewise has a `FieldValidatorSupport` abstract class that implements `FieldValidator` and extends `ValidatorSupport`.

All of this is, of course, a preface to saying that all you need to do to implement your own custom validator is to extend one of these abstract classes and code the `validate()` method. Let's look at a `FieldValidator` that makes sure an entered `String` property's length is within a certain range.[3] This can be useful when you're going to put the text into a database column and want to make sure you don't get JDBC exceptions from having more characters than the size of the field in the table. Listing 13.12 shows the implementation of the `StringLengthFieldValidator`.

> **Listing 13.12 StringLengthFieldValidator, which validates the length of a String property**

```
public class StringLengthFieldValidator
        extends FieldValidatorSupport {
    private boolean doTrim = true;
    private int maxLength = -1;
    private int minLength = -1;

    public void setMaxLength(int maxLength) {
        this.maxLength = maxLength;
    }

    public int getMaxLength() {
        return maxLength;
    }

    public void setMinLength(int minLength) {
        this.minLength = minLength;
    }

    public int getMinLength() {
        return minLength;
    }

    public void setTrim(boolean trim) {
        doTrim = trim;
```

---

[3] The `StringLengthFieldValidator` started as an example here for building a custom validator, but it seemed useful; so, now it's one of the prepackaged validators.

```
        }

        public boolean getTrim() {
            return doTrim;
        }

        public void validate(Object object)
                throws ValidationException {
            String fieldName = getFieldName();
            String val = (String) getFieldValue(fieldName, object);

            if (doTrim) {
                val = val.trim();
            }

            if ((minLength > -1) && (val.length() < minLength)) {
                addFieldError(fieldName, object);
            } else if ((maxLength > -1)
                    && (val.length() > maxLength)) {
                addFieldError(fieldName, object);
            }
        }
    }
}
```

The `StringLengthFieldValidator` adds the properties `maxLength`, `minLength`, and trim, and uses them to check against the length of the `String`. The `getFieldName()`, `getFieldValue()`, and `addFieldError()` methods are implemented in the abstract base class and make it trivial to write new validators.

Once you've created a new `Validator` class, all that's left is to register it with the Validation Framework, to be able to use it as a named validator in your *-validation.xml files. All that has to be done is to add this line to the validators.xml file:

```
<validator name="stringlength"
        class="com.opensymphony.xwork.validator.validators.
        ⟶StringLengthFieldValidator"/>
```

After doing this, you can add the validator to any field (it should be a `String` property) using the name `stringlength`.

13.3.2 *Validating with different contexts*

Removing validations from your action classes is a nice benefit, but the validations you've seen so far could easily be coded in a `validate()` method. In fact, if your actions have only one entry point method (like the `execute()` method of the `action` interface), then it's often best to put your validations directly in your `validate()` method, because doing so makes testing easy and fast. However, in real-world systems, it often makes sense to put multiple entry point methods on one action class and map them to different aliases in your xwork.xml file. This can prevent the explosion of action classes that can happen when you stick strictly to the "one action = one Command" idea.

Unfortunately, if you want different validations for different entry points, this approach can make managing your validations somewhat complex. Although it's possible to figure out which method is being called in your validate() method and have a series of if...else blocks, it's not pretty. The Validation Framework makes this much simpler by allowing you to define different validations for different contexts. In this case, the context name is the action alias. The filenames take the form of *ActionName-aliasName*-validation.xml. For an action class named CreateUser mapped with an alias named createUserPrepare, which also extends a base action class named BaseAction, the order of loading of validation definitions would be like this:

1 BaseAction-validation.xml

2 BaseAction- createUserPrepare-validation.xml

3 CreateUser-validation.xml

4 CreateUser- createUserPrepare-validation.xml

The framework looks first to the default validations for the parent classes (BaseAction-validation.xml) for validations (this also includes any implemented interfaces), then to the context-specific validations for the parent classes (BaseAction-createUserPrepare-validation.xml), then to the default validations for this class (CreateUser-validation.xml), and finally to the specific validations for this class and context (CreateUser-createUserPrepare-validation.xml). Because these validations are all built up and added to a list, it's important to think about what validations you put where. Only validations that are common to all contexts should be put in the class-level validation files. Similarly, only validations that are common to all subclasses should be put in parent class validation files.

13.3.3 *Short-circuiting validation*

It's sometimes the case that one validation failing means no other validations should be run. For example, if an email field is required, and it's null, you don't need to check whether it's a valid email address. In order to enable this, a short-circuit property was added to the Validation Framework in WebWork 2.1. Here's an example of an email field using the short-circuit attribute:

```
<field name="user.email">
    <field-validator type="requiredstring" short-circuit="true">
        <message>You must enter a value for email.</message>
    </field-validator>
    <field-validator type="email" short-circuit="true">
        <message>Not a valid e-mail.</message>
    </field-validator>
</field>
```

If the field is null or empty, the `email` validator[4] isn't called because the `short-circuit` attribute is set to `true` for the `requiredstring` validator.

The `short-circuit` option checks whether any error messages are added during the execution of that validator. For field validators, as shown earlier, it checks for errors added for this field. If any errors are added for this field, validations for this field are short-circuited, but other validations continue. If the `short-circuit` attribute is added for an action validator, it checks for any errors added to the action-level error message list. If any errors are added, *all* validations are short-circuited. This means no more validations are run. As we noted earlier, validations are inherited from parent classes, so it's important to be careful not to short-circuit validations that you don't mean to.

13.3.4 *The ExpressionValidator*

The `ExpressionValidator` and `FieldExpressionValidator` are basically the same; the only thing that changes is where error messages are added, the first adding them to the action-level error list, the second adding them to the list mapped to the field name. They both allow you to apply any OGNL expression that returns a `boolean` value as a validator. If the expression evaluates to `true`, the validation passes. If it evaluates to `false` (or if it returns a non-`boolean` value), the validation fails and the error message supplied (either with the message key or the default message) is added. The following example validation definition ensures the sum of two numeric properties of the action is less than a constant maximum value:

```
<validator type="expression">
    <param name="expression">
    @example.ValidatedBean@MAX_TOTAL > (number + number2)
    </param>
```

---

[4] Note here that validators *should* be written to be completely independent, so a validator that checks the value of a property against some rule (for instance, checking that a `String` makes a valid email address) shouldn't add an error message if the property is null. The `email` validator does this. This way, you can apply this validator to a nonrequired field and not get extra error messages when it's empty.

```
<message key="invalid.total">Invalid total!</message>
</validator>
```

The @example.ValidatedBean@MAX_TOTAL part of the expression gets the value of a static constant from the ValidatedBean class, which is then compared with the sum of the number and number2 properties of the action. If these two properties add up to more than the static constant MAX_TOTAL, an error message is added.

13.3.5 *Reusing validations with the visitor field validator*

Validations aren't specific to action classes. The Validation Framework can be used without the rest of WebWork to provide a generic object validation framework for domain objects. It's often the case that you'll want to define validation rules for your domain objects or model objects and reuse them across all the actions or other classes that use those objects, but you need a way to trigger the Validation Framework to use those validations. In order to do this, the Validation Framework comes with the VisitorFieldValidator.

Applying the VisitorFieldValidator

The VisitorFieldValidator tells the Validation Framework to look up and use the validations for the object in the named property of the action. Let's look at how you could centralize validations for your User objects and refactor your CreateUser action to use these validations. Listing 13.13 shows the contents of User-validation.xml, which defines the validations for the User class. This file sits directly beside the User class file in the same package.

Listing 13.13 User-validation.xml

```
<!DOCTYPE validators PUBLIC
    "-//OpenSymphony Group//XWork Validator 1.0//EN"
    "http://www.opensymphony.com/xwork/xwork-validator-1.0.2.dtd">
<validators>
    <field name="firstname">
        <field-validator type="requiredstring">
            <message>First name is required!</message>
        </field-validator>
    </field>
    <field name="lastname">
        <field-validator type="requiredstring">
            <message>Last name is required!</message>
        </field-validator>
    </field>
    <field name="username">
        <field-validator type="requiredstring">
            <message>Username is required!</message>
```

```
                </field-validator>
            </field>
            <field name="password">
                <field-validator type="requiredstring">
                    <message>Password is required!</message>
                </field-validator>
            </field>
            <field name="email">
                <field-validator type="requiredstring">
                    <message>Email name is required!</message>
                </field-validator>
            </field>
        </validators>
```

This validation file defines the same field validators you've been using, required
String validators on the firstname, lastname, username, and email fields of the
User object. Now let's look at how you tell the Validation Framework to use it.
Listing 13.14 shows the new CreateUser-validation.xml file, which uses the
VisitorFieldValidator to tell the Validation Framework to use the User-
validation.xml file.

Listing 13.14   CreateUser-validation.xml

```
<!DOCTYPE validators PUBLIC
    "-//OpenSymphony Group//XWork Validator 1.0//EN"
    "http://www.opensymphony.com/xwork/xwork-validator-1.0.dtd">
<validators>
    <field name="user">
        <field-validator type="visitor">
            <message>User: </message>
        </field-validator>
    </field>
</validators>
```

The visitor field validator you define here tells the Validation Framework to look
up the validations for the class of the object it gets from calling the getUser()
method. Because it gets back a User object, it looks for a User-validation.xml file
next to the User class in the same package. It then tells the Validation Framework
to execute the validations defined in that file against the User object while adding
any error messages back to your action. This chaining of validations can be
applied to single-value properties, like the user property, but can also be applied
to Collections and Arrays of objects; the Validation Framework looks up validations for each object it finds based on the class of the object.

The `<message>` element shown in listing 13.14 gives a `String` that is prepended to the beginning of every message applied by the validators for the visited object. For instance, if the name is invalid for your `User` object, the final message will be *User: You must enter a name.* This is a combination of the message from the `VisitorFieldValidator` in listing 13.14 (*User:*), and the message added by the validator in listing 13.13 (*You must enter a name.*).

Using other validation contexts for visited objects

In the previous example, you created a User-validation.xml file. This file defines the default validations for the `User` object; but as you've seen, you can have different validation sets for different contexts. In fact, in the previous example, the context for validating the action is `createUser`, the name of the alias of the action as defined in the `<action>` element in xwork.xml. This context is passed along to the `visitor` validator; so, if you wanted to have context-specific validations, you could define them in a file named User-createUser-validation.xml. This file would be used when the `visitor` field validator was applied from the `createUser` action alias, along with the default validations for the `User` object, as defined in the User-validation.xml file in listing 13.13. If you had another action that was mapped with the alias editUser which also applied the `VisitorFieldValidator` to a `User` object, it would try to load a file named User-editUser-validation.xml along with your User-validation.xml file.

It's often the case that you'll have a small number of validation contexts for a domain object and wish to map the many places it's used to those contexts. As an example, an application might have a set of validations that only apply for online editing of domain objects, and a different set of validations that apply for batch processing. For the `User` object, this would give your User-validation.xml file as the default validations, plus User-online-validation.xml and User-batch-validation.xml defining the online and batch specific validations, respectively.

The `VisitorFieldValidator` accommodates this by allowing you to specify the validation context to use, rather than just using the validation context being used by the parent object. To do this, you provide a parameter named `context` using the `<param>` element, as follows:

```
<!DOCTYPE validators PUBLIC
    "-//OpenSymphony Group//XWork Validator 1.0//EN"
    "http://www.opensymphony.com/xwork/xwork-validator-1.0.dtd">
<validators>
    <field name="user">
        <field-validator type="visitor">
            <param name="context">online</param>
```

```
        <message>User: </message>
    </field-validator>
  </field>
</validators>
```

Using this validation file, the Validation Framework looks for the User-validation.xml file and the User-online-validation.xml file when finding validations for the User object.

The validation context set using the <param> element as shown here becomes the new default validation context. This means that if the User object defines any VisitorFieldValidators (for instance, to an Address object), then the online validation context will be used unless overridden again as we've shown. This allows you to define the validations for your domain object using a small number of contexts (such as online and batch), map the action validations to the domain objects using the VisitorFieldValidator and the <param> element, and have the validation context flow through all the validation relationships as defined using VisitorFieldValidators.

13.4 Summary

Validating form data is central to web applications, and WebWork provides many ways to implement validation. The most direct method for validating values is coding the validations directly in your execute() method. This approach mixes validations and business logic, so it's often better to consolidate your validation code in the validate() method from the Validateable interface and use an interceptor to make sure it's called before the execute() method.

For more advanced validation requirements and validation reuse, WebWork provides a meta-data driven Validation Framework. This Validation Framework allows you to define validations in XML files that are automatically loaded by the framework based on the filename.

Many different prebuilt validators are bundled with WebWork, including simple ones like the required field validator and complex ones like the expression validator (which allows you to use any OGNL expression as a validator). The VisitorFieldValidator is a prebuilt validator that lets you tell the framework to validate the property value (including arrays and collections) using the validations defined for the property's type. This allows you to centralize validations for your domain objects and have them used by any action that uses the domain type.

Internationalization

14

Developing internationalized web applications is hard, and we can't hope to cover all aspects of this challenging topic. The extensive facilities provided by WebWork can help you tackle the technical aspects of building an internationalized application, leaving you to only externalize your text messages, manage the translation process, internationalize your data, and so on—that is, to do the hard part. Web-Work's internationalization facilities can also be used in noninternationalized applications to format dates and numbers for the screen, and we'll also look at this usage.

14.1 *Exploring a quick internationalization example*

During this chapter, we'll explore an internationalized version of CaveatEmptor that shows a tree of categories with localized text for labels and for the category data itself. The example also lets the user choose a language: English, German, Spanish, or French. Figure 14.1 shows the initial page you see when you access the example app (actually, the page you see depends on the default locale of your browser; but this is the default page, because the default locale is en_US).

As you can see, you're shown a tree of category names, a link to create a new category, and the option to choose another language. All of these values are in the

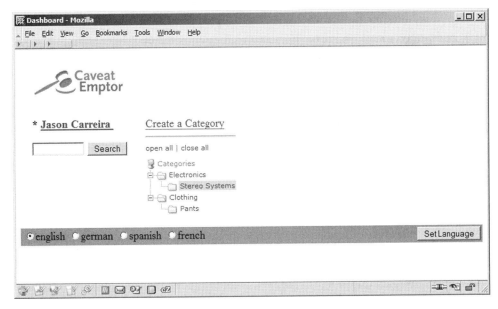

Figure 14.1 When you first access the example application, you see the item list in your default language.

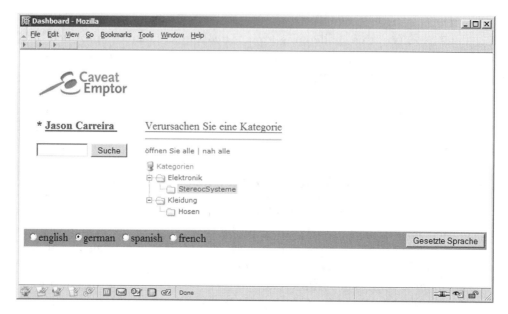

Figure 14.2 The same view items page looks like this after you select German for the language.

correct language and are correctly formatted for the default locale, en_US; but if you were building a web app just for US usage, it would look the same. Let's look at what happens when you choose another language and click the Set Language button.

Figure 14.2 shows the same page after you've selected German and clicked Set Language. Note that not only are the category names localized to their German equivalents, but so are the labels and button texts. Also note that the German texts use non-ASCII characters such as ö.

Throughout the rest of this chapter, we'll look at how this example application works as we discuss the i18n facilities provided by WebWork.

14.2 *Sources for messages*

In order to provide different texts for different locales, you need a source for the application to find the correct texts for a given locale. Fortunately, Java provides these facilities for you in the form of the java.util.ResourceBundle abstract class. The JDK ships with two implementations of ResourceBundle: java.util.Property-ResourceBundle and java.util.ListResourceBundle.

The PropertyResourceBundle is the more commonly used ResourceBundle; it looks for a set of similarly named properties files in the classpath. For instance, in the example application, you'll be loading a ResourceBundle named CreateLocal-izedCategory. This looks for a set of properties files named like this:

- CreateLocalizedCategory.properties
- CreateLocalizedCategory_de.properties
- CreateLocalizedCategory_en.properties
- CreateLocalizedCategory_es.properties
- CreateLocalizedCategory_fr.properties

These properties files should contain a set of *key=value* pairs mapping the keys you want to use to look up the texts to the correct text for that locale.

It's also possible to programmatically build the ResourceBundle, and the List-ResourceBundle provides an abstract base class to make this easier. When Resource-Bundle.getBundle() is called, it searches first for a class with the correct name of the ResourceBundle (including the language and country suffixes—for example, ItemDescriptions_fr.class). If the class extends java.util.ResourceBundle, it's used; otherwise ResourceBundle looks for properties files with the correct names. All of the WebWork facilities go through the ResourceBundle.getBundle() method, so either properties files or classes can be used for your ResourceBundles; however, things like the class hierarchy searching are more difficult when you have to extend ResourceBundle.

The example application includes three different ResourceBundles.org.hibernate.auction.i18n is a default ResourceBundle (see section 14.2.2) with message texts for things like formatting dates and numbers (see section 14.3.3). The org.hibernate.auction.web.actions.localized.CreateLocalizedCategory Resource-Bundle[1] is the ResourceBundle for the CreateLocalizedCategory action and holds action specific message texts like the title and the field label texts. The org.hibernate.auction.localization.LocalizedMessages ResourceBundle is implemented as Java classes and accesses localized texts from the database. Because it's not associated with an action, it isn't automatically loaded; it's directly loaded in your JSP page. Next we'll look at how these different ResourceBundles are loaded.

---

[1] Although ResourceBundle names can use either the com/example/MyResourceBundle or com.example.MyResourceBundle naming convention, the JavaDocs for PropertyResourceBundle specify that the .java class name form is preferred.

14.2.1 *Understanding the ResourceBundle search order*

When WebWork looks for a message text, it searches for a ResourceBundle based on a class or object you give it. This allows you to easily define message texts at different levels and have them be found, with more specific texts taking precedence over more general ones. Let's look at the general search order as shown in figure 14.3.

1 WebWork searches for a ResourceBundle based on the class passed in (or the class of the object passed in), including the interfaces and superclasses of that class. This process looks for a ResourceBundle with the same name and package as the class passed in. The search order for class hierarchy searching is as follows:

  a Look for the message in a ResourceBundle for the class.

  b If not found, look for the message in a ResourceBundle for each implemented interface.

  c If not found, traverse up the class's hierarchy to the parent class, and repeat from step 1.

2 If the message text isn't found in the class hierarchy search and the object implements ModelDriven,[2] WebWork calls getModel() and does a class hierarchy search for the class of the model object.

3 If the message text still isn't found, WebWork searches the class hierarchy for default package texts. For the package of the original class or object, you look for a ResourceBundle named package in that package. For instance, if the class is org.hibernate.auction.ExampleClass, you look for a ResourceBundle named org.hibernate.auction.package. You continue along this line for each superclass in turn.

4 If WebWork hasn't found the text yet, it tries to see if the message key refers to a property of an object on the value stack. If looking for user on the value stack returns a non-null object, and the text key you're looking for is user.label.address, you use the user object's class to search for the text key label.address, searching up its class hierarchy, and so on, as in previous steps.

5 The last resort is to search for the text in the default ResourceBundles that have been registered as described in the next section.

---

[2] For a refresher on modeldriven actions, see chapter 4, section 4.6.

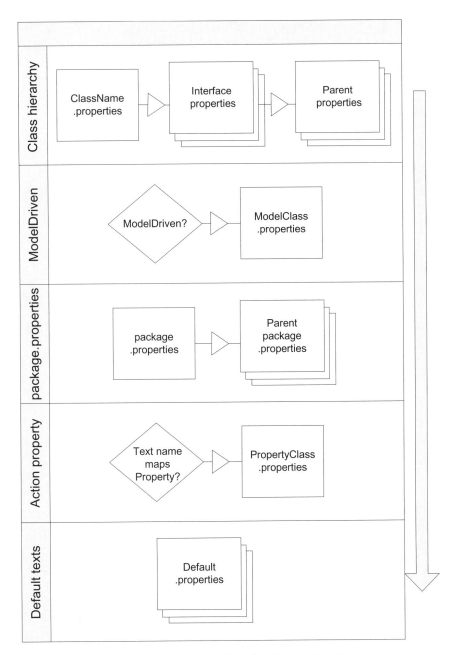

Figure 14.3 WebWork searches a series of locations for localized texts.

As you can see, there are many opportunities to set default texts at different levels and have them picked up automatically for all classes under their scope. For the most part, however, you'll probably use action-level `ResourceBundles` and default `ResourceBundles`, which we'll look at next.

14.2.2 *Adding default resource bundles*

You'll often have a set of messages that you use throughout your application and that you'll always want to be available when getting a localized text. WebWork provides the ability to register default `ResourceBundles` either through a configuration property or programmatically. The example application includes an `i18n` `ResourceBundle`, which you want to add as a default `ResourceBundle`. In order to do this, you add this line to the `webwork.properties` file:

```
webwork.custom.i18n.resources=org.hibernate.auction.i18n
```

At startup, this `ResourceBundle` is added to the list of default `ResourceBundles`. Note the path before the `i18n` part of the `ResourceBundle` name: This indicates that the `ResourceBundle` can be found in the package `org.hibernate.auction`. Alternatively, this `ResourceBundle` could be added in a startup class, such as a `ServletContext-Listener`, by making a call to the `com.opensymphony.xwork.util.LocalizedText-Util` class:

```
LocalizedTextUtil
    .addDefaultResourceBundle("org.hibernate.auction.i18n");
```

Either way you register default `ResourceBundles`, they're available to the i18n facilities of WebWork when it searches for texts in default `ResourceBundles`. When WebWork searches the default `ResourceBundles`, it does so last to first; so, default `ResourceBundles` registered later take precedence over earlier ones.

14.2.3 *The <ww:i18n> tag*

In addition to the default `ResourceBundle` searching, you can explicitly make a `ResourceBundle` available inside a JSP page using the `<ww:i18n>` tag. The i18n tag puts an object implementing `com.opensymphony.xwork.TextProvider` and holding the `ResourceBundle` specified onto the value stack. Calls to `getText()` by tags find this object and get the message texts from the specified `ResourceBundle`. Listing 14.1 shows the segment of the example JSP that builds the table of items.

Listing 14.1 `<ww:i18n>` tag, which makes a ResourceBundle available for calls to `getText()`

```
<%--Push the resource bundle for
item descriptions onto the stack--%>
<ww:i18n
    name="org.hibernate.auction.localization.LocalizedMessages">
    <ww:select label="%{getText('text.parent', null, null)}"
               name="category.parentCategory"
               value="category.parentCategory.id"
               list="#categoryPicker.categories"
               listKey="id"
               listValue="#indent({top, ''}) + getText(name)"
    />
</ww:i18n>
```

In listing 14.1, the i18n tag is used to push a ResourceBundle named org.hibernate.auction.localization.LocalizedMessages onto the value stack, so that the call to getText(name) in the listvalue of the <ww:select> tag can access those texts.

One thing to remember when you're using the <ww:i18n> tag is the scope where localized texts will be found. In listing 14.1, the 'text.parent' text is provided in a default ResourceBundle, not the LocalizedMessages ResourceBundle provided by the <ww:i18n> tag. Because the <ww:i18n> tag is already providing a ResourceBundle, the search order listed earlier isn't used to find a ResourceBundle that has the given text. If a text isn't found, the default value is returned, which is the name of the text key unless otherwise specified. Thus if your label attribute looked like this:

```
label="%{getText('text.parent')}"
```

you'd end up with a label of text.parent displayed to the user.

The example code uses a value stack trick to make it keep searching for the appropriate text. By adding the two extra null parameters, you ensure that the default value is null. Because the value stack is designed to keep searching down the stack for a property if it gets null, this causes the value stack to skip the TextProvider that the <ww:i18n> tag has pushed onto the value stack and fall back to the action. The call to getText() on the action triggers the search for a ResourceBundle and eventually finds the default resource bundle with the text.parent entry. You can use this method to find messages from any outside scope while inside a <ww:i18n> tag.

Now that you've experimented with loading localized texts, let's look at how to use them.

14.3 Using internationalized messages

Loading ResourceBundles is all well and good, but the point is to *use* the texts. WebWork provides facilities for finding the correct localized texts that use the ResourceBundle searching you looked at in the previous section. In addition to the places like the <ww:text> tag and calls to getText(), which are explicitly designed to take a message text key, you can use Object Graph Navigation Language (OGNL) expressions to get localized message texts in the attributes of the WebWork tags.

The <ww:text> tag

The <ww:text> tag is the simplest and most direct way to write a localized text message out to the page. It has one required attribute, name, which gives the message text key. The name attribute can be a hard-coded key, or it can be evaluated if you wrap the expression using the %{...} syntax. The header for the Create Category page uses the <ww:text> tag with a hard-coded text key to get a localized page title, as you see here:

```
<head>
  <title><ww:text name="text.createCategory"/></title>
</head>
```

14.3.1 Parameterizing localized texts

You'll often want to put values into your messages that are only known at runtime. WebWork provides two ways of putting runtime values into your message texts:

- Any expressions in the body of your text that are enclosed in brackets beginning with ${ and ending with } like ${expr} are evaluated against the value stack as OGNL expressions, and the value of that expression is put in the place of the ${expr} part of the message text.

- Message texts can also use message formatting as done by the java.text.MessageFormat class. For instance, arguments can be passed in to be put into the message to replace numbered placeholders {0} through {9}. Check out the JavaDocs for MessageFormat for more details on the formatting options. You'll see some of them when we look at formatting dates and numbers.

When you're using numbered placeholders in a MessageFormat String for your message text, you need to pass parameters to be used to fill in these placeholders. With calls to getText() on your actions, you can optionally pass in a List of objects to be put into the correct spots in the message. When you're using the `<ww:text>` tag, there are two ways to pass values to be put into the placeholders:

- Use the `value0...value3` attributes of the `Tag`. This way is deprecated, but it still works well—especially when you have just one or two simple parameters. It's also more concise and can save some lines of JSP code.

- Use the `<ww:param>` tag to add unnamed properties. This method is more flexible and allows more properties to be added. It also allows for whole chunks of text, even text dynamically generated with other JSP tags, to be passed in as parameters to the message. You'll see this advanced usage discussed in section 14.4.3.

These two `<ww:text>` tag uses are functionally equivalent:

```
<ww:text name="format.date" value0="created"/>

<ww:text name="format.date"><ww:param value="created"/></ww:text>
```

You can pass up to 10 parameters to be put into the message using the `<ww:param>` tags; their order depends on the order of the `<ww:param>` tags inside the `<ww:text>` tag. The `value` attribute of the `<ww:param>` tag is evaluated as an OGNL expression against the value stack, and the return value is put into the `<ww:text>` tag's parameters. You can also use the `<ww:param>...</ww:param>` form of the tag to put any text you like (including dynamically generated text) into the message parameters.

14.3.2 *Using getText() in taglib attributes*

WebWork tag attributes can all be evaluated against the value stack, so it makes sense that you can get properties and call methods on your action from the attributes of the tags using OGNL. When you don't need to pass any parameters to the formatted message text, the `<ww:text>` tag's functionality can be replicated by using a `<ww:property>` tag. These two do the same thing:

```
<ww:text name="text.createCategory "/>
<ww:property value="getText('text.createCategory')"/>
```

More useful, however, is to use `getText()` calls to get localized texts for labels for UI elements. Here's an example of a text field with a localized label text:

```
<ww:textfield label="%{getText('text.name')}" name="category.name"/>
```

This gets the `text.name` localized text and puts it into the label for your textfield.

14.3.3 *Formatting dates and numbers*

Formatting dates and numbers consistently throughout an application can be tricky, regardless of whether you're building an internationalized app. Fortunately, `java.text.MessageFormat` and WebWork's localized message text support can help you use a consistent format string everywhere in your site. The example application shows localized dates and amounts for the items. As you saw earlier, a date can be written out using the `<ww:text>` tag like so:

```
<ww:text name="format.date" value0="created"/>
```

A monetary value can be written out like this:

```
<ww:text name="format.money" value0="price"/>
```

You're passing in the `price` and `created` properties of the item to be formatted using the appropriate text format `String`. The `format.money` and `format.date` texts are defined in the i18n.properties file, as shown here:

```
format.money={0,number,currency}
format.date={0,date,short}
```

The `format.money` and `format.date` texts use `java.text.MessageFormat` formatting. Note that you don't need different versions of these texts for different locales, because `MessageFormat` takes care of that for you. Without having to change the format string or know anything about the user in the JSP, the dates and numbers are automatically formatted according to the correct locale. Here you define the formats in a default `ResourceBundle`, but they could be defined (or overridden) in action-specific `ResourceBundle`s.

These are relatively simple `MessageFormat` formatting strings, but much more can be done by `MessageFormat`. The JavaDocs for `MessageFormat` are the best resource for these advanced usages.

14.3.4 *Using localized messages in validations*

In chapter 13, "Validating form data," we discussed different validation strategies for your actions; but you always hard-coded the validation error messages in the code or XML file. For an internationalized application, you need not only the main text of the pages to be internationalized, but also any messages you show to the user, especially messages telling them they've entered something incorrectly.

Using localized messages in the validation framework is designed to be easy by allowing you to specify your message text key in your *-validation.xml file. Here's a snippet of a validation file for a field named baz:[3]

```
<field name="baz">
    <field-validator type="int">
        <param name="min">0</param>
        <message key="baz.range">Could not find baz.range!</message>
    </field-validator>
</field>
```

The key attribute here is used to specify a message text key to be used in a call to getText(). If the validation fails to find the localized error message text, it uses the default text found between the open and close <param> tags. These message texts can't expect arguments as in the MessageFormat strings, because there's no way to supply them. They can, however, use the ${expr} notation we discussed earlier. In the test resource bundle, the baz.range text is defined like so:

```
baz.range=${getText(fieldName)} must be greater than ${min}
```

Here you see the ${expr} notation used to call a method, getText(), to get a localized version of the label for this field name. It also uses the min property from the field validator object itself, picking up the value that was set into it as a property. This works because when you're evaluating the validations, the validator instances themselves are pushed onto the value stack. Thus you can access properties of the validator and the action (and any other object on the value stack) transparently from your validation message text.

14.3.5 *Using internationalized texts for type conversion messages*

As you saw in chapter 12, type-conversion errors can add a message to your field error messages. The default message is Invalid value '${value}' for field xxx, which leaves a lot to be desired, especially for an internationalized application. Fortunately, before defaulting back to this message, WebWork looks for a text named invalid.fieldValue.xxx. You can use this to provide a better, and localized, message text. All you need to do is to provide a message text for each property in a ResourceBundle that is accessible from the action (that is, the action's Resource-Bundle, one of the parent classes ResourceBundle, or a default ResourceBundle).

---

[3] This example comes from the test suite for XWork, where the validation framework is built and tested. Test suites can be some of the best documentation for the usage of a library, so don't be afraid to dig in and see what they're testing.

Localized texts for Collections

Many times, you'll have collections of objects, each of which you're exposing to the web page via indexed properties. You'll have form field names like `items[0].name`, `items[1].name`, and so on. You may not even know how many of these you'll have, because the page writes them out as it scrolls through a collection. If you had to provide type-conversion error messages for every one of these, you'd see things like `invalid.fieldValue.item[0].name=...`, `invalid.fieldValue.item[1].name=...`, and, because you don't know how many of these you may have, there's no guarantee that you'll have them all covered. Fortunately, someone pointed this out to us, and it's been fixed.[4] In order to provide a type-conversion error message for *all* item names, you can use a localized text key like this:

```
invalid.fieldValue.items[*].name=Some type conversion message here
```

This is primarily of use in type-conversion text lookup, but the `[*]` notation can be used anywhere to match all indexes of a text key with a `[0]` type notation.

Setting a different default conversion error message

You may not want to set type-conversion error texts for all your properties, but want to have a different default error conversion message. The default error message is looked up from the default `ResourceBundles` registered with the `LocalizedTextUtil` class using the text key `xwork.default.invalid.fieldvalue`. The previous default is defined in a `ResourceBundle` that is automatically added to the default `ResourceBundles`. It's looked up with one parameter passed in: the property name. The default type conversion error message looks like this:

```
xwork.default.invalid.fieldvalue=Invalid field value for field "{0}".
```

If you define this property in your default `ResourceBundle`, which is registered with the `LocalizedTextUtil` (see section 14.2.2), your custom type-conversion message will be used. You can also use this to make your default type-conversion error message be localized, because the default `ResourceBundle` bundled in Web-Work isn't. Make localized versions of your default `ResourceBundle` texts, and the correct one will be used.

Now that you've seen the basic usage of the internationalization features, let's look at how you can solve more complex problems.

---

[4] OK, we admit it. We didn't think of everything the first time ... or the second.

14.4 Tips and tricks

We've looked at the facilities provided by WebWork that allow you to (more) simply internationalize your application, but that's not all there is to it. Internationalizing applications is as much an art as a science, depending on how different platforms determine default character encodings, the whims of browser makers in sending the correct locale headers, and so on. Those are more the subject of a good QA department, but you'll build a toolbox of tricks that help control what you can control when building internationalized applications.

14.4.1 Programmatically setting the locale

In figures 14.1 and 14.2, the example application shows a list of items with correctly localized messages for the selected locale. Because we went to the trouble of translating the text to the other languages, let's see it again, this time in French, in figure 14.4.

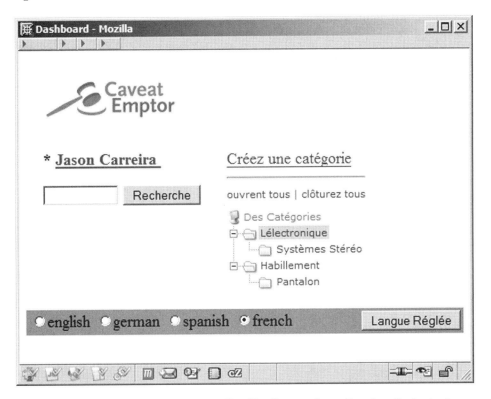

Figure 14.4 The example application looks like this after you choose French as the language.

Normally, the locale is set from the request. The servlet container sets the locale in the request based on the HTTP headers it receives from the browser, which are based on the user's system settings and browser preferences. This normally works well to get the correct language for the user; but if you're trying to test a localized application, or if you want to let your users choose their own language, you need to find a different method. Knowing, as you do, that the framework uses the `ActionContext ThreadLocal` to get the locale (which is set by the `ServletDispatcher`), the issue becomes figuring out which locale the user is trying to set and putting it into the `ActionContext`. If this seems like a good task for an interceptor to you, then you're right.

The `I18nInterceptor` was originally created by Aleksei Gopachenko and added to the OpenSymphony wiki.[5] It will be added to WebWork by the 2.2 release. The basic idea is to look in the request for a particular named parameter (the parameter name is configurable) and set the specified locale into the session. Regardless of whether the parameter was found, you look up the locale that's been set into the `Session` and put it into the `ActionContext` to be used by the framework. Now all you need is a form to allow the user to choose a language and submit it back to the same action, where the `I18nInterceptor` can find the request parameter and do its work. Listing 14.2 shows the JSP that creates the form at the bottom of the page to allow the user to choose a locale.

Listing 14.2 JSP that renders the form to allow the user to choose a locale

```
<ww:bean id="locales"
    name="org.hibernate.auction.localization.Locales"/>
<form action="<ww:url includeParams="get" encode="true"/>"
     method="POST">
<table width="100%" bgcolor="#8888BB" >
  <tr>
    <td>
    <ww:radio name="request_locale"
            list="#locales.locales"
            listKey="value"
            listValue="key"
            theme="simple"
            value="(#session['webwork_locale'] == null) ?
                   locale : #session['webwork_locale']"/>
    </td>
```

---

[5] See http://wiki.opensymphony.com/pages/viewpage.action?pageId=10 for the full source of this interceptor.

```
    <td align="right">
      <input type="Submit"
        value="<ww:text name="text.setLanguage"/>"/>
    </td>
  </tr>
  </table>
  </form>
```

This JSP uses a bean, `org.hibernate.auction.localization.Locales`, which provides a `Map` of `String` names (english, german, and so on) to the correct locales (`Locale.US`, `Locale.GERMANY`, and so forth). The interesting part is the `<ww:radio>` tag. It creates a set of radio buttons, each named `request_locale`, with values like `en_US` and `de_DE`. The `value` attribute uses a bit of OGNL to set the value, which tells the `<ww:radio>` tag which of the buttons should be preselected. If the locale hasn't been set in the `Session`, the expression calls `getLocale()` and uses that as the selected value; otherwise, it uses the value in the `Session`. When this form is submitted, the `I18nInterceptor` finds the parameter `request_locale` and creates the requested locale, and then puts it in the `Session` with the key `webwork_locale`. The interceptor also checks the `Session` for this key, whether it was just set or not, and, if it finds a `Locale` in the session, puts it in the `ActionContext` to be used by the rest of the framework. One other point of interest is the `<ww:submit>` tag, which uses `getText()` for the value to put a localized version of Choose Language on the button.

14.4.2 *Implementing ResourceBundles as classes*

In section 14.2, we mentioned that `ResourceBundles` can be implemented as classes that extend `java.util.ResourceBundle` instead of using properties files. When you want to load message texts from the database, this is the only way. When you're building `ResourceBundles`, you're free to do it however you'd like, as long as they extend `java.util.ResourceBundle` at some level. The JDK provides the `java.util.ListResourceBundle` to be used as a base class for your own `ResourceBundle` classes, but we find that directly implementing the abstract methods of `java.util.ResourceBundle` is more straightforward. Listing 14.3 shows the `org.hibernate.auction.localization.LocalizedMessages` class.

Listing 14.3 `LocalizedMessages`: a `ResourceBundle` that gets the texts from a `LocalizedTextDAO` component

```java
public class LocalizedMessages extends ResourceBundle {
  private LocalizedTextDAO getLocalizedTextDao() {
    ActionContext ctx = ActionContext.getContext();
    ComponentManager cm =
      (ComponentManager) ctx
        .get(ComponentInterceptor.COMPONENT_MANAGER);
    if (cm == null) {
      return null;
    } else {
      return (LocalizedTextDAO)
        cm.getComponentInstance(LocalizedTextDAO.class);

    }
  }

  public Enumeration getKeys() {
    Map texts = getTexts();
    if (texts == null) {
      return null;
    }
    return new IteratorEnum(texts.keySet().iterator());
  }

  protected Object handleGetObject(String key) {
    LocalizedTextDAO dao = getLocalizedTextDao();
    if (dao == null)  {
      return null;
    }

    LocalizedText localizedText =
      dao.getLocalizedText(getLocaleForTexts(),key);
    if (localizedText == null) {
      return null;
    } else {
      return localizedText.getText();
    }
  }

  protected Map getTexts() {
    LocalizedTextDAO dao = getLocalizedTextDao();
    if (dao == null) {
      return null;
    }

    List textList = dao.getTexts(getLocaleForTexts());
    Map texts = new HashMap();
    for (Iterator iterator = textList.iterator();
        iterator.hasNext();) {
```

```
        LocalizedText text = (LocalizedText) iterator.next();
        texts.put(text.getKey(),text.getText());
      }
      return texts;
    }

    protected Locale getLocaleForTexts() {
      return null;
    }
  }
```

In listing 14.3, the LocalizedMessages class initializes itself with an application-level LocalizedTextDAO component and delegates to that component for retrieving texts. getKeys() and handleGetObject() are the abstract methods of ResourceBundle that a subclass must implement. The LocalizedTextDAO that the LocalizedMessages instance looks up in the component manager reads persistent LocalizedText objects from the database, which are mapped to a table using Hibernate. Listing 14.4 shows the getTexts(Locale locale) method from LocalizedTextDAO.

Listing 14.4   getTexts(), which uses a named query to get the localized texts for a given locale

```
  /**
   * Get a List of the LocalizedTexts for the specified Locale
   * @param locale the specified Locale to find the texts for
   */
  public List getTexts(Locale locale) throws InfrastructureException {
    try {
      Query q = persistenceManager.getSession()
          .getNamedQuery("localeTexts");
      q.setString("localeStr",
                  (locale == null) ? null : locale.toString());
      return q.list();
    } catch (HibernateException ex) {
      throw new InfrastructureException(ex);
    }
  }
```

The localeTexts named query is defined like this:

```
<query name="localeTexts"><![CDATA[
    select text from LocalizedText text
    where text.localeStr = :localeStr
]]></query>
```

Because this class represents the default texts for this ResourceBundle, it uses null for the locale. Let's look at one of the locale-specific subclasses of LocalizedMessages. Listing 14.5 shows org.hibernate.auction.localization.LocalizedMessages_en, which overrides getLocaleForTexts() to return the correct locale.

Listing 14.5   LocalizedMessages_en subclass of LocalizedMessages

```
public class LocalizedMessages_en extends LocalizedMessages {
    protected Locale getLocaleForTexts() {
        return Locale.US;
    }
}
```

The LocalizedMessages_en subclass of LocalizedMessages only has to return the correct locale. Similarly, there are subclasses LocalizedMessages_de, Localized-Messages_es, and LocalizedMessages_fr. The appropriate locale is passed along to LocalizedTextDAO when the texts are retrieved and allows the LocalizedTextDAO to find the correct localized texts.

14.4.3   Using the <ww:param> tag to pass dynamically generated text to message texts

As we mentioned in section 14.3.2 on parameterizing message texts, you can use the <ww:param> tag not only to pass simple values to your message texts but also to dynamically generate text blocks. By putting JSP tags inside your <ww:param> tag, you can build a complex text block that is put into your text message at the proper location. This JSP content can even call <ww:text> to get other localized texts inside the body of the <ww:param> tag.

Let's take a common example. Many applications need to provide paged data when there are too many items to show on one page. You could hard-code this paging to put the numbers in the page, but not all languages use the same numbering schemes. If you're going to the trouble of internationalizing your application, it's best not to forget these little details, so let's examine how you can use JSP tags inside a <ww:param> tag to solve this problem. First, let's see what the example looks like when it runs. Figure 14.5 shows the paging example; it's nothing special, but what's interesting is how it's generated.

As another prelude to jumping into the JSP, let's look at the action, Paging-Action, in listing 14.6 (getters and setters omitted).

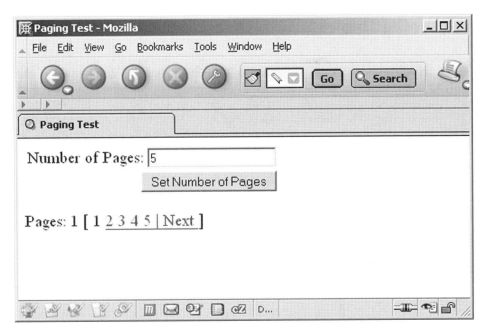

Figure 14.5   The paging example shows the available pages with links to navigate to the other pages.

Listing 14.6   `PagingAction`

```
public class PagingAction extends ActionSupport {
    private int numPages = 5;
    private Integer currentPage = new Integer(1);
    private List pages = new ArrayList();

    public String execute() throws Exception {
        for (int i = 1; i <= numPages; i++) {
            pages.add(new Integer(i));
        }
        return super.execute();
    }

    public boolean hasNextPage() {
        return currentPage.intValue() < numPages;
    }
}
```

PagingAction sets up a List of page numbers and keeps track of the number of pages (settable from the form on the page) and the current page number. Let's also look at the properties resource bundle for the `PagingAction`. Listing 14.7 shows the PagingAction.properties file's contents.

Listing 14.7 PagingAction.properties

```
pages.label= Pages:
pages.total = {0,number,integer} [{1}]
pages.item = {0,number,integer}
pages.next = | Next
numPages.label=Number of Pages
numPages.button=Set Number of Pages
```

Some of the pieces of the final page are obvious, such as the label texts, but the rest only makes sense in the context of the JSP that uses it to render the page numbers. You're ready now to look at the JSP for generating the paging (we'll skip the JSP to create the form to change the number of pages); see listing 14.8.

Listing 14.8 JSP that renders your paging

```
<ww:text name="pages.label"/>
<ww:text name="pages.total">
  <ww:param value="currentPage"/>
  <ww:param>
    <ww:iterator value="pages">
      <ww:if test="!currentPage.equals(top)">
        <ww:url id="url" value="paging.action">
          <ww:param name="currentPage" value="top"/>
          <ww:param name="numPages" value="numPages"/>
        </ww:param>
        <a href="<ww:property value="#url"/>">
      </ww:if>
      <ww:text name="pages.item">
        <ww:param value="top"/>
      </ww:text>
      <ww:if test="!currentPage.equals(top)">
        </a>
      </ww:if>
    </ww:iterator>
    <ww:if test="hasNextPage()">
      <ww:url id="url" value="paging.action">
        <ww:param name="currentPage"
                  value="currentPage + 1"/>
        <ww:param name="numPages" value="numPages"/>
      </ww:url>
      <a href="<ww:property value="#url"/>">
        <ww:text name="pages.next"/>
      </a>
    </ww:if>
```

```
  </ww:param>
</ww:text>
```

Let's look through this JSP from the top. The first line gets a localized text for the key pages.label, which is `Pages:` in the PagingAction.properties file. Next you get the localized text for the key `pages.total`, which is `{0,number,integer} [{1}]` in the properties file. This text expects two parameters to be passed to it (the first a number), and it puts them in the appropriate spots in the final text. The first `<ww:param>` is a simple property, passing in the `currentPage` property of the action. The second `<ww:param>` takes up the majority of the code listing and contains JSP tags to generate the page numbers with links, and so on. The `<ww:iterator>` tag iterates over each page number; the tags inside it decide whether it needs a link (if that page number isn't the current page), and then a `<ww:text>` tag formats the current page number.

Finally, this code checks whether it needs a Next link by calling `hasNextPage()` on the action and creates an appropriate link if it's needed. After the code renders all this and iterates over all the pages, the resulting text is passed as the second parameter to the `pages.total` text you saw earlier. The text is put inside the `[...]` in the text, and you see the page numbers and possibly the Next link in the final page. This method can be used to pass in complex generated text and put it in the correct spot in a localized message text.

14.4.4 *Setting the encoding: here, there, and everywhere*

Now that you've gone through all the trouble of internationalizing your application, it would be a shame to have the text get mangled on the way to the user because of using the wrong character encoding somewhere along the line. It's a good idea to be redundant with setting the character encoding for the pages. Here's the beginning of create.jsp:

```
<%@ page contentType="text/html; charset=UTF-8"%>
<%@ taglib uri="webwork" prefix="ww"%>
<html>
  <head>
    <title><ww:text name="text.createCategory"/></title>
    <META HTTP-EQUIV="content-type" CONTENT="text/html; charset=UTF-8">
  </head>
```

The page uses two different methods for setting the character encoding. Some combinations of servers and browsers may not pick up on one or the other, so set both. Redundancy here doesn't hurt, so it's better to be safe than sorry. This applies everywhere you touch the output stream, so make sure all your included JSPs set the correct character encoding, any filters you apply do the same, and so on.

You may also need to set your IDE to use a specific character encoding when saving files. If the JSP file is saved with a different character encoding than it sets, some servers may pick up on the file's character encoding and use that instead. In IntelliJ IDEA, for instance, you can set the character encoding under Settings > General > File Encoding.

14.4.5 *A note on Java PropertyResourceBundles*

Unfortunately, Java throws another obstacle in your way. The JavaDocs for the `java.util.Properties` class have this to say about character encodings: "When saving properties to a stream or loading them from a stream, the ISO 8859-1 character encoding is used. For characters that can't be directly represented in this encoding, Unicode escapes are used." For `ResourceBundles` implemented using .properties files, this means characters that aren't represented in the ISO 8859-1 character encoding must be escaped in the .properties file. For example, the text for Items for Auction in German appears like this on the page:

```
Einzelteile für Auktion
```

In the `CreateLocalizedCategory_de.properties` file, it's written like this:

```
text.itemsAuction=Einzelteile f\u00FCr Auktion
```

The ü character has been escaped as the `\u00FC` Unicode escape string. Escaping these texts by hand can be tedious, so it's best to find a tool to help you. Unfortunately, there aren't any completely polished tools in this space; however, the Resource Editor from Make Technologies (http://www.maketechnologies.com) works pretty well, although it's still kind of flaky.

14.4.6 *A final note*

We've looked at how to localize the texts in your web application, but that's only part of the picture. You also need to translate images, get localized data from your database, and handle a host of other issues. Remember, it's not just translation—there are also issues of page layouts, because not all languages read left to right. To make a truly internationalized application, you have to think about i18n for *everything*.

14.5 Summary

Developing internationalized applications can be challenging, but with the help of the right tools, it can be manageable. WebWork provides a comprehensive toolbox for building internationalized applications and managing your localized texts. WebWork provides facilities for looking up `ResourceBundle`s as sources for localized message texts at many different levels. The search order for `Resource-Bundle` resources in WebWork makes it easy to set up default texts for your entire application, sections of the app, or down to the action and property level.

WebWork's internationalization facilities are tied into all the parts of the framework, allowing for localized message texts for validation messages, type-conversion messages, form field labels, and so on. WebWork's tag library provides easy access to your localized texts, and the built-in formatting options using OGNL expressions and `java.text.MessageFormat` formatting strings allow for dynamic message texts and advanced formatting of dates and numbers. The abstractions in WebWork on top of the Servlet APIs let you implement different strategies for determining the correct locale and finding `ResourceBundle`s. Taken all together, WebWork's internationalization tools should provide everything you need to build an internationalized web application (or at least as much as a web framework can provide).

Best practices

15

This chapter covers

- Testing methodologies
- Extending the UI tag library and taking full advantage of its features
- Preventing duplicate form submissions
- Automatically displaying a "please wait" page
- Writing generic Create, Read, Update, Delete (CRUD) actions

Best practices with a language, development environment, or framework make the difference between just getting the job done and being really productive. In this chapter, we discuss best practices not just for using the WebWork framework but also for general development practices as they apply to a WebWork project. Environment setup can also have a large impact on productivity, so we'll look at setting up an environment that gives the fastest turnaround to your code-deploy-test cycle.

One of the driving motivations behind the WebWork framework has always been testability. Decoupling actions from the Web, programming to interfaces with replaceable implementations, and the loose coupling provided by the Inversion of Control container can all be attributed to this design influence. As such, it shouldn't be surprising that it's relatively easy to test WebWork actions at many levels, from unit tests to integration tests to full in-container tests.

WebWork also offers many opportunities for reuse and modularization, so we'll discuss how you can build reusable components in WebWork to capture your best practices for the entire team to use. Interceptors are an obvious place to start with extracting common code, so we'll present some interceptor tricks to solve complicated issues in a reusable component. The WebWork tags provide an example of creating user interface components, so we'll look at how you can customize and extend the tags as well as other methods for creating UI components to be shared across screens.

Next, we'll examine techniques and advanced features that can totally alter the workflow and behavior of your actions, without modifying your actions one bit. This is accomplished through the loose coupling and power provided by Web-Work's interceptors. Finally, we'll look at one of the most common patterns requested by WebWork developers: building actions to handle creating, reading, updating, and deleting entries in a database.

15.1 Setting up your environment

The first step to being able to develop, test, or debug a WebWork application is setting up the development environment to make you as productive as possible. This includes setting up an automated build to compile your source code and run your tests, setting up the IDE to let it automate many of the repetitive tasks for you, and configuring your web application to minimize the number of times you have to restart the container to pick up configuration changes. If you're not already familiar with and using Ant (http://ant.apache.org/, an automated build tool) and JUnit (http://www.junit.org/index.htm, a Java unit testing framework), we recommend that you download them now and start learning them as you go through this chapter.

15.1.1 *Setting up your IDE*

We'll assume you've already got your project set up to the point that you can code and compile, but setting up an efficient environment for development is another thing altogether. The steps are IDE specific, but the basics are as follows:

1   Set up a web resource directory that mirrors your WAR file structure. This directory will hold all your JSPs as well as your WEB-INF directory with the web.xml file. Different IDEs have different requirements and different capabilities, so you may not need to mimic your WAR file structure exactly. You want IDE support for JSP editing with error highlighting and code completion; having your web resource directory mirror the WAR file structure helps some IDEs understand your JSPs.

2   Make sure your IDE can find the tag library descriptors of any taglibs your web application uses (webwork.tld, for instance). This allows your IDE to do the error highlighting and code completion in JSP editing.

3   Associate the source codes for the open source libraries you use in your IDE. Don't be afraid to trace into the code of the libraries; that's a good way to learn how they work and the only way to find any bugs (although we hope this is infrequent). It's also helpful when you're plugging into a library at its extension points (such as WebWork interceptors) because you can see other implementations of the extension point and how they're called.

4   Set up a web application module or application profile that the IDE can automatically deploy or debug. Ideally, doing so will allow for editing the JSPs and automatically pick up changes to the JSPs without requiring an application reload.

Assuming your IDE provides support, this can use the tool your IDE provides. Make sure you look at what you have to do to get it to pick up JSP edits (for example, a build to synchronize the edits or build and deploy the WAR file).

Alternatively, you can set up a Servlet container's main method to be executed directly like any other application and pass it the configuration information it needs to automatically pick up your web application. For example, to set up Resin 2.1 from Caucho (www.caucho.com) as a standalone application pointing to a project-specific configuration file, you would set parameters as follows:

- Main class—`com.caucho.server.http.HttpServer`
- VM parameters—`-Dresin.home=. -Xdebug -Xnoagent -Djava.compiler=NONE -Xrunjdwp:transport=dt_socket,server=y,suspend=n,address=12345`
- Program parameters—`-conf resin.xml`
- Working directory—Root directory of your project
- Classpath—Classpath of your project plus the Resin JARs

The resin.xml file specified in the parameters sets up the classpath and specifies the web application root as shown in listing 15.1, allowing you to edit the JSPs and let Resin automatically pick up the changes.

Listing 15.1   resin.xml

```
<caucho.com>

    <system-property org.apache.commons.logging.Log=
        "org.apache.commons.logging.impl.SimpleLog"/>
    <system-property
        org.apache.commons.logging.simplelog.defaultlog="warn"/>

    <log id="/log" href="stderr:" timestamp="[%Y-%m-%d %H:%M:%S.%s]"/>

    <http-server error-log="build/resin-error.log">
        <doc-dir>src/webapp</doc-dir>
        <http port="8080"/>
        <host id="">
            <web-app id="/">
                <work-dir>../../build/work</work-dir>
                <temp-dir>../../build/tmp</temp-dir>
                <cache-mapping url-pattern="/*" expires="2"/>
                <class-update-interval>
                    100000000
                </class-update-interval>
                <jsp jsp-update-interval="1s"/>

                <classpath id="../../build/java"/>
                <classpath id="../../lib/core" library-dir="true"/>
            </web-app>
        </host>
    </http-server>
</caucho.com>
```

15.1.2   *Reloading resources*

After setting up your project to allow you to edit JSPs and have the changes automatically picked up by your Servlet container, you're most of the way to having an efficient environment. But what if you need to change your configuration or edit your resource bundles to change your localized texts? You can set a couple of flags to let the framework know you'd like to reload configuration files when they change:

- `webwork.configuration.xml.reload`—This property name is somewhat misleading, because it does more than just make the XML configuration file reload. If this property is set to `true` in webwork.properties, then your xwork.xml configuration files, *-validation.xml validation configuration files, and *-conversion.properties type conversion configuration files will all be reloaded when they change.

- `LocalizedTextUtil.setReloadBundles(boolean reloadBundles)`—If you call `LocalizedTextUtil.setReloadBundles(true)` on `com.opensymphony.xwork.-util.LocalizedTextUtil`, then your `ResourceBundles` will be cleared from the `ResourceBundle` cache before each load. This allows you to edit your `Resource-Bundle` property files and have those changes picked up without restarting. Note that this reload flag doesn't work with all `ResourceBundle` implementations, but it should work with property file `ResourceBundles`. Listing 15.2 shows a `Servlet-ContextListener` that automatically sets this flag when your web application starts.

Listing 15.2   `ServletContextListener` that sets a flag to automatically reload `ResourceBundles`

```
public class DebugServletContextListener
        implements ServletContextListener {
    public void contextInitialized(ServletContextEvent event) {
        LocalizedTextUtil.setReloadBundles(true);
    }

    public void contextDestroyed(ServletContextEvent event) {}
}
```

These settings have some overhead, so it's good to set them up in your development environment but have them stripped out for your production builds.

15.2   Unit-testing your actions

Unit testing involves testing the smallest working unit of code, usually a class or method, to validate its behavior. Unit tests should be very fast to execute, so that there is little barrier to running them often. A good suite of unit tests is an important part of your regression test suite (but not all of it) to make sure changes don't break anything else. Unit tests with good code coverage (the amount of your code they test) can provide a nice safety net to catch you when doing refactorings; they also give you more freedom to experiment, because you can have some assurance that you haven't broken things if all your tests pass.

Unfortunately, unit-testing web applications has traditionally been one of the trickiest and most fragile parts of building them. Web frameworks that are heavily tied to the Servlet container and Http* classes must run inside either a Servlet container or some servlet-mimicking scaffolding. Running unit tests in a Servlet container is much, *much* slower than running them directly in your IDE and/or Ant script, which means you'll run them less often. Running inside a scaffolding framework is more complex, and there's also some question of whether it adequately represents the environment where the code will be deployed.

One of the core principles of WebWork is to be easily testable. WebWork actions aren't tied to the Servlet container, nor do they depend on Http* classes. Simple actions are as easy to test as plain Java objects; you create an instance, set property values, execute the action, and verify that the values held by the action are as expected. However, unless your actions are extremely simple (on the order of taking two numbers and computing their sum), they probably have external dependencies. Unit tests are all about testing one bit of code, so you need other strategies for decoupling your action from its dependencies for unit testing.

15.2.1   Using mock objects

The point of unit testing your classes is to test them in isolation from their dependencies, but your code expects to be able to call methods on its dependencies; thus you need a way to provide your classes with simpler versions of the objects on which they're dependent. When you provide the implementation of the dependency, you have more control over the behavior of that dependency, and your tests don't change as the real implementation changes (as long as the interface and class contract don't also change). This is what the mock objects idea is designed to give you. There are a few implementations of these ideas, including MockObjects (http://www.mockobjects.com) and EasyMock (http://www.easymock.org), but you'll use the MockObjects library in the examples as we look at tests from the CaveatEmptor codebase. Mock objects come in two flavors:

- *Static mocks* are classes that implement the interfaces or extend abstract classes used by your classes to provide simple implementations. Mock implementations are provided for interfaces such as `javax.servlet.http.HttpServlet-Request/HttpServletResponse` and JMS interfaces such as `javax.jms.Queue` in the MockObjects package. These can be easy to use when the types you're using are already implemented by the MockObjects framework, but many times not all the methods of the type being mocked are implemented; then you'll have to extend the framework class to add the functionality you need.

- *Dynamic mocks* are created by the framework using dynamic proxies based on the interface you're trying to use. This allows you to easily create mock instances of your own interfaces without having to create classes. Both MockObjects and EasyMock provide this functionality.

The main functionality that mock objects libraries give you beyond implementing or proxying your interfaces is to set up expected calls, including setting constraints on expected method parameters and setting up return values. Both Mock-Objects and EasyMock provide this and allow you to validate your mock instance, checking that the expected method calls on the mock instance were made.

Listing 15.3 shows code from the `setUp()` and `tearDown()` methods of a JUnit `TestCase` that uses a dynamic mock.

Listing 15.3   JUnit `TestCase` `setUp()` and `tearDown()` methods

```java
protected void setUp() throws Exception {
    super.setUp();
    user = new TestUser();
    user.setId(userId);
    userDaoMock = new Mock(UserDAO.class);
    userDaoMock.matchAndReturn("getUserById",
            C.args(C.eq(userId), C.IS_FALSE), user);
    userDAO = (UserDAO) userDaoMock.proxy();
    session = new HashMap();
    session.put(AuthenticationFilter.USER, user);
}

protected void tearDown() throws Exception {
    super.tearDown();
    userDaoMock.verify();
}
```

The `matchAndReturn()` method tells the `userDAO` that for calls to `getUserById(Long id, boolean lock)` where the ID is your predefined `Long id` value and `lock` is `false`, it should return your `User` object. The `proxy()` method returns a `DynamicProxy` that implements the interface the mock was passed in its constructor. This proxy can be cast to the interface and any methods from the interface can be called on it, but an exception will be thrown if the mock hasn't been told the method will be called using one of the `expect*` or `match*` methods. The `expect*` methods are more strict than the `match*` methods because you must match the number of calls to the `expect*` methods with the number of times your code calls the method. In practice, you often end up testing your implementation more than is necessary with the `expect*` methods; so in the examples, you'll see more `match*` methods used.

15.2.2 *The advantage of IoC for testing*

As you've seen, you want to control the dependencies that are passed into your actions before you execute the actions in your unit tests. As you saw in chapter 6, "Inversion of Control," controlling and managing the dependencies of your actions and having them passed in rather than looking them up is what Inversion of Control is all about. Because actions that are developed for IoC have methods for passing in dependencies (the enabler *Aware interfaces implemented by your action), it's easy to build mocks of the dependencies and set them on the action as you see in the previous example, where you create a mock version of the `UserDAO` interface and pass it in to be used by the action. In the previous example, take special note of how `userDAO`, a private field, is set in `setUp()` and is now ready to be applied to an action during the actual test.

Compare this with the complex setup and teardown code that would be needed to test actions that look up their dependencies from a static registry or a JNDI context, and you can see why IoC and test-driven design often go hand in hand. To test a JNDI application, for instance, you would have to set up a `jndi.properties` file that tells JNDI which `javax.naming.InitialContext` class to use; you'd also have to set up a `javax.naming.InitialContext` class to mock a real JNDI context and then create mocks of your dependencies and bind them in the mock context. It's much easier to create the mock of your dependency and call a setter on your action.

15.2.3 *Handling statics and ThreadLocals*

WebWork has a couple of features that can make testing a little trickier. The first is the configuration, which is held in a static configuration instance, so having more than one test run in a JVM can lead to issues with one test seeing the configuration of another. The second is the `ActionContext`, which holds the state of an action execution in a `ThreadLocal`, which likewise can make for difficult-to-diagnose issues if not handled carefully. Normal JUnit execution has an interesting way of avoiding these types of problems: Each test method is executed in its own JVM instance after the `setUp()` method and before the `tearDown()` method. Although this is the safest method for executing tests, it's also the slowest. Running unit tests in a JUnit `TestSuite` or running them in an IDE usually opens one JVM to run the tests (still one at a time), so unit tests that all run successfully in your Ant build using the `<junit>` ant task set to fork a new JVM per test may suddenly start breaking when run in your IDE.

Listing 15.4 shows the `setUp()` and `tearDown()` methods of a JUnit `TestCase` subclass that takes the `Configuration` and `ActionContext` issues into account.

> **Listing 15.4** `setUp()` and `tearDown()` combination that cleans up static and
> `ThreadLocal` state

```
protected void setUp() throws Exception {
    ConfigurationManager.destroyConfiguration();
    ConfigurationManager.addConfigurationProvider(
        new MockConfigurationProvider());
    ConfigurationManager.getConfiguration().reload();

    OgnlValueStack stack = new OgnlValueStack();
    ActionContext.setContext(new ActionContext(stack.getContext()));
}

protected void tearDown() throws Exception {
    ConfigurationManager.clearConfigurationProviders();
    ConfigurationManager.destroyConfiguration();
    ActionContext.setContext(null);
}
```

The `setUp()` method creates a new `MockConfigurationProvider` and adds it after destroying any previous configuration; then it tells the `ConfigurationManager` to rebuild from this one provider. This process empties all previous configuration held by the static `Configuration` instance and reloads it from the one `ConfigurationProvider` you've provided. It also creates a new `ActionContext` and sets it into the `ActionContext ThreadLocal`.

Note that if you don't clean up this issue, this `ActionContext` and `Configuration` will be left over for the next test if it's run in the same `Thread`. This is where the `tearDown()` method from JUnit comes in. It's always called after your test runs, so it's used to clean up the `Configuration` and set the `ThreadLocal` to null (which causes it to be reinitialized the next time it's asked for). If all your unit tests clean up not only any resources they open (such as file or database connections) but also static or `ThreadLocal` resources, you should be able to run your unit tests much faster in your IDE or using `TestSuites`.

15.3 Putting the pieces together: integration testing

So far, we've looked at unit-testing WebWork actions; that is, you've done your best to isolate your actions from any dependencies or configuration setup. Although unit testing is definitely important, as you might imagine, a whole range of potential problems can't be caught by unit tests. Is your xwork.xml set up correctly? Will your configured set of interceptors correctly set up properties on your action and set the parameters of your action from the request? This is where integration tests come in: to allow you to test a larger portion of the system. Again, this isn't the whole system, because we won't look at testing inside the container to validate the HTML produced by your pages (system or functional testing, which is outside the scope of this book); but it gives you a better test of how the pieces of your app come together.

The downside of integration tests is that they take longer to run. How much longer depends on what your integration tests are doing, but a comprehensive integration test suite can easily stretch to over 30 minutes. So, it's better to have them run as part of an automated build system.

15.3.1 Testing your configuration

One area where integration testing can help is when your unit tests are passing but the code in your web app isn't working as expected. Often the problem turns out to be a disconnect between the expectation of how things are configured that is coded into your unit test and the reality of your web app configuration. For example, if the `component` interceptor is left out of your interceptor stack for the `Update-User` action being tested in listing 15.3, then the expectation that a `UserDAO` instance is set onto your action before `prepare()` or `execute()` is called is incorrect. Although your unit test will pass, you'll get a mysterious `NullPointerException` when you hit the page in the web app. In this case, you should test the interaction of the framework, the configuration, and your code.

Listing 15.5 shows the important methods from the `UpdateUser` action. In the `prepare()` method, the action gets the `User` object from the session that is put there by the `AuthenticationInterceptor` during login.

Listing 15.5 `UpdateUser` action, which loads the `User` object in the `prepare()` method

```
public void prepare() throws Exception {
    Long id = ((User) session.get(
        AuthenticationInterceptor.USER)).getId();
    user = userDAO.getUserById(id, false);
}

public String execute() throws Exception {
    userDAO.makePersistent(user);
    return SUCCESS;
}
```

This is important because the configuration in the xwork.xml file for the `Update-User` action has the `prepare` interceptor applied before the `parameter` interceptor. So, the `User` object loads before you try to set the parameters from the request onto it and save it. Let's look at an integration test that guarantees this process is working as expected.

Listing 15.6 shows the test method for the integration test. It shows an example of a couple of advanced integration testing techniques: setting up the `Action-Proxy` the way the `ServletDispatcher` would, and registering mock components to be supplied to your action.

Listing 15.6 Integration test that sets up an `ActionProxy`

```
public void testInterceptorStackLoadsBeforeSettingProperties()
        throws Exception {
    Map extraContext = new HashMap();
    DefaultComponentManager dcm = new DefaultComponentManager();
    dcm.addEnabler(UserDAO.class,UserDAOAware.class);
    dcm.registerInstance(UserDAO.class,userDAO);
    extraContext.put(ComponentInterceptor.COMPONENT_MANAGER,dcm);
    extraContext.put(ActionContext.SESSION,session);
    Map params = new HashMap();
    // these are all required
    params.put("user.firstname", "Jason");
    params.put("user.lastname", "Carreira");
    params.put("user.username", "jcarreira");
    params.put("user.password", "password");
    params.put("user.email", "jcarreira@gmail.com");
```

```
        extraContext.put(ActionContext.PARAMETERS,params);
        // let's make sure this happens
        userDaoMock.expect("makePersistent", C.args(C.isA(User.class)));
        ActionProxy proxy = ActionProxyFactory.getFactory()
            .createActionProxy("/secure",
                               "updateProfile",
                               extraContext);
        assertNotNull(proxy);
        proxy.setExecuteResult(false); // don't need to try
                                       // to dispatch to a JSP
        assertEquals(Action.SUCCESS,proxy.execute());
        assertSame(user,((UpdateUser)proxy.getAction()).getUser());
        assertEquals("Jason", user.getFirstname());
        assertEquals("Carreira", user.getLastname());
        assertEquals("jcarreira", user.getUsername());
        assertEquals("password", user.getPassword());
        assertEquals("jcarreira@gmail.com", user.getEmail());
    }
```

The first part of the test method sets up the extraContext map to hold the objects
the ServletDispatcher normally sets up for the ActionProxy before creating it. The
extraContext holds things like the request parameters, a map wrapping the
HttpSession, a map wrapping the application, the component manager, and so on.
First you set up the component manager with the mock UserDAO you looked at in listing 15.3. This component manager now sets your mock UserDAO onto your action
when the component interceptor executes. Next you put the session map you used
in listing 15.3 (which holds the User object) into the extraContext. Finally, you set
up the parameters that would be the request parameters if you were executing
through the ServletDispatcher and put that map into the extraContext.

Now that the extraContext map is set up, you're ready to create the ActionProxy.
You can do so by calling ActionProxyFactory.getFactory().createActionProxy. It
automatically accesses your configuration, loading your xwork.xml file so you're testing your real configuration. You call setExecuteResult(false) so it won't try to do
an HTTP dispatch to a JSP page after executing the action. You check the result code
returned by the ActionProxy when you execute it, to make sure it executed successfully, and then start verifying the results.

First you check that the User object in the action is the same one you put into
the session map. Next you check that the request parameters you set up at the top
were set onto your User object. Doing so verifies that the interceptors called the
prepare() method first, loading the User from the session, before the parameter
interceptor executed to set the request parameters onto the User.

As you can see, this test is straightforward when you break it down into the steps it's going through. It's simplified by isolating only the pieces you want to test together and mocking the others. By mocking the component manager and the UserDAO in this test, you're able to keep this test from having to access the database, which is usually a good idea if possible. Integration tests could be set up to test the configuration of every action in your application and all the layers of your application together; but writing integration tests can be a lot more work than writing unit tests, and the configuration of many of your actions will be the same. It generally makes sense to only create integration tests for complex configuration points and areas where you find problems.

15.3.2 *Seeing the configuration with the config browser*

Rather than have to write a new integration test every time you have a question about your configuration, it can be helpful to get a view of your configuration at runtime as the framework sees it. WebWork comes with a utility to do this called the config browser. To install the config browser, do the following:

1 Get the webwork-config-browser.jar file, which is part of the WebWork distribution, and put it into the WEB-INF/lib directory of your web application.

2 Edit xwork.xml to include the configuration file for the config browser, like this:

```
<include file="config-browser.xml"/>
```

3 Edit your velocity.properties file to add the macros used by the config browser templates:

```
# Velocity Macro libraries.
# The webwork.vm comes standard with webwork.
# The tigris-macros.vm comes with the config browser.
velocimacro.library = webwork.vm, tigris-macros.vm
```

Once you've done these steps and restarted your web application, you can access the config browser using a URL like this: http://localhost:8080/*myApp*/config-browser/actionNames.action. The server name and port should point to your Servlet container, and *myApp* is replaced by the context of your web application in the Servlet container. When you hit this URL, it should open a page that looks like figure 15.1.

The config browser's main page shows the namespaces available in your web application and the action aliases available in the default namespace. Clicking one of the other namespaces takes you to the same page with the action names

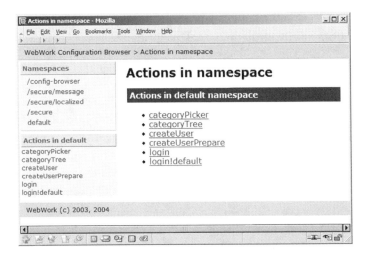

Figure 15.1   The main page for the config browser shows the namespaces of your web application and the action names in the default namespace.

available in that namespace. Clicking one of the action names takes you to a page like that shown in figure 15.2.

The action information page gives general information about the action alias (name, class, and so on) and also provides a tabbed interface to see the details of the results, interceptors, properties, and validators applied to this action configuration. The Interceptors tab and the Validators tab are particularly helpful

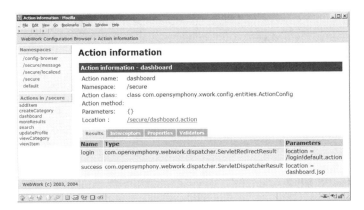

Figure 15.2   The action information page gives details about the action alias and tabs for getting details of the results, interceptors, properties, and validators.

in tracking down issues. Each of them shows the interceptors or validators in a table in the order they will be applied.

15.4 *Testing validations*

An important consideration for any new framework feature you decide to use should be, "How am I going to test this?" Testing is key, and one of the strengths of WebWork is the way action classes are decoupled from the web environment where they run, because this allows for reuse and—above all—testability. It's important, therefore, to think about how you'll test your validations and how your validations will (or won't) affect the testing of your action's functionality.

15.4.1 *Testing programmatic validations*

Testing validations written directly into your execute() method is simple. You can't help but test them as you're testing the functionality of the action itself. This can also be a problem, because you can't individually test your validations and your action's business logic. Thus it's preferable to put your validations in the validate() method instead, if possible. By putting your validations in the validate() method, you can manually test your action's business logic and validations separately.

Listing 15.7 shows what a test looks like that tests the HelloWorld action when your validation is coded directly into the execute() method.

> **Listing 15.7   Testing an action with validations defined in the execute() method**

```
public class HelloWorldActionTest extends TestCase {
    public void testFieldErrorAddedWhenNoUserName() throws Exception {
        HelloWorldAction action = new HelloWorldAction();
        assertEquals(Action.INPUT, action.execute());
        assertTrue(action.hasFieldErrors());
        Map fieldErrors = action.getFieldErrors();
        assertTrue(fieldErrors.containsKey("user.name"));
        …
    }
}
```

15.4.2 *Testing validation.xml files*

Testing validations declared in validation XML files is a little more work than directly calling your action classes, but not much. You don't have to execute your actions to test the validations; you can use the same method the validation interceptor uses:

```
ActionValidatorManager.validate(object, context);
```

This method is the entry point to the validation framework and looks up the validators applied for the class of the object passed in. The context parameter is the validation context to validate for and is used as part of the filenames as you saw in chapter 13 ("Validating form data"). When the validation interceptor calls this method, the context parameter is the name of the action alias as mapped in xwork.xml.

Let's look at how you test the validations applied to an action, in this case the CreateUser action. Listing 15.8 shows the CreateUser-validation.xml file that defines validations for CreateUser.

Listing 15.8   CreateUser-validation.xml

```
<!DOCTYPE validators PUBLIC
    "-//OpenSymphony Group//XWork Validator 1.0//EN"
    "http://www.opensymphony.com/xwork/xwork-validator-1.0.2.dtd">
<validators>
    <field name="user">
        <field-validator type="visitor">
            <message/>
        </field-validator>
    </field>
</validators>
```

The CreateUser-validation.xml file defines one validator: a visitor field validator that calls the validators for the User object. It calls the validations for the User object, so let's look at those. Listing 15.9 shows the User-validation.xml file.

Listing 15.9   User-validation.xml

```
<!DOCTYPE validators PUBLIC
    "-//OpenSymphony Group//XWork Validator 1.0//EN"
    "http://www.opensymphony.com/xwork/xwork-validator-1.0.2.dtd">
<validators>
    <field name="firstname">
        <field-validator type="requiredstring">
            <message>First name is required!</message>
        </field-validator>
    </field>
    <field name="lastname">
        <field-validator type="requiredstring">
            <message>Last name is required!</message>
        </field-validator>
    </field>
    <field name="username">
        <field-validator type="requiredstring">
```

```
                <message>Username is required!</message>
            </field-validator>
        </field>
        <field name="password">
            <field-validator type="requiredstring">
                <message>Password is required!</message>
            </field-validator>
        </field>
        <field name="email">
            <field-validator type="requiredstring">
                <message>Email name is required!</message>
            </field-validator>
        </field>
    </validators>
```

The User-validation.xml file defines `requiredstring` validators for several fields of the `User` class, so let's set up some tests to make sure these are working as you expect. First let's look at the `setUp()` method that's called before each test in the test class:

```
public void setUp() throws Exception {
    super.setUp();
    user = new User();
    user.setFirstname("Jason");
    user.setLastname("Carreira");
    user.setUsername("jcarreira");
    user.setPassword("");
    user.setEmail(null);
}
```

As you can see, this `setUp()` method creates a `User` object and sets some values into its properties. The `password` field is set to an empty string and the `email` field is set to null, so those are the fields you'd expect the `requiredstring` validators to add error messages for. Listing 15.10 shows the `testUserValidationsFromCreateUser()` test method, which uses the validation framework to execute the validations of the `CreateUser` action.

Listing 15.10 testUserValidationsFromCreateUser() method

```
public void testUserValidationsFromCreateUser()
        throws ValidationException {
    CreateUser createUser  = new CreateUser();
    createUser.setUser(user);

    ActionValidatorManager.validate(createUser,"");

    Map fieldErrors = createUser.getFieldErrors();
    assertNotNull(fieldErrors);
    assertEquals(2, fieldErrors.size());
    assertTrue(fieldErrors.containsKey("user.password"));
    assertTrue(fieldErrors.containsKey("user.email"));
}
```

This test method is straightforward. It creates a CreateUser instance and puts the User object created in setUp() into it. Next it calls ActionValidatorManager.validate() to apply the validations to the CreateUser instance, which also calls the User instance validations because of the visitor field validator in the CreateUservalidation.xml file. Finally, it checks that the two expected field errors have been added to the action.

What if you want to test the validations on a domain model class like User? The extra trick you need here is to give the validation framework somewhere to put the error messages so you can retrieve them. To do this, you need another signature for the ActionValidatorManager.validate() method:

```
ActionValidatorManager.validate(object, context, validatorContext)
```

This extra parameter is an instance of the ValidatorContext interface, which extends TextProvider and ValidationAware to provide localized texts and store messages. Listing 15.11 shows the testUserValidationsDirectly() test method that uses this method to validate the User instance built in the setUp() method.

Listing 15.11 testUserValidationsDirectly() method

```
public void testUserValidationsDirectly()
        throws ValidationException {
    ValidationAware validationAware = new ValidationAwareSupport();
    ValidatorContext validationContext =
        new DelegatingValidatorContext(validationAware);

    ActionValidatorManager.validate(user,"",validationContext);

    Map fieldErrors = validationAware.getFieldErrors();
```

```
        assertNotNull(fieldErrors);
        assertEquals(2, fieldErrors.size());
        assertTrue(fieldErrors.containsKey("password"));
        assertTrue(fieldErrors.containsKey("email"));
    }
```

The unit test uses a `DelegatingValidatorContext` to pass to the `validate()` method. The `DelegatingValidatorContext` takes an object in its constructor that it tries to delegate calls to. If the object passed in implements `ValidationAware`, then calls to set messages will be passed along to this object. If the object implements `TextProvider`, then calls to get localized texts will be delegated to the object. In this case, you're just interested in being able to get the error messages that are generated by the validators, so you create a `ValidationAwareSupport` that implements `ValidationAware` and pass it to the new `DelegatingValidatorContext`. Now you can just validate the `User` object and then check the error messages that are put into the `ValidationAwareSupport` instance. (Note here that because you're not going through the `visitor` field validator, the field names are `password` and `email` instead of `user.password` and `user.email`.) Using this method of testing, you can now test validations on any class in your application.

15.5 Advanced UI tag usage

When we introduced the UI tags in chapter 11, we said that the real power comes from the ability to override templates, create new UI tags, and design entirely new themes. These types of customizations are what WebWork is all about: provide great default features, but allow for even better functionality through customizations and extension points.

In this section, we'll first look at the common requirement of a pop-up calendar integrated into your web application's forms. You'll implement this requirement in three different ways, highlighting the various extension points that WebWork's UI tags offer.

In addition to the calendar requirement, we'll also address the number one question that developers ask when using the UI tags: "Do I really have to structure my forms using a two-column design?" The answer is "No." Using WebWork's support for themes, we'll show you how to create your own unique look and feel for your applications, using any form layout you wish.

15.5.1 *Overriding existing templates*

Looking at the calendar requirement again, let's start by defining how the calendar should look. Figure 15.3 contains the sample form from chapter 11, but with the addition of the Birthdate field. Notice that it looks very much like a textfield, with a small icon to the right of it. When clicked, the icon pops up the calendar, as shown in the figure, which lets the user easily select a date.

Figure 15.3   The calendar pop-up

Because the textfield with the mini-calendar icon (which pops up a working calendar) looks almost exactly like a textfield, the first implementation you'll implement is one in which you override the templates with the existing default theme, xhtml. Remember from chapters 10 and 11 that Velocity templates are loaded from both the classpath and the web application directly. The template used for the textfield tag is located in the webwork JAR at /template/xhtml/text.vm.

Recall that the original text.vm contents are as follows:

```
#parse("/template/xhtml/controlheader.vm")
#parse("/template/simple/text.vm")
#parse("/template/xhtml/controlfooter.vm")
```

You override this file by creating a file with the same name and path in the web application:

```
#parse("/template/xhtml/controlheader.vm")
#if ($parameters.calendar)
  #set ($parameters.size = 10)
#end
#parse("/template/simple/text.vm")
#if ($parameters.calendar)
  <script language="JavaScript">
  var cal_${parameters.name} =
      new calendar2(
          document.forms['$parameters.form.name']
              .elements['$parameters.name']);
  cal_${parameters.name}.year_scroll = true;
  cal_${parameters.name}.time_comp = false;
```

```
      </script>
      <a href="javascript:cal_${parameters.name}.popup();">
          <img src="/shared/images/cal.gif" border="0"/>
      </a>
    #end
    #parse("/template/xhtml/controlfooter.vm")
```

You replace the default text.vm implementation with a new one that modifies the template to show a calendar pop-up. You do this by checking for the existence of a `calendar` parameter. If the parameter is supplied, you force the size of the text-field to 10 (this is done before rendering the core tag from the simple theme) and then print out necessary JavaScript and HTML to show the calendar icon.

Now, rendering a calendar from a JSP is as simple as this:

```
<%@ taglib prefix="ww" uri="webwork"%>
<html>
  <head>
    <title><ww:text name="title"/></title>
    <script language="JavaScript"
            src="/shared/javascript/calendar2.js"></script>
  </head>

  <body>
    <ww:form action="updateProfile" method="post">
      ...
      <ww:textfield label="Birthdate" name="birthdate">
        <ww:param name="calendar" value="true"/>
      </ww:textfield>
      ...
    </ww:form>
  </body>
</html>
```

This is an example of overriding a template and accepting new parameters that aren't part of the JSP tag library. This type of encapsulation and extendibility is very powerful and allows you to begin to build robust and reusable UI components—even ones not used in forms.

Let's look at an alternative implementation that demonstrates the possibilities when customizing these templates. Recall that the xhtml theme's textfield implementation includes controlheader.vm and controlfooter.vm. Suppose you only need one calendar in the entire application, so modifying text.vm seems like overkill. What about providing a generic way to place content after the main form element is rendered? Instead of creating a modified text.vm file, you can modify controlfooter.vm:

```
$!{parameters.after}</td>
  </tr>
```

Recall that the default controlfooter.vm is as follows:

```
</td>
</tr>
```

With this change, a JSP that shows the calendar would now be this:

```
<%@ taglib prefix="ww" uri="webwork"%>
<html>
  <head>
    <title><ww:text name="title"/></title>
    <script language="JavaScript"
            src="/shared/javascript/calendar2.js"></script>
  </head>

  <body>
    <ww:form action="updateProfile" method="post">
      <ww:textfield label="Birthdate" name="birthdate" size="10">
        <ww:param name="after">
<script language="JavaScript">
var cal_birthdate =
    new calendar2(document.forms['updateProfile']
        .elements['birthdate']);
cal_birthdate.year_scroll = true;
cal_birthdate.time_comp = false;
</script>
<a href="javascript:cal_birthdate.popup();">
    <img src="/shared/images/cal.gif" border="0"/>
</a>
        </ww:param>
      </ww:textfield>
    </ww:form>
  </body>
</html>
```

In this example, you use a normal textfield, setting the size to 10, with the addition of some general content after the form element is rendered. Because the change was made to controlfooter.vm, you can use this trick for any UI tag in the xhtml theme, not just textfield. You can even use this trick to render two templates, one using the xhtml theme and one using the simple theme, in a single row:

```
<ww:textfield label="Zip code" name="zip">
  <ww:param name="after">
    - <ww:textfield theme="simple" name="extendedZip"/>
  </ww:param>
</ww:textfield>
```

Adding new parameters, whether in a single template or in a common file used by an entire theme, is a perfect way to customize WebWork's template library. However, although what you've seen thus far is great when you need to reuse a component once or a few times, it isn't ideal when you wish to create a component that can easily be reused many times over. Let's see how WebWork facilitates this level of reusability.

15.5.2 *Writing custom templates*

Recall from chapter 11 the component tag. Its purpose is to allow easy creation of entirely new components. There are two ways to do this. The first, and simpler, way is to create a new Velocity file, such as calendar.vm, and reference it in the JSP as follows:

```
<ww:component template="calendar"
              label="Birthdate"
              name="birthdate"/>
```

Assuming that calendar.vm looks like the following, the expected component is rendered without the need to pass in any sort of custom parameter as you had to do in the previous examples:

```
#parse("/template/xhtml/controlheader.vm")
#set ($parameters.size = 10)
#parse("/template/simple/text.vm")
<script language="JavaScript">
var cal_${parameters.name} =
    new calendar2(document.forms['$parameters.form.name']
        .elements['$parameters.name']);
cal_${parameters.name}.year_scroll = true;
cal_${parameters.name}.time_comp = false;
</script>
<a href="javascript:cal_${parameters.name}.popup();">
    <img src="/shared/images/cal.gif" border="0"/>
</a>
#parse("/template/xhtml/controlfooter.vm")
```

As you can see, this is similar to text.vm overrides sans the `$parameters.calendar` check. This works great for most situations. You can even pass in additional parameters to your new components by using the `ww:param` tag. However, sometimes you'll wish the parameters were more easily known, especially if you're using an IDE that can do code-completion in JSPs. Consider the following JSP snippet:

```
<ce:calendar label="Birthdate" name="birthdate"/>
```

A new tag library has been created, allowing you to narrow down which parameters you're interested in. (Consult the WebWork tag library definition (TLD) file for the definition of the `component` tag for a list of the default parameters it supports.) A sample tag might look like the following:

```
package org.hibernate.auction.web.tags;

import com.opensymphony.webwork.views.jsp.ui.ComponentTag;
import com.opensymphony.xwork.util.OgnlValueStack;

public class CalendarTag extends ComponentTag {
    String foo;

    protected String getDefaultTemplate() {
        return "calendar";
    }

    public String getFoo() {
        return foo;
    }

    public void setFoo(String foo) {
        this.foo = foo;
    }

    protected void evaluateExtraParams(OgnlValueStack stack) {
        addParameter("foo", findValue(foo));
    }
}
```

In this example, a new foo attribute is made available (provided the TLD also indicates this). The expression of the value of foo is evaluated against the value stack and added to the $parameters map, making it available in calendar.vm as $parameters.foo. Once you get the hang of extending ComponentTag, then you can start to crank out tons of reusable UI components.

15.5.3 *Writing custom themes*

The last, and most commonly misunderstood, aspect of the UI tags we'll discuss is theme extension and creation. Almost every time a developer looks at WebWork's default UI tags (using the xhtml theme), the tags are dismissed as being too restrictive. This section shows that the complete opposite is the case.

Suppose your UI design calls for all forms to be rendered in a three-column technique: the first column the label, the second column the form element, and the third column an optional description or example input value. Novice Web-Work developers either give up on the UI tags entirely, or find themselves writing JSPs like so:

```
<ww:form action="foo">
  <tr>
    <td>
      <table border="0">
```

```
      <ww:textfield label="Username" name="username"/>
    </table>
  </td>
  <td>
    <i>Enter the screen name you wish to be identified by...</i>
  </td>
</tr>
...
</ww:form>
```

This technically may work, but clearly what was helpful has now become a hindrance: The UI tags aren't working for you but actually against you. Instead, we recommend something like this:

```
<ww:form action="foo">
  <ww:textfield label="Username" name="username">
    <ww:param name="desc">
      <i>Enter the screen name you wish to be identified by...</i>
    </ww:param>
  </ww:textfield>
</ww:form>
```

Then you can override controlfooter.vm as follows:

```
</td>
  <td>$!parameters.desc</td>
</tr>
```

But what if you sometimes want two-column forms and other times want three-column forms? This is where themes come into play. Rather than modifying and overriding the xhtml theme every time, it's recommended that you branch off the xhtml theme entirely and create your own theme. Let's call this three-column theme 3c.

To create the new theme, copy all the files in /template/xhtml in the Web-Work JAR file (you may need to unjar or unzip it), and place them in the directory /template/3c in your web application. You now have an exact copy of the xhtml theme named "3c". Modify controlheader.vm and controlfooter.vm as you see fit. When you wish to display a three-column form, you can do this:

```
<ww:form theme="3c" action="foo">
  <ww:textfield theme="3c" label="Username" name="username">
    <ww:param name="desc">
      <i>Enter the screen name you wish to be identified by...</i>
    </ww:param>
  </ww:textfield>
</ww:form>
```

This works, but having to specify the theme for every UI component is tedious. You have two options. First, you can change the default theme globally to 3c by setting the `webwork.ui.theme` property in webwork.properties. However, doing so requires that all your `xhtml` components specify the `xhtml` theme. Fortunately, there is a second option.

All of WebWork's UI components use the following order to determine the theme:

1 Use whatever theme is specified for the tag.

2 Look in the `page`, `request`, `session`, and `application`-scoped attributes for a value associated with the attribute key theme.

3 Fall back to the default theme specified in webwork.properties (xhtml by default).

You've seen the first and last ways to specify the theme, but you haven't seen the second. Because all four contexts are searched (`page`, `request`, `session`, and `application`), the possibilities for configuration become very interesting. Using the previous example, you can eliminate the need to set the theme in multiple UI tags by doing this:

```
<ww:set scope="page" name="theme" value="3c"/>
<ww:form action="foo">
  <ww:textfield label="Username" name="username">
    <ww:param name="desc">
      <i>Enter the screen name you wish to be identified by...</i>
    </ww:param>
  </ww:textfield>
</ww:form>
```

It's also important to note that the theme is looked up in the session. This gives you an easy way to skin your application for different users. The possibilities are endless, and we encourage you to not shy away from creating your own themes.

Now that we've discussed just about every way to customize the look of your HTML forms, let's look at a unique way to adapt the behavior of your forms and make them more robust when faced with eager and click-happy users.

15.6 Using form tokens to prevent duplicate form submissions

As a web application developer, the stateless nature of web applications can cause a number of problems for your application. The issue is that requests are controlled by the client, and you can get requests in a different order than you expect or even get the same request multiple times. This can happen if the user clicks the Submit button on a web form more than once, because the browser sends each

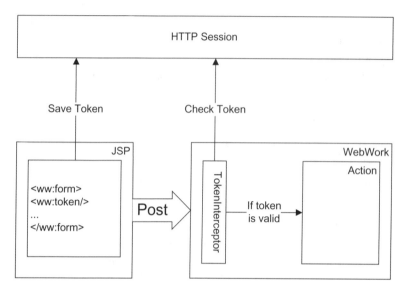

Figure 15.4 The `token` tag and `token` interceptor work together to check for valid tokens before executing the action.

click as a duplicate form post request, or even if the user just clicks the Reload button in their browser on a page built after a form post. This can be especially dangerous because posting a form is usually a signal to the server to *do* something, and many server actions—for example, transferring money between two accounts—shouldn't be done more than once.

One of WebWork's advanced features is prebuilt support for preventing duplicate form posts through the use of unique form tokens. This support comes in the form of a `<ww:token>` JSP tag on the view side and applying an interceptor to check for the proper form token before allowing the action to execute on the controller side. As you see in figure 15.4, these two pieces work together by saving state in the session and checking for the proper token name/token value in the session before allowing the action to execute. Note that form tokens are only part of the answer. To minimize the chances of users accidentally resubmitting a form, you should use `redirect` results after processing a form post.

15.6.1 Using the <ww:token> tag

The `<ww:token>` tag creates a new form token, saving the token in the session using the token name as the key. The token values generated are cryptographically strong UUIDs, so there is no worry about duplicate token values or users guessing a different token value. This is the case because the token is in the form of 32 random characters (including A–Z and numbers): 32^36 possible values, which would take thousands of lifetimes to guess. Listing 15.12 shows a simple example of using the `token` tag.

Listing 15.12 The token tag, which builds a form token

```
<ww:form action="saveCategory">
  <ww:token name="category.token"/>
  <ww:if test="category.id != null">
    <ww:hidden name="categoryId" value="%{category.id}"/>
  </ww:if>
  <ww:select label="%{getText('text.parent')}"
             name="category.parentCategory"
             value="category.parentCategory.id"
             list="#categoryPicker.categories"
             listKey="id"
             listValue="#indent({top, ''}) + name" />
  <ww:textfield label="%{getText('text.name')}"
                name="category.name"/>
  <ww:submit value="Save"/>
</ww:form>
```

You see here that the `token` tag is given a `name` attribute. If this `name` attribute is left out, a default token name is used. Each token name, whether it's the default token name or a supplied token name, has a maximum of one valid token value at any time. This means you can use different token names to protect different parts of your web application. The `token` tag creates two hidden input fields in the form, one for the token name and one for the token value. These form fields are read by the `token` interceptor when the form is posted back to the server. The hidden fields for the example `<ww:token>` tag shown earlier look like this:

```
<input type="hidden"
       name="webwork.token.name"
       value="category.token"/>
<input type="hidden" name="category.token"
       value="F0DVU9PRT393S28Z3EO5K5JNNLCA6NQJ"/>
```

The first hidden field specifies the name of the actual form token—in this case, `category.token`, because that's what you specified. The second maps this token name to a cryptographically strong token value.

15.6.2 *Applying the TokenInterceptor*

The `com.opensymphony.webwork.interceptor.TokenInterceptor` can be applied to an action to ensure that a valid token was included in the parameters coming from the web request. Doing so makes sure that:

- The `token` tag was in the form to generate a token value and save it in the session
- The current token value was the last one saved for this token name
- The token has not already been used to verify a previous request

The `TokenInterceptor` uses utility classes to find the token from the request. The basic flow is as follows:

1 Find the token name by looking for the standard token `name` parameter in the request. If this parameter exists in the request, it gives the name of the token to look for.

2 If the token name was found, find the token value by looking for a `request` parameter with that name.

3 If the token value was found in the `request` parameters, get the token value for this token name in the session.

4 If the token value from the session equals the token from the request, then remove this session attribute (to prevent the token from being used again) and call `handleValidToken(invocation)`; if not, call `handle-InvalidToken(invocation)`.

This last step is important because, as you'll see in a moment, another token interceptor subclasses `TokenInterceptor` to override these methods. In the `TokenInterceptor`, `handleInvalidToken()` adds an error message to the action (if it implements `ValidationAware`) and returns `INVALID_TOKEN_CODE`, a constant return code defined in the `TokenInterceptor` as `invalid.token`. This return code is returned to look up a result without executing the action, so you can be sure your action only executes for valid token values. In the action configuration, a result can be mapped for `invalid.token` to allow a special page to be displayed for duplicate posts. `TokenInterceptor`'s `handleValidToken()` method calls `invocation.invoke()` to call the rest of the interceptors and the action in order. This interceptor effectively acts as a gateway, blocking duplicate posts or requests coming in without a valid token.

15.6.3 *Transparently re-rendering pages with the TokenSessionStoreInterceptor*

The `com.opensymphony.webwork.interceptor.TokenSessionStoreInterceptor` extends the `TokenInterceptor` to override the `handleInvalidToken()` and `handleValidToken()` methods. In the `TokenSessionStoreInterceptor`, `handleValidToken()` saves an object containing the `ActionInvocation` and the token value in a `Map` in the session. If duplicate posts come in, reusing the same token, this object is retrieved from the session, and the result page is re-rendered using the saved state without executing the action again. This lets you prevent duplicate posts from executing the action more than once while also giving the user a nicer experience: They see the same page again, rather than an error page.

Although the `token` and `token-session` interceptors can help prevent duplicates posts being submitted and processed, there is another common problem with web applications and users who click too frequently: Long-running pages are often resubmitted multiple times. The `token-session` interceptor can transparently address this issue, but sometimes having a simple Please Wait page while the action executes gives the user a better sense of confidence with your application. The `execAndWait` interceptor does that for you.

15.7 *Displaying wait pages automatically*

The `execAndWait` interceptor allows you to make the action run in a separate thread while returning a page to the user in the meantime. Let's look at an example of a web application that shows a working page when you go to buy airline tickets online. Figure 15.5 shows a screen from Northwest Airlines' website.

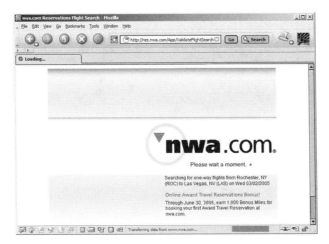

**Figure 15.5
nwa.com shows a wait page
while doing some long-running
processing.**

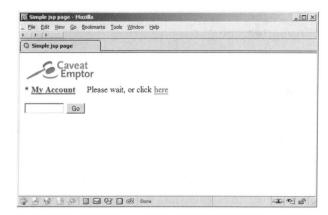

Figure 15.6
CaveatEmptor uses a wait page
while doing a search.

While the nwa.com site is doing some long-running processing, it shows users a page to let them know that something is happening. Without this page, it might seem the site is hung, and the user might keep refreshing, posting the flight search again and again. Figure 15.6 shows the wait page from CaveatEmptor that is displayed during a search.

How do you separate the processing to do the work of the action from returning a page for the user? First, let's take another look at the normal processing in WebWork. Figure 15.7 shows the flow of a request coming from the user.
As you can see, all the work is done in the action before the page comes back to the user. However long it takes to execute the action and render the page is the time the user waits for a response. Figure 15.8 shows an overview of separating the work from the final view shown to the user using the execAndWait interceptor.

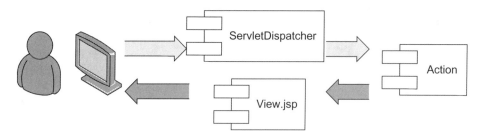

Figure 15.7 In normal action processing, all the work is done in the action before the page is rendered for the user.

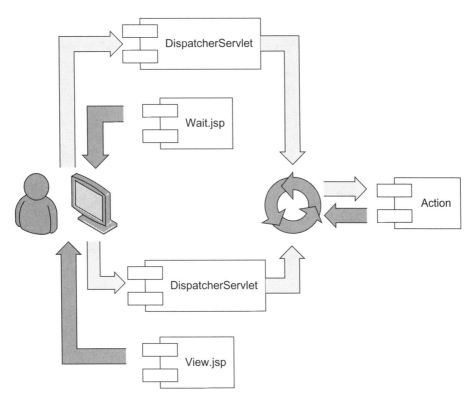

Figure 15.8 Using the `execAndWait` interceptor, the request to start the processing and the request to show the final page to the user are separated.

Figure 15.8 shows that with the `execAndWait` interceptor, the first request starts a thread to run the action, returning a wait.jsp view to the user to let them know the application is working. This wait.jsp page also serves another purpose: It includes a meta-refresh to tell the browser to make the request again in some number of seconds. As long as the processing of the action is going on, the wait.jsp view is returned and sets the timer to refresh again. Eventually, the action finishes; the next time the page refreshes, it returns the result from the action and renders the view.jsp to show the user the work done by the action.

Listing 15.13 shows the configuration for the `search` action from CaveatEmptor.

Listing 15.13 Configuration for the `search` action, which includes the `execAndWait` interceptor

```
<action name="search"
        class="org.hibernate.auction.web.actions.Search">
    <interceptor-ref name="default"/>
    <interceptor-ref name="execAndWait"/>
    <result name="wait">search-wait.jsp</result>
    <result name="success"
            type="redirect">moreResults.action</result>
</action>
```

The `execAndWait` interceptor is added after the default interceptor stack. It's important that `execAndWait` be the last interceptor, because it stops the execution and no further interceptors will be called. In the thread created by the `execAndWait` interceptor, only the action is executed, so any interceptors after the `execAndWait` will never be run.

The other piece you need to set up is the page that is returned to the user while they wait for the action to complete. Listing 15.14 shows the search-wait.jsp returned by the `search` action.

Listing 15.14 search-wait.jsp

```
<%@ taglib prefix="ww" uri="webwork"%>
<html>
  <head>
    <title>Simple jsp page</title>
    <meta http-equiv="refresh"
          content="5;url=<ww:url includeParams="all"/>"/>
  </head>
  <body>
    Please wait, or click
    <a href="<ww:url includeParams="all"/>">here</a>
  </body>
</html>
```

The search-wait.jsp page includes a meta `refresh` command in the page header that tells the browser to refresh the page after 5 seconds. The `<ww:url>` tag builds a URL with all the parameters from the request included (both GET parameters in the URL and POST parameters coming from a form post). It also tells users what is happening and gives them the same link to click to refresh manually. The wait page should always send users back to the same URL so the `execAndWait` interceptor can correctly identify the original request to check if the thread has completed.

Now that you've seen how to change the behavior of your web interface by adding interceptors such as `token-session` or `execAndWait`, let's take one last look at a best practice for developing actions responsible for creating, reading, updating, and deleting entities from your application: CRUD actions.

15.8 A Single action for CRUD operations

As a final look at using WebWork, let's examine one of the most common use cases for a web framework. The most basic functionality implemented in web applications is CRUD operations for records from the database. CRUD stands for Create, Read, Update, and Delete, and it's the basic administrative functionality required for applications that work with persistent data. The most straightforward CRUD implementation would have separate action classes for each operation, easily three or four classes with configuration for each. When you start down this path, you quickly find a lot of commonality between these classes and opportunities to refactor them down to fewer classes. How far to take this refactoring and whether to use the pattern as shown here is a stylistic choice, but it provides an opportunity to discuss some advanced usage patterns. Listing 15.15 shows the `EditCategory` action that provides the CRUD operations for `Category` entities.

> **Listing 15.15 EditCategory action, which is mapped to all operations for CRUD of categories**

```
public class EditCategory extends AbstractCategoryAwareAction
        implements Preparable {
    private Long categoryId;
    private Category category;

    public void prepare() throws Exception {
        if (categoryId != null) {
            category =
                categoryDAO.getCategoryById(categoryId,false);
        }
    }

    public String saveCategory() {
        if (category == null) {
            return INPUT;
        }
        categoryDAO.makePersistent(category);
        return SUCCESS;
    }
}
```

Before we go into the code, let's look at the configuration for the aliases of this action in xwork.xml. Listing 15.16 shows the action configurations for the four aliases.

Listing 15.16   Four aliases for the `EditCategory` action, representing CRUD operations

```
<action name="newCategory"
        class="org.hibernate.auction.web.actions.categories.-
EditCategory">
    <result name="success">createCategory.jsp</result>
</action>

<action name="viewCategory"
        class="org.hibernate.auction.web.actions.categories.-
EditCategory">
    <interceptor-ref name="editStack"/>
    <result name="success">viewCategory.jsp</result>
</action>

<action name="editCategory"
        class="org.hibernate.auction.web.actions.categories.-
EditCategory">
    <interceptor-ref name="editStack"/>
    <result name="success">createCategory.jsp</result>
</action>

<action name="saveCategory"
        class="org.hibernate.auction.web.actions.categories.-
EditCategory" method="saveCategory">
    <interceptor-ref name="crudStack"/>
    <result name="input">createCategory.jsp</result>
    <result name="success"
            type="redirect" >dashboard.action</result>
</action>
```

The first thing to notice is that the `saveCategory` alias is the only one that declares a different method, `saveCategory()`. All the others default to the `execute()` method that is the default implementation in `ActionSupport`, returning `Action.SUCCESS` without doing anything else. For the others, the only code is in the `prepare()` method. Let's look at each of these aliases in turn.

15.8.1 *Creating new categories with newCategory*

The `newCategory` alias is the simplest. Since no `categoryId` parameter is passed to it, the `prepare()` method doesn't do anything. In fact, the only thing that happens is the return of `SUCCESS` from `execute()`. When the page goes to render, the property reads for subproperties of Category (such as category.parentCategory) get null for the category, and WebWork creates a new Category object.[1] This new Category object is set back onto the action so that its properties may be called. Let's look at the JSP page that renders the form before we move on; listing 15.17 shows the form from createCategory.jsp.

Listing 15.17   createCategory.jsp

```
<ww:form action="saveCategory">
  <ww:token/>
  <ww:if test="category.id != null">
  <ww:hidden name="categoryId" value="%{category.id}"/>
  </ww:if>
  <ww:select label="%{getText('text.parent')}"
             name="category.parentCategory"
             value="category.parentCategory.id"
             list="#categoryPicker.categories"
             listKey="id"
             listValue="#indent({top, ''}) + name" />
  <ww:textfield label="%{getText('text.name')}"
                name="category.name"/>
  <ww:submit value="Save"/>
</ww:form>
```

This form has just two visible fields: a drop-down list of all categories from which to choose the parent category, and a text field in which to enter the category name. The form fields default to the values from the Category held by the action. When the select tag evaluates the category.parentCategory expression, if the category is null, it creates a new Category as discussed earlier. If you're editing a previous Category, the select list is preselected with that category's parent.

The form also includes a <ww:token> tag, which, as you saw in section 15.6, prevents duplicate form submissions when combined with a token interceptor. Next is a check to see if you're creating a new Category or editing a preexisting Category by looking at the category ID to decide whether it should include a hidden form field with the ID.

15.8.2   *Reading and updating with viewCategory and editCategory*

Loading a Category to view isn't really a CRUD operation, but functionally it's the equivalent of loading it for editing: take the Category ID and load it from the

---

[1] See chapter 12 for a discussion of null value handling.

database, then render the appropriate page. In the case of the `viewCategory` action, this is viewCategory.jsp; for the `editCategory` action, it's createCategory.jsp. The important thing to notice in the configuration shown in listing 15.16 is that both of these action configurations use the `editStack` interceptor-ref. Listing 15.18 shows the definition of the `editStack` interceptor stack.

Listing 15.18 The `editStack` interceptor

```
<interceptor-stack name="editStack">
    <interceptor-ref name="auth"/>
    <interceptor-ref name="component"/>
    <interceptor-ref name="servlet-config"/>
    <interceptor-ref name="static-params"/>
    <interceptor-ref name="params"/>
    <interceptor-ref name="prepare"/>
    <interceptor-ref name="model-driven"/>
    <interceptor-ref name="conversionError"/>
    <interceptor-ref name="workflow"/>
</interceptor-stack>
```

The important change between this interceptor stack and the default interceptor stack used by `newCategory` is the order of the `parameter` interceptor and the `prepare` interceptor. In `editStack`, the `parameter` interceptor is set before the `prepare` interceptor. The `categoryId` property is set by the `parameter` interceptor and then used in the `prepare()` method to load the `Category` from the database. Once the correct `Category` has been loaded, the action's `execute()` method is called (remember that it doesn't do anything besides return SUCCESS) and the page is rendered, using the values from the loaded `Category`.

15.8.3 *Saving categories with saveCategory*

Both the `newCategory` and `editCategory` actions go to the createCategory.jsp page, which POSTs its form to `saveCategory.action`. This action either saves a new `Category` instance or updates an existing `Category` instance in the database. To start to understand how it works, let's look at its interceptor stack. Listing 15.19 shows the definition for the `crudStack`.

Listing 15.19 `crudStack`, which defines an interceptor stack

```
<interceptor-stack name="crudStack">
    <interceptor-ref name="auth"/>
    <interceptor-ref name="token"/>
    <interceptor-ref name="component"/>
```

```
    <interceptor-ref name="servlet-config"/>
    <interceptor-ref name="static-params"/>
    <interceptor-ref name="params"/>
    <interceptor-ref name="prepare"/>
    <interceptor-ref name="model-driven"/>
    <!-- We have params here twice because we use
         the first set of params to retrieve our
         model, then set the params on that -->
    <interceptor-ref name="params"/>
    <interceptor-ref name="conversionError"/>
    <interceptor-ref name="validation"/>
    <interceptor-ref name="workflow"/>
</interceptor-stack>
```

As you can see, the `crudStack` is using the same `parameter -> prepare` technique you saw earlier in the `editStack` to load a `Category` from the database. However, as the comment points out, you have the parameter interceptor applied again. The order of steps is as follows:

1 The `token` interceptor validates that a valid token is passed with the form submission.

2 The `parameter` interceptor sets the `categoryId` property on the action if it's passed.

3 The `prepare` interceptor calls `prepare()` on the action, causing it to load the specified `Category` from the database if the `categoryId` parameter was passed (for editing an existing `Category`).

4 The `parameter` interceptor is called again, this time setting the properties of the `Category` instance from the form fields.

5 The action's `saveCategory()` method is called, saving the `Category` instance to the database.

It's important to understand that, like any other example where values are set directly from the form parameters, this one has a potential security hole. You must either trust that the HTTP requests won't be modified by a malicious user, or you must add a security layer between the setting of the fields and the storage of them.

One way to handle this type of security is to use the Proxy pattern—that is, wrap a proxy object around every business object that lets the proxy decide whether the current user is allowed to set (or get) particular fields.

15.8.4 *Setting the parentCategory*

Looking back at the `createCategory.jsp` shown in listing 15.17, two form fields set properties on the loaded `Category` instance: a textfield named `category.name` and a select list named `category.parentCategory`. They set the name of the category and its parent category, obviously; but note that the value of the select box is set to the parent category's ID (`category.parentCategory.id`), whereas the field-name is just `category.parentCategory`. You're setting the actual `parentCategory` property, which is of type `Category`, by depending on WebWork's type conversion. The parent category's ID is trying to be set as the `parentCategory` property, so WebWork figures out that it needs to use a type converter. Listing 15.20 shows the `convertValue()` method of the `CategoryConverter` class.

Listing 15.20 The `CategoryConverter` class

```
public Object convertValue(Map map, Object target, Member member,
                           String propertyName, Object value,
                           Class toClass) {
  if (toClass.getName().equals(Category.class.getName())) {
    if (value instanceof Category) {
      return value;
    }
    CategoryDAO dao =
        (CategoryDAO) getComponent(CategoryDAOAware.class);
    Long id = getLongId(value);
    if (id != null) {
      return  dao.getCategoryById(id,false);
    }
  } else if (toClass.getName().equals(String.class.getName())) {
    if (value instanceof String) {
      return value;
    }
    if (value instanceof Category) {
      return ((Category)value).getId().toString();
    }
  }
  return null;
}
```

Because you use the DAO and assume that conversions are from the `String` representation of the ID and back, your converter is pretty simple. In fact, with a little refactoring, it's easy to create one converter that can convert any of your persistent classes. As this example shows, it can simplify your CRUD actions and any other actions that are dealing with entity relationships considerably and allow you to more naturally describe the semantics intended (such as setting the category's parent category rather than setting the ID).

15.9 Summary

We covered a wide range of topics in this chapter, and although some of them may not seem related (such as IDE settings and UI components), they all have one thing in common: Their advanced and unique features are made possible by the underlying philosophy of WebWork. WebWork makes the framework work *for* you, not the other way around; WebWork makes it *easy* to test your code; and WebWork makes it *possible* to extend without being too complex.

WebWork is about making *you* productive. In this chapter, you learned about ways to increase that productivity, whether through better deployment of your app server using Resin, or by knowing how to extend the UI tag library. We've reached the end of the book, and not only have you learned the basic features WebWork offers, such as internationalization, validation, type conversion, and UI templates, but you've also seen how to extend all those features to begin building many tools and components you can add to your toolbox.

It's time to begin creating your own set of tools: useful type converters, UI themes, IoC components, or custom validators. The most important thing you should remember when using WebWork is that it was developed specifically to make you productive. Never be complacent about unproductive development. Always look for ways to extend and utilize your frameworks and libraries, WebWork included, to their maximum potential. And when you reach that maximum, push some more—you'll likely make the next release that much better.

We hope you enjoy WebWork as much as we do, and we hope to see you soon in the WebWork community.

Appendix:
WebWork architecture

As you first learned way back in chapter 1, "An overview of WebWork," WebWork is made up of two parts. The foundation of WebWork is XWork, a generic Command pattern framework. WebWork adds an MVC web application framework implemented as a wrapper on top of XWork. The core concepts of the framework, including actions, interceptors, and results, are defined by XWork. WebWork extends the basic implementations of these concepts to support web application development. This appendix discusses the core design of XWork and WebWork.

We laid out the separation between XWork and WebWork in chapter 1, so in this appendix we'll discuss the framework architecture without too much focus on which parts are XWork and which are WebWork.

A.1 *Implementing the Command pattern*

At its core, WebWork is a Command pattern implementation. The Command pattern takes units of code that would be methods in normal functional or OO programming, and makes them into classes called *commands* or *actions*, which all implement a common interface. As you can see in figure A.1, action instances can then be created and passed to be executed by code that doesn't have to know which command class it's executing, as long as it implements the command interface.

If you use a command execution framework, the framework can encapsulate the execution of the action. Because you're calling actions through a framework, you can configure the framework to add services around the call, like saving the command objects to replay them backward for undo, or saving them to a log, or sending them off to be executed somewhere else. The client code, which executes the

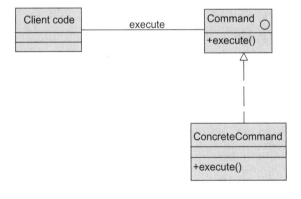

Figure A.1
**The simplest possible Command
pattern implementation**

Appendix: WebWork architecture

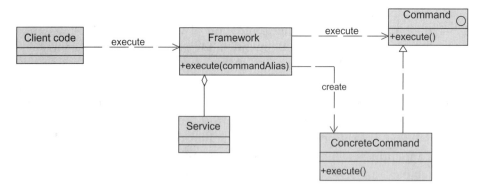

Figure A.2   Calling commands through a Command pattern framework allows the client code to be decoupled from the command implementation and lets the framework add other services transparently.

action through the framework, doesn't need to know what other services may be called, or even which action class is being executed, as you can see in figure A.2.

Because you don't directly call the classes, but rather make the calls through the framework, you can change the behavior of your commands by configuring the framework without having to change your command classes. How the framework is configured and what services are available is implementation specific; but as we discuss in chapter 3, "Setting up WebWork," WebWork actions are configured in an XML file named xwork.xml.

A.1.1   Basic Command pattern features

WebWork provides the standard features of a Command pattern framework, as well as advanced features not found in any other command framework. The standard features of a Command pattern implementation include the following:

- Configuring an action class to be executed based on an alias name, decoupling the caller from the implementing command object. This is done through the xwork.xml configuration file, which we look at in detail in chapter 3.

- Allowing configuration-time parameters to be set onto the action instance before execution. These parameters can be set in the xwork.xml file. See chapters 3 and 5 ("Adding functionality with interceptors") for more information.

- Setting request-specific parameters onto the action instance before execution. This is handled by an interceptor, as discussed in chapter 5.

- Providing a mapping between command return codes and a result to be executed. This mapping is done in the xwork.xml file, also discussed in chapter 3.

- Chaining multiple commands together via configuration to provide support for composition of macros from many actions. This is handled by the combination of a result mapped in xwork.xml and an interceptor. Action chaining is covered in detail in chapter 7, "Using results."

A.1.2 Advanced Command pattern features

WebWork also provides many advanced features, some of which aren't found in any other command framework:

- Per-class and per-property type conversion support when you're setting properties onto the action instance. This flexible type conversion allows you to use domain objects with more complicated property types, rather than all String FormBeans as in Struts or other frameworks. Type conversion is covered in detail in chapter 12.

- Localized text message support with a message inheritance model based on action class hierarchies. Internationalization support is covered in chapter 14.

- Error message support at the class instance and field level. This allows you to save error messages for display to the user at either the action level or at the per-field level. Managing error messages is covered in chapter 4, "Implementing WebWork actions."

- Configurable interceptors to provide before and after processing around the execution of the action instance. Interceptors are configured via the xwork.xml file and are discussed in detail in chapter 5.

- An XML metadata-driven validation framework to validate action and domain object values. This lets you define your validations external to your code and provide different validations for different usage scenarios. Validation is covered in chapter 13.

A.2 Actions

The core unit of functionality in WebWork is the action. Actions are the command objects in WebWork's implementation of the Command pattern discussed in section A.1. Actions implement the com.opensymphony.xwork.Action interface, which defines only one method:

```
public String execute() throws Exception
```

This method is the default entry point (the method the framework calls when executing the action) for execution in your action classes. You can configure your action alias to call a method other than `execute()`, and even have multiple different action aliases pointing to different methods in the same action class with different interceptors, results, and so on.

The `com.opensymphony.xwork.ActionSupport` class implements `Action` and several optional interfaces and can be used as a base class for your own action classes to extend to inherit implementations of these interfaces. In chapter 4, we look in detail at implementing your own actions and the default implementations provided by `ActionSupport`.

A.3 *Interceptors*

Interceptors in WebWork allow you to encapsulate code to be executed around the execution of an action. These are extra services the Command pattern framework can provide, transparently,[1] to the execution of your actions. They're defined outside the action class, yet have access to the action and the action execution environment at runtime, letting you componentize cross-cutting code and provide separation of concerns. Cross-cutting code can be anything from timing and logging your action execution to setting up resources such as database connections and transactions and cleaning them up after execution. Many WebWork features, including core functionality like setting properties on the action instance, are implemented as interceptors. This is code many of your actions will need, but you don't want to be forced to see it in every action, either through cut-and-paste or complex class inheritance hierarchies. Instead, the modular approach to executing an action allows you to customize the action execution to do just the pieces you need.

If you think this sounds like Aspect-Oriented Programming (AOP), you're right. It shares many concepts with the idea of method interception from AOP; but it doesn't require any preprocessing or byte-code modification, because the callers and called actions are decoupled and the interception is internal to the framework. We take a detailed look at interceptors in chapter 5, and we'll examine a sequence diagram of the interactions that occur in executing an action later in this appendix when we discuss what happens inside the `ActionProxy` and `ActionInvocation`.

---

[1] The level of transparency depends on what the interceptor is doing. Some interceptors, like `timer` and `logger`, don't change the behavior of the action at all. Other interceptors, like `parameter` and `prepare`, may be key to the operation of the action, and not including them would break things.

A.4 Results

The `com.opensymphony.xwork.Result` interface represents a generic outcome of an action execution. This is basically anything you want to happen after the action is executed. The `Result` interface defines only one method:

```
public void execute(ActionInvocation invocation) throws Exception
```

Results can be used to produce any kind of output needed from the action execution, such as displaying a web page, generating a report, or sending an email. WebWork provides results for doing servlet dispatch (used to dispatch to a JSP for rendering), servlet redirects, Velocity, FreeMarker, JasperReports (which allows you to generate PDF, CSV, XML, and so on), XSLT rendering, and the `Action-ChainResult`, which can be used to chain processing from the current action to another action.

Results are mapped to a result code in your action configuration in xwork.xml. We discuss this in detail in chapter 3; but for now, all you need to know is that you can tell WebWork to execute a different result based on the return code of your action's `execute()` method. Each different return code can have its own result to be executed. Results are discussed in detail in chapter 7.

A.5 Value stack

The value stack is central to the dynamic context-driven nature of XWork and WebWork. It's a stack of objects against which expressions can be evaluated to find property values dynamically, by searching for the first object (from the top of the stack down) that has a property of that name. WebWork builds up the value stack during execution by pushing the action onto the stack.

Many WebWork JSP tags and Velocity macros access the value stack and may push or pop objects to/from it. The value stack is built on and around Object Graph Navigation Language (OGNL) and acts as an extension of OGNL's single-object root concept to support the multiple-object stack. We'll discuss OGNL and the interaction between OGNL and the value stack more in the next section.

A.5.1 OGNL

OGNL (see http://www.opensymphony.com/ognl) lets you evaluate expressions to navigate properties on JavaBeans for either getting or setting property values. OGNL also provides advanced expression features such as static or instance method execution, projection across a collection, and lambda expression definition for expression reuse. OGNL also provides a rich type-conversion model that has been extended in XWork and WebWork. Type conversion is covered in detail in chapter 12.

The basics of the OGNL language are simple and should cover 90 percent of common usages. Basic bean properties are accessed using the property name. For example, the expression `count` is evaluated by trying to find a getter for a property named `count`, like `getCount()`. Similarly, the expression `address.street` calls `getAddress().getStreet()` if you're getting a property, or `getAddress().setStreet()` if you're setting a property. Other features of OGNL are similarly straightforward; for instance, the expression `hashCode()` calls the hash code method on the current object in the OGNL context.

We discuss OGNL syntax in detail in chapter 8, including the WebWork extensions to OGNL. But for now the expressions used in the examples should be self-explanatory, and we'll comment them where they're not.

A.6 *ActionProxy / ActionInvocation*

The `ActionProxy` serves as client code's handle to execute an action. Because you're executing the action through the framework, you use this proxy rather than the action instance itself so that it may encapsulate the extra functionality of the interceptors, results, and so on. Figure A.3 shows the relationship between the `ActionProxy`, the `ActionInvocation`, the action instance, the interceptors, the results, and the `ActionContext` (which we'll cover in the next section).

The `ActionProxy` holds an `ActionInvocation`, which represents the current state of the execution of the action. The `ActionInvocation` holds the action instance, the interceptors to be applied (in order), the map of results (mapped from return code to result instance), and an `ActionContext` (more on this in the next section).

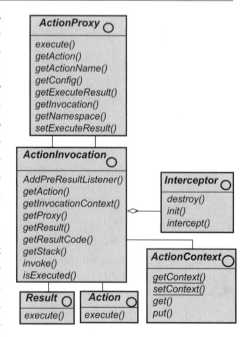

Figure A.3 Class diagram of the classes involved in executing an ActionProxy

The `ActionProxy` is created by a dispatcher—such as the `ServletDispatcher` in WebWork—using the static `ActionProxyFactory` instance, in this way:

```
ActionProxy proxy = ActionProxyFactory.getFactory()
    .createActionProxy(namespace, actionName, context);
```

After creating the `ActionProxy` with the context (which includes the request parameters, the application map, the session map, the locale, and the `ServletRequest` and `ServletResponse`), the `ServletDispatcher` executes the `ActionProxy` by calling the `execute()` method. Figure A.4 shows the sequence of calls in the `execute()` method of the `DefaultActionProxy` (the default implementation of the `ActionProxy` interface).

The `ActionProxy` sets up the execution context for the `ActionInvocation` (you'll see more about this in a moment when we discuss the `ActionContext`) and then calls `invoke()` on the `ActionInvocation`. The `ActionInvocation` `invoke()` method finds the next interceptor that hasn't been executed and calls `intercept()` on it. The interceptor can do any preprocessing using the `ActionInvocation` before calling `invoke()` again on the `ActionInvocation`. This reentrant behavior can make `ActionInvocation` somewhat confusing. The `ActionInvocation` maintains its state to know which interceptors have been executed; and, if there are more interceptors, it calls `intercept()` on the next one. If there are no more interceptors to be called, the action instance is executed. The return code from the action is used to look up the result to use, and it's executed. Finally, the `invoke()` method returns, returning control to the last interceptor in the stack. This interceptor can do any post-processing necessary and then return from the `invoke()` method, allowing the previous interceptor to do its post-processing, and so on, until all the interceptors have returned. Finally, the `ActionProxy` cleans up some state and returns.

One consequence of passing the `ActionInvocation` into the interceptors and depending on it to continue processing the other interceptors and finally the action is that interceptors can choose to *not* continue processing (thus shortcutting action execution) and just return a result code. This allows, as an example, a `SecurityInterceptor` to prevent action execution if the user doesn't have permissions to the action.

The `ActionProxyFactory/ActionProxy/ActionInvocation` architecture also allows for different strategies for executing actions. For example, using this architecture, you could build a Java Message Service (JMS) dispatcher to allow asynchronous action processing and a client dispatcher that allows rich clients to call to a server, to have actions executed on the server side with the required parameters and

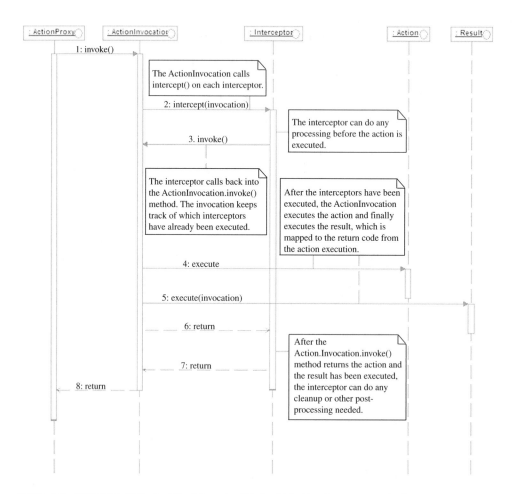

Figure A.4   Sequence diagram of the internals of `DefaultActionProxy.execute()`

then return to the client to be rendered for the user. This is already being done for the project MessageWork, which was recently added to http://dev.java.net.

A.7 *ActionContext*

The `ActionContext` is a `ThreadLocal Map` with helpers for getting and setting predefined values such as the application and session maps, the `ActionInvocation`, request parameters, the locale, and so on. An `ActionContext` is associated with a particular `ActionInvocation/ActionProxy` pair and is associated with the `Thread` during the execution of that `ActionInvocation`.

In the previous section, we said that the `ActionProxy` sets up some state before invoking the `ActionInvocation` and cleans up some state afterward. This setup associates the `ActionContext` with the current `Thread` so that it's available during the `ActionInvocation` execution. Let's look at what the `ActionProxy` is doing before and after invoking the `ActionInvocation`; see figure A.5.

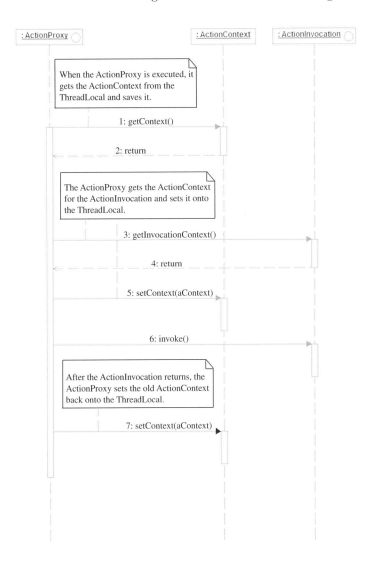

Figure A.5 Sequence diagram of the `ActionContext` setup and teardown done by `DefaultActionProxy` before and after invoking the `ActionInvocation`

Figure A.5 shows the sequence of calls made by the `DefaultActionProxy` before and after the `ActionInvocation`'s `invoke()` method is called. The `ActionContext` is created during the `ActionInvocation` and `ActionProxy` construction and stored until the `ActionProxy` is executed, when it's associated with the `Thread`. During interceptor, action, and result execution, your code can use the `ActionContext.getContext()` method to get the `ActionContext` from the `ThreadLocal` and thus get the current execution context.

The `ActionContext` contains valuable information about the environment during execution. These context values are set up by the `ServletDispatcher` before creating the `ActionProxy` and are passed in the `extraContext` `Map` to the `createActionProxy()` method on the `ActionProxyFactory`. The properties found in the `ActionContext` are as follows:

- `ActionInvocation`—`getActionInvocation()` gives access to the current `ActionInvocation`, which is associated with this `ActionContext`.

- `Application`—`getApplication()` gives you a `java.util.Map` implementation that wraps the application scope using the `ServletContext`. You can read and write to the application scope using this map.

- `ConversionErrors`—`getConversionErrors()` returns a `Map` of field name to field value pairs for all fields that had type-conversion errors. We discuss this in detail in chapter 12.

- `Locale`—`getLocale()` gets the locale of the current request. This locale is used for finding localized text messages, as you see in detail in chapter 14.

- `Name`—`getName()` gets the name of the current action. This is from the part of the request that identifies the action to execute and corresponds to the action name mapped in the xwork.xml file.

- `Parameters`—`getParameters()` returns the `Map` of parameters from the request. This `Map` is from `String` parameter names to `String[]` values—because the parameters from an `HttpServletRequest` can have multiple values for each parameter name, the `Map` gives you `String` arrays.

- `Session`—`getSession()` returns a `java.util.Map` implementation that wraps the `HttpSession` attributes. You can get and set values to/from the session using this `Map`.

- `ValueStack`—`getValueStack()` returns the value stack of the current request.

Along with these predefined values, you can use the `put()` and `get()` methods to set your own values into the `ActionContext` to be available later, without having to pass the values explicitly. You could do so, for instance, to associate a database connection to be used during processing of the interceptors and the action with the current `ActionContext ThreadLocal`. In that way, your code can retrieve the database connection anywhere it's needed without having to pass it in every method call. Your code can also skip the thread-safety that would be needed for a static storage solution, because the `ActionContext` is associated with only one `Thread`.

A.7.1 *ThreadLocal storage*

The `ActionContext` is implemented as a `ThreadLocal` so that it's always available without having to be passed along in every method call. `ThreadLocals` (`java.lang.ThreadLocal`) were added in Java 1.2. They provide `Thread`-specific storage, where each `Thread` has its own instance of the `Object`. Accessors for getting the `ThreadLocal` value can be static methods, allowing the `ThreadLocal` value to be retrieved anywhere; it need not be passed as a method parameter.

Listing A.1 shows the `ThreadLocal`-specific code in `ActionContext`.

Listing A.1   ActionContext's ThreadLocal-specific code

```
static ThreadLocal actionContext = new ActionContextThreadLocal();

public static void setContext(ActionContext aContext) {
    actionContext.set(aContext);
}

/**
 * Returns the ActionContext specific to the current thread.
 *
 * @return ActionContext for the current thread
 */
public static ActionContext getContext() {
    ActionContext context = (ActionContext) actionContext.get();

    if (context == null) {
        OGNLValueStack vs = new OGNLValueStack();
        context = new ActionContext(vs.getContext());
        setContext(context);
    }

    return context;
}

private static class ActionContextThreadLocal extends ThreadLocal {
    protected Object initialValue() {
        OGNLValueStack vs = new OGNLValueStack();
```

```
        return new ActionContext(vs.getContext());
    }
}
```

Looking at the getContext() and setContext() methods, you see that they use the ThreadLocal set() and get() methods. The ThreadLocal set() method associates an Object with the ThreadLocal for later retrieval. The ThreadLocal get() method retrieves the Object currently associated with the ThreadLocal for this Thread.

The only other implementation detail is the ActionContextThreadLocal inner class. It's a specialized subclass of ThreadLocal that overrides the initialValue() method from ThreadLocal to set up a default value for the ThreadLocal, so that the first call to get() on the ThreadLocal doesn't return null.

One note about using ThreadLocals: They're notoriously tricky in unit testing. Take proper care to set up and tear down ThreadLocals before and after unit tests, to ensure that the tests don't interfere with one another. If you look at the unit tests in XWork and WebWork, you can see the effort involved to make sure the unit tests don't leave any side effects that can cause unforeseen interactions.

A.8 *The servlet dispatcher*

The ServletDispatcher is the main entry point of requests in WebWork. It's a servlet that is normally mapped to an extension (typically *.action, although *.jspa is another common extension used by the WebWork community). It uses the request path to determine which action to execute, as discussed in section 3.2.2 on namespaces. The ServletDispatcher serves as the adapter between the HTTP request/response world of servlets and WebWork and the generic Command pattern action/result world of XWork.

The ServletDispatcher creates the context for executing an action by setting up java.util.Map implementations that wrap the application-, session-, and parameter-scoped attributes. It then uses the ActionProxyFactory to create an ActionProxy, returning an error to the user if no action is mapped to the requested name. Finally, the ServletDispatcher executes the ActionProxy, which, as you saw earlier, includes executing any associated interceptors, the action itself, and whichever result is mapped to the result code returned from the action. This result could, for instance, render a web page or create a PDF document. The ServletDispatcher also handles wrapping the request for multipart file-upload requests (discussed in chapter 4) and handling error codes, and is generally the glue that ties WebWork together.

A.9 Summary

At its heart, WebWork is a Command pattern implementation (XWork) wrapped with an MVC web application framework (WebWork). The framework handles command execution, allowing the calling code to be decoupled from the concrete action classes and allowing the framework to add services around the action execution. These services are provided in the form of interceptors in WebWork, and they handle much of the framework's core functionality.

In order to add these services, the framework encapsulates the execution of an action in an `ActionProxy`/`ActionInvocation` pair. The `ActionProxy`/`ActionInvocation` wraps the action, includes the interceptors and the result, and manages when each is called during execution. Interceptors are called in order and can do whatever they need to before and after executing the rest of the `ActionInvocation` (including the other interceptors). During the action execution, the action, interceptors, and result can access a `ThreadLocal` storage space called the `ActionContext`, which is managed by the `ActionProxy` and is available only during the `ActionProxy.execute()` method.

`ActionProxy` instances are created by the `ServletDispatcher` using the static `ActionProxyFactory` instance. The `ServletDispatcher` maps HTTP requests coming into an action namespace and action alias, which are used to create the correct `ActionProxy` by the `ActionProxyFactory`. The `ServletDispatcher` then executes the `ActionProxy`, which handles executing the interceptors, action, and result (such as a web page or a PDF).

index